THE FORCE OF POETRY

THE FORCE
OF POETRY

CHRISTOPHER RICKS

CLARENDON PRESS · OXFORD

1984

Oxford University Press, Walton Street, Oxford OX2 6DP

London New York Toronto
Delhi Bombay Calcutta Madras Karachi
Kuala Lumpur Singapore Hong Kong Tokyo
Nairobi Dar es Salaam Cape Town
Melbourne Auckland

and associated companies in
Beirut Berlin Ibadan Mexico City Nicosia

Oxford is a trade mark of Oxford University Press

Published in the United States
by Oxford University Press, New York

British Library Cataloguing in Publication Data
Ricks, Christopher
The force of poetry.
1. English poetry—History and criticism
I. Title
821′009 PR502
ISBN 0-19-811722-1

Library of Congress Cataloging in Publication Data
Ricks, Christopher B.
The force of poetry.
Includes index.
1. English poetry—History and criticism—Addresses,
essays, lectures. 2. English language—Style—Addresses,
essays, lectures. I. Title.
PR503.R55 1984   821′.009   84-4951
ISBN 0-19-811722-1

Typeset by DMB (Typesetting), Oxford
and printed in Great Britain
at the Alden Press, Oxford

'In this passage is exerted all the force of poetry, that force which calls new powers into being, which embodies sentiment, and animates matter . . .'
(Johnson, *The Rambler*, No. 168, 26 October 1751)

PREFATORY NOTE

This is a gathering of essays, not a march of chapters, but the essays have some interdependence in that each attends to an aspect, feature, or resource of the language manifested in poetry. Summarily: the essay on Gower gives salience to diction and formulae. That on Marvell, to a particular figure of speech. That on Milton, to sound and sense. That on Johnson, to metaphors dead or alive. Those on Wordsworth, first, to line-endings, and second, to a part of speech, the preposition. That on Beddoes, to the vitality of language in relation to the celebration of death. That on Housman, to manner and move-ment. That on Empson, to the images and the story. That on Stevie Smith, to the resources of bathos. That on Lowell, to a particular kind of pun. That on Larkin, to tone. Those on Hill, to transition and punctuation, brackets and hyphens. The four essays at the end are in some ways more generally couched, and are on clichés, lies, misquotations, and American English in its relation to the transitory.

I have published two essays on allusion, in the sense of the use made of the words and phrases of previous poets. These essays I have not collected here, because I intend them to be part of a book on allusion; but the one on Dryden and Pope ('Allusion: The Poet as Heir') may be found in *Studies in the Eighteenth Century, III*, ed. R. F. Brissenden and J. C. Eade (Australian National University Press, 1976), and that on Tennyson ('Tennyson Inheriting the Earth') in *Studies in Tennyson*, ed. Hallam Tennyson (Macmillan, 1981).

ACKNOWLEDGEMENTS

All of these essays except the last have previously been published. Small changes have been made throughout, and substantial changes to the following: Beddoes, Stevie Smith, Robert Lowell, Geoffrey Hill (the second essay), and Clichés. I am grateful to the publishers, journals, and editors. I am also grateful to Christ's College, Cambridge, for meeting the cost of the typing.

Gower:	*Gower's 'Confessio Amantis' : Responses and Reassessments*, ed. A. J. Minnis (D. S. Brewer, 1983).
Marvell:	*Approaches to Marvell : The York Centenary Lectures*, ed. C. A. Patrides (Routledge & Kegan Paul, 1978).
Milton:	*Essays by Divers Hands : Being the Transactions of the Royal Society of Literature*, new series, xxxix, ed. John Press (Oxford University Press, 1977); the Tredegar Memorial Lecture, 1974.
Johnson:	*Essays in Criticism*, xvi:3 (July 1966).
Wordsworth, 1:	*Essays in Criticism*, xxi:1 (January 1971).
Wordsworth, 2:	*Harvard English Studies 2*, ed. Reuben A. Brower (Harvard University Press, 1971).
Beddoes:	*Grand Street*, i:2 (Winter 1982), and iii:4 (Summer 1984).
Housman:	*Essays in Criticism*, xiv:3 (July 1964).
Empson:	*William Empson : The Man and His Work*, ed. Roma Gill (Routledge & Kegan Paul, 1974).
Smith:	*Grand Street*, i:1 (Autumn 1981).
Lowell:	adapting a BBC talk, part of which was published in *The Listener*, 10 March 1977.
Larkin:	*Larkin at Sixty*, ed. Anthony Thwaite (Faber & Faber, 1982).
Hill, 1:	the W. D. Thomas Memorial Lecture, University College of Swansea, 1978; published by the College, and then *The Times Literary Supplement*, 30 June 1978.
Hill, 2:	*Geoffrey Hill: Essays on his Work*, ed. Peter Robinson (Open University Press, 1984).

Clichés: *The State of the Language*, ed. Leonard Michaels
                    and Christopher Ricks (University of California
                    Press, 1980). This drew on an essay on Hill,
                    London Magazine, November 1964.
Lies: *Critical Inquiry*, ii:1 (Autumn 1975).
Pater, Arnold and
misquotation: *The Times Literary Supplement*, 25 November 1977.
American
English: previously unpublished; adapting a talk given
                    to the British Institute of the United States,
                    meeting at Boston University in April 1983.

The author and publisher are grateful for permission to reprint the
following copyright material.

W. H. Auden: 'Let us honour if we can . . .', copyright 1934
                    and renewed 1962 by W. H. Auden; extract
                    from 'Lay your sleeping head, my love',
                    copyright 1940 and renewed 1968 by W. H.
                    Auden, both from *W. H. Auden: Collected Poems*,
                    edited by Edward Mendelson. Reprinted by
                    permission of Faber & Faber Ltd., and Ran-
                    dom House, Inc.
John Berryman: 'Dream Song 7' and extract from 'Dream Song
                    27' from *77 Dream Songs*, copyright © 1959,
                    1962, 1963, 1964 by John Berryman; 'Dream
                    Song 118' from *His Toy, His Dream, His Rest*,
                    copyright © 1964, 1965, 1966, 1967, 1968 by
                    John Berryman. Reprinted by permission of
                    Faber & Faber Ltd., and Farrar, Straus &
                    Giroux, Inc.
J. V. Cunningham: 'A Century of Epigrams', No. 60 from *The Col-
                    lected Poems and Epigrams* by J. V. Cunningham,
                    1971, Swallow Press. Reprinted with the per-
                    mission of The Ohio University Press, Athens.
Bob Dylan: extracts from: *Is Your Love in Vain*, copyright ©
                    1978 Special Rider Music (ASCAP); *I Threw It
                    All Away*, copyright © 1969 Big Sky Music; *If
                    You See Her Say Hello*, copyright © 1974, 1975
                    Ram's Horn Music; *No Time to Think*, copy-

right © 1978 Special Rider Music (ASCAP); *When You Gonna Wake Up*, copyright © 1979 Special Rider Music; *I Pity the Poor Immigrant*, © 1968 Dwarf Music; *Visions of Johanna*, © 1966 Dwarf Music. Used by permission. All rights reserved. Extracts from: *Love Minus Zero/No Limit*, © 1965 Warner Bros, Inc; *I Shall be Free*, © 1963 Warner Bros, Inc; *Masters of War*, © 1963 Warner Bros, Inc; *I'll Keep It With Mine*, © 1965 Warner Bros, Inc; *All I Really Want to Do*, © 1964 Warner Bros, Inc; *To Ramona*, © 1964 Warner Bros, Inc; *Don't Think Twice, It's Alright*, © 1963 Warner Bros, Inc; and from *When The Ship Comes In*, © 1963 Warner Bros, Inc. Used by permission. All rights reserved.

T. S. Eliot: extracts from 'Marina', 'Burnt Norton', 'The Dry Salvages', 'The Waste Land', 'The Love Song of J. Alfred Prufrock' and from 'East Coker' from *Collected Poems 1909-1962*, copyright © 1963, 1964 by T. S. Eliot. Reprinted by permission of Faber & Faber Ltd., and Harcourt Brace Jovanovich, Inc. Extracts from the introductory essay to 'London: A poem and The Vanity of Human Wishes' by Samuel Johnson (1930); from *The Atheneum*, 11 April 1919; from 'Introduction to a translation of Valéry's Art of Poetry'; from *TLS*, 27 September 1928; from *Dial*, lxxi (1921); from *Dial*, lxxii (1922) from *TLS*, 2 September 1926; all from uncollected works of T. S. Eliot by permission of Mrs. Valerie Eliot and Faber & Faber Ltd.

William Empson: from *Collected Poems of William Empson*, copyright 1949, 1977 by William Empson. Reprinted by permission of Chatto & Windus Ltd., and Harcourt Brace Jovanovich, Inc.

David Ferry: 'The Soldier', copyright © 1957 by David Ferry, from *On The Way to the Island* (Wesleyan, 1960). Reprinted by permission of Wesleyan University Press.

Roy Fuller: 'The Truth About Pygmalion' from *Buff* (1965).
                      Reprinted by permission of André Deutsch
                      Ltd.

Robert Graves: 'To bring the dead to life, ...'. Reprinted by
                      permission of A. P. Watt Ltd., for the author.

Seamus Heaney: extracts from *Death of a Naturalist, Door Into the
                      Dark, Wintering Out* and *Field Work*, copyright
                      © 1976, 1979 by Seamus Heaney. Reprinted
                      by permission of Faber & Faber Ltd., and Far-
                      rar, Straus & Giroux, Inc.

Geoffrey Hill: extracts from *Mercian Hymns* (1971), *Tenebrae*
                      (1978), *For the Unfallen* (1959) and from *King
                      Log* (1968). Reprinted by permission of André
                      Deutsch. Extracts from *The Mystery of the Charity
                      of Charles Péguy* reprinted by permission of André
                      Deutsch in association with Agenda Editions.
                      Uncollected poems are quoted with the permis-
                      sion of Geoffrey Hill.

A. E. Housman: 'I to my perils' (Poem VI from *More Poems*) and
                      extract from 'The sigh that heaves the grasses'
                      (*Last Poems*, xxvii) and 'When the bells justle in
                      the tower' (*Additional Poems*, ix) from *The Col-
                      lected Poems of A. E. Housman*, copyright 1922,
                      1939, 1940, © 1965 by Holt, Rinehart and
                      Winston, Inc; copyright 1950 by Barclays Bank
                      Ltd, copyright © 1967, 1968 by Robert E.
                      Symons. Reprinted by permission of The
                      Society of Authors as the literary representative
                      of The Estate of A. E. Housman, Jonathan
                      Cape Ltd., as publishers of *Collected Poems*, and
                      Holt, Rinehart and Winston, Inc.

Ted Hughes: extract from 'A Kill' from *Crow*, copyright ©
                      1971 by Ted Hughes. Reprinted by permission
                      of Faber & Faber Ltd., and Harper & Row
                      Publishers, Inc.

Philip Larkin: 'An Arundel Tomb', 'Talking in Bed' and ex-
                      tracts from 'Mr Bleaney', 'Ambulance' and
                      'Ignorance' all from *The Whitsun Weddings*. Re-
                      printed by permission of Faber & Faber Ltd.

Michael Longley: extract from 'The Corner of An Eye: King-
                      fisher' from *An Exploded View*; extracts from
                      'Mole', 'Ars Poetica' and from 'Last Rites:

Death-Watch' all from *Man Lying On a Wall.* Reprinted by permission of Victor Gollancz Ltd.

Robert Lowell: '1790' from *Poems 1938-1949*, copyright 1950 by Robert Lowell. Reprinted by permission of Faber & Faber Ltd., and Harcourt Brace Jovanovich, Inc; 'Memories of West Street and Lepke' from *Life Studies*, copyright © 1958, 1959 by Robert Lowell; 'Non-violent' and an extract from 'History' both from *History*, copyright © 1967, 1968, 1969, 1970, 1973 by Robert Lowell; from 'The Day' from *Day By Day*. Reprinted by permission of Faber & Faber Ltd., and Farrar, Straus & Giroux, Inc.

Paul Muldoon: extracts from *New Weather* and from *Mules*. Reprinted by permission of Faber & Faber Ltd.

Ezra Pound: extract from Canto LXXX, from *The Cantos of Ezra Pound*, copyright 1948 by Ezra Pound. Reprinted by permission of Faber and Faber Ltd., and New Directions Publishing Corp.

Jon Silkin: from *The Poetry of Geoffrey Hill*. Reprinted by permission of the author.

Stevie Smith: from *The Collected Poems of Stevie Smith* (Allen Lane/New Directions), copyright 1937, 1938, 1950, © 1957, 1966, 1971, 1972 by Stevie Smith. Reprinted by permission of James MacGibbon as literary executor and by New Directions Publishing Corporation.

CONTENTS

JOHN GOWER:
METAMORPHOSIS IN OTHER WORDS

Any lover of Gower should begin with a confession. Mine is that, no medievalist, I confess my not being competent to substantiate—from the larger linguistic and literary context—those verbal felicities which I believe that I apprehend in Gower. Saying this may be suicidal of me, but I prefer to think of it as a cry for help. The crucial question, at any rate, is no different for those who are indeed scholars of fourteenth-century poetry. C. S. Lewis—who wrote the best criticism of Gower as of so much else—put this question most answerably:

All plain styles, except the very greatest, raise a troublesome question for the critic. Are they the result of art or of accident?[1]

In the half-century since Lewis wrote those words, literary theorists have discovered a good many problems in this whole matter of intentionalism, and have invented a bad many more. Those of us who still hold to the belief that it is sadly possible for a reader to take an unwarrantable pleasure in a writer's words are not obliged to equate intention with fully conscious decision; felicities are a coinciding of the happily unplanned with the deliberated. Lewis himself simply acknowledged a complication: 'Not all that is unconscious in art is therefore accidental'.

Take the case of John Aubrey, who thrusts upon us the choice between apprehending his prose as genius or as ingenuousness. As in this death sentence from the life of Sir William Davenant:

He was next a servant (as I remember, a Page also) to Sir Fulke Grevil, Lord Brookes, with whom he lived to his death, which was that a servant of his (that had long wayted on him, and his Lordship had often told him that he would doe something for him, but did not, but still putt him off with delayes) as he was trussing up his Lord's pointes comeing from Stoole (for then their breeches were fastned to the doubletts with points; then came in hookes and eies; which not to have fastened was in my boy-hood a great crime) stabbed him.

[1] *The Allegory of Love* (1936), p. 203.

The flashing naked surprise of those last two words—'stabbed
him'—is a re-enactment of the crime, made the more horrible
by the juxtaposition of a truly great crime with the observations
about tailoring and about the need to adjust one's dress. The
world of daily banality (lavatories and fly-buttons) is one where
the moments of possible social embarrassment (as with eating
and making love) are indeed the moments of great vulner-
ability, and are monstrously continuous with murder. Then
the three bracketed parentheses, which occupy two-thirds of
the sentence and which settle into stubborn procrastination
(from six words to thirty and twenty-nine), dilate with a murderous impatience at the Lord's delays, throbbing at once with
a sharp pun on 'wayted on': '(that had long wayted on him, and
his Lordship had often told him that he would doe something
for him, but did not, but still putt him off with delayes) . . .'
What could more dramatically realize the scene, its unfulfilled
promises and its mounting tensions, than Aubrey's own putting us off with delays? Yet all the while the sentence's plot is
undisguised even within delay's swaddlings: '. . . with whom
he lived to his death, which was that a servant of his . . . stabbed
him'. Are the 'pointes' (tags) both pointed towards and at odds
with 'stabbed him'? Are the breeches alive to such contrarieties
as those in *Macbeth*, where a breach is stabbed between 'breach'
and 'breeched'?

> Here lay *Duncan*,
> His Silver skinne, lac'd with his Golden Blood,
> And his gash'd Stabs, look'd like a Breach in Nature,
> For Ruines wastfull entrance: there the Murtherers,
> Steep'd in the Colours of their Trade; their Daggers
> Unmannerly breech'd with gore.   (II iii)

Is Aubrey's prose truly instinct with something of Shakespeare's genius, or am I imagining all this, transubstantiating
clumsiness to felicity? There were those who thought Aubrey a
maggotty-headed credulous fellow, and it is possible that his
especial attraction is for those of us who are maggotty-headed
credulous fellows.[2]

[2] For a comparison of Aubrey and Clarendon in such matters, see my essay on
'The Wit and Weight of Clarendon' in a forthcoming volume in honour of Irvin
Ehrenpreis: *Augustan Studies*, ed. Douglas Lane Patey.

Gower is cooler, but the critical argument can be heated. Is he an ordinary writer, or one who uses the ordinary? Are clichés and verbal formulae passive within his poetry, or active? Making use of the textual findings of Gower's great editor G. C. Macaulay, and of Macaulay's most authoritative reviewer (W. P. Ker), Lewis seized upon their instance of revision as a nub, at what has long been acknowledged as one of Gower's great moments in *Confessio Amantis*:

> And as sche caste hire yhe aboute,
> Sche syh clad in o suite a route
> Of ladis, wher thei comen ryde
> Along under the wodes syde:
> On faire amblende hors thei sete,
> That were al whyte, fatte and grete,
> And everichon thei ride on side.
> The Sadles were of such a Pride,
> With Perle and gold so wel begon,
> So riche syh sche nevere non;
> In kertles and in Copes riche
> Thei weren clothed, alle liche,
> Departed evene of whyt and blew;
> With alle lustes that sche knew
> Thei were enbrouded overal.
> Here bodies weren long and smal,
> The beaute faye upon her face
> Non erthly thing it may desface;
> Corones on here hed thei beere,
> As ech of hem a qweene weere . . .
>   (iv 1305-24)

That Gower always, or often, calculated . . . those reticences which delight us in his poetry, is very unlikely. But there is evidence that he knew, in his own way, what he was about. The famous line
    The beaute faye upon her face
attained its present form only by successive revisions—revisions which demonstrate, so far as such things can be demonstrated, the working of a fine, and finely self-critical, poetic impulse. The first version—
    The beaute of hire face schon
    Wel bryhtere than the cristall ston,
—is just what would have contented the ordinary 'unconscious' spinner of yarns in rhyme; but it did not content Gower.[3]

---

[3] *The Allegory of Love*, p. 204.

Not, then, the ordinary spinner of yarns; instead

> The spider's touch, how exquisitely fine!
> Feels at each thread, and lives along the line.[4]

The non-medievalist might wish to learn from his informed colleagues whether it is fanciful to feel that some of the felicity is in the way in which the lines move in and out of the plural and the distributive singular, even though the plain sense is, of course, of plurals throughout. 'Her face' means 'their faces', yes, but Gower modulates from 'Here bodies', through 'her face', to 'here hed'. Given that the triumph of the lines is both the evocation of uncompetitive beauty (even while the lines speak of the nullity of any earthly competition) and the evocation of benign interchangeability ('As ech of hem a qweene weere'), it would be possible to imagine that Gower's act of imagining these singularly lovely women involves some dissolving of anything singular within a plurality, such as the linguistic norms of his age made unobtrusively convenient. Possible, but possibly mistaken. With a poet like T. S. Eliot, undulatingly alive always to the relations of singular and plural, such speculation would not be far-fetched; with Gower, the reader who is not a Gower-scholar must seek guidance from his betters. Sometimes his betters are not only stringent but astringent.

J. A. W. Bennett wrote:

'No earthly thing or person can compare with them for the other-worldly beauty in their faces'. The couplet has been justly praised, its meaning not always grasped.[5]

But this still leaves some questions about those delicacies of meaning for which the word 'grasped' is too robust. That Gower's word 'thing' needs to be expanded as 'thing or person' is itself important—and no word is more important to Gower than 'thing'. Not less suggestive is the difference between Bennett's translation of 'desface' here—'can *compare* with them'—and the translation which he gives in his glossary under 'desface': 'disfigure, mar'. For the reader needs to know what play, if any, there is over the features of the word 'desface'; needs to know, that is, whether the rhyme of 'face' and 'des-

---

[4] Pope, *An Essay on Man*, i 217-8.   [5] *Selections from John Gower* (1968), p. 150.

face'—despite or because of the medieval conventions about such rhyming[6]—might have been alive as at least a different kind of rhyme from those which flank it (*overal/smal*, and *beere/weere*). The poignant hopelessness of any earthly competition would then be limned in the move from 'face' to 'desface', the latter a word which may foolishly try to annul the former but which succeeds only in ending up saying it again. The rhyme of the earlier version—

> The beaute of hire face shon
> Wel bryhtere than the cristall ston

—is in comparison a merely predictable reflection.

'No earthly . . .' has become a cliché (no earthly use, no earthly good) now that its heavenly contrast has been lost; but a modern poet such as Geoffrey Hill can create his exact sad meaning out of refusing to acquiesce in the uncontrasting cliché, and out of swerving at the last moment back to the unearthly:

> I love my work and my children. God
> Is distant, difficult. Things happen.
> Too near the ancient troughs of blood
> Innocence is no earthly weapon.
> ('Ovid in the Third Reich')

It was this 'no earthly' of Hill's which brought to mind some other lines of his which may clarify what is at issue in Gower's rhyme of 'face'/'desface'. In what is likewise an evocation of the enduring dead (though far from the world of faery), Hill has written:

> Grass resurrects to mask, to strangle,
> Words glossed on stone, lopped stone-angel;
> But the dead maintain their ground—
> That there's no getting round—
> ('The Distant Fury of Battle')

The impossibility is lodged not only in the argumentativeness of the clichés but also in *round*'s being so obdurately lodged in *ground*. Is such an art of language unthinkably remote from Gower's art? Bennett does seem to be in two minds. 'Can

---

[6] Medieval writers regarded such rhyming as technically commendable and aesthetically pleasing. See J. A. Burrow, *Ricardian Poetry* (1971), pp. 20-1, 148.

compare with them' proffers 'desface' as entirely abstract, its features all worn away, having no relation to those faces with which the poet rhymes it; but Bennett's gloss 'disfigure' would keep in play some possibility of features. Is Gower's word quite without such an intimation of mortality as 'can put them out of countenance'? Has it no continuity with Adam's cry in *Paradise Lost* (ix 900-1)?

> How art thou lost, how on a sudden lost,
> Defac't, deflourd, and now to Death devote!

The two most potent words in Gower are 'soft' and 'thing', words of entirely different texture which yet have in common a high degree of plasticity such as is altogether germane to Gower's supreme concern: metamorphosis. 'Soft' has internal plasticity, the plasticity which can greatly change its shape (and Gower's 'soft' still includes the internal plasticity of silence— 'Thei speken alle, and sche was softe', i 2564). 'Thing' has external plasticity, the plasticity of being applicable to a great number of shapes. 'Soft' and 'thing' are likely to be found animating most of the great passages in Gower; and Gower's greatest feats are likely to call upon—to be called into being by—the two words together.

> And thus when that thi liht is faded
> And Vesper scheweth him alofte,
> And that the nyht is long and softe,
> Under the cloudes derke and stille
> Thanne hath this thing most of his wille.
> (iv 3208-12)

'Soft' is clearly at one with one side of Gower's art, one side of its gentleness. 'Gower's language', said W. P. Ker, 'is never strained, and it is never anything but gentle'.[7] But gentleness is not weakness, and so is not simply softness; Lewis therefore, probably remembering what Ker had said and needing strongly to qualify it, was urgent:

His true quality comes out rather in the ring of such a line as
    The newe schame of sennes olde,
where we are surprised at this element of iron in a poet elsewhere so gentle, so fanciful, and so at peace.[8]

[7] *Essays on Medieval Literature* (1905), p. 107.   [8] *The Allegory of Love*, p. 212.

It is this feeling for the iron, only against which can softness truly be felt, that gives such sinister biding life to the lines which capture Pauline's being lured by the false priests to spend the night in the temple:

And al withinne in prive place
A softe bedd of large space
Thei hadde mad and encourtined,
Wher sche was afterward engined.
(i 875-8)

A gin-trap is iron and unyielding; the 'softe bedd' is welcoming and yielding; and the horror is in the very softness of the trap, so soft and so untender, just as the horror is in the bedroom's cloistered erotic privacy ('in prive place'), waiting to be violated, and in the taunting equanimity with which the amplitude of the bed—'A softe bedd of large space'—will prove to be the confines of a narrow trap. There is nothing soft about the head which sees this grimly corrupted softness of a bed, or about the heart which feels the happily uncorrupted one, as in the well-known relaxed comedy of the dwelling-place of the God of sleep:

And for he scholde slepe softe,
Upon a fethrebed alofte
He lith with many a pilwe of doun:
The chambre is strowed up and doun
With swevenes many thousendfold.
(iv 3019-23)

The word 'softe' is drawn from the inner world of sleep ('he scholde slepe softe') out to the outer world that ministers to sleep ('softe, / Upon a fethrebed alofte'), by a progression that is affectionately paralleled in the way that the dreams from the inner world turn out to litter genially the room, dreams as daily and indubitable as, say, pillows:

He lith with many a pilwe of doun:
The chambre is strowed up and doun
With swevenes many thousendfold.

The transition—effecting this Saul Steinberg tactility of humour in the solid soft dreams—is managed through that *rime riche* on 'doun': at first the down of the pillows, and then at once the happy adverbial carelessness of 'strowed up and doun'. Once again the non-medievalist stands in need of being told about the conventions of such rhyming in Gower's day, though this would not have to involve accepting the belief that if something were a convention, this would mean that it was thereby not available for discreet creative suggestion. When Ker, who quoted with pleasure the description of sleep's home ('it is good writing')[9], chose to end his twenty-three-line excerpt halfway through the *doun/doun* couplet, he robbed the passage of one of its lovely slumberous untossing turns.

'Soft' feels the shaping spirit of imagination within itself: 'thing' challenges the shaping spirit of imagination, partly by the sheer width of its applicability, and partly by its propensity to offer itself as a contrast to the imagined. 'Things and imaginings' (Samuel Beckett). 'No ideas but in things' (William Carlos Williams). 'Not Ideas about the Thing but the Thing Itself' (Wallace Stevens). To value an art such as Gower's which can make so much of 'things', it is necessary to see as only a half-truth the insistence that in poetry the concrete is to be preferred to the abstract. (F. W. Bateson used to ask, 'What could be more abstract than Leavis's use of the word ''concrete''?') It is necessary to return to some sense of the imagination's power as exactly the power of abstracting and generalizing.

It is the combination in the word 'thing' of the most daily and solid object-ness, thinginess, with the most generalizing of abstract gestures, that leads Wordsworth to love and need the word, so that it rolls through all things of his; just as it leads the philosopher Austin, who knows how to do things with words including the word 'thing'; and as it leads Empson, whose six-line poem 'Let it go' finds the word unobtrusively inescapable in three of its lines, and whose poem 'The Scales' ends with a great conjunction which is both a casual gesture towards the socially known and a taking upon itself of the mystery of things:

> Say (she suspects) to sea Nile only brings
> Delta and indecision, who instead
> Far back up country does enormous things.

---

[9] *Essays on Medieval Literature*, p. 119.

Gower can make all the depredations of time pivot upon the
word 'thing', as when Venus says to the aged lover: 'The thing
is torned into was' (viii 2435)—a line in comparison with whose
meticulous indecorum the linguistic innovation of Hopkins
sounds melodramatic:

> This to hoard unheard,
> Heard unheeded, leaves me a lonely began.
> ('To seem the stranger lies my lot . . .')

There is a fine fitness in the very words with which Richard II
is said to have urged Gower to his enterprise:

> And bad me doo my besynesse
> That to his hihe worthinesse
> Som newe thing I scholde boke . . .
> (*Prologus* 49-51*)

The 'newe thing' is the re-casting of the old, and this is clear
in Gower's metamorphosis of Ovid's *Metamorphoses*. Gower's
enterprise is a meta-metamorphosis. In saying that for Gower
'the *Metamorphoses* had a powerful direct appeal', Bennett is
drawn naturally to such a word as 'transformation', a word
which is right both for the plasticity within the stories and for
the plasticity with which Gower treats Ovid. Once again there
is a congruence of the internal and the external. 'It is the
miraculous transformation of human lovers into bird, beast, or
tree that most excites his sympathy and touches him to pity and
to poetry';[10] this, and the scarcely less miraculous transformation of poetry into poetry. When Bennett says with much
truth that 'his renderings of the stories of Alcione and Philomela show how much more he was than a mere translator', one
might add that it is the congruity of such a word as 'renderings'
both to the feats within Gower's poetry and to the feats of
Gower's poetry that animates his art; and therefore that what is
then offered by Bennett as the contrastive notion of 'a mere
translator' is no more than a polemical convenience.

Behind Bennett's use of the word 'transformation' is Derek
Pearsall's, in his fine essay on Gower's narrative art.[11] When
Pearsall says of the story of Tereus, Philomela and Procne, that

---

10 *Selections*, p. xii.
11 'Gower's Narrative Art', *P.M.L.A.*, lxxxi (1966), 475-84.

'the transformations, which follow, are nothing in Ovid, but are developed by Gower with great charm and tenderness', or says that the story of Ceix and Alceone 'makes a similar use of the transformations to suggest human values in poeticized form', the word 'transformations' is perfectly applied to the narrative and is at the same time perfectly applicable to the narrative art.[12]

How, though, does Gower incarnate within his very words the metamorphoses which are his ancient and novel preoccupation? What metamorphosis in other words do his words realize? One might start with the simplicity of genius in the turn within the penitent beast-like Nebuchadnezzar:

> And so thenkende he gan doun bowe,
> And thogh him lacke vois and speche,
> He gan up with his feet areche,
> And wailende in his bestly stevene
> He made his pleignte unto the hevene.
> He kneleth in his wise and braieth,
> To seche merci and assaieth
> His god, which made him nothing strange,
> Whan that he sih his pride change.
>
> (i 3022-30)

It is the minutest change of the unspoken 'prayeth' to the ringing 'braieth' upon which these lines turn. G. C. Macaulay speaks levelly of Nebuchadnezzar as 'braying for mercy' (p. xxxix). 'Braieth' is everything that is still unredeemedly animal ('his bestly stevene'), and yet it is within an air's-breath of being human. (No animal can pray.) You must prick up your ears to make quite sure what word you have heard: prayeth? brayeth? 'Kneleth', before this word, and 'merci' after it, exert a mild but irresistible pressure to release the word 'prayeth'.[13] But then when Nebuchadnezzar brays, he does pray; the distinction beautifully falls away within God's forgiveness, and Gower's brayer is answered. Nebuchadnezzar may 'lacke vois and speche', but nevertheless 'He made his pleignte unto the hevene'.

---

[12] Charles Tomlinson has a subtle account of these things, particularly in modern poetry, in *Poetry and Metamorphosis* (1983).

[13] See i 933-4:   And she began to bidde and preie
                      Upon the bare ground knelende.

The 'change' of which the last line speaks is therefore not only the explicit change from Nebuchadnezzar's pride to his humility, voiced when he 'braieth', but it also listens back to the punitive change which had come upon him when he was transformed into this beast, and then it listens forward to the merciful change which will now come upon him when he will be transformed ('in a twinklinge of a lok') back to a man; all this is incarnate in the 'change' of 'prayeth' to 'braieth'. Moreover, the 'pride' of which the last line speaks is not Nebuchadnezzar's alone. Gower's art of admonition permits us no easy superiority to his exemplary sinners, and there is a well-judged warning against complacency—against an audience's complacency—couched within the *brayeth/prayeth* turn. For though prayer may be heard as everything, it must also be held in all humility to be nothing. What perhaps, in the ears of God, is praying but braying? George Herbert's amazing list of kennings for prayer, in 'Prayer', comes short of Gower in this one respect.

So when Ker praises in Gower 'the polite simplicity, the perfect ease of conversation, which was the peculiar gift of the French poets',[14] one might wish to press the word 'conversation' to release from within itself the word 'conversion', since Gower's ease of conversation is necessarily at one with an art of conversion, both in converting French virtues into English ones and in engaging—as in the stories of Nebuchadnezzar and Midas—with conversion in every sense of the word.

It was the highly coloured and even exhibitionist lines of Tourneur and of Middleton which T. S. Eliot found to

exhibit that perpetual slight alteration of language, words perpetually juxtaposed in new and sudden combinations, meanings perpetually *eingeschachtelt* into meanings, which evidences a very high development of the senses, a development of the English language which we have perhaps never equalled. ('Philip Massinger')[15]

But it will be by marrying this formulation to another of Eliot's great formulations about alteration—'to be original with the *minimum* of alteration, is sometimes more distinguished than to be original with the *maximum* of alteration'[16]—that we will be

[14] *Essays on Medieval Literature*, pp. 114-5.
[15] *Selected Essays* (1932), 1951 edn, p. 209.
[16] Introductory Essay to *London* and *The Vanity of Human Wishes* (1930), p. 11.

able to apprehend the particular development of the English
language which is not only recorded but is in process in the art
of an unflamboyant poet like Gower, devoted to deep quiet
alterations as the medium, the element, and the subject of his
poetry.

The difference between Gower's capability, which scarcely
ever slept, and his high power, which can instil 'Such sober
certainty of waking bliss' (or woe), can be glimpsed in the juxtaposition of two of his metamorphoses. First, the story of
Acteon and the naked Diana:

> Bot he his yhe awey ne swerveth
> Fro hire, which was naked al,
> And sche was wonder wroth withal,
> And him, as sche which was godesse,
> Forschop anon, and the liknesse
> Sche made him taken of an Hert,
> Which was tofore hise houndes stert,
> That ronne besiliche aboute
> With many an horn and many a route . . .
>
> (i 366-74)

This is fluent and serviceable, and is better poetic narration
than all but a very few English poets have managed; and yet
nothing in it gives unforgettable life to the moment of metamorphosis. Gower's equanimity is not felt here to be in tension
with the fear or delight which would validate equanimity as
something other than equability. Then compare the metamorphosis effected on the next page not by Diana but by Medusa
and her sister-Gorgons:

> What man on hem his chiere caste
> And hem behield, he was als faste
> Out of a man into a Ston
> Forschape, and thus ful manyon
> Deceived were, of that thei wolde
> Misloke, wher that thei ne scholde.
>
> (i 413-8)

Once again a man is 'forschape'; but here the language is instinct with the change. It is not only the compact prepositional
immediacy (in both senses) of the line 'Out of a man into a
Ston' (the effect is of a grim 'hey presto', even while such

words are unimaginable in Gower); it is also the apprehensive power of the rhyme *caste/faste*. For though 'faste' means 'quickly', it petrifies and is locked fast under the Gorgonian pressure of 'caste' before it and of 'Ston' after it;[17] and though 'caste' means 'threw' ('his chiere caste'), it too becomes petrified.

> Cast noght thin yhe upon Meduse,
> That thou be torned into Ston. . .
> (i 438-9)

No sooner said than done, if you say 'Cast'. To cast is 'to throw anything plastic or fluid into a particular shape' (as in *Cursor Mundi*, 1300); it is a wondrous necessary word to a poet of metamorphosis and forshaping, and Gower is at once fixed and various in his transformations of the rhyme *cast/fast*, all rhyming being by its very nature an act of casting and of making fast. C. S. Lewis said of some instances of Gower's art that 'In all these—and there are many more—the poetry is so pure in its own kind that no analysis can resolve it into elements'.[18] But though Gower's purity is indeed a challenge to the analytic critic, there will be some purchase when the subject is itself the resolving of elements into other elements or combinations.

Metamorphosis may run not only from but into the fluid, and Gower's fluency is adapted to catch these escapes and escapades, as in another moment of forshaping, in the wrestling of Hercules and Achelons:

> This Geant wot he mai noght longe
> Endure under so harde bondes,

[17] 'Fast' is an instance of what Freud discusses in 'The Antithetical Sense of Primal Words' (1910). See i 519-22, on Ulysses and the Sirens:

> That noman of his compaignie
> Hath pouer under that folie
> His Ere for no lust to caste;
> For he hem stoppede alle faste.

v 3603-7:
> Sche tok him thanne a maner glue,
> The which was of so gret vertu,
> That where a man i wolde caste,
> It scholde binde anon so faste
> That noman mihte it don aweie.

v 4068-70:
> Sche tok Eson in bothe hire armes,
> And made him forto slepe faste,
> And him upon hire herbes caste.

[18] *The Allegory of Love*, p. 202.

> And thoghte he wolde out of hise hondes
> Be sleyhte in som manere ascape.
> And as he couthe himself forschape,
> In liknesse of an Eddre he slipte
> Out of his hond, and forth he skipte . . . (iv 2104-10)

The 'bondes' of the rhyme—(and every rhyme, again, is an act of bonding, the bonds of trust or of bondage, and not necessarily what Milton called 'the troublesom and modern bondage of Rimeing')—fail to hold the gliding Protean elider. 'Out of hise hondes' at the end of one line slides blithely on into 'Out of his hond' at the beginning of a subsequent line; the repetition is alive with relief, as of a wish that has exactly come to pass, a hope answered in act. The act of escaping is the act of forshaping, as the rhyme *ascape/forschape* instances; and the slipperiness of the snake gives body to what could so easily have been a clichéd abstractness in 'out of his hond', so that Gower's lines are like a muted version of Robert Lowell's evocation of Cleopatra's pain when it seems that death may elude her:

> Poisonous snakes gave up their secrets,
> you held them with practiced hands,
> you showed your breasts. Then bolder, more ferocious,
> death slipping through your fingers,
>
> how could you go aboard Octavian's galleys,
> how could you march on foot, unhumbled,
> to crown triumphant Caesar's triumph—
> no queen now, but a private woman?
> ('Cleopatra', an 'imitation' of Horace, Odes, Book I, 37)

In Gower it is the movements within the verse itself, and not Lowell's saddened elusive use of cliché ('slipping through your fingers'), which animate these metamorphoses, and which are continuous with Gower's 'devotion to movement and progression, his preoccupation with things that change as you watch them'.[19]

A third form—or process—of metamorphosis comes when the wonder is not the changes effected upon the characters, whether into fixity or fluidity, but rather the changes effected by the characters. The touch of Midas, say. The cumulative power of Gower's verse here—a cumulative power in touch

---

[19] *The Allegory of Love*, p. 207.

with avarice as essentially cumulative and with horror as no less so—asks ample quotation. Midas wonders whether to choose delight, or worship, or profit.

And thus upon the pointz diverse
Diverseliche he gan reherce
What point him thoghte for the beste;
Bot pleinly forto gete him reste
He can no siker weie caste.
And natheles yit ate laste
He fell upon the coveitise
Of gold; and thanne in sondri wise
He thoghte, as I have seid tofore,
Hou tresor mai be sone lore,
And hadde an inly gret desir
Touchende of such recoverir,
Hou that he mihte his cause availe
To gete him gold withoute faile.
Withinne his herte and thus he preiseth
The gold, and seith hou that it peiseth
Above al other metall most:
'The gold,' he seith, 'may lede an host
To make werre ayein a King;
The gold put under alle thing,
And set it whan him list above;
The gold can make of hate love
And werre of pes and ryht of wrong,
And long to schort and schort to long;
Withoute gold mai be no feste,
Gold is the lord of man and beste,
And mai hem bothe beie and selle;
So that a man mai sothly telle
That al the world to gold obeieth.'
Forthi this king to Bachus preieth
To grante him gold, bot he excedeth
Mesure more than him nedeth.
Men tellen that the maladie
Which cleped is ydropesie
Resembled is unto this vice
Be weie of kinde of Avarice:
The more ydropesie drinketh,
The more him thursteth, for him thinketh
That he mai nevere drinke his fille;
So that ther mai nothing fulfille

The lustes of his appetit:
And riht in such a maner plit
Stant Avarice and evere stod;
The more he hath of worldes good,
The more he wolde it kepe streyte,
And evere mor and mor coveite.
And riht in such condicioun
Withoute good discrecioun
This king with avarice is smite,
That al the world it myhte wite:
For he to Bachus thanne preide,
That wherupon his hond he leide,
It scholde thurgh his touche anon
Become gold, and therupon
This god him granteth as he bad.
Tho was this king of Frige glad,
And forto put it in assai
With al the haste that he mai,
He toucheth that, he toucheth this,
And in his hond al gold it is,
The Ston, the Tree, the Lef, the gras,
The flour, the fruit, al gold it was.
Thus toucheth he, whil he mai laste
To go, bot hunger ate laste
Him tok, so that he moste nede
Be weie of kinde his hunger fede.
The cloth was leid, the bord was set,
And al was forth tofore him fet,
His disch, his coppe, his drinke, his mete;
Bot whanne he wolde or drinke or ete,
Anon as it his mouth cam nyh,
It was al gold, and thanne he syh
Of Avarice the folie.
And he with that began to crie,
And preide Bachus to foryive
His gilt, and soffre him forto live
And be such as he was tofore,
So that he were noght forlore.
This god, which herde of his grevance,
Tok rowthe upon his repentance,
And bad him go forth redily
Unto a flod was faste by,
Which Paceole thanne hyhte,
In which as clene as evere he myhte

He scholde him waisshen overal,
And seide him thanne that he schal
Recovere his ferste astat ayein.
This king, riht as he herde sein,
Into the flod goth fro the lond,
And wissh him bothe fot and hond,
And so forth al the remenant,
As him was set in covenant:
And thanne he syh merveilles strange,
The flod his colour gan to change,
The gravel with the smale Stones
To gold thei torne bothe at ones,
And he was quit of that he hadde,
And thus fortune his chance ladde.
And whan he sih his touche aweie,
He goth him hom the rihte weie.

(v 217-316)

There is much here to weigh, even as gold is weighed ('hou that it peiseth'). Gower's, like Milton's, is an art endlessly firm and tactful in prolepsis. So when Midas delights in the fact that 'Gold is the lord of man and beste', he is averting his eyes from the implications of that lordship and of his being a man; and when he delights in the fact 'That al the world to gold obeieth', he refuses to see what is to come, when he will see undelighted all delight, himself doomed to obey gold beyond all previous manner of obedience. 'Withoute gold mai be no feste': and with gold—if you have the touch of Midas—there may be no feast either.

The word 'gold' is tolled, and as with all repetitions, the word is at once made fuller and fuller and emptier and emptier by the repetition. The word becomes a hypnotic pressure and an oppressive evacuation, in a way that beautifully and chillingly answers to the addictive ambition and its negation. The word comes ten times in twenty-four lines, at the heart of which is the litany ('The gold . . .', at the head of every other line for eight lines) before which Midas prostrates himself. In the later evocation of doom just starting to recognise itself, Gower's touch is perfect:

And forto put it in assai
With al the haste that he mai,
He toucheth that, he toucheth this,

> And in his hond al gold it is,
> The Ston, the Tree, the Lef, the gras,
> The flour, the fruit, al gold it was.

How obdurately the gratification of 'al gold it is' hardens into the ominous 'al gold it was'. Ten lines later, this turn ('al gold it is' / 'al gold it was') has returned, and turned upon itself. No longer at the end of the line but at its head, its words are turned in admonition:

> Bot whanne he wolde or drinke or ete,
> Anon as it his mouth cam nyh,
> It was al gold . . .

Once again Gower uses the turn of a rhyme to combine a turn of phrase and a turn of fortune or a turning of shape. The rhyme of *fille* and *fulfille*, despite what may be truly said of medieval conventions, could perhaps still feel different from the rhyme which succeeds it (*appetit/plit*); and the rhyme of *laste/laste* is the nemesis of *rime riche*, locked by the rich touch of Midas:[20]

> Thus toucheth he, whil he mai laste
> To go, bot hunger ate laste
> Him tok; so that he moste nede
> Be weie of kinde his hunger fede.

The metamorphic sequence is there within the tactful word 'touch'. At its first appearance it is all innocent abstraction: 'Touchende of such recoverir' ('concerning . . .'). But then, at Midas' prayer of his precious bane, it becomes the touch of this hand:

> For he to Bachus thanne preide,
> That wherupon his hond he leide,
> It scholde thurgh his touche anon
> Become gold, and therupon
> This god him granteth as he bad.

[20] Baudelaire has some telling rhymes when thinking of Midas, in 'Alchimie de la Douleur':

> Hermès inconnu qui m'assistes
> Et qui toujours m'intimidas,
> Tu me rends l'égal de Midas,
> Le plus triste des alchimistes;
> Par toi je change l'or en fer
> Et le paradis en enfer.

The word 'touch' compacts the daily and the miraculous, not only in a general way because of the saints' touch (the king's evil), but in particular because of the metallurgical assaying in the word:

> And forto put it in assai
> With al the haste that he mai,
> He toucheth that, he toucheth this . . .

For a little while, this touch is childlike and ingenuous; Gower's syntax lets us feel Midas' new and foolish pleasure in testing out his touch: 'He toucheth that, he toucheth this . .'. It works! But when, four lines later, the words have darkened with the sombre turn 'Thus toucheth he . . .', the bale and the bane are imminent. In the end, the word 'touch' returns, but in order to go away for good: 'And whan he sih his touche aweie . . .' But this absolution would not have been possible if Midas had not prayed for forgiveness. Where Nebuchadnezzar was forgiven when he brayed/prayed, Midas is forgiven when he acknowledges a different compacting, the compacting of his sin and its illusory golden rewards:

> And preide Bachus to foryive
> His gilt . . .

Humility takes him back:

> Forthi this king to Bachus preieth
> To grante him gold . . .

The taint of guilt (gilt) and of avarice will be washed away; the mercenary connotations of 'quit' (redeem a debt) are there at the end only to be redeemed by the metamorphosis of the gravel to gold:

> And thanne he syh merveilles strange,
> The flod his colour gan to change,
> The gravel with the smale Stones
> To gold thei torne bothe at ones,
> And he was quit of that he hadde,
> And thus fortune his chance ladde.
> And whan he sih his touche aweie,
> He goth him hom the rihte weie . . .

W. P. Ker may have been thinking of this unsuffering scape-goat of a stream when he said:

It is not easy without long quotations to show how good Gower can be; one cannot tell the beauty of a stream from looking at a selected inch or two.[21]

The relation between the turning of a phrase, the turning of someone into someone or something else, and the bodily act of turning: this is the hinge in the story of Florent and the loathly lady.

> The prive women were asent,
> That scholden ben of his assent:
> Hire ragges thei anon of drawe,
> And, as it was that time lawe,
> She hadde bath, sche hadde reste,
> And was arraied to the beste.
> Bot with no craft of combes brode
> Thei myhte hire hore lockes schode,
> And sche ne wolde noght be schore
> For no conseil, and thei therfore,
> With such atyr as tho was used,
> Ordeinen that it was excused,
> And hid so crafteliche aboute,
> That noman myhte sen hem oute.
> Bot when sche was fulliche arraied
> And hire atyr was al assaied,
> Tho was sche foulere on to se:
> Bot yit it may non other be,
> Thei were wedded in the nyht;
> So wo begon was nevere knyht
> As he was thanne of mariage.
> And sche began to pleie and rage,
> As who seith, I am wel ynowh;
> Bot he therof nothing ne lowh,
> For sche tok thanne chiere on honde
> And clepeth him hire housebonde,
> And seith, 'My lord, go we to bedde,
> For I to that entente wedde,
> That thou schalt be my worldes blisse:'
> And profreth him with that to kisse,

---

[21] *Essays on Medieval Literature*, p. 116.

As sche a lusti Lady were.
His body myhte wel be there,
Bot as of thoght and of memoire
His herte was in purgatoire.
Bot yit for strengthe of matrimoine
He myhte make non essoine,
That he ne mot algates plie
To gon to bedde of compaignie:
And whan thei were abedde naked,
Withoute slep he was awaked;
He torneth on that other side,
For that he wolde hise yhen hyde
Fro lokynge on that foule wyht.
The chambre was al full of lyht,
The courtins were of cendal thinne,
This newe bryd which lay withinne,
Thogh it be noght with his acord,
In armes sche beclipte hire lord,
And preide, as he was torned fro,
He wolde him torne ayeinward tho;
'For now,' sche seith, 'we ben bothe on'.
And he lay stille as eny ston,
Bot evere in on sche spak and preide,
And bad him thenke on that he seide,
Whan that he tok hire be the hond.
    He herde and understod the bond,
How he was set to his penance,
And as it were a man in trance
He torneth him al sodeinly,
And syh a lady lay him by
Of eyhtetiene wynter age,
Which was the faireste of visage
That evere in al this world he syh.
                              (i 1743-1805)

The first turn is that of understandable revulsion:

> And whan thei were abedde naked,
> Withoute slep he was awaked;
> He torneth on that other side,
> For that he wolde his yhen hyde
> Fro lokynge on that foule wyht.

At which point, it is confirmed to us—though not yet dawning
upon Florent—that all will be well. For the division of the

couplet is such as to make its second line swing open like a great door to let in the light:

> . . . hyde
> Fro lokynge on that foule wyht.
> The chambre was al full of lyht,

—it has all the simplicity of literalness and all the suggestiveness of symbolism. Florent is to turn again. The lady's prayer is an appeal to his honour; she

> preide, as he was torned fro,
> He wolde him torne ayeinward tho . . .

At the climactic moment, the climax not of love but of honour, Florent does turn; the rhyme of 'hond' and 'bond' is again a sacrament of two made one, as a rhyme may delight to be (as well as recalling the *honde/housebonde* rhyme of thirty lines earlier):

> And bad him thenke on that he seide,
> Whan that he tok hire be the hond.
>   He herde and understod the bond,
> How he was set to his penance,
> And as it were a man in trance
> He torneth him al sodeinly,
> And syh a lady lay him by
> Of eyhtetiene wynter age,
> Which was the faireste of visage
> That evere in al this world he syh . . .

'In trance' is poised between before and after, an intersection of time and the timeless. 'He *torneth* him al sodeinly' catches the precipitancy with which a reluctant decision is irreversibly willed into act, since before and after this act of turning the tenses are not present but past. Relief and release, of both of which Gower is a master, are alive in the heartfelt evocation of young beauty: 'of eyhtetiene wynter age'. For winter, though it makes perfect sense and could be said only to mean 'years', cannot but call up the old age which has just been completely metamorphosed into youth and yet which cannot be forgotten, not least because Florent has still, it seems, another decision to take: not, this time, the decision as to whether to be honourable, but whether to have the lady be young by day or by night.

That Gower is aware of how the 'wynter' of years may either
be held parallel to old age or be held at right angles to youth
is clear from the story of Jason and Medea. There we hear of
'a Raven, which was told / Of nyne hundred wynter old'
(v 4133-4); and then, thirty lines later, the potion works its
magic:

> And tho sche yaf him drinke a drauhte,
> Of which his youthe ayein he cauhte,
> His hed, his herte and his visage
> Lich unto twenty wynter Age;
> Hir hore heres were away,
> And lich unto the freisshe Maii,
> Whan passed ben the colde schoures,
> Riht so recovereth he his floures.
>   (v 4167-74)

'Wynter old' belongs naturally with 'nyne hundred', whereas
'wynter Age' poignantly dissents from 'twenty' (as it did from
'eyhtetiene'), as is intimated by the immediate reversion to
'hore heres'. Yet these grey hairs are mentioned only because
they 'were away', and if the 'colde schoures' then continue to
keep the memory grey, they are at once rhymed away, spelled
away, by 'floures'.

Gower makes us feel the very moment of metamorphosis by
so tactfully keeping in touch with the old and the new/young:

> He torneth him al sodeinly,
> And syh a lady lay him by
> Of eyhtetiene wynter age . . .

Gower's tact is the clearer if we set his lines beside what George
Meredith (a poet, after all, of more than talent) makes of a
loathly-lady story, in 'The Song of Courtesy':

> When that evil lady he lay beside
> Bade him turn to greet his bride,
> What, think you, he did?
>   O, to spare her pain,
> And let not his loathing her loathliness vain
>   Mirror too plain,
>   Sadly, sighingly,
>   Almost dyingly,
> Turned he and kissed her once and again.

> Like Sir Gawain, gentles, should we?
> *Silent, all!* But for pattern agree
> There's none like the Knight of Courtesy.
>
> Sir Gawain sprang up amid laces and curls:
> Kisses are not wasted pearls:-
> What clung in his arms?
>   O, a maiden flower,
> Burning with blushes the sweet bride-bower,
>   Beauty her dower!

The physical act of 'Turned he' is forceless in comparison with Gower's act of turning, just because of the complete absence in Meredith of any incarnation of the other great turning, the metamorphosis; the moment is skipped: 'What clung in his arms?' Likewise the flower is mere rhyming prettiness (*flower/ bower/dower*), whereas in Gower's Jason the flowers are the ineffaceability of winter within the gratitude of spring:

> His hore heres were away,
> And lich unto the freisshe Maii,
> Whan passed ben the colde schoures,
> Riht so recovereth he his floures.

As for the simplicity in Gower of 'eyhtetiene wynter age', and its tacit discrimination, these are like the song at its best; in Wyatt, say; or in Bob Dylan, who sings (in 'The Lonesome Death of Hattie Carroll') of the young assailant that he 'had twenty-four years' but of the assailed woman that she 'was fifty-one years old'.

Gower is at his deepest in such metamorphoses as these of Florent and the loathly lady, or Jason and Medea, because they so directly relate to something crucial both to all life and to his art—or, more exactly, to that conjunction of life and art which Lewis so cogently praises in *Confessio Amantis*. For though we are none of us likely to be metamorphosed as are those in Ovid, we are all of us sure—should we live long enough—to be metamorphosed by time. Life has a way of changing 'eyhtetiene wynter age' into some other reckoning within which the word 'wynter' sits more happily and unhappily. Pondering the human and technical difficulty presented by the obligation to have an honourable palinode, Lewis says of Gower: 'He finds in his own experience—the experience of an old man—how

Life itself manages the necessary palinode; and then manages
his in the same way'. But this palinode is so exquisitely appropriate to Gower's enterprise because it is metamorphosis, none
the less miraculous for being in the fullest sense a daily occurrence. It is this which makes me question two words in Lewis's
touching account:

> This lover is separated by a fatal barrier from the 'yonge lusti route'
> of his rivals. He is old. The *Confessio Amantis*, written by an old poet,
> in failing health, appropriately tells the story of an old man's un-
> successful love for a young girl.[22]

For 'fatal barrier' is not altogether right; there is no fatal *barrier*
between the young and the old, since the one is inexorably and
at every moment being metamorphosed into the other. This is
of no comfort to the aged lover, but barriers are a different
matter. William Empson once said to me, à propos of the difficulty of writing at the age of nearly 70 a piece in honour of the
80th birthday of his old supervisor, I. A. Richards, that one
trouble with getting old is that you all become the same age.

The elements which are metamorphosed within Gower's
poetry are often the irreducibly minimal within the language.
There is a particular life, for instance, in Gower's pronouns.
The story of Iphis is the old story of the birth of a daughter
when what the father wanted was a son. It looks set to be Ligdus
and Son, a pre-commercial *Dombey and Son*. The decision to
save the life of the newborn unwanted girl by pretending that it
is a boy turns naturally to the most ordinarily serviceable word
'it'. The word comes at first with what looks like simple abstraction:

> and that thei scholden seie
> It were a Sone:

But there the 'it' could be, not the abstract fact, but the actual
child; and so at once into the deception of the word 'him':

> and that thei scholden seie
> It were a Sone: and thus Iphis
> Thei namede him, and upon this
> The fader was mad so to wene.
>   (v 466-9)

22 *The Allegory of Love*, pp. 217-8.

The compacted deception is in the slide from 'and thus Iphis   /
Thei namede . . .', since this is within their power and they
may name the baby anything (even something deceptive, a
male name), into 'and thus Iphis / Thei namede *him*'. For this
is not just a performative, but a transformative. Gower could
have said 'her', but the use of 'him' makes it seem that the
transformation is indeed effected. Like 'the fader', we too are
'mad so to wene'. To all intents and purposes (but not all, it
will turn out), Iphis might seem now to be a boy. But if the king
is deceived, Nature is not, and Gower's 'it' keeps alive the
biding deception:

> And thus in chambre with the qweene
> This Iphis was forthdrawe tho,
> And clothed and arraied so
> Riht as a kinges Sone scholde.
> Til after, as fortune it wolde,
> Whan it was of a ten yer age,
> Him was betake in mariage
> A Duckes dowhter forto wedde,
> Which Iante hihte, and ofte abedde
> These children leien, sche and sche,
> Which of on age bothe be.
>
> (v 470-80)

'Sche and sche' is superb in its interchangeability and equanimity. 'Sche and sche': it is magnificent, but it is not marriage. Fortunately Cupid has pity on the pair of them, and
changes Iphis into what she could best be:

> Forthi Cupide hath so besett
> His grace upon this aventure,
> That he acordant to nature,
> Whan that he syh the time best,
> That ech of hem hath other kest,
> Transformeth Iphe into a man,
> Wherof the kinde love he wan
> Of lusti yonge Iante his wif;
> And tho thei ladde a merie lif . . .
>
> (v 496-504)

At last 'he' and 'his' ring true, in an act of loving transformation at once supernatural and poetical, an act which for a
moment transforms Iphis into Iphe, in a moment of onomastic

magic which is the 'merie' counterpart to the onomastic sadness in Milton which speaks, for the one and only time in that
poem, not of Lycidas but of Lycid: 'To strew the Laureat Herse
where *Lycid* lies'. For 'he' does not; only an 'it', the thought of
him.

The chastening miracle that is age's metamorphosis has as
its bracing complement the chaste miracle that is art's metamorphosis. The story of Pygmaleon, itself a work of imagination, may be compared to Adam's dream; except that instead
of going on 'he awoke and found it truth', we should have to
say of Pygmaleon and the 'image', that he awoke it and found
truth.

> I finde hou whilom ther was on,
> Whos name was Pymaleon,
> Which was a lusti man of yowthe:
> The werkes of entaile he cowthe
> Above alle othre men as tho;
> And thurgh fortune it fell him so,
> As he whom love schal travaile,
> He made an ymage of entaile
> Lich to a womman in semblance
> Of feture and of contienance,
> So fair yit nevere was figure.
> Riht as a lyves creature
> Sche semeth, for of yvor whyt
> He hath hire wroght of such delit,
> That sche was rody on the cheke
> And red on bothe hire lippes eke;
> Wherof that he himself beguileth.
> For with a goodly lok sche smyleth,
> So that thurgh pure impression
> Of his ymaginacion
> With al the herte of his corage
> His love upon this faire ymage
> He sette, and hire of love preide;
> Bot sche no word ayeinward seide.
> The longe day, what thing he dede,
> This ymage in the same stede
> Was evere bi, that ate mete
> He wolde hire serve and preide hire ete,
> And putte unto hire mowth the cuppe;
> And whan the bord was taken uppe,

> He hath hire into chambre nome,
> And after, whan the nyht was come,
> He leide hire in his bed al nakid.
> He was forwept, he was forwakid,
> He keste hire colde lippes ofte,
> And wissheth that thei weren softe,
> And ofte he rouneth in hire Ere,
> And ofte his arm now hier now there
> He leide, as he hir wolde embrace,
> And evere among he axeth grace,
> As thogh sche wiste what he mente:
> And thus himself he gan tormente
> With such desese of loves peine,
> That noman mihte him more peine.
> Bot how it were, of his penance
> He made such continuance
> Fro dai to nyht, and preith so longe,
> That his preiere is underfonge,
> Which Venus of hire grace herde;
> Be nyhte and whan that he worst ferde,
> And it lay in his nakede arm,
> The colde ymage he fieleth warm
> Of fleissh and bon and full of lif.
>
> (iv 371-423)

The greatness of Gower is his entire freedom from prurience. 'And ofte his arm now hier now there/He leide': this is reticent and unforthcoming, not prurient, and yet the difference is solely one of tone, since those very same words could so easily snigger. Donald Davie praised Gower within a context of 'The Chastity of Poetic Diction' (the larger context being *Purity of Diction in English Verse*):[23] 'it is in Gower that we find a chaste diction'.

To attend to the moment of this metamorphosis in other poets is to feel how cool and true is Gower's sense of it all, how free the spirit is. There is John Marston's 'The Metamorphosis

---

[23] (1952), p. 32, and see p. 68. Also '. . . Whan I, that mai noght fiele hir bare, / Mai lede hire clothed in myn arm' (iv 1140-1). 'The elegantly turned antithesis between "bare" and "clothed" in the last two lines releases all the sensuality latent in the word "clothed", so that its very sound (as in Keats's "wealth of *globed* peonies") becomes luxurious. One feels the touch of the lady on the lover's arm' (Burrow, *Ricardian Poetry*, p. 30).

of Pigmalions Image':

> Yet all's conceit. But shadow of that bliss
> Which now my Muse strives sweetly to display
> In this my wondrous metamorphosis.
> Daine to beleeve me, now I sadly say:
> > The stonie substance of his Image feature,
> > Was straight transform'd into a living creature.
>
> For when his hands her faire form'd limbs had felt,
> And that his armes her naked wast imbraced,
> Each part like Waxe before the sunne did melt,
> And now, oh now, he finds how he is graced
> > By his owne worke. Tut, women will relent
> > When as they finde such moving blandishment.
> > > (Stanzas 28-9)

But nothing in Marston's words brings alive 'this my wondrous metamorphosis' at the moment when the statue is
brought alive. 'Straight transform'd' is said and not felt, and
why should we 'daine to beleeve' Marston? The internal rhyme
of 'wast [waist] imbraced' ('naked wast imbraced') thickens,
and the melting wax is alien to all wonder, issuing naturally in
the knowing cynicism that decodes the story for us:

> > Tut, women will relent
> When as they finde such moving blandishment.

Or there is Dryden, who in translating Ovid is more honest
than Marston about his mixed feelings but is no better at
catching the moment of miracle or at keeping his hands off his
handiwork:

> The Youth, returning to his Mistress, hies, }
> And impudent in Hope, with ardent Eyes, }
> And beating Breast, by the dear Statue lies. }
> He kisses her white Lips, renews the Bliss,
> And looks, and thinks they redden at the Kiss;
> He thought them warm before: Nor longer stays,
> But next his Hand on her hard Bosom lays:
> Hard as it was, beginning to relent,
> It seem'd, the Breast beneath his Fingers bent;
> He felt again, his Fingers made a Print,
> 'Twas Flesh, but Flesh so firm, it rose against the Dint:
> The pleasing Task he fails not to renew:
> Soft, and more soft at ev'ry Touch it grew;

> Like pliant Wax, when chafing Hands reduce
> The former Mass to Form, and frame for Use.
> He would believe, but yet is still in pain, ⎫
> And tries his Argument of Sense again,   ⎬
> Presses the Pulse, and feels the leaping Vein. ⎭
> Convinc'd, o'erjoy'd, his studied Thanks and Praise,
> To her who made the Miracle, he pays:
> Then Lips to Lips he join'd; now freed from Fear,
> He found the Savour of the Kiss sincere:
> At this the waken'd Image op'd her Eyes,
> And view'd at once the Light and Lover, with surprize.
>   ('Pygmalion and the Statue' 72-95)

The 'surprise' is too much hers, too little Pygmalion's or ours.
But Gower makes us catch our breath in catching the moment.

> Bot how it were, of his penance
> He made such continuance
> Fro dai to nyht, and preith so longe,
> That his preiere is underfonge,
> Which Venus of hire grace herde;
> Be nyhte and whan that he worst ferde,
> And it lay in his nakede arm,
> The colde ymage he fieleth warm
> Of fleissh and bon and full of lif.

The 'it' of the statue is at odds with the 'his' of 'his nakede
arm'—'And it lay in his nakede arm'—but will be so only for
a moment longer:

> And it lay in his nakede arm,
> The colde ymage he fieleth warm
> Of fleissh and bon and full of lif.

The miraculous metamorphosis is in the trice. 'The cold ymage
he fieleth warm': at the start of the line, still a statue, and at the
end a woman, with 'fieleth' concentrating in itself—like a
hinge—both the past and the sudden present, since he is said to
feel the cold image warm. The process, which would in a comic
context resemble an Irish Bull, is one that makes sense by
courtesy of metamorphosis. Here, it is the metamorphosis of
joy: in a characteristic Johnson line from *The Vanity of Human
Wishes*, like 'Now pall the tastless Meats, and joyless Wines'
(how could they pall if they were tasteless and joyless?), it

might be the metamorphosis of disillusionment. The confidence of Gower's joy—he shares Pygmaleon's joy in his art—is fulfilled in the final line:

> The colde ymage he fieleth warm
> Of fleissh and bon and full of lif.

'Warm / Of fleissh' is fine, and—though miraculous—only to be expected; but 'warm / Of fleissh and bon and full of lif' is something else again, and goes very deep. It is as though the very bones (what in the woman might most recall the hardness of the statue) can be felt as warm;[24] and the double *and* ('Of fleissh and bon and full of lif') surges on into achieved bliss. For if Pygmaleon is in some respects a true type of the artist, he is also in some respects a true type of the lover, at once transfigurer and transfigured. 'It is only in his love that the Lover is transfigured' (Lewis).[25]

For Gower's triumph is a triumph over more than one kind of bad feeling. Prurience is one; another is misogyny. The story of Pygmaleon and the statue[26] began, after all, as a story about a man's being disgusted by women, and it is still a story which lends itself naturally either to the fiercenesses of misogyny or to the fiercenesses which are turned against misogyny, as in Ian McEwan's story about a man in love with a shopwindow-dummy ('Dead as They Come'), or in Roy Fuller's repudiation of the belief that for Pygmaleon the ending was a happy one:[27]

THE TRUTH ABOUT PYGMALION

> Do not imagine I was glad she breathed.
> My ear was pressed against the ivory:
> Suddenly appetite and longing seethed.

[24] The 'bone' is taken seriously, deeply, within 'flesh and bone' elsewhere in Gower too—

i 1530-2:
> A lothly wommannysch figure,
> That forto speke on fleisch and bon
> So foul yit syh he nevere non.

iv 3679-81:
> Hou it is torned fleissh and bon
> Into the figure of a Ston:
> He was to neysshe and sche to hard.

v 4208-9:
> Anon therof the fyr sprong oute
> And brent hir bothe fleissh and bon.

[25] *The Allegory of Love*, p. 216.
[26] For an account of what the Victorians made of the story of Pygmaleon, see Richard Jenkyns, *The Victorians and Ancient Greece* (1980), pp. 141-6.
[27] From *Buff* (1965).

Since to an ideal form I had bequeathed
All that ennobled and disquieted me
Do not imagine I was glad she breathed.

It was a trap that I myself had teethed
To find that in my virgin private she
Suddenly appetite and longing seethed.

I took away my arms that had been wreathed
About the flanks of perfect slavery:
Do not imagine I was glad she breathed.

The territory was deeply cleft and heathed
Where, art turned back into reality,
Suddenly appetite and longing seethed.

To sense the puny sword that had been sheathed,
To know the unequal clash that had to be,
Do not imagine I was glad. She breathed.
Suddenly appetite and longing seethed.

The revulsion is as much from this metamorphosis as from women: art here does not turn into reality, it turns *back* into reality.

Gower's achievement is to rise above all such disgusts and angers (which is not to deny that those too can rise to art), just as he is magnanimously indifferent to the comedy or the disgust which might attend upon the fondler of statues. The lucid dignity of Gower's creation may be set against the good-humoured preposterousness of the eighteenth-century bibliophile Henry George Quin. In Florence in 1785, Quin visited the Medici Venus every day.

I placed a chair by the pedestal, and mounting on it, I applied my lips to different parts of the statue. At first I kissed it as one would any piece of marble, but upon my conscience, at last I began to conceive it was real flesh and blood, and my favours increasing in proportion, I don't know what I should have done had not my sensual Reverie been interrupted by an ill-looking fellow who came into the room and jawed me terribly for dusting the chair-covers.

Have found out a happy *Succedaneum* for Cantharides. Put a smooth doe-skin glove on your hand, get up on a chair by the Venus de Medici and shutting your eyes pass your hand gently over all the parts of its body, this operation being repeated two or three times the nervous system will be thrown into an agreeable and innoxious state of Pride.

I shall preserve the stocking [which he tried on the statue] as a sacred relic and treasure it up in the same place with the tin fig-leaf which I stole from the Nudities of the Apollo of Belvedere.[28]

All this is, to put it mildly, very different from the steely mildness with which Gower meets the bizarrerie of his stories.

The art of Gower is a moral and spiritual metamorphosis. He transforms stories that are stonily inhuman or swampily subhuman, stories that are alive to the sick absurdities of sexual perversion and to the humiliations which the sexes visit upon each other, into a poetry of free simplicity. The poetry itself—six hundred years later—is still warm of flesh and bone and full of life. C. S. Lewis' words about Gower—'All plain styles, except the very greatest, raise a troublesome question for the critic'—might suggest that Gower's simplicity is never of the very greatest. But could there be a greater simplicity than this?

> The colde ymage he fieleth warm
> Of fleissh and bon and full of lif.

Such simplicity, as T. S. Eliot knew, can be feelingly incarnated in words provided it is known not to be a matter of words alone:

Great simplicity is only won by an intense moment or by years of intelligent effort, or by both. It represents one of the most arduous conquests of the human spirit: the triumph of feeling and thought over the natural sin of language.[29]

---

[28] Arthur Rau, 'Portrait of a Bibliophile, XIII: Henry George Quin, 1760-1805', *The Book Collector*, xii (1964), 449-62.

[29] *The Athenaeum*, 11 April 1919.

ANDREW MARVELL:
'ITS OWN RESEMBLANCE'

I

The Mind, that Ocean where each kind
Does streight its own resemblance find.
('The Garden')

A characteristic figure of speech in Marvell is that which goes beyond saying of something that it *finds* its own resemblance, and says instead, more wittily and mysteriously, that something *is* its own resemblance. When William Empson remarked such a figure in Shelley—

So came a chariot in the silent storm
Of its own rushing splendour. . . .

And others mournfully within the gloom
Of their own shadow walked, and called it death.
('The Triumph of Life')

—Empson called it a self-inwoven simile or a short-circuited comparison.[1] Others have since called it reflexive imagery. Often it signs itself with the word 'own'. It is at home to the acknowledged characteristics of Marvell's poetry: balance and yet conflict; inclusion and yet exclusion; withdrawal and yet emergence; microcosm and yet macrocosm; self and yet all else. It is at home with, and accommodates too, both the phases of seventeenth-century wit:

Contradiction is at the centre of poetic wit in the seventeenth century. In its pure form it becomes paradox in the first half of the century, and antithesis in the second; that is, contraries are reconciled in the one, and opposed in the other.[2]

For the self-inwoven simile is a figure which both reconciles and opposes, in that it describes something both as itself and as something external to it which it could not possibly be. In one of its most teasing forms, something finds itself compared to both of the terms within a comparison.

[1] *Seven Types of Ambiguity* (1930), 1947 edn, pp. 160-1.
[2] George Williamson, *The Proper Wit of Poetry* (1961), p. 95.

With a range of mood, intent, and form, Marvell uses it in
every important kind of poem that he writes; and showing so is
the first half of what I want to do here. In his political-religious
poetry, for instance, it figures the largest knowledge—of all
past, present, and future—which we must try to imagine and
which we must also acknowledge as unimaginable. Marvell
sets the terms for his own poetic providence in the opening of
'A Poem upon the Death of O.C.':

> That Providence which had so long the care
> Of *Cromwell's* head, and numbered ev'ry hair,
> Now in its self (the Glass where all appears)
> Had seen the period of his golden Years.

Here the turn witnesses to the wonder of a religious paradox;
Providence is seen as (and yet can scarcely be visualized as)
that which sees, that which is seen, and that wherein is seen.
Abraham Cowley speaks of this same paradox in his *Davideis*,
Book ii: 'Shap'd in the *glass* of the divine *Foresight*'; but Cowley,
unlike Marvell, found no shape for the paradox such as would
express it rather than speak of it, for there is no greater mystery
in his line of verse than in the equable prose with which he
glosses the glass: 'It is rightly termed a *Glass* or *Mirror*, for God
foresees all things by looking only on himself, in whom all
things always are.' Marvell's lines inspire awe at Providence as
the seer, the seen, and the seen in. As so often with reflexive
imagery, literal reflections also catch the light, with their paradoxes of identity and difference, transposition, unreal reality,
and substantial insubstantiality. Rosalie Colie remarked,
à propos of Marvell's 'On a Drop of Dew', that 'the mirror
image is taken as both thinking (reflection, speculation), and
the instrument to stimulating thinking'.[3]
   Marvell inaugurates his poem on the death of Cromwell with
this mystery set before us with the greatest lucidity; the wit is
subdued, and time is suspended in the high unimaginability of
Providence's relation to time. The obvious contrast, one that
here is to Marvell's honour, is with Milton's time-ridden
elaboration of Providence's paradox in Book iii of *Paradise Lost*,
of which J. B. Broadbent remarked with imaginative pertin-
ence: 'He leads us into a corridor of verbal mirrors in which

---

[3] *Paradoxia Epidemica* (1966), p. 282.

unbodied concepts are defined by their antitheses so all we can do is mark time with our lips.'[4] If we ask why Marvell succeeds where Milton fails, the answer is not only that Marvell does not subdue his momentaneous insight to the doled-out world of discourse, but that Marvell seizes upon a simply literal fact which incarnates the metaphysical paradox, the fact that the eye is itself a mirror, and can be the seer, and the seen in.[5] 'Looking babies' is one form of this teasing reality, as the lover gazes into the loved one's eyes; another is the military proximity, eyeball to eyeball, which is accorded the highest honours in 'An Elegy upon the Death of my Lord Francis Villiers':

> Lovely and admirable as he was,
> Yet was his Sword or Armour all his Glasse.
> Nor in his Mistris eyes that joy he tooke,
> As in an Enemies himselfe to looke.

'By Andrew Marvell', wrote the honest and excellently informed George Clarke in his copy of the poem about 250 years ago; and there is something characteristic of Marvell, though not unique to him, in the turn with 'himselfe': 'As in an Enemies himselfe to looke', where there is both 'he himselfe' and the reflexive verb 'looke himselfe':

> And for a Glass the limpid Brook,
> Where *She* may all *her* Beautyes look.
> ('Upon Appleton House' 701-2)

Within one kind of religious poetry, then, the vast outward vistas of Providence are glimpsed through this telescopic figure. Within another kind, the meditative poem, the same turn is used microscopically for a no less characteristic miniature miracle of inward vistas:

> How it the purple flow'r does slight,
> Scarce touching where it lyes,

---

[4] *Some Graver Subject* (1960), p. 147.

[5] Proust created his own hyperbolical version of this hyperbole, by making spectacles their own spectacle:

'But isn't the Princess on the train?' came in ringing tones from Brichot, whose huge spectacles, resplendent as the reflectors that laryngologists attach to their foreheads to throw a light into the throats of their patients, seemed to have taken their life from the Professor's eyes, and, possibly because of the effort that he was making to adjust his sight to them, seemed themselves, even at the most trivial moments, to be gazing at themselves with a sustained attention and an extraordinary fixity. (*Cities of the Plain*, in *Remembrance of Things Past*, trans. C. K. Scott Moncrieff, 1929 (reprinted 1941), viii 28).

> But gazing back upon the Skies,
>   Shines with a mournful Light;
>   Like its own Tear,
> Because so long divided from the Sphear.
>   ('On a Drop of Dew')

The assonantal rhyme-sequence (*slight/lyes/Skies/Light*) is given a further delicate weightiness by the mourning head-words too:

> But gazing back upon the *Skies*,
>   *Shines* with a mournful *Light*;
>   *Like* its own Tear;

—at which the self-infolded comparison is at its most succinct. 'Like its own Tear': this invites us to see the dew drop as a tear wept by itself; to see it therefore both as eye and tear, a vision which is unimaginable and yet is more than clear, is plausible, because of that shared liquidity of shape which Proust observed with saddened grotesquerie:

He slipped his other hand upwards along Odette's cheek; she fixed her eyes on him with that languishing and solemn air which marks the women of the old Florentine's paintings, in whose faces he had found the type of hers; swimming at the brink of her fringed lids, her brilliant eyes, large and finely drawn as theirs, seemed on the verge of breaking from her face and rolling down her cheeks like two great tears.

(How strange is the metamorphosis there from 'she fixed her eyes on him'—*elle le regarda fixement*—to the image of her weeping her eyes out.)

She looked back at him with eyes welling with affection, ready to detach themselves like tears and to fall upon his face.

> (*Swann in Love*)[6]

The author of 'Eyes and Tears' might have appreciated Proust's repeated fancy, at once painful and comic; yet the poignancy of Marvell's vistas of regression and involution comes from a sense of division—'Because so long divided from the Sphear'— not *within* but *from*. There is a chastened tone in Marvell's figure, 'Like its own Tear', that is animated by a fear of the rounded yet ephemeral sufficiencies of self, with this form of

---

[6] *Swann's Way* in *Remembrance of Things Past*, ii 20-1, 224.

reciprocity—that of the eye and the tear—itself too self-infolded; so that the effect is that Marvell's line shares something with Wilfred Owen's Virgilian feeling for

> Whatever shares
> The eternal reciprocity of tears.
> ('Insensibility')

What is missing from the lines of Richard Crashaw which Marvell probably knew—

> Each Ruby there,
> Or Pearle that dare appeare,
> Be its owne blush, be its owne Teare.
> ('Wishes. To his (supposed) Mistresse')

—is such a sense of awed transposition; for there is no haunting interminability, such as exists when we try to imagine a drop of water wept by itself, between a pearl and 'its owne Teare'; instead of Marvell's fluid windows, we are handed something which crystallizes as cleverness.

In another poetic kind, the love poem, Marvell contemplates very different tears but again under the aspect of this same figure of speech.

> And, while vain Pomp does her restrain
> Within her solitary Bowr,
> She courts her self in am'rous Rain;
> Her self both *Danae* and the Showr.
> ('Mourning')

Whereas the dew drop's tear was chastened, this turn is chastening. For it puts the sardonic, though thrillingly musical, point of view of those ('Yet some affirm . . .') who are sceptical of her tears and believe them to be a self-indulgence. She loves her love and her self, her grief and her tears. Dead Strephon once courted her, now she courts herself. The ancient ingenuity of Zeus' rape-seduction of Danae, ensconced by her father in her tower but not safe from a golden shower of amorous rain, is matched by the modern ingenuity of this turn. The effect of 'Her self both *Danae* and the Showr' is to give to the previous line, 'She courts her self in am'rous Rain', a taunting quality of understatement or—looked at from the other end—of overstated courtesy. Can Zeus fairly be said finally to have *courted*

Danae? The lady is fancied to be both of the partners in a rape-
seduction story. The air of the lines is wonderfully easy, yet, in
such a story, ease is cause of wonder. (The tone altogether precludes the fevers and chills endemic in the sort of word which
Harold Toliver uses about all such moments in Marvell: 'homo-
erotic', 'auto-erotic', and 'mono-virginal'.[7]) The psychological
acumen and delicacy of the insight into the gratification of grief
must rank with those manifested in *Twelfth Night*'s capacious
understanding of Olivia; Marvell's lyrical succinctness compacts the reflexive verb and the reflexive image—

> She courts her self in am'rous Rain;
> Her self both *Danae* and the Showr.

—in an acknowledgement of one strange yet natural form
which self-infolded self-division may take.

Self-division is the animation of another of Marvell's notable
kinds, the debate poem. The Soul has the first word in 'A Dialogue between the Soul and Body':

> O who shall, from this Dungeon, raise
> A Soul inslav'd so many wayes?
> With bolts of Bones, that fetter'd stands
> In Feet; and manacled in Hands.
> Here blinded with an Eye; and there
> Deaf with the drumming of an Ear.

The very faculties of the body incapacitate, and they preclude
what they seem to promise, since they offer travesties of true
and incorporeal faculties. Yet how various and unpriggish are
the forms which Marvell gives to this age-old spiritual or soul-
ish grievance.[8] 'Here blinded with an Eye' is something other
than a mere easy reversal, since it arms itself with a love-cliché

---

[7] *Marvell's Ironic Vision* (1965).

[8] Ted Hughes seems to me to subtract in force what he adds in violence, in 'A Kill'
(*Crow*, 1970):

> Flogged lame with legs
> Shot through the head with balled brains
> Shot blind with eyes
> Nailed down by his own ribs
> Strangled just short of his last gasp
> By his own windpipe
> Clubbed unconscious by his own heart
> Seeing his life stab through him, a dream flash
> As he drowned in his own blood

to compound its disapproval of the Body. Lovers are always being blinded by eyes (and the Body is to blame for this), but lovers—indeed all of us—are mistaken to think that it is the eyes of others which most blind us: it is our own eyes. 'Deaf with the drumming of an Ear' finds its persuasive power elsewhere (again, though, vigilant not to offer a mere reversal): in the simple fact of the ear-drum, which is used to press the spiritual claim that, far from being made to hear by the eardrum, we are permanently deafened by the drumming of the ear. Even the strictures which seem most bald have their play of variety; 'that fetter'd stands / In Feet' rises above the jingle of polemic, since 'fetter'd' is etymologically cognate with 'Feet'; and 'manacled in Hands' repeats and yet does not repeat this, since 'manacled' is not etymologically cognate with 'Hands' and yet Latin beckons. . . . (The sheer resourcefulness of the Soul's recriminations can be felt if you simply substitute 'handcuffed in hands'.) But with only the spectral tacit etymology of 'manacled', and with no physical counterpart such as lends colour to the accusation against the eardrum, there remains to hand another cliché to be retorted with. For though, if there is one thing you can't be manacled with, it is your own hands, the Soul's turn of speech inspiredly or perversely seizes upon something which was often said, and something which is again apt to the Soul's indictment of the Body: that other people's hands manacle you. As when Robert Herrick warned that women's

> Armes, and hands, and all parts else,
> Are but Toiles, or Manicles
> Set on purpose to enthrall
> Men, but Slothfulls most of all.
> ('Disswasions from Idlenesse')

'And manacled in Hands': for something of the same teasing knot of clarity and inconceivability, we might go to Steinberg's fantastical—or Escher's realistic—drawing of a hand drawing a hand. E. H. Gombrich has said of Escher: 'What all these prints have in common is that they compel us to adopt an initial assumption that cannot be sustained as we try to follow it through',[9] and it is this challenging tension—to visualize the

---

[9] 'Illusion and Visual Deadlock' (1961), in his *Meditations on a Hobby Horse* (1963), 1971 edn, p. 155.

unvisualizable—which Dr Leavis pinned down as just the quality which cannot be pinned down in a poem like 'A Dialogue between the Soul and Body': 'Of its very nature it eludes, defies and transcends visualization. . . . That undoubted force . . . is not in the least a matter of their compelling us to *visualize* anything; it is that they are paradoxes the essence of which is to elude or defy visualization.'[10]

Compel, no; challenge, yes, as is implied by the word 'defy'. Then with perfect equipollence or evenhandedness, the figure with which the Soul challenged the Body is retorted by the Body against the Soul:

> O who shall me deliver whole,
> From bonds of this Tyrannic Soul?
> Which, stretcht upright, impales me so,
> That mine own Precipice I go;

The Body is both what falls and what it falls down, by a nightmare of self-division such as induces a vertigo in the mere thought (the mere unthinkable thought); and 'impales' even adds some fear that the Body, 'stretcht upright', is not only that which falls and that which it falls down, but also that which it falls upon: 'impales me so'.

> O the mind, mind has mountains; cliffs of fall
> Frightful, sheer, no-man-fathomed.
> (Hopkins, 'No worst, there is none')

Marvell's lines are to me more frightening, less melodramatic, than Hopkins's, and than William Golding's fierce stroke in *Pincher Martin* when the rock to which the man clings is felt to be the tooth within his own head. There is in Marvell a resilience and a vibrancy of anger such as intimate a nobler fear.

Within Marvell's pastoral poetry, fear is called up but to be fended off. The flooding of the meadows need cause no perturbation, but it causes the astonishment which Marvell's figure delights to recognize:

> The River in it self is drown'd,
> And Isl's th'astonish'd Cattle round.
> ('Upon Appleton House' 471-2)

---

[10] 'The Responsible Critic', *Scrutiny*, xix (1953), 166.

By enlarging so that it becomes more than itself, the river loses
its self; but fortunately it is lost only to be found again later.
Yet even so, when the flooding has gone and the river is restored,
at this moment too Marvell must have recourse to his reflexive
paradox:

> No *Serpent* new nor *Crocodile*
> Remains behind our little *Nile*;
> Unless it self you will mistake,
> Among these Meads the only Snake.
> (629-32)

The miraculous abiogenesis of the great Nile, breeding snakes
from its mud, is outdone by the humble English counterpart,
'our little Nile', since this river breeds, inconceivably, the snake
of itself. The good-natured reproof to such credulity—

> Unless it self you will mistake,
> Among these Meads the only Snake —

itself evolves into a mistake, since the next lines take the fancy
as having an established life:

> See in what wanton harmless folds
> It ev'ry where the Meadow holds. . . .

How gently, with what paradisal innocence, this snake holds
something in its folds.

But such implications, famous as they rightly are in the
appreciation of Marvell, are not what I want to follow. For it is
the variety and ubiquitousness of the self-infolded simile in
Marvell which I have wished first of all to establish. It is grist to
my mill—indeed, is itself both grist and mill—that T. S. Eliot,
when he wished to deplore the related (though not strictly
reflexive) images which finally close up 'Upon Appleton House'
within their Chinese boxes or their Russian dolls:

> But now the *Salmon-Fishers* moist
> Their *Leathern Boats* begin to hoist;
> And, like *Antipodes* in Shoes,
> Have shod their *Heads* in their *Canoos*.
> How *Tortoise like*, but not so slow,
> These rational *Amphibii* go?
> Let's in: for the dark *Hemisphere*
> Does now like one of them appear.

—that Eliot, deploring these lines, should himself have succumbed to this very Marvellian image: 'images . . . which support nothing but their own misshapen bodies'.[11] For it may be said of many of Marvell's reflexive images that, as Empson said in paraphrasing one of Shelley's, 'it sustains itself by supporting itself'. Marvell's lines here, characteristically, at once expand and contract, in a double perspective which calmly blinks; I am reminded of a newspaper advertisement I once saw which began 'expanding contracting industry requires draughtsmen. . . .'

The political-religious poem, the meditative poem, the love poem, the debate poem, the pastoral poem—there remains certainly one kind of poem which mattered greatly to Marvell: satire. So let me round off this first half of my round-up by quoting four lines from *The Last Instructions to a Painter*. The attribution of the poem to Marvell seems to me to gain some weight from the masterly turn within—and not just the presence of—such a reflexive image as this:

> But when he came the odious Clause to Pen,
> That summons up the *Parliament* agen;
> His Writing-Master many a time he bann'd,
> And wish'd himself the Gout, to seize his hand.
>   (469-72)

Wished himself to be his own gout? Wished for himself gout? Either way—or, if Marvell, both ways—it has the ring of an authentic Marvellian reflexive image. Like all such images, it has clear affinities with much else in Marvell, particularly his recourse to balance and to mirroring. For, like those, the reflexive image is at once two and one—and is all the more crucial then to such metaphysical poetry as is genuinely metaphysical in its preoccupation (as James Smith argued in *Scrutiny*, 1933) with the metaphysical problem of the One and the Many.

> Nature that hateth emptiness,
> Allows of penetration less.
>   ('An Horatian Ode')

But art delights to outdo nature, and to make two things occupy the one space; and Marvell's is famously, and in both senses, an art of penetration.

[11] 'Andrew Marvell' (1921), in his *Selected Essays* (1932), 1951 edn, p. 297.

II

The self-inwoven simile burgeoned in the poems of Marvell and his contemporaries as never before. (And as never since? Not altogether so, since I shall claim that it is at the heart of the achievement of a recent group of poets.) In the predecessors of Marvell, the figure seldom carries full conviction and seems rather to be awaiting its later consummation. When, for instance, it shows itself in Donne, some part of our surprise is not at the turn itself but at its being Donne who unexpectedly expects it to serve his turn:

> For thee, thou needst no such deceit,
> For thou thy selfe art thine own bait.
>
> ('The Baite')
>
> And on the hatches as on Altars lyes
> Each one, his owne Priest, and owne Sacrifice.
>
> ('The Calme')

Both of those have something unfulfilled and prophetic, an unripeness. For the particular kind of half-convinced levity in those lines from 'The Baite' sounds more like a Caroline poet than the innermost Donne,[12] and the particular kind of half-convinced gravity in those lines from 'The Calme' sounds more like the Dryden of *Annus Mirabilis* than the innermost Donne. It is only in the sombre magnificence of the *Devotions*— 'But I doe nothing upon my selfe, and yet am mine owne *Executioner*' (*Twelfth Meditation*)—that Donne's imagination is profoundly stirred to an apprehension of ineradicable human perversity through the perversity of this figure of speech.

If for the moment we pass over Marvell and his contemporaries, we may sketch a literary history for the self-inwoven simile such as accords with the larger history as it has been argued by Eliot and Leavis. For this figure is a witty and mysterious one, and the eighteenth and the nineteenth centuries were both, in different ways, unhappy with the integration of wit and mystery characteristic of much seventeenth-century poetry. Augustan poetry has its favourite fascinations, exerted

---

[12] 'The Baite' imitates Marlowe's 'The Passionate Shepherd to his Love'; Walton described Donne's lines as 'made to shew the world that hee could make soft and smooth Verses, when he thought them fit and worth his labour'.

upon it and by it, in the matter of incongruity and surprise; but its 'common Sense' found pretentious and vulgar any large attempt to imagine this particular form of the unimaginable.

And when the same Lady goes into the Bath, the Thought (as in justness it ought) goes still deeper.

> Venus *beheld her, 'midst her Crowd of Slaves,*
> *And thought* Herself *just risen from the Waves.*

How much out of the way of common Sense is this Reflection of *Venus*, not knowing herself from the Lady?

> (*Of the Art of Sinking in Poetry*, 1728, ch. vii)

Yet notice how 'Reflection'—'this Reflection of *Venus*'—half concedes that there is a 'common Sense' explanation for, or at least intermediary towards, this two-in-one self-mistaking:

> And its yet muddy back doth lick,
> Till as a *Chrystal Mirrour* slick;
> Where all things gaze themselves, and doubt
> If they be in it or without.
>
> ('Upon Appleton House' 635-8)

Of the Art of Sinking in Poetry presses on:

Of the same nature is that noble Mistake of a frighted Stag in full Chace, of which the Poet,

> *Hears his own Feet, and thinks they sound like more;*
> *And fears the hind Feet will o'ertake the fore.*

So astonishing as these are, they yield to the following, which is *Profundity* itself,

> *None but* Himself *can be his Parallel.*
> [Theobald, *Double Distress*]

unless it may seem borrow'd from the Thought of that *Master of a Show in Smithfield*, who writ in large Letters, over the Picture of his Elephant,

> *This is the greatest Elephant in the World, except* Himself.

Wittily done. Yet in simply ruling out, on simple principle, such turns (whether or not these particular ones are effective), such Augustan criticism was cutting itself off from a certain form of poetic apprehension which genuinely 'is *Profundity* itself'.

> So hand in hand they passd, the lovliest pair
> That ever since in loves imbraces met,
> *Adam* the goodliest man of men since borne
> His *Sons*, the fairest of her Daughters *Eve.*
>   (*Paradise Lost*, iv 321-4)

So that the best Augustan uses of this figure are merely deft, unpretentiously and unmysteriously witty.

> Such Piles of Buildings now rise up and down;
> *London* itself seems going out of Town.
> (James Bramston, *The Art of Politicks*, 1729)

That does not so much tease the mind, leave alone tease it at once into and out of thought, as tickle it. When Charles Dickens had recourse to the same turn, he gave it a context which is less wittily pointed but more poignantly mysterious, and more strongly related—as a reflexive image most revealingly may be—to the powers and the limitations of the imagination itself:

> It [Washington] is sometimes called the City of Magnificent Distances, but it might with greater propriety be termed the City of Magnificent Intentions; for it is only on taking a bird's-eye view of it from the top of the Capitol, that one can at all comprehend the vast designs of its projector, an aspiring Frenchman. Spacious avenues, that begin in nothing, and lead nowhere; streets, mile-long, that only want houses, roads and inhabitants; public buildings that need but a public to be complete; and ornaments of great thoroughfares, which only lack great thoroughfares to ornament—are its leading features. One might fancy the season over, and most of the houses gone out of town for ever with their masters. To the admirers of cities it is a Barmecide Feast; a pleasant field for the imagination to rove in; a monument raised to a deceased project, with not even a legible inscription to record its departed greatness.   (*American Notes*, ch. viii)

Though the witty possibilities there are deliberately dampened, the profundity is at one with humour, a grounded lugubrious humour. Elsewhere Dickens used the self-infolded self-divided figure of speech in one of his greatest evocations of the self-infolded self-divided nature of guilty fear, in the true derangements of imagination that haunt the murderer Jonas Chuzzlewit:

> Dread and fear were upon him, to an extent he had never counted on, and could not manage in the least degree. He was so horribly afraid of

that infernal room at home. This made him, in a gloomy, murderous, mad way, not only fearful *for* himself, but *of* himself; for being, as it were, a part of the room: a something supposed to be there, yet missing from it: he invested himself with its mysterious terrors; and when he pictured in his mind the ugly chamber, false and quiet, false and quiet, through the dark hours of two nights; the tumbled bed, and he not in it, though believed to be; he became in a manner his own ghost and phantom, and was at once the haunting spirit and the haunted man.   (*Martin Chuzzlewit*, ch. xlvii)[13]

In its vital imagining of a nemesis of the short-circuited comparison in the short-circuiting that is madness,[14] this suggests that some particular triumphs were made possible by the nineteenth-century separating of such a figure from its witty possibilities; and yet it is characteristic of Dickens that even this grimmest instance should have its full nature only when it is seen as complementing the genuine though painful humour which has made play with the self-involved comparison throughout *Martin Chuzzlewit*:

Mr Pecksniff. . . . certainly did not appear to any unusual advantage, now that he was alone. On the contrary, he seemed to be shrunk and reduced; to be trying to hide himself within himself; and to be wretched at not having the power to do it.   (ch. xxx)

'I want a man as is his own great-coat and cloak, and is always a-wrapping himself up in himself. And I have got him too', said Mr Tapley.   (ch. xxxiii)

He [Mr Nadgett] went about so stealthily, and kept himself so wrapped up in himself, that the whole object of his life appeared to be, to avoid notice and preserve his own mystery.   (ch. xxxviii)

So that when we come at last to 'He became in a manner his

[13] Thom Gunn uses the climax of this paragraph as the epigraph to Part 2 of *Jack Straw's Castle* (1976).

[14] Compare *The Diary of Alice James*, ed. Leon Edel (1965), p. 149 (26 October 1890):

As I used to sit immovable reading in the library with waves of violent inclination suddenly invading my muscles taking some one of their myriad forms such as throwing myself out of the window, or knocking off the head of the benignant pater as he sat with his silver locks, writing at his table, it used to seem to me that the only difference between me and the insane was that I had not only all the horrors and sufferings of insanity but the duties of doctor, nurse, and strait-jacket imposed upon me, too.

Also Melville, *The Confidence Man*, ch. iii: 'I have been in mad-houses full of tragic mopers, and seen there the end of suspicion: the cynic, in the moody madness muttering in the corner; for years a barren fixture there; head lopped over, gnawing his own lip, vulture of himself'.

own ghost and phantom', we can take 'in a manner' as not
merely meaning 'as it were', since we have seen some other
manners in which a man may be self-infolded.

But the nineteenth-century propensity to isolate the witty
(and the humorous) from the mysterious is evident in what
mostly happens to the reflexive image. The poet to whom it
came naturally, as Empson saw, was Shelley, but what also
came naturally to Shelley was the disjunction of the figure's
mystery from all possibility of wit or humour. Let me acknowledge an excellent essay by William Keach on 'Reflexive Imagery in Shelley' [15] (though I had better add that it generously
acknowledges as a spur to its thinking some thoughts of mine
about Marvell, and I risk being suspected of self-infolded or
short-circuited self-congratulation). Mr Keach sensitively
shows that Empson does less than justice to Shelley in saying:
'when not being able to think of a comparison fast enough he
compares the thing to a vaguer or more abstract notion of
itself'; and likewise in saying: 'Shelley seldom perceived profit-
able relations between two things, he was too helplessly excited
by one thing at a time, and that one thing was often a mere
notion not conceived in action or in an environment.' For this
not only does not do justice to Shelley, it does not do justice
either to Empson's own intuition, since he at once added: 'But,
even with so limited an instrument as the short-circuited comparison, he could do great things.' Keach is able to show how
reflexive images in Shelley act 'as verbal representations' of the
'process of reflexive imaginative projection', by dramatizing
sometimes 'a self-inclosed psychic experience', sometimes 'the
mind's involuted descent into the depths of its own reflexiveness'. It is a strength of Keach's argument, as it is of Shelley's
poetry, that this strange power of the imagination is shown by
the same figure of speech to take both benign and malign
forms. Imaginative self-sufficiency may be solipsism, madness.
Yet it remains true, and is to my mind a grave limitation even
of the best such images in Shelley, that their tone is itself obdurately self-enclosed, impervious to—though not invulnerable
to—wit and humour. There is a self-gratification, an ease of

continuity, in Shelley's use of the word 'mournfully', too at
home with 'gloom' and 'shadow' and 'death':

> And others mournfully within the gloom
> Of their own shadow walked, and called it death.

Whereas Marvell's word 'mournful' has a various play of light
against the surrounding words 'Shines' and 'Light', achieving
a fluctuant iridescence:

> But gazing back upon the Skies,
> Shines with a mournful Light;
> Like its own Tear.

What Marvell achieves cannot, I believe, be justly caught in
Keach's formulation about those lines: 'It is Marvell who sets
the standard for the sheer intellectual wit reflexive images can
yield.' For Marvell has a luminosity of pathos. If we wish to
use an antithesis of 'sheer intellectual wit' against 'psychic
expressiveness', it is not in the seventeenth-century writers but
in the nineteenth-century writers that such a choice, often misguidedly, is made. 'In emulation of Leander and Don Juan, he
swam, I hear, to the opposite shores the other day, or some
world-shaking feat of the sort, himself the Hero whom he went
to meet' (Meredith, *The Ordeal of Richard Feverel*, ch. xxxv). The
pun on Hero and the full iambic rounding—'Himself the Hero
whom he went to meet'—so plump out the reflexive image as to
make it seem that it is not Richard Feverel, about whom those
words are penned in a letter, or even Adrian Harley, who pens
them, but the author of them, Meredith, who really breathes
the air of self-congratulation. At the opposite end, even
Clough, who was creatively dissatisfied with the Victorian disjunctions, was able to animate only one half of this figure's
paradoxical powers, the Shelleyan mournfulness:

> Though tortured in the crucible I lie,
> Myself my own experiment.
> *(Adam and Eve, I ii)*

When Eliot praised in Marvell 'this alliance of levity and
seriousness (by which the seriousness is intensified)', he was
urging the twentieth century to renew such an alliance in its
poetry as in his own poetry. The self-infolded simile, moreover

folding in itself both wit and mystery, has found itself at home again. As when Harold Massingham addresses the spider, with a felicity that is not the less comic in being rueful about the imagination:

> You know the knack, don't you?
> Imagination's envy.
> You're your own yoyo, aren't you?
> ('Spider', *Black Bull Guarding Apples*, 1965)

Or as when the American poet David Ferry moves from the spider's self-infoldedness to the larger infoldings of love and duty, submission and self-submission, within a remarkable constellation of reflexive images:

THE SOLDIER

> Saturday afternoon. The barracks is almost empty.
> The soldiers are almost all on overnight pass.
> There is only me, writing this letter to you,
> And one other soldier, down at the end of the room,
> And a spider, that hangs by the thread of his guts,
> His tenacious and delicate guts, Swift's spider,
> All self-regard, or else all privacy.
> The dust drifts in the sunlight around him, as currents
> Lie in lazy drifting schools in the vast sea.
> In his little sea the spider lowers himself
> Out of his depth. He is his own diving bell,
> Though he cannot see well. He observes no fish,
> And sees no wonderful things. His unseeing guts
> Are his only hold on the world outside himself.
> I love you, and miss you, and I find you hard to imagine.
> Down at the end of the room, the other soldier
> Is getting ready, I guess, to go out on pass.
> He is shining his boots. He sits on the edge of his bunk,
> Private, submissive, and heedful of himself,
> And, bending over himself, he is his own nest.
> The slightest sound he makes is of his being.
> He is his mother, and nest, wife, brother, and father.
> His boots are bright already, yet still he rubs
> And rubs till, brighter still, they are his mirror.
> And in this mirror he observes, I guess,
> His own submissiveness. He is far from home.
> (*On the Way to the Island*, 1960)

Yet this, though a very fine poem, is an isolated instance; in so far as it calls up the same figure in other recent American poets such as Richard Wilbur, it calls them up too as instances rather than as a constellation. The more important affinity with Marvell and his contemporaries is the gifted group of Ulster poets: Seamus Heaney, Michael Longley, Derek Mahon, and Paul Muldoon. Like Marvell and his contemporaries, they write out of an imagination of civil war. But before speculating on the relation between civil war and the reflexive image, let me show how variously pervasive is the self-infolded simile in these Ulster poets.

Seamus Heaney

The burn drowns steadily in its own downpour.
('Waterfall', *Death of a Naturalist*, 1966)

Then notes stretch taut as snares. They trip
To fall into themselves unknowingly.
('The Play Way')

The leggy birds stilted on their own legs,
Islands riding themselves out into the fog . . .

. . . things founded clean on their own shapes.
('The Peninsula', *Door into the Dark*, 1969)

The breakers pour
Themselves into themselves.
('Girls Bathing, Galway 1965')

[of an eel]
. . . . a wick that is
its own taper and light
through the weltering dark.
('A Lough Neagh Sequence: The Return')

You had to come back
To lean how to lose yourself,
To be pilot and stray—witch,
Hansel and Gretel in one.
('The Plantation')

The tawny guttural water
spells itself: Moyola
is its own score and consort.
('Gifts of Rain', *Wintering Out*, 1972)

like an eel swallowed
in a basket of eels,
the line amazes itself.
('Viking Dublin: Trial Pieces', *North*, 1975)

As if he had been poured
in tar, he lies
on a pillow of turf
and seems to weep

the black river of himself
('The Grauballe Man')

Who dreamt that we might dwell among ourselves
In rain and scoured light and wind-dried stones?
('Triptych:1', *Field Work*, 1979)

a quill flourishing itself.
('In Memoriam Sean O'Riada')

As you swayed the talk
and rode on the swaying tiller
of yourself.
('Elegy')

Words entering almost the sense of touch
Ferreting themselves out of their dark hutch.
('Glanmore Sonnets: II')

Fetch me the sandmartin
skimming and veering
breast to breast with himself
in the clouds in the river.
('Homecomings')

Michael Longley
a knife-thrower
hurling himself.
('The Corner of An Eye: Kingfisher', *An Exploded View*, 1973)

Who bothers to record
This body digested
By its own saliva . . .
('Mole', *Man Lying on a Wall*, 1976)

I go disguised as myself, my own beard
Changed by this multitude of distortions
To stage whispers, my hair a give-away,
A cheap wig, and my face a mask only—

So that, on entering the hall of mirrors
The judge will at once award the first prize
To me and to all of my characters.
('Ars Poetica:3')

I keep my own death-watch:
Mine the disembodied eye
At the hole in my head . . .
And no one there by myself,
My own worst enemy.
('Last Rites: Death-watch')

Derek Mahon

And heard, in the whispering gallery of his soul,

His own small, urgent discord echoing back.
('De Quincey in Later Life', *Night Crossing*, 1968)

To whom, in my will,
This, I have left my will.
('An Image from Beckett', *Lives*, 1972)

It is here that the banished gods are in hiding,
Here they sit out the centuries
In stone, water
And the hearts of trees,
Lost in a reverie of their own natures.
('The Banished Gods', *The Snow Party*, 1975)

Paul Muldoon

The snail moves like a
Hovercraft, held up by a
Rubber cushion of itself.
('Hedgehog', *New Weather*, 1973)

Its head in the clouds

Of its own breath.
('Thinking of the Goldfish')

I believed in your riding all night
Lathered by your own sweat.
('The Radio Horse')

Seeing the birds in Winter
Drinking the images of themselves
Reflected in a sheet of ice.
('Vampire')

> You hold yourself as your own captive.
>   ('Elizabeth')

>   [two stars]
>   They yawned and stretched
>   To white hides,
>   One cutting a slit
>   In the wall of itself
>   And stepping out into the night . . .

>   It had learned
>   To track itself
>   By following the dots
>   And dashes of its blood.
>   ('The Year of the Sloes')

>   The girls in the poolroom
>   Were out on their own limbs.
>   ('The Girls in the Poolroom', *Mules*, 1977)

>   I had gone out with the kettle
>   To a little stream that lay down in itself.
>   ('Armageddon, Armageddon')

Many of those are creatively grateful to Marvell; Heaney's

>   and seems to weep
>   the black river of himself

may be bred from the union of 'Like its own Tear' and 'The
River in it self is drown'd'. But so urgent and diverse a preoccupation with the same figure of speech, in poets who though
close to each other are very different, is not likely to have arisen
from a narrowly literary influence, let alone a single literary
influence. It is more likely that there is at least some relevance
in the deep affinity between Marvell's England and these
poets' Ulster, racked by civil war that both is and is not religious. Christopher Hill's pioneering attempt to relate the con-
flicts within Marvell's poems to those of the Civil War might
here be complemented.[16] There are indeed other important
affinities between the poetry of Marvell's age and the poetry of
the 1960s and 1970s, such as are obviously germane to the reflexive image: first, an intense self-reflexive concern with the

---

[16] 'Society and Andrew Marvell' (1946), *Puritanism and Revolution* (1958).

art of poetry itself in poems; and second, a thrilled perturbation at philosophical problems of perception and imagination (Marvell's late-night reflexive wittiness is more than a joke: 'Th' *Astrologers* own Eyes are set', 'Two Songs at the Marriage of the Lord Fauconberg'). But to these should be added the way in which the short-circuited comparison is itself apt to civil war. It is not only a language for civil war (desolatingly two and one), but also, in its strange self-conflict, a civil war of language and of the imaginable. The peculiar attraction of the figure, though, is that while it acknowledges (as truth must) such a civil war, it can yet at the same time conceive (as hope must) a healing of such strife. For what Keach says of the reflexive image and the mind may be applied to the reflexive image and society:

Reflexive images call unusual attention to the act of mind they presuppose, an act of mind which combines a moment of analysis and division, in which an aspect is separated from the idea to which it belongs, and a moment of synthesis and reunion, in which the separated aspect is put back into relationship with the idea: 'His eyes beheld / Their own wan light . . .' (*Alastor*, lines 469-470). 'Wan light' is simultaneously separate from 'eyes' and thus capable of becoming the direct object of what the eyes 'beheld', and inseparable from 'eyes', since their object is an aspect of themselves . . . A reflexive image makes the reader aware of the mind's ability not only to perceive relationships but to create them in a context of unity and identity.

Reunion, unity, and identity: these may embody, as they do in the work of Marvell and of Heaney, not only philosophical and psychological hopes, but also civil and political ones.

The reflexive image simultaneously acknowledges the opposing forces and yearns to reconcile them. It is, like all paradoxes, 'a composition of contraries', and composition is not only a literary term but a civic one, of peace after differences. This is so whether or not the reflexive images in Marvell and in the Ulster poets deal directly with civil war, as they sometimes do and often do not. For the self-divided image flourishes in those unflourishing times when it will have to be said not only of the ignoble man but of the noble man that he

> Did thorough his own Side
> His fiery way divide.
> ('An Horatian Ode')

At its best, the wit of the self-infolded comparison is brave in its
consciousness of danger or threat, and this is true even of the
preposterous peril in Steinberg's drawings: a man putting a
revolver to an apple on his own head, or a man sitting fishing
on a whale which is about to swallow his bait. Those are as
good as the report by the Food Standards Committee objecting
to the digestive biscuit: 'To justify its name, said the committee's chairman, Professor Alan Ward, yesterday, the biscuit
should have the power of digesting itself' (*The Times*, 12 May
1977). Or, in the words of Stanley Fish, *Self-Consuming Artifacts.*

When Marvell and his contemporaries, like the Ulster poets
of the 1960s and 1970s, were so wittily serious and resourceful
with the self-infolded simile, they were at once recognizing and
resisting the perverse infoldings and divisions, surmounting
them with resilient paradox. Thomas Stanley's silkworm
makes her destiny her choice, or at least her very being:

> See with what pains she spins for thee
> The thread of her own Destinie

—where 'pains' calls up pain but fends it off, in a way that con-
soles the lover for the pains he takes and receives.

Richard Lovelace's poems teem with everyday wonders that
are comically *outré* and yet divertingly apt to human life and its
large perplexities. When Lovelace goes to the ant, he sees a
rebuke to the sluggard the oddity of which—'Thou, thine own
Horse and Cart'—goes beyond even the preposterous, since
the preposterous (*praeposterus*, before-behind) means putting the
cart before the horse, and how could that be posited of a creature who is his own horse and cart? The witticism, itself a compliment to witty nature, ushers in a serious anti-Aesopian
fable. Again, the battle between 'The Toad and Spyder' jests
about war (as does 'Upon Appleton House'), but its alliance of
levity and seriousness calls upon the short-circuited comparison, passing from a prayer to Athena ('Heaven's blew-eyed
Daughter, thine own Mother!'), through a self-laceration
('Chaf'd in her own black fury wet'), to the climactic oddity:

> Till he but one new Blister is,
> And swells his own Periphrasis.

Yet the same figure of speech which may swell as a destructive

excess of self may also be a valued feat of self-involvement, as
when Lovelace praises Eldred Revett, 'That to thine own self
hast the Midwife play'd'. What is charming about that compliment to Revett's poems is that it infolds the very figure of
speech which Revett delightingly shared with Lovelace—and
with Marvell. For Revett's poems, when they come to life, are
alive with the self-infolded comparison:

> And a winding river steals
> That with it self drunk curling reels.
> ('The Land-schap between two hills')
>
> Thou dost as it doth round thee flow
> In thine own cloud (invelop'd) go. . . .
> As properly I might thee name
> Thine own fair picture in a frame.
> ('To a Lady with black hair')
>
> So a but peradventure fall
> Awakes the sleeping *Harpsychall*.
> Which since the Artist finger'd last,
> Lay lull'd in its own musick (fast).
> ('On *Mr. Gambles* composing of *Mr. Stanleyes* Odes')
>
> When I retir'd back to her eyes to see,
> If this were wanton prodigality;
> But in those fair lights by some smarting wounds,
> Their griefs seem'd carv'd by their own Diamonds.
> ('Lycoris weeping')
>
> She is her *own close mourning in*
> (At Natures Charge) a *Cypress skin*. . . .
> Thou dost not to our dear surprise
> Thine own *white marble* statue rise.
> ('One Enamour'd on a *Black-moor*')
>
> Rivers that chide upon their shelves
> Caught, are made fetters for themselves.
> ('Winter')

And there is 'The Centaure':

> Who usher to no Woman kind,
> But *Ride before*, your *own behind*.
> And when you over-ridden sweat,
> Walk (your *own Hostler*) down the Heat.

Lovelace paid a compliment to Revett's Centaur in the opening of 'The Snayl', and then proceeded to outdo Revett in wit
and substantiality.

So let me end, before I become my own periphrasis, with
Lovelace's most acutely delightful eliciting of the powers latent
within the self-infolded simile, his two poems on 'The Snayl':

> Wise Emblem of our Politick World,
> ·Sage Snayl, within thine own self curl'd.

Like Paul Muldoon with his snail, Lovelace himself creates
a wise emblem, since he apprehends through this figure of
speech so many of the taxing contrarieties of life, the self-
divisions and self-infoldings, and yet suggests that the seriously
witty imagination will rise to them and above them.

> Compendious Snayl! thou seem'st to me,
> Large *Euclids* strickt Epitome.

There is the largest life of nature, which is both distinct from us
and yet alive in us, as when the snail is his own sunrise:

> And thou from thine own liquid Bed
> New *Phoebus* heav'st thy pleasant Head.

There is the life of family, which is both distinct from us and
yet alive in us:

> Thou thine own daughter then, and Sire,
> That Son and Mother art intire,
> That big still with thy self dost go,
> And liv'st an aged Embrio.

There is death, strangely alive inside us and outside us:

> And as thy House was thine own womb,
> So thine own womb, concludes thy tomb.

Yet there is the religious life:

> Now hast thou chang'd thee Saint; and made
> Thy self a Fane that's cupula'd;
> And in thy wreathed Cloister thou
> Walkest thine own Gray fryer too.

Lovelace's second poem on the snail likewise opens out
and clamps together the paradoxes not only of activity and
passivity—

> That moveth him by traverse Law,
> And doth himself both drive and draw;

and of host and guest—

> That when the Sun the South doth winne,
> He baits him hot in his own Inne;

and of controller and controlled—

> I heard a grave and austere Clark,
> Resolv'd him Pilot both and Barque;

but also of the inconceivable ability to lift oneself up by one's own bootstraps:

> Yet the Authentick do beleeve,
> Who keep their Judgement in their Sleeve,
> That he is his own Double man,
> And sick, still carries his Sedan.

The snail carries himself in his own sedan chair; would Eliot have called this an image which supports nothing but its own misshapen body?

Marvell honoured Lovelace, as is clear from his celebratory poem, 'To his Noble Friend Mr. Richard Lovelace, upon his Poems', which speaks of what the Civil War had done to poetry: 'Our Civill Wars have lost the Civicke crowne'. Marvell must have admired, that which his own art exemplifies, the alliance of levity and seriousness in the self-infolded simile which concludes Lovelace's second poem on the snail, a wistful weighty joke, at once personal and civic, about personal integrity and civil disintegration:

> But banisht, I admire his fate
> Since neither Ostracisme of State,
> Nor a perpetual exile,
> Can force this Virtue change his Soyl;
> For wheresoever he doth go,
> He wanders with his Country too.

JOHN MILTON:
SOUND AND SENSE IN *PARADISE LOST*

Comparison and analysis, as T. S. Eliot said, are the chief tools
of the critic; and we can gain a sense of the particular nature of
Milton's achievement by looking first of all at the relations of
sound and sense in some poetry other than his.

First, Dr. Johnson.

> How small, of all that human hearts endure,
> That part which laws or kings can cause or cure.
> (Johnson, contributed to Goldsmith's *The Traveller*)

The network of sounds is delicate and various. 'Endure' rhymes
with 'cure', and yet their senses face in opposite directions;
'small' rhymes internally with 'all', narrowing down with
'small' as against widening out with 'all'; 'hearts' rhymes with
'part', and 'laws' with 'cause'; 'or' is repeated as 'or' (and
rhymes with 'laws' and 'cause'); 'that' is repeated as 'that',
but with a different sense; the alliteration within the first
line—'how', 'human'—plays its story against that within the
second line: 'kings', 'can', 'cause', 'cure'. If we set aside the
three humble words 'How', 'of', and 'which', the only two
words which do not rhyme with anything are 'human' in the
first line and 'kings' in the second, and those two words present
the plot of this stoical couplet. Yet the salience, the prominence,
of 'human' and 'kings' does not lift them aloofly above the
couplet's auspices, since each alliterates with the word that
follows it. Johnson's achievement here is that these interlacings
of sound—which create and enforce nuances of meaning and of
feeling—never harden into a diagram. The suppleness of the
rhythm sees to that.

If there is a 'network of sounds', we should ask what the net
catches. First, one of the great conservative apophthegms, a
poignant rebuke to the social and political optimism that postu-
lates the infinite plasticity of man. Yet the profound adjuration
of the couplet is not merely asserted; its manner and movement
give it the weight of something which Johnson has not merely
thought of but is thinking about. Its pondering unites thought

and feeling, and is wonderfully free of that suspect pleasure which so often taints stoical sentiments, taints them with a relish which combines with their generality to make them seem vicarious. The network, then, catches a great deal; what is it that Johnson's network here does not catch? What is not caught, and is not sought, is any inward sense of experiencing those things which human hearts have to endure, any such felt pain. Yet the lines are informed by experience, are weighty with it, so what experience is it? It is the experience of contemplating the grim facts of human experience; not the original, dramatic if you like, pains, but the pain which recognizes that laws and kings can cause or cure so little (not nothing, which would be an easier because more total dismay, but so little). What we feel in the lines is not the immediacy or inwardness of being in pain, but the chastened generality of being pained— and not in a casual or social sense of pained. And it is this which we feel in Milton's great lines:

> Not that faire field
> Of *Enna*, where Proserpin gathring flours
> Her self a fairer Floure by gloomie *Dis*
> Was gatherd, which cost *Ceres* all that pain
> To seek her through the world;
> (*Paradise Lost*, iv 268-72)

There is pain in the lines, but the pain we feel is that of contemplating the pain felt by a mother as she searches for her daughter; we are—painfully—*not* allowed to pretend to ourselves that we share Ceres' pain. 'All that pain': it is known to us but *not* ours. Nothing in us thinks 'all *this* pain'; our pain is less than hers, and different from hers, and Milton's art here embodies a noble warning about what may be the true limits of the sympathetic imagination.

The difference between this mediated pain, in Johnson and in Milton, and the immediacy of pain may be clear from a great passage in which Shakespeare presents the heart and what it has to endure.

Horatio. You will lose this wager, my Lord.
Hamlet. I doe not thinke so, since he went into France, I have beene in continual practice; I shall winne at the oddes: but thou wouldest not thinke how ill all's heere about my heart: but it is no matter.

Horatio. Nay, good my Lord.

Hamlet. It is but foolery; but it is such a kinde of gain-giving as would
perhaps trouble a woman.

Horatio. If your minde dislike any thing, obey. I will forestall their
repaire hither, and say you are not fit.

Hamlet. Not a whit, we defie Augury; there's a speciall Providence in
the fall of a sparrow. If it be now, 'tis not to come: if it bee not to
come, it will bee now: if it be not now; yet it will come; the readi-
nesse is all.   (V ii)[1]

Shakespeare's genius is at its most profound here, and the
heart of this passage about the heart and what it can endure is
this: 'but thou wouldest not thinke how ill all's heere about my
heart'. We feel intensely with Hamlet, we share his pain and
premonition, and the very uttering of the words is astonish-
ingly at one not only with such pain but with the *hearing* of the
uttered words. There can be no easy saying or hearing of them,
partly because of the perilous thickening within 'how ill all's
heere', partly because there is no natural fluency of linkage
between any of the words in the sequence 'how ill all's heere
about my heart', partly because of the precarious breathy hesitation of the alliteration on 'h'—'how', 'heere', 'heart'—
groping against the vowelled cautious openings for 'ill', 'all's',
'about'. The effect is intensely dramatic, in its combination of
the most intimate sharing of experience with the most awed
sense of our being so extraneous to Hamlet, his being—despite
Horatio's love for him—so terribly isolated. Yet the greatness
is, as always, a moral as well as an artistic thing. For in admitting so painfully to his pain—'but thou wouldest not thinke
how ill all's heere about my heart'—Hamlet is indeed making
clear just what it is that his courage must meet, and yet he is
never further from self-pity than when acknowledging his pain.
The lucid and disciplined confidence with which he replies to
Horatio is no kind of boast, it is the sheerest serenity of confidence, and yet without complacency ('I shall winne at the
oddes'):

Horatio. You will lose this wager, my Lord.

Hamlet. I doe not thinke so, since he went into France, I have been in
continuall practice; I shall winne at the oddes:

---

[1] The Folio text, but emending the Folio's 'how all heere about my heart' from
Quartos 2-4.

Yet Hamlet feels at once that though he will win he will lose. How beautifully 'I doe not thinke so' becomes 'but thou wouldest not thinke how ill all's heere about my heart'; how revealing is that 'but', and then how finely Hamlet at once reaffirms his courage, his heart, by rounding mildly upon himself with a second 'but' that reverses the impulse of the first:

Hamlet. . . . . but thou wouldest not thinke how ill all's heere about my heart: but it is no matter.

(He needs 'but' again twice in his next effort of imaginative will, with its brave jest: 'It is but foolery; but it is such a kinde of gain-giving as would perhaps trouble a woman.') The tissue of feelings and perceptions is at one with the very sounds; notice how Horatio's proper negativity of prudence, 'and say you are not fit', becomes the vaulting resolution of Hamlet's 'Not a whit', and so into the bleakly ominous 'it' which rings out five times.

Those words—'but thou wouldest not thinke how ill all's heere about my heart'—have an extraordinary physical immediacy which springs from the fact that they seem to compact a sense of pain in the heart with a sense of pain in the lungs. They speak of the heart, and they dilate with everything which this play has made us feel about the heart, from its opening:

> And I am sicke at heart   (I i)

through Hamlet's soliloquies:

> But breake my heart . . .   (I ii)
>
> Hold my heart . . .   (I v)
>
> Must (like a Whore) unpacke my heart with words
>   (II ii)

through the antagonism of Claudius to Hamlet—Hamlet's journey to England

> shall expell
> This something setled matter in his heart
>   (III i)

('but thou wouldest not thinke how ill all's heere about my heart; but it is no matter'); through the antagonism of Hamlet to Rosencrantz and Guildenstern: 'You would pluck out the

heart of my Mysterie' (III ii); down to this last scene of the
play, which moves from Hamlet's words to Horatio:

> Sir, in my heart there was a kinde of fighting

and

> If thou did'st ever hold me in thy heart

to Horatio's words of Hamlet:

> Now cracks a Noble heart.

Hamlet's heart—'but thou wouldest not thinke how ill all's
heere about my heart'—is at the moment of his death his whole
self, his feelings and his courage.

But breath labours in those words too, that breath of which
Hamlet at his first appearance knows the pain-pretending
travesty:

> Nor windy suspiration of forc'd breath   (I ii)

the breath of which so much is made here in the play's last
scene:

> Why doe we wrap the gentleman in our more rawer breath?
>   (V ii)[2]

> If it please his Majestie, 'tis the breathing time of day with me:
> let the Foyles bee brought.

> *King.* 'Our sonne shall win.'
> *Queen.*   'He's fat, and scant of breath.'

and—the pain of the heart and of the breath—

> If thou did'st ever hold me in thy heart,
> Absent thee from felicitie awhile,
> And in this harsh world draw thy breath in paine,
> To tell my Storie.

A full response, then, to 'but thou wouldest not thinke how
ill all's heere about my heart' leads us to Keats's poignant
sense of breathing and the heart, of that tragic solicitude which
informs the very greatest poetry:

However among the effects this breathing is father of is that tremen-
dous one of sharpening one's vision into the heart and nature of

---

[2] Quartos 2-4.

Man—of convincing ones nerves that the World is full of Misery and
Heartbreak, Pain, Sickness and Oppression—[3]

Convincing one's nerves: it is a great phrase in its compacting
of the highest understanding with the most inwardly physical
experiencing. To think back to Dr. Johnson—

> How small, of all that human hearts endure,
> That part which laws or kings can cause or cure.

—is to recognize both that there can be great poetry which does
not seek to convince the nerves and that the very greatest poetry
does this among the many things it does. William Empson has
seen, though he has rightly not plucked out, the heart of this
mystery:

Critics often say or imply casually that some poetic effect conveys
a direct 'physical' quality, something mysteriously intimate, something which it is strange a poet could convey, something like a sensation which is not attached to any one of the senses . . . Probably it is
in this way, as a sort of taste in the head, that one remembers one's
own past experiences, including the experience of reading a particular poet. Probably, again, this mode of apprehension is connected
with the condition of the whole body, and is as near as one can get to
an immediate self-knowledge.[4]

An immediate self-knowledge, and at one with an immediate
knowledge of another person: this is there in the words: 'but
thou wouldest not thinke how ill all's heere about my heart.'
No one will find these claims surprising who remembers the
words to which the First Quarto reduces Hamlet's whole speech
here, words in greatness's stead:

Hamlet. Beleeve me *Horatio*, my heart is on the sodaine Very sore, all
here about.

Milton's genius was radically un-Shakespearean (on this,
Dr. Leavis's arguments stand like Teneriff or Atlas unre-
moved). This does not mean that Milton 'forfeits all possibility
of subtle or delicate life in his verse'[5] (on this, Dr. Leavis's
arguments should themselves suffer 'dislodgment'), but it does
mean that Milton's achievement more resembles that of

[3] To Reynolds, 3 May 1818.
[4] *Seven Types of Ambiguity* (1930); 1947 edn, pp. 16-17.
[5] *Revaluation* (1936), p. 53.

Dr. Johnson's 'human hearts' than of Hamlet's heart. This
should not surprise us; for one thing, Milton was in many respects an Augustan poet (and not only as being a contemporary
of Waller, Denham, Marvell, and Dryden); for another, it was
of Dr. Johnson's poetry that Dr. Leavis found himself able to
say, truly, both that 'This is great poetry' and that 'nothing
could be remoter from the Shakespearean use of language . . .
than the Johnsonian'. Dr. Leavis's stricture on Milton—'We
are often in reading him, moved to comment that he is "external" or that he "works from the outside"' is to me unquestionably right, except as a stricture. For although the highest art is the
dramatic inwardness of Shakespeare, or that which accommodates such inwardness while not limiting itself to even that, it
is not true that no great poetry can be external or can work
from the outside. Dr. Johnson works so, and so does the poet
whose subject again and again elicits from him a terrible sense
of what it is to be outside, to be external, to be excluded:

> And wisdome at one entrance quite shut out.
>
> (iii 50)

> The Stairs were then let down, whether to dare
> The Fiend by easie ascent, or aggravate
> His sad exclusion from the dores of Bliss.
>
> (iii 523-5)

> They looking back, all th'Eastern side beheld
> Of Paradise, so late thir happie seat,
> Wav'd over by that flaming Brand, the Gate
> With dreadful Faces throng'd and fierie Armes.
>
> (xii 641-4)

That Milton has a different conception of the external (a conception for which there is something to be said) comes out if we
consider what—in ways different from Johnson and from
Shakespeare—he makes of the word 'heart'. Take its first
occurrence in *Paradise Lost*, in the opening aspiration:

> And chiefly Thou O Spirit, that dost prefer
> Before all Temples th'upright heart and pure,
> Instruct me, for Thou know'st.   (i 17-19)

Nothing there, it is true, makes us feel as if that heart were
beating in our body; no sounds in its vicinity collaborate with
it to make it beat. Yet 'Instruct' brings home that Milton is

imaginatively engaged; since it is Latin *instruere*, to build, it perfectly links those Temples which are built and that *upright* heart which is to be instructed. (Four lines later, 'what is low raise and support'.) Milton makes the upright and instructed heart as visible, as externally monumental, and at least as valuable as the temples; his concern is not with the intimate recesses of the heart, but with its public attestation. So that though the words do indeed work externally, they are not unfelt; what is alive in them is not the feeling of a fleshly heart but the heartfelt aspiration towards a spiritual heart.

Later in Book i, we hear of Satan's heart. Here Milton does bring sound into play; the word 'Darts' darts forward into 'heart' (assimilating Satan's heart to its aggressive impulses), and then 'heart' hardens into the word 'hardning', *t* into *d* (as the aggression indurates itself):

> He through the armed Files
> Darts his experienc't eye, and soon traverse
> The whole Battalion views, thir order due,
> Thir visages and stature as of Gods,
> Thir number last he summs. And now his heart
> Distends with pride, and hardning in his strength
> Glories. (i 567-73)

Yet here too we feel no distending heart within ourselves; we experience something, indeed, but what we experience is an awed and fearful contemplation—the 'experienc't eye' is Satan's, the experiencing eye is ours. Milton wishes to exclude us from certain intimacies of feeling, he wishes to preclude our softening towards Satan's hardening. The poetry is of a kind which is deeply suspicious of the treacherous glissade from empathy to sympathy.

Even when Adam's heart is in distress, Milton does not use his words to enforce a sense of that heart within us, but to intimate the spiritual context which here makes a missed heartbeat so momentously unlike any which we have ever felt. Adam waits for Eve to return; our unshared sense of a premonition felt in another's heart is quite different from that which we share with Hamlet's premonition at his heart.

> Yet oft his heart, divine of something ill,
> Misgave him; hee the faultring measure felt.
> (ix 845-6)

Milton's effort is not to make us feel with Adam ('hee the faultring measure felt'); it is to make us feel very differently— to feel a quite different dismay from any which he feels, and to feel it retrospectively through what is for him the prospective pressure of 'divine of something ill', where 'divine' means more than just 'divining' and is an ominous word (twenty lines later, Eve is offering him the fruit as 'of Divine effect'); and through the pressure of 'Misgave', which means more than just a feel- ing of misgiving and is an ominous word (the *Oxford English Dictionary* has under misgive 'bestow amiss', 1611 and 1639-40; soon we watch Eve as 'She gave him of that fair enticing Fruit'); and through the pressure of 'the faultring measure', where 'faultring' is ominous with Adam's and Eve's fall, fault and faltering, and where 'measure' is not only that of the heart but also the shattered temperance.[6] All these pressures shape Milton's lines, but they do not work from the inside and with a proper obstinacy they do not make us feel what Adam felt; what he feels with the immediate dismay of an imminent pros- pect we feel with the alienated dismay of an inveterate retrospect. Such an art is in its way external, but it is not unexperiencing.

It is the relationship of sound to sense which most enables a poet's words to be at once fully an experience and fully an understanding. The large claims that can—and should—be made for Milton therefore have to face the complaint made by T. S. Eliot against him:

It is at least more nearly possible to distinguish the pleasure which arises from the *noise*, from the pleasure due to other elements, than with the verse of Shakespeare, in which the auditory imagination and the imagination of the other senses are more nearly fused, and fused together with the thought. ('A Note on the Verse of Milton', 1936[7])

Many of the great Miltonic moments are of imagining some- thing which cannot be felt, or rather can be felt only in the imagination. One of the greatest of such moments is the superb line in Book iii,

Love without end, and without measure Grace

6   But Knowledge is as food, and needs no less
       Her temperance over Appetite, to know
       In measure what the mind may well contain.
                              (vii 126-8)
[7] Reprinted as 'Milton I' in *On Poetry and Poets* (1957); p. 161.

What is felt in the line is less the existent actuality of such love and grace than its infinite possibility; the line offers perhaps the most beautiful chiasmus (*a/b/b/a*) in the language: Love and Grace stand as the supports which suspend between them all the bridging possibilities, so that the line flings itself out with the trusting arc of a great suspension bridge. (How finely the line chooses not to end with its word 'end', and how lovely this metre's 'measure'.) What secures the arc, makes it so sure a hope, is the firmness of its rhyme. For 'Grace' rhymes with 'face' two lines earlier, and it rhymes again with grace three lines later:

> Man therefore shall find grace,
> The other none: in Mercy and Justice both,
> Through Heav'n and Earth, so shall my glorie excel,
> But Mercy first and last shall brightest shine.
> Thus while God spake, ambrosial fragrance fill'd
> All Heav'n, and in the blessed Spirits elect
> Sense of new joy ineffable diffus'd:
> Beyond compare the Son of God was seen
> Most glorious, in him all his Father shon
> Substantially express'd, and in his face
> Divine compassion visibly appeerd,
> Love without end, and without measure Grace,
> Which uttering thus he to his Father spake.
> O Father, gracious was that word which clos'd
> Thy sovran sentence, that Man should find grace;
> For which both Heav'n and Earth shall high extoll
> Thy praises, with th'innumerable sound
> Of Hymns and sacred Songs, wherewith thy Throne
> Encompass'd shall resound thee ever blest.
>
> (iii 131-49)

Here the 'ineffable' is truly spoken of; here love and grace have 'visibly appear'd' (patently so), and are indeed 'substantially express'd' (expressed in words as in the face of God); here, grace resounds, as the word 'sound' resounds in the word 'resound'. Yet grace, with miraculous simplicity, is as sweetly obvious, as effortless, as the rhyme of 'grace' and 'face'. What saves the lines from the sureness of complacency, though, is the crucial point of punctuation, the fact that Milton's climactic line ends not with a full stop but with a comma. If you or I had had the genius and grace to create the line 'Love without end, and without measure Grace', we should have succumbed to the pride that would have made it the conclusive crescendo:

>   and in his face
> Divine compassion visibly appeer'd,
> Love without end, and without measure Grace.

But such a full stop would have been a self-congratulatory roll of drums. The beauty and moral delicacy of Milton's line are alive in its pausing so little, its being impelled at once into the simple narrative, risking anti-climax, of the next line:

> Love without end, and without measure Grace,
> Which uttering thus he to his Father spake.

'Which uttering': for all its triumphant effortlessness, it is astonishing, for 'which' here has to mean 'Love without end, and without measure Grace'—Christ uttered all *that*.

The poetry is superb, and it is quite without *superbia*. But it asks to be praised in terms that do not deny that it is in its way external, it does work from the outside. It praises a verity external to itself. It externally feels what it is to imagine something (and grace is itself the highest act of imagination), rather than what it is to feel the immediacy of something. Not human immediacy, divine mediation: Christ 'His dearest mediation thus renewd'.

T. S. Eliot would not be justified in deploring the sound-effect of Milton's rhymes here as mere '*noise*'; and yet Eliot's own poetry does show us what kind of greatness he himself was desirous of. Put Milton's rhyming of 'grace' and 'face' beside Eliot's lines in 'Marina' which tell how all those who mean Death

> Are become unsubstantial, reduced by a wind,
> A breath of pine, and the woodsong fog
> By this grace dissolved in place
>   What is this face, less clear and clearer
> The pulse in the arm, less strong and stronger—
> Given or lent? more distant than stars and nearer than the eye.

The conjunction of 'unsubstantial', 'grace' and 'face' recalls Milton's 'Substantially', 'grace', and 'face', but Eliot's lines work upon us quite differently; they emulate the inwardness of that pulse and the nearness of that eye, so that they intimate an intimacy, a privacy, distant from Milton's distance, his ritual of public profession. Milton here is delicate but not tentative; he is altogether without any factitious tentativeness, but this does mean that he cannot sound some notes which Eliot can sound, notes of a true tentativeness such as we hear in Eliot's rhyming of 'grace' there against 'place' and 'face' (the effect upon us is 'less clear and clearer' than Milton's magnificent lines), or such as we hear in *Little Gidding*:

> See, now they vanish,
> The faces and places, with the self which, as it could,
> loved them.

The unstriving simplicity there of 'faces and places' is qualified by the wavering tentative movement of the rhythm and syntax, so that 'as it could' is at once a minimal recognition and a firm assurance:

> See, now they vanish,
> The faces and places, with the self which, as it could,
> loved them.

It may seem odd to take rhymes as one's instance of sound and sense in *Paradise Lost*, despite the fact that rhymes do have the advantage of being more clear-cut, more credibly isolable, than other subtleties of sound which can be so haunting. For did not Milton preface his poem with a note on 'The Verse'?

The measure is *English* Heroic Verse without Rime, as that of *Homer* in *Greek*, and of *Virgil* in *Latin*; Rime being no necessary Adjunct or true Ornament of Poem or good Verse, in longer Works especially, but the Invention of a barbarous Age, to set off wretched matter and lame Meeter. . . .

Yet the poet who so sardonically clashes 'matter' against 'Meeter' there is not indifferent to rhyme, and he had earlier created the masterly rhyming of 'Lycidas'; it has long been remarked that *Paradise Lost* deploys rhymes, though fairly infrequently, with great skill. Milton may applaud the example he has set, 'the first in *English*, of ancient liberty recover'd to Heroic Poem from the troublesom and modern bondage of Rimeing'; but we may allow his word 'lame' and his metaphor, liberation, to remind us of the words of T. S. Eliot in his 'Reflections on "Vers Libre"' (1917):

This liberation from rhyme might be as well a liberation *of* rhyme. Freed from its exacting task of supporting lame verse, it could be applied with greater effect where it is most needed.[8]

Three hundred years ago, a few months before Milton died in November 1674, the second edition of *Paradise Lost* was published, and with it Andrew Marvell's commendatory verses. He ended with ten lines about Milton's lofty refusal to rhyme:

> I too transported by the Mode offend,
> And while I meant to Praise thee must Commend.
> Thy Verse created like thy Theme sublime,
> In Number, Weight, and Measure, needs not Rhime.

Yet one rhyme-word of which Marvell twice availed himself is notable; for Marvell's opening verse-paragraph ends by telling of Marvell's fear that Milton would ruin the sacred truths:

> (So *Sampson* groap'd the Temples Posts in spight)
> The World o'rewhelming to revenge his sight.[9]

And Marvell's penultimate verse-paragraph (followed only by the coda on rhyming) ends:

> Just Heav'n thee like *Tiresias* to requite
> Rewards with Prophesie thy loss of sight.

Whether Marvell was conscious of it or not, 'sight' and its rhymes are of supreme importance to Milton.

Why is the line in Book iii, when Milton speaks of his blindness:

> And wisdome at one entrance quite shut out.

so magnificent a marriage of sound and sense? It does not make you *feel* blindness (as the opening of Eliot's 'Marina': 'What seas what shores what grey rocks and what islands', makes you feel something akin to the recovery of sight); instead

---

[8] *To Criticize the Critic* (1965), p. 189.
[9] 'Spite' is Satan's bitter recoiling rhyme in ix 171-8:

> Revenge, at first though sweet,
> Bitter ere long back on it self recoiles;
> Let it; I reck not, so it light well aim'd,
> Since higher I fall short, on him who next
> Provokes my envie, this new Favorite
> Of Heav'n, this Man of Clay, Son of despite,
> Whom us the more to spite his Maker rais'd
> From dust: spite then with spite is best repaid.

it superbly makes you feel 'quite shut out' from any imagin-
ability of unimaginable blindness. The anguished dignity of
blinded Gloucester's cry—'All dark and comfortless'—is a
very different thing; 'comfortless' pulls us within his pain, into
the inward deeply ensconced need for comfort. The totality of
that particular exclusion, blindness, one whole sense wholly
lost, is in the curt but stoical clippedness of those three monosyllables each ending with its finality of t: 'quite shut out'.
Three times it tolls, and Eliot would hardly be able to speak
here of 'the pleasure which arises from the *noise*'. But a fuller
sense of Milton's fullness—of his supple yet assured felicities of
sound and sense—asks a long passage, asks not just the opening of Book iii but also the ending of Book ii. There are many
attentivenesses which would be rewarding, but the one that is
to the purpose is the rhyme of light against night:

> But now at last the sacred influence
> Of light appears, and from the walls of Heav'n
> Shoots farr into the bosom of dim Night
> A glimmering dawn; here Nature first begins
> Her fardest verge, and *Chaos* to retire
> As from her outmost works a brok'n foe
> With tumult less and with less hostile din,
> That *Satan* with less toil, and now with ease
> Wafts on the calmer wave by dubious light
> And like a weather-beaten Vessel holds
> Gladly the Port, though Shrouds and Tackle torn;
> Or in the emptier waste, resembling Air,
> Weighs his spread wings, at leisure to behold
> Farr off th'Empyreal Heav'n, extended wide
> In circuit, undetermind square or round,
> With Opal Towrs and Battlements adorn'd
> Of living Saphire, once his native Seat;
> And fast by hanging in a golden Chain
> This pendant world, in bigness as a Starr
> Of smallest Magnitude close by the Moon.
> Thither full fraught with mischievous revenge,
> Accurst, and in a cursed hour he hies.

Notice how 'light' rhymes with 'Night' (positioned as the
rhyme); notice how, half a dozen lines later, the two blend into
this rhyme:

> Wafts on the calmer wave by dubious light.

Notice, too, that the invocation to light which then begins the
next book will now present the quite un-dubious light. The
'sacred *influence* / Of light' will now appear, with a different impulse, as 'Bright *effluence*'. The breathless alliteration of hatred
which ends Book ii, 'he hies', will at once be succeeded and
redeemed by the same alliteration devoted now to the aspiring
breath of prayer: 'Hail holy light.' The whole of the great
opening revolves upon the crucial words that rhyme with
'light':

Book iii

> Hail holy light, ofspring of Heav'n first-born,
> Or of th'Eternal Coeternal beam
> May I express thee unblam'd? since God is light,
> And never but in unapproached light
> Dwelt from Eternitie, dwelt then in thee,
> Bright effluence of bright essence increate.
> Or hear'st thou rather pure Ethereal stream,
> Whose Fountain who shall tell? before the Sun,
> Before the Heavens thou wert, and at the voice
> Of God, as with a Mantle didst invest
> The rising world of waters dark and deep,
> Won from the void and formless infinite.
> Thee I re-visit now with bolder wing,
> Escap't the *Stygian* Pool, though long detain'd
> In that obscure sojourn, while in my flight
> Through utter and through middle darkness borne
> With other notes than to th'*Orphean* Lyre
> I sung of *Chaos* and *Eternal Night*,
> Taught by the heav'nly Muse to venture down
> The dark descent, and up to reascend,
> Though hard and rare: thee I revisit safe,
> And feel thy sovran vital Lamp; but thou
> Revisit'st not these eyes, that rowle in vain
> To find thy piercing ray, and find no dawn;
> So thick a drop serene hath quencht thir Orbs,
> Or dim suffusion veild. Yet not the more
> Cease I to wander where the Muses haunt
> Cleer Spring, or shadie Grove, or Sunnie Hill,
> Smit with the love of sacred song; but chief
> Thee *Sion* and the flowrie Brooks beneath
> That wash thy hallowd feet, and warbling flow,
> Nightly I visit: nor somtimes forget

Those other two equal'd with me in Fate,
So were I equal'd with them in renown,
Blind *Thamyris* and blind *Maeonides*,
And *Tiresias* and *Phineus* Prophets old.
Then feed on thoughts, that voluntarie move
Harmonious numbers; as the wakeful Bird
Sings darkling, and in shadiest Covert hid
Tunes her nocturnal Note. Thus with the Year
Seasons return, but not to me returns
Day, or the sweet approach of Ev'n or Morn,
Or sight of vernal bloom, or Summers Rose,
Or flocks, or herds, or human face divine;
But cloud in stead, and ever-during dark
Surrounds me, from the chearful waies of men
Cut off, and for the Book of knowledg fair
Presented with a Universal blanc
Of Natures works to mee expung'd and ras'd,
And wisdome at one entrance quite shut out.
So much the rather thou Celestial light
Shine inward, and the mind through all her powers
Irradiate, there plant eyes, all mist from thence
Purge and disperse, that I may see and tell
Of things invisible to mortal sight.

This speaks often of the beauties of sound, and might alert us
to the relation of sound and sense, there for instance in the
lucid audacity which rhymes the second line and the seventh
line, each beginning with 'Or' and postulating an alternative
way of conceiving of light:

Or of th' Eternal Coeternal beam . . .

Or hear'st thou rather pure Ethereal stream . . .

The rhyme asks us to see that these alternatives can accommodate each other as the rhyme can, for the beam which is
light can play upon a stream, and light can stream as a beam
does. But the integrating rhyme, or rather the living principle
of the passage, is *light*, which moves from the first line to
become positioned as a rhyme in line 3 and then at once to
rhyme with itself in line 4, with the indubitability of such a
massive simple clinching return.[10] 'Bright' then rhymes both

---

[10] 'Light' ends a line fifty or so times in the poem: only here does it end two succeeding lines. But Christ's resurrection rhymes 'dawning light' with 'dawning light'

with 'light', and with itself in line 6. Line 12 then gives us a very different word positioned as the rhyme:

> Won from the void and formless infinite.[11]

Three lines later, again positioned as the rhyme, comes that word which could mean cowardice but here means courage:

> In that obscure sojourn, while in my flight

Three lines later again, and again positioned as a rhyme, Night makes the entry for which we have waited since the end of Book ii:

> I sung of *Chaos* and *Eternal Night.*

But when Night returns (in line 32), it has been made more mild ('Nightly I visit'), and we are ready for the other crucial word in this constellation of related rhymes, the word which brings together 'light' and 'bright' and 'night': 'sight':

> Or sight of vernal bloom, or Summers Rose,

The last half-dozen lines of this great verse-paragraph move with touching and instant resolution from the dark finality of

> And wisdome at one entrance quite shut out.

—to a brightening courage which rhymes 'light' with its conclusive 'sight':

> So much the rather thou Celestial light
> Shine inward, and the mind through all her powers
> Irradiate, there plant eyes, all mist from thence
> Purge and disperse, that I may see and tell
> Of things invisible to mortal sight.

The aspiration and the affirmation are at one in the complete-

across a line's interval as of his days of death, in the fullness of an irresistible reviving:

> so he dies,
> But soon revives, Death over him no power
> Shall long usurp; ere the third dawning light
> Returne, the Starres of Morn shall see him rise
> Out of his grave, fresh as the dawning light,
> (xii 419-23)

[11] Pronounced so, as when Donne rhymes 'infinite' and 'unite'; compare *Paradise Lost*, v 596 ending 'infinite' and 600 ending 'Light'; and iii 373 which ends with 'Infinite' and then has 'Light' (375), 'brightness' (376), and 'bright' (380).

ness of that final assured and simple rhyme.[12] Such poetry does indeed 'shine inward';[13] it does not shine outward from a feeling of inwardness, as it would if the poet were working from the inside; rather, it assumes that the truth is in its way as 'external' to us as is the light of day. Certain truths about truth can be seized by such externality, such likening of it to light. Those truths are brought home through felicities of rhyme which embody Arthur Hallam's profound restatement of the nature of rhyme: 'Rhyme has been said to contain in itself a constant appeal to Memory and Hope.' Yet the memory has to confront loss, and the hope is a perpetual striving against that which it can resist but cannot extirpate.

Book iii begins 'Hail holy light', but it ends with the dark alighting of Satan upon earth, he too in flight being permitted his rhyme of flight against light as he

> Throws his steep flight in many an Aerie wheele,
> Nor staid, till on *Niphates* top he lights.

We may remember Dr. Johnson's remark that 'The word "light" is one of Shakespeare's favourite play-things', a remark which elsewhere he phrased so that 'delights' chimes with 'light': 'There is scarcely any word with which Shakespeare so much delights to trifle as with "light", in its various significations.' Milton too saw the profound possibilities here, whether in the buoyancy of a crackling brightness:

> Light as the Lightning glimps they ran, they flew.   (vi 642)

---

[12] A comparable serenity, at once liquid and firm, informs the magnificent evocation of light and sight in vii 359-69:

> Of Light by farr the greater part he took,
> Transplanted from her cloudie Shrine, and plac'd
> In the Suns Orb, made porous to receive
> And drink the liquid Light, firm to retaine
> Her gather'd beams, great Palace now of Light.
> Hither as to thir Fountain other Starrs
> Repairing, in thir gold'n Urns draw Light,
> And hence the Morning Planet guilds his horns;
> By tincture or reflection they augment
> Thir small peculiar, though from human sight
> So farr remote, with diminution seen.

[13] But not with the same effect as Ben Jonson:

> Light, I salute thee, but with wounded nerves . . .

—a line praised by T. S. Eliot, a poet who in both senses makes much of nerves. Contrast the soothing truth of Milton:

> To resalute the World with sacred Light.   (xi 134)

Or in the lightsomeness of a peaceful dawn:

> Now morn her rosie steps in th'Eastern Clime
> Advancing, sow'd the Earth with Orient Pearle,
> When *Adam* wak't, so customd, for his sleep
> Was Aerie light, from pure digestion bred,
> And temperat vapors bland, which th'only sound
> Of leaves and fuming rills, *Aurora*'s fan,
> Lightly dispers'd . . .   (v 1-7)

(Lovely to think of sleep as being 'lightly dispers'd' at dawn.)
Or there is the weaponry of a warlike dawn:

> others from the dawning Hills
> Lookd round, and Scouts each Coast light-armed scoure.
>   (vi 528-9)

Or the sardonic hopelessness of Adam at the curses which

> On mee as on thir natural center light
> Heavie.   (x 740-1)

Or the 'Celestial Ardors' of angelic energy:

> Vaild with his gorgeous wings, up springing light.   (v 250)

Or the credulity of diabolical complacency, making Hell all the
more sombre:

> This horror will grow milde, this darkness light,   (ii 220)

But this last instance is the more telling, for it moves on:

> This horror will grow milde, this darkness light,
> Besides what hope the never-ending flight
> Of future days may bring.   (ii 220-2)

Belial's appalling jauntiness, his tacit gullibility as to the kind
of 'never-ending flight' which time may proffer, is caught with
dreadful pathos in the fleeting rhyme (there is no punctuation
after 'never-ending flight').

It is not possible to chart all of Milton's various, beautiful,
and new feats with the word 'light'. Again and again he places
it at the end of a line; frequently he rhymes it with a word also
at the end of a line, and even more frequently he rhymes it with
many a word within the lines in its immediate vicinity. Hardly
ever does he place it within a line and *not* give it one or more

rhymes within, say, five lines. Perhaps the most delightfully audacious is the back-to-back climax of 'night' and 'light' here:

All night the dreadless Angel unpursu'd
Through Heav'ns wide Champain held his way till Morn,
Wak't by the circling Hours, with rosie hand
Unbarr'd the gates of Light. There is a Cave
Within the Mount of God, fast by his Throne,
Where light and darkness in perpetual round
Lodge and dislodge by turns, which makes through Heav'n
Grateful vicissitude, like Day and Night;
Light issues forth . . .   (vi 1-9)

But there is something greater than audacity in the enlightened gentleness of Uriel's words, the more so as they are words to the disguised Satan; Uriel speaks of light and of the night, as he misguidedly guides the disguised Satan towards the earth:

Look downward on that Globe whose hither side
With light from hence, though but reflected, shines;
That place is Earth the seat of Man, that light
His day, which else as th'other Hemisphere
Night would invade, but there the neighbouring Moon
(So call that opposite fair Starr) her aide
Timely interposes, and her monthly round
Still ending, still renewing through mid Heav'n,
With borrowd light her countenance triform
Hence fills and empties to enlighten the Earth,
And in her pale dominion checks the night.
                                   (iii 722-32)

The concluding night here is not 'Chaos and Eternal Night'; it has the equanimity of a pacific rhyme, just as the moon's dominion checks the night both in setting limits to night's power and in chequering the night. (The *OED* cites Robert Greene, 1590: 'checkt the night with the golden rays'.) True dominion is as effortlessly gentle, and as creative of beauty, as the moon's checking chequerwork—the artistic claim is also a moral and spiritual one. Such poetry does 'enlighten the Earth', three hundred years after the death of its poet, and it is an experience, not a mere assertion. It is external, as the moon's light is external to us, and indeed as the moon's light is external to her ('With borrowd light'), but it is not unfelt. It interposes its timely aid, and its dominion checks the night.

SAMUEL JOHNSON:
DEAD METAPHORS AND
'IMPENDING DEATH'

It has itself become something of a cliché that Johnson's best poetry finds its force in a renovation of cliché. The excellent criticism of T. S. Eliot and F. R. Leavis[1] was developed by Donald Davie in *Purity of Diction in English Verse* (1952), which showed that the metaphorical life in the poems of Johnson is often a matter of invigorating dead or flat metaphor, of using clichés so that their pristine force is recreated or so that they are seen in a new perspective. In *The Vanity of Human Wishes*, the defeated Xerxes 'gains' the sea—and that is all he does gain, the cliché sardonically intimates. In *London*, 'Greenwich smiles upon the silver Flood', not simply because this is a pastoral moment of 'transient calm', but because *silver* grimly refuses to stay put as just a pastoral word—in London 'smiles are sold'.

Such a use of metaphor is a corollary of Johnson's convictions about life and literature. 'What is new is opposed, because most are unwilling to be taught; and what is known is rejected, because it is not sufficiently considered, that men more frequently require to be reminded than informed' (*The Rambler*, No. 2, 24 March 1750). If this begins by recognising the role of those who proclaim the new, its conclusion reveals that Johnson's own heart was more in the latter duty, of 'reminding' men. (Unlike the reiterations of information a reminder acts more indirectly—as metaphor does.) Life and literature are for Johnson in more danger from our forgetting or losing the things that we possess than from our failing to gain new things. In *The Rambler*, No. 3 (27 March 1750) he once again puts the two duties fairly before us, but he devotes more of his words to the alternative that had his particular allegiance:

The task of an author is, either to teach what is not known, or to recommend known truths by his manner of adorning them; either to let new light in upon the mind, and open new scenes to the prospect,

[1] Introductory Essay to *London* and *The Vanity of Human Wishes* (1930); 'The Augustan Tradition', *Revaluation* (1936).

or to vary the dress and situation of common objects, so as to give them fresh grace and more powerful attractions, to spread such flowers over the regions through which the intellect has already made its progress, as may tempt it to return, and take a second view of things hastily passed over, or negligently regarded.

Johnson varies the dress and situation of common metaphors, giving them fresh grace and more powerful attractions, so that phrases which we have regrettably but inevitably come to pass over hastily or regard negligently can at their best recapture their original force. There is, as is natural in a great writer, a congruence of life and literature, so that the phrasing which Johnson uses when speaking of our sense of mortality applies as truly to our sense of language: 'This conviction, however forcible at every new impression, is every moment fading from the mind' (*The Idler*, No. 103, 5 April 1760). So too with 'the great art of piety', which resembles the art of literature, and consists in 'the perpetual renovation of the motives to virtue' (*The Rambler*, No. 7, 10 April 1750).

A sidelight is thrown upon this poetic practice of Johnson's by a youthful or schooldays translation of his which was not published in its entirety until 1964, in the Yale edition of the poems. Addison's *Proelium inter Pygmaeos et Grues* ('Battle of the Pygmies and Cranes', 1698) is a Latin imitation of the pseudo-Homeric *Batrachomyomachia* ('Battle of the Frogs and Mice'), and Johnson's 170-line translation of Addison, now printed among his Juvenilia or his Early Poems, is 'noteworthy as Johnson's only known verse translation from a modern Latinist'. To the critic it is noteworthy for the way in which it handles clichés. Repeatedly Johnson either chooses to employ a cliché when he might have avoided one, or adds clichés where there is no equivalent for them in Addison. But already in this apprentice exercise Johnson renovates what is dead. The clichés are brought disconcertingly to life by the subject of the poem, since Johnson selects such as relate in some way to the battle and the birds.

> In vain from heavens black Concave, like a Cloud
> Fresh foes descending glut their swords with blood.
> (20-1)

As Professor Davie would say, in such a style all swords glut themselves with blood, and in his *Irene* (I i) Johnson was to give us the cliché quite dead: 'No more the glutted Sabre thirsts for Blood'. But here the metaphor is sharply alive, because the swords of the cranes are their beaks. The cranes are endowed with swords which they can indeed glut with blood. Moreover there is no equivalent in the Latin (Johnson is imaginatively expanding):

> *Exiguosque canam pugiles, Gruibusque malignos*
> *Heroas, nigrisque ruentem e nubibus hostem.*

One notices too that Johnson's 'from heavens black Concave, like a Cloud' is also an unobtrusive amplification of the Latin, which simply says that the foe descends from the black clouds. 'Like a Cloud' invigorates the old metaphor which sees a multitude of birds or insects as a cloud (Spenser's gnats, Milton's locusts), and it does so by suggesting that there were so many birds that they actually darkened the air (Milton: 'the wing'd air dark't with plumes'). Such must once have been part of the idea that presented itself to the person who first used what is now a cliché and spoke of a cloud of insects. Johnson allows us access to the original act of imagination which created the metaphor. His 'Cloud' hovers between the literal and metaphorical, and in the ambiguity each fortifies the other.

'Glut their swords' adds to the Latin; 'like a Cloud' amplifies it. Both are examples of the resurrection of metaphors, but the interest of the poem is in the persistence of the habit, and not in any single knock-down instance. The Miltonic phrase which precipitated Addison's poem does itself contain a sardonic pun not so very different from those which Johnson creates:

> For never since created man,
> Met such imbodied force, as nam'd with these
> Could merit more than that small infantry
> Warr'd on by Cranes.
>
> (*Paradise Lost*, i 573-6)

Addison's poem has many latinised Miltonisms; that Johnson recalled the original context in Milton is suggested by his taking up the word 'embodied' (78) from it.

Johnson establishes his strategy for this military poem in the opening lines:

Feather'd Battalions, Squadrons on the wing
And the sad fate of Pygmie Realms I sing.
Direct O Goddess, my advent'rous song
In warring Colours shew the warring throng
Teach me to range my troopes in just array
Whilst beaks and swords engage in bloody fray
And paint the horrors of the dreadfull day.

The additions to Addison are notable:

Pennatas acies, et lamentabile bellum
Pygmeadum refero: parvas tu, Musa, cohortes
Instrue; tu gladios, mortemque minantia rostra,
Offensosque Grues, indignantesque pusillam
Militiam celebra; volucrumque hominumque tumultus.

Johnson was not content simply to translate *pennatas acies* as
'Feather'd Battalions'—he immediately expands it with
'Squadrons on the wing', where 'on the wing' conveys both the
literal meaning and the metaphorical urgency of war (*OED*:
'moving swiftly and briskly, astir', including a quotation from
Rasselas). The phrase carries conviction because of its literal
meaning, and it has force because it recaptures the energy of
the mind which originally glimpsed and summed up a precipitate energy by describing it as 'on the wing'.

Johnson's metaphor then is one which amplifies Addison's
text. But there is nothing in the Latin which corresponds to his
pun 'In warring Colours shew the warring throng'—the Latin
has merely *celebra*. 'Warring Colours' is a trite figure for the
contrast and opposition of colours; Johnson, by paralleling
style and subject, renovates the cliché. Not as strongly as Pope
was to do in the description of Buckingham's death, when he
converted the strife between the colours into one in which each
tried to outdo the other in squalor ('In the worst inn's worst
room . . . Where tawdry yellow strove with dirty red').[2] Johnson
was not equally successful on each occasion in this juvenile
poem—it is rather the poetic practice which is important. Just
as he added the 'Colours', so he adds the stock phrasing of
'paint the horrors'. To 'paint' in such a context is usually nothing more than one of countless interchangeable synonyms for
'describe', whereas Johnson's sequence, 'warring Colours . . .

2 'Epistle to Bathurst' 299-304.

beaks and swords engage in bloody fray. . . . paint the horrors',
is one that puts unexpected pressure on 'paint' so that it suggests to daub with blood.

These first seven lines show on three occasions a pressure on
dead metaphor, either by amplification or modification of
Addison's Latin. That it was by no means inevitable for a
translator to deploy such metaphors is suggested by the fact
that none of the three standard eighteenth-century translations
of Addison's poem employs any of them. William Warburton's
translation in 1724 flatly offers this:

> I sing the Crane and Pygmy up in arms,
> And brandish'd tucks oppose to pointed beaks.
> Raise, muse, the fury of the feather'd foe,
> Lead the low cohorts to the dusty field,
> And men and birds in rude encounter join.

The pygmies, Johnson tells us, lived

> In a low vale by rocks that pierce the skies
> Guarded from all but winged enemies.
>   (24-5)

The cliché 'pierce the skies' is Johnson's addition; Addison has
inhospita saxa. But the local context puts a pressure on 'pierce'
(the pygmies are 'guarded', by things that pierce, from their
'enemies'), and so does the general context of beaks, swords
and wounds. 'Pierce' is given just the point which it must
originally have had when somebody was emboldened to describe
high sharp rocks with such a metaphor. A wording which is
now as dead as our *skyscraper*, and which was once as bold as
that was, is restored to us. There is a similar effect later in the
poem; Johnson has been telling how the war began because the
pygmies smashed the nests and eggs of the cranes:

> And crush'd the yet unanimated young
> From hence the seeds of Discord first arose.
>   (49-50)

But 'seeds of discord' shows Johnson adding a cliché; the Latin
says *Hinc causae irarum, bella hinc, fatalia bella*. Johnson prefers a
sardonic irony, one which Warburton stumbles on the edge of
with his 'War, fatal war, from these dire seeds arose'. Crush-
ing the eggs brought to life the seeds of discord. Thomas

Newcomb's translation offers a different cliché, and an irrelevant one: 'From this dire spring immortal discords rose'.
How does Johnson embody the discords? He makes no attempt to translate Addison's words *confusaque mortis imago*, which Warburton renders as 'grisly deaths in different forms confused', and which James Beattie in 1766 paraphrases with an irrelevant metaphor: 'Death's grim visage scares the Pigmy-realms'. Johnson remembers what we say about Death, and he remembers the subject of the poem, and he gives us: 'Death exulting stalk'd along the land' (53). The cliché about death (*OED*: *stalk* 4c, 'of quasi-personified maleficent agencies', from 1593) is combined with a reminder about the birds (*OED*: *stalk* 4, 'to walk like a long-legged bird', where the first example, 1530, comes pat: 'He stalketh lyke a crane'). Johnson's feeling for context, together with his responsibility towards language, gives more force to his usage than is present in, for example, Collins' talk of how Danger 'stalks his Round' ('Ode to Fear').
The cranes gather for war:

> *omnesque simul, quas Strymonis unda,*
> *Aut stagnum Mareotidis, imi aut uda Caystri*
> *Prata tenent, adsunt; Scythicaque excita palude,*
> *Et conjurato volucris descendit ab Istro,*
> *Stragesque immensas et vulnera cogitat absens.*

Johnson adds a cliché, but with a difference:

> When all conspiring leave Maeons lake
> And warm Cäyster's flowing banks forsake
> To Mareotis fen the rumour flies
> From Isther's flood unnumberd flocks arise
> Which whet their beaks, for flight their wings prepare.
> (66-70)

Ever since Book iv of the *Aeneid*, rumour has 'flown', so frequently indeed that one might pervert the question of Tennyson's Lancelot: 'I hear of rumours flying through your court . . . When did not rumours fly?' Johnson's rumour conspires with the birds and imitates them. Addison had pinpointed the moment as if the cranes were merely migrating: *Ergo ubi ver nactus proprium*. Johnson expands this into a time-honoured metaphor, which on this occasion is acutely relevant: 'when o'er Winters sway, prevail'd the spring' (72). Yet it is as well to

be reminded of the greater effect in *The Vanity of Human Wishes*
(208): 'And Winter barricades the Realms of Frost'. That line
is a touchstone, a reminder not to overestimate the intrinsic
worth of Johnson's schoolboy effort, though at the same time it
serves to show the continuity of his habits of mind and of
creation.

The pygmies are marshalled for battle:

> *Nec minor in terris motus, dum bella facessit*
> *Impiger, instituitque agmen, firmatque phalangas,*
> *Et furit arreptis animosus homuncio telis:*
> *Donec turma duas composta excurrat in alas,*
> *Ordinibusque frequens, et marte instructa perito.*

Johnson strengthens his lines with a decorous pun:

> Meantime the Pygmies with undaunted hearts
> Temper their swords and point their missive darts
> The steely troops embodied closely stand.
>
> (76-8)

'Undaunted . . . temper' enforces the old sense of 'obdurate'
for *steely*, whereas 'swords . . . darts' reminds us too of the steel
of arms and armour.

> But now their cruel enemies draw near
> And first a sound invades th' astonish'd ear.
>
> (90-1)

In bad Augustan verse all sounds invade the ear instead of
simply being heard (*OED* from 1673). Yet Johnson is right in
thinking that suffocating under the phrase is what was once
a boldly imaginative metaphor. To use the phrase immediately
after telling us how the 'cruel enemies draw near' is to bring
that metaphor back to martial life. All that Addison had said
was *Jamque procul sonus auditur.*

For a while the outcome of the battle is uncertain: *Armorum
pendet fortuna.* Johnson sees the relevance to this particular battle
of the tacit metaphor in *pendet.* So he expands this in a way
which is still traditional but which makes it more birdlike: 'And
victory hangs doubtfull o'er the field' (a line which has the further ominous point of hinting that the cranes will win). Johnson
had prepared for this expansion by his treatment of the immediately preceding lines:

Mox defessa iterum levibus sese eripit alis,
Et vires reparata iterum petit impete terras.
Armorum pendet fortuna.

Johnson anticipates the renewed metaphor of victory hanging
doubtful:

> Breathless at length they leave th'unfinish'd war
> And hang aloft suspended in the air.
> But their lost strength and vigour soon return
> They clap their wings, and with new fury burn;
> Then, swift as thought, by headlong anger driv'n
> Descend, impetuous, from the vault of Heav'n.
> Their foes the shock sustain in Battle skill'd,
> And victory hangs doubtfull o'er the field.
>
> (102-9)

The pressure on *pendet* is a matter of metaphorical expansion
and not of addition, and the same is true of Johnson's choice of
'headlong anger' as well as 'impetuous' (both deriving from
Addison's *impete*). It is a commonplace to describe anger as
headlong, but here the cranes are swooping to earth.

A huge crane carries off the pygmy-chief into the air, and the
pygmies mourn:

> *frustra Pygmaei lumine moesto*
> *Regem inter nubes lugent, solitoque minorem*
> *Heroem aspiciunt Gruibus plaudentibus escam.*

Johnson's pun is simply carried over from the Latin, though he
reinforces it: 'The joyfull Cranes triumphant clap their wings'.
But his next two lines add a tacit metaphor:

> While the sad Pygmies mourn with weeping eyes
> Their Godlike Hero strugling in the skies.
>
> (128-9)

Addison had not explicitly said 'Godlike', although *heroem*
implies demi-god; nor had he said 'in the skies', but *inter nubes*.
Johnson's sequence, 'mourn . . . Godlike . . . skies', may add
a mock-heroic suggestion which does not seem to be part of
Addison's meaning: that the pygmy is being translated into the
skies to become a star. Like, for example, that other great
soldier, Julius Caesar, whose death provides the final metamorphosis in Book xv of Ovid. In the translation by Leonard

Welsted (in Samuel Garth's collection, 1717), as Venus stands
over the dying Caesar:

> Her *Caesar's* heav'nly Part she made her Care,
> Nor left the recent Soul to waste to Air;
> But bore it upwards to its native Skies:
> Glowing with new-born Fires she saw it rise;
> Forth springing from her Bosom up it flew,
> And kindling, as it soar'd, a Comet grew:
> Above the Lunar Sphere it took its Flight,
> And shot behind it a long Trail of Light.

The poem draws to an end, but Johnson has one superbly
reticent pun still in store:

> *ergo pars vertere terga*
> *Horribili perculsa metu, pars tollere vocem*
> *Exiguam; late populus Cubitalis oberrat.*
> *Instant a tergo volucres, lacerantque trahuntque*
> *Immites, certae gentem extirpare nefandam.*
>
> Part turn their Backs, part seiz'd with wild surprise
> Utter sad groans and lamentable cries.
> Impending death they strive to 'scape in vain ⎫
> For fear retards their flight, the cruell Crane ⎬
> Scatters their breathless bodies o'er the plain. ⎭
>   (146-50)

Impending death, indeed. A latent metaphor (death is hanging
over them) is brought vividly to a manifest life, and is perhaps
supported by speaking, with a sardonic pun, of the pygmies'
unattainable 'flight'—which like 'impending' has no strict
counterpart in the original.

   Johnson's translation is not a work of great intrinsic merit,
though it does include some remarkable felicities. Its importance lies in the demonstration, even in a juvenile and circum-
scribed poem, that the metaphorical skill he would best deploy
would be a revivification of dead metaphors into a disconcertingly relevant prominence, varying their dress and situation 'so
as to give them fresh grace and more powerful attractions'.

WILLIAM WORDSWORTH 1:
'A PURE ORGANIC PLEASURE
FROM THE LINES'

I

There is reason to think that Wordsworth was aware of a discussion about the difference between poetry and prose in Erasmus Darwin's *Loves of the Plants*; aware, too, 'almost certainly', of an article in *The Monthly Magazine* for July 1796 on 'Is Verse Essential to Poetry?'[1] Such arguments are ancient, and usually yield only to fatigue. Robert Lowell said, 'I no longer know the difference between prose and verse'.[2] T. S. Eliot towards the end of his life declared: 'the moment the intermediate term *verse* is suppressed, I do not believe that any distinction between prose and poetry is meaningful'.[3] That was in 1958; but thirty years earlier, when the usual arguments were being rehearsed in *The Times Literary Supplement*, Eliot had come up with a very suggestive formulation: 'Verse, whatever else it may or may not be, is itself a system of *punctuation*; the usual marks of punctuation themselves are differently employed' (*TLS*, 27 September 1928).

The punctuation of which poetry or verse further avails itself is the white space. In prose, line-endings are ordinarily the work of the compositor and not of the artist; they are compositorial, not compositional. Without entering into some traditional problems of distinction, and without claiming here[4] that it is line-endings alone which importantly distinguish poetry (or at any rate such poetry as is not also verse) from prose, one may at least urge that the poet has at his command this further 'system of punctuation'. The white space at the end of a line of poetry constitutes some kind of pause; but there need not be

[1] W. J. B. Owen, *Wordsworth as Critic* (1969), pp. 17-20.

[2] In an interview with D. S. Carne-Ross, *Delos*, i (1968).

[3] Introduction to a translation of Valéry's *Art of Poetry* (1958), p. xvi.

[4] See my review of John Sparrow's *Visible Words* (1969), in *Essays in Criticism*, xx (1970). Geoffrey N. Leech's *A Linguistic Guide to English Poetry* (1969) has some good instances of the effects created by lineation.

any pause of formal punctuation, and so there may be only equivocally a pause at all. A non-temporal pause? Unless the rhythm or the sense or the formal punctuation insists upon it, the line-ending (which cannot help conveying some sense of an ending) may not be exactly an ending. The white space may constitute an invisible boundary; an absence or a space which yet has significance; what in another context might be called a pregnant silence.

Just how much a line-ending may effect has been finely shown in two classic passages of literary criticism. Dr. F. R. Leavis commented on two lines from Keats's 'To Autumn':

> And sometimes like a gleaner thou dost keep
> Steady thy laden head across a brook;

'As we pass across the line-division from "keep" to "steady" we are made to enact, analogically, the upright steadying carriage of the gleaner as she steps from one stone to the next.'[5] The perfect steadiness of rhythm matches the simply steady movement of the syntax; the sense that such steadiness has to be achieved, that it is laden and not just casual, is enforced by the line-ending, across which—it stands for the unseen brook which we are *not* looking down at—the steady movement must be made.

Such a line-ending creates its effect mimetically and without recourse to any type of ambiguity. But a line-ending—and here the classic piece of criticism is by Donald Davie—may create its significance by a momentary ambiguity:

> Then feed on thoughts, that voluntarie move
> Harmonious numbers; as the wakeful Bird
> Sings darkling, and in shadiest Covert hid
> Tunes her nocturnal Note.
>   (*Paradise Lost*, iii 37-40)

The language is deployed, just as the episodes are in a story, so as always to provoke the question 'And then?'—to provoke this question and to answer it in unexpected ways. If any arrangement of language is a sequence of verbal events, here syntax is employed so as to make the most of each word's eventfulness, so as to make each key-word, like each new episode in a well-told story, at once surprising and just. The eventfulness of language comes out for instance in 'Then feed on

---

[5] 'Mr. Eliot and Milton', *The Common Pursuit* (1952), p. 17.

thoughts, that voluntarie move', where at the line-ending 'move' seems intransitive, and as such wholly satisfying; until the swing on to the next line, 'Harmonious numbers', reveals it (a little surprise, but a wholly fair one) as transitive. This flicker of hesitation about whether the thoughts move only themselves, or something else, makes us see that the numbers aren't really 'something else' but are the very thoughts themselves, seen under a new aspect; the placing of 'move', which produces the momentary uncertainty about its grammar, ties together 'thoughts' and 'numbers' in a relation far closer than cause and effect.[6]

Before now pointing to the kinds of effect, subtle and various, which Wordsworth achieved with line-endings, I need to suggest some of the ramifications. For the use of line-endings can be a type or symbol or emblem of what the poet values, as well as the instrument by which his values are expressed.

First there is Wordsworth's commitment to those ample relationships which yet do not swamp or warp the multiplicities which they accommodate.[7] No fragmentation into separateness; but also no dissolution within a greedily engrossing unity. Such a commitment asks an analogous literary feat: that the relationship between the line of verse and the passage of verse be just such a relationship. The poetic achievement is itself to embody the values to which the poet has allegiance. The separate line of verse must not be too simply separate, and yet it must have its individuality respected. Nothing must be viewed 'In disconnection dead and spiritless' (*The Excursion*, iv 962). Everything must be free, 'Itself a living part of a live whole' (*The Prelude*, iii 625). The might of poetry is, like that of mind and world, a 'blended might',[8] something which overrides 'our puny boundaries' (*The Prelude*, ii 223).

'Beyond, though not away from': Geoffrey Hartman's shrewd paradox is therefore as right for the verse as for the vision. Beyond, though not away from: such, after all, is the relation of tenor to vehicle within a metaphor, and such is the relation of verse-paragraph to verse-line, or of poem to verse-paragraph. Wordsworth said:

6 'Syntax and Music in *Paradise Lost*', in *The Living Milton*, ed. Frank Kermode (1960), p. 73.
7 John Jones is invaluable here; see in particular pp. 32, 33, 47, 68, 84, and 85 of *The Egotistical Sublime* (1954).
8 See *Poetical Works*, ed. E. de Selincourt and H. Darbishire, v (1949), 339.

The Imagination also shapes and *creates*; and how? By innumerable processes; and in none does it more delight than in that of consolidating numbers into unity, and dissolving and separating unity into number. (*Preface to Poems*, 1815)

'Consolidating numbers': the words cannot but bring to mind the other sense of *numbers*, 'harmonious numbers', that poetic imagination which consolidates numbers into unity by creating poetic numbers within poetic unity.

So it is not surprising that a characteristic Wordsworthian effect should be that in which line gives way to line with the utmost intangibility of division. James Smith has written exquisitely of 'Michael':

The verse of the poem is a delicate thing. It has almost ceased to beat, and seems maintained only by the flutter of tenuous hopes and sickening fears.

> the unlooked-for claim
> At the first hearing for a moment took
> More hope out of his life than he supposed
> That any old man ever could have lost.

Wordsworth, who was so often an imitator, here speaks with his own voice; and the verse is the contribution he makes to prosody.[9]

Yet Wordsworth made more than one contribution to prosody (even though we might agree that this was his greatest); and similar considerations bear upon verse of a quite different tone and tempo.

> and oftentimes
> When we had given our bodies to the wind,
> And all the shadowy banks, on either side,
> Came sweeping through the darkness, spinning still
> The rapid line of motion; then at once
> Have I, reclining back upon my heels,
> Stopp'd short, yet still the solitary Cliffs
> Wheel'd by me, even as if the earth had roll'd

---

[9] *Scrutiny*, vii (1938), 53. A related point is excellently made by Jonathan Wordsworth (*The Music of Humanity*, 1969, p. 139); he quotes 'The Ruined Cottage' 379-80:

> She did not look at me. Her voice was low,
> Her body was subdued;

and he remarks that 'The end-stop after "low" allows Wordsworth the effect, without the triteness, of a single line with heavy caesura: "Her voice was low,   her body was subdued"'.

> With visible motion her diurnal round;
> Behind me did they stretch in solemn train
> Feebler and feebler, and I stood and watch'd
> Till all was tranquil as a dreamless sleep.
>
> (*The Prelude*, i 478-89)

'Stopp'd short': yet these lines are about—and supremely evoke—the impossibility of stopping short. There can be no cutting off the sequential, and the verbal sequences themselves tell their tale. Within the first three lines, *and* comes twice (not to return for eight lines). Next, within three lines, *sweeping, spinning*, and *reclining* (all continuing, yet with no such participles recurring thereafter). Next, within three lines, *Stopp'd, Wheel'd*, and *roll'd* (with the 'Stopp'd short' unable to prevent the emergence of such a sequence, and with 'watch'd' waiting to appear three lines later). Last, *and* three times within the single line, embodying the perfect rallentando and diminuendo which chasten the childish expectation that it might be possible to stop short:

> Behind me did they stretch in solemn train
> Feebler and feebler, and I stood and watch'd
> Till all was tranquil as a dreamless sleep.

The pleasure which one takes—like the understanding which one gains—in such an evolution through a dozen lines is itself 'a pure organic pleasure from the lines'. Such verse is a triumphant vindication of the severe judgment which Wordsworth passed on Macpherson's Ossian:

In nature every thing is distinct, yet nothing defined into absolute independent singleness. In Macpherson's work, it is exactly the reverse; every thing (that is not stolen) is in this manner defined, insulated, dislocated, deadened,—yet nothing distinct. (*Essay, Supplementary to the Preface*, 1815)

It is characteristic of Wordsworth's sturdiness that he wanted to know where he stood. Blank verse was (in Milton's words) to have 'the sense variously drawn out from one verse into another'. The heroic couplet was to practise its natural determinations. Any mongrel verse was more than disapproved of by Wordsworth—it physically and psychically disconcerted him:

I have indeed, a detestation of couplets running into each other, merely because it is convenient to the writer;—or from affected imitation of our elder poets. Reading such verse produces in me a sensation like that of toiling in a dream, under the night-mair. The Couplet promises rest at agreeable intervals; but here it is never attained—you are mocked and disappointed from paragraph to paragraph. (Letter to Hans Busk, 6 July 1819)

Second, there is Wordsworth's understanding of how easily one sense may tyrannize over the others—and in so doing may moreover fail to realise its own fullest potentialities.

> for I had an eye . . .
> Which spake perpetual logic to my soul,
> And by an unrelenting agency
> Did bind my feelings, even as in a chain.
> (*The Prelude*, iii 156-67)

The eye and the ear (and not only those two senses) must be reconciled, neither lording it over the other. This too must have as its counterpart and embodiment a literary achievement. Reading should itself be a type of the proper relation of eye to ear; and the poet's lines—the relationships which he creates between the single line and its accommodating passage—must effect such a relationship of eye and ear.

Did the printing press minister to a situation in which literature itself could not but tyrannize through the eye? No, because of the subtly complementary relationship of eye to ear as we read—or rather, as we read such literature as is delicately aware. The fluidity and suppleness of line-endings, especially in true blank verse (such as must always remember the warning 'Blank verse seems to be verse only to the eye'[10]), create an equivocal relationship to the eye; a relationship which creates its own checks and balances. As Hartman says, 'Wordsworth's later thought is constantly busy with the fact that the eye is or should be subdued . . . He now sees into the life of things not by a defeat of the eye which drives it on, but rather "with an eye made quiet by the power / Of harmony, and the deep power of joy"'.[11]

Since the verse is to epitomise such harmony and balance, it is natural that the word *line* or *lines* should figure so often in Wordsworth's lines, sometimes with a covert metaphorical

[10] Johnson's *Life of Milton*.
[11] *Wordsworth's Poetry 1787-1814* (1964), p. 114.

application to the verse-lines themselves. Pope had used such a self-referring:

> The spider's touch, how exquisitely fine!
> Feels at each thread, and lives along the line.
>
> *(An Essay on Man,* i 217-18)

'Line' there is not a mere repetition of 'thread'; by giving us both, Pope ensures our noticing that the verse-line too is evoked, itself to be as exquisitely fine, as feeling, as alive. Wordsworth evokes both the line and the line-ending:

> Dreamlike the blending also of the whole
> Harmonious Landscape, all along the shore
> The boundary lost—the line invisible
> That parts the image from reality;
>
> *(Home at Grasmere* 574-7)

The boundary is also that which we cross when we pass from one 'line' to another; 'the line invisible' (following the dash—) is also that which separates one line from another, 'invisible' because it is emblematised on the page by the white space, and not, for instance, by the line of a dash. Invisible, but not non-existent; there is no thing solidly there, no formal punctuation, but there is nevertheless the parting—by means of a significant space, a significant vacancy—of one thing from another. Consider too the self-referring effect created in the skating episode by invoking 'The rapid line of motion'. Or there is the disconcerting mixture of gains and losses—as so often—in the two versions of *The Prelude,* i 588-93:

1805   even then,
> A Child, I held unconscious intercourse
> With the eternal Beauty, drinking in
> A pure organic pleasure from the lines
> Of curling mist, or from the level plain
> Of waters colour'd by the steady clouds.

1850   even then,
> I held unconscious intercourse with beauty
> Old as creation, drinking in a pure
> Organic pleasure from the silver wreaths
> Of curling mist, or from the level plain
> Of waters coloured by impending clouds.

1850 has the richly proleptic suggestion of 'impending', and it retains the crucial inaugurations of the last two lines, both *Of*. But it weakens the force of the other prepositions, removing *With* from the head of the line and *in* from the end of the line, thereby abolishing the engrossing energy of the enjambment: 'drinking in / A pure organic pleasure'. (The *1850* line-break at 'drinking in a pure / Organic pleasure' is altogether ineffectual.) But the superiority of *1805* is clearest in the change from 'the lines / Of curling mist' to 'the silver wreaths / Of curling mist'. On the one hand, the austerity of *lines* has been sacrificed to prettiness; on the other, a suggestiveness too has been sacrificed. For the word *lines* unobtrusively related Wordsworth's delight in 'the eternal Beauty' to his own beautiful lines which are here speaking; we were given a sense of what that 'pure organic pleasure' was, by experiencing its literary counterpart, a 'pure organic pleasure' of a literary kind, drinking it in from these very *lines*. It is a bad bargain which trades away both austerity and suggestiveness. Just for a handful of silver wreaths.

It is the placing of *lines* at the end of the line there which should especially alert us. A quiet paradox informs this stanza (added in 1815) of 'I wandered lonely as a cloud':

> Continuous as the stars that shine
> Or twinkle on the milky way,
> They stretched in never-ending line
> Along the margin of a bay:
> Ten thousand saw I . . .

Not literally a 'never-ending' line of daffodils, of course—any more than the line of verse itself is never-ending. Yet the fact that the verse-line is not brought to an end by punctuation, the fact that it opens into unending space, allows the other aspect of the paradox to impinge on us too. The effect of the lines would be quite different if they were re-punctuated:

> Continuous as the stars that shine
> And twinkle on the milky way,
> They stretched in never-ending line.
> Along the margin of a bay,
> Ten thousand saw I . . .

Third, there is Wordsworth's insistence that a proper surprise is something serene not crashing: 'a gentle shock of mild surprise' (*The Prelude*, v 407). Life necessitates transitions, indeed it thrives on them, but a true transition is one which finds its spontaneity and its surprise somewhere other than in violence. Such transitions and transformations can be set by the poet before your very eyes; they can be the transitions and successions by which a line is taken up by a sequence of lines without being impaired, without ceasing to be itself. In Davie's words, 'a little surprise, but a wholly fair one'. The mutuality and reciprocity within the poem itself are witnesses to those mutualities and reciprocities which engaged Wordsworth's mind and heart, and they are to surprise not startle us. The transitions within the poem, from line to line, are to parallel the great transitions to which all life moves. One season gives way to another—gives way, but does not collapse or succumb; the seasons change, but with no sudden or brutal dismissal. 'The seasons came . . .'—and their coming leads naturally to the word 'inobtrusive' (*The Prelude*, ii 307, 316). Or there is the coming of dawn. In what does the superiority of *1850* over *1805* consist in the following example?

1805   But I have been discouraged; gleams of light
           Flash often from the East, then disappear
                                            (i 134-5)

1850   That hope hath been discouraged; welcome light
           Dawns from the east, but dawns to disappear

The second line now itself *dawns*; the silent self-referring metaphor then tautens the whole line.

We may therefore wish to apply a word like *passage*, so justly used by Hartman, to the passage of verse itself; everything that Hartman here says has its stylistic counterpart or obligation:

Change is not destruction, transition is not violence, and the passage from one mode of being to another should resemble the storm at the beginning of 'Resolution and Independence' which passes into the calm, sunny energies of a new day . . .

[Wordsworth's] aim [is] to render the advent of a new season without defining it into absolute, independent singleness. The passage from one season to another as from one state of being to another is thought of as a gentle transfer of energies.   (p. 203)

Such a gentle transfer of energies must be both effected and symbolised in the transfer of energies from one line to the next, in such a *passage*. In Hartman's words, 'transformations can occur without injury': that they can do so is something which the transforming movement of the verse itself must not only state but epitomise.

II

Lineation in verse creates units which may or may not turn out to be units of sense; the 'flicker of hesitation' (Davie's term) as to what the unit of sense actually is—a flicker resolved when we round the corner into the next line—can create nuances which are central to the poet's enterprise. 'Again and again I must repeat, that the composition of verse', Wordsworth said, 'is infinitely more of an art than men are prepared to believe; and absolute success in it depends upon innumerable minutiae'.[12] Take the conclusion of one of the greatest passages in *The Prelude*:

> in my thoughts
> There was a darkness, call it solitude,
> Or blank desertion, no familiar shapes
> Of hourly objects, images of trees,
> Of sea or sky, no colours of green fields;
> But huge and mighty Forms that do not live
> Like living men mov'd slowly through my mind
> By day and were the trouble of my dreams.
>   (i 420-7)

As we move forward through the lines, it seems that they are asserting, and not just intimating, that the huge and mighty forms do not live; then as we reach the next line, we realise that what may be being said is rather that they live but do not live as men live—or is it that they do not live whereas men do? The ambiguity is not removed by the *1850* punctuation, though the movement within the inaugurating line is thereby changed. Although the ambiguity would still exist if the lines were simply deployed as prose with no change of word-order, the ambiguity would then be less tangible, since there would not be the possi-

---

[12] Letter to William Rowan Hamilton, 22 November 1831.

bility (created by the line-ending and its non-temporal pause) that the unit of sense is conterminous with the line-unit, 'But huge and mighty Forms that do not live'. Redeployed as prose, the following 'Like . . .' would come too hard upon the heels of 'that do not live', and would hardly permit of much of a 'flicker of hesitation'.

The instance is a famous one, and it is central to Wordsworth, since the question of whether such mighty forms do not live or whether they do indeed live but not as men live (rather as 'unknown modes of being') is one which his poetry never ceased to revolve. Indeed William Empson drew attention to the fugitive suggestiveness of the line-ending at this very point:

> my brain
> Work'd with a dim and undetermin'd sense
> Of unknown modes of being;
> (*The Prelude*, i 418-20)

'There is a suggestion here from the pause at the end of the line that he had not merely "a feeling of" these unknown modes but something like a new "sense" which was partly able to apprehend them—a new *kind* of sensing had appeared in his mind'.[13]

The white space, then, may act somewhat as does a rest in music; it may be a potent absence. One might give a new application to Wordsworth's remark in the Preface to *Lyrical Ballads* that 'To these qualities he [the poet] has added a disposition to be affected more than other men by absent things as if they were present'. Like all poets, Wordsworth creates meanings which take into account those absent senses of a word which his verse is aware of fending off:

> I saw him riding o'er the Desert Sands,
> With the fleet waters of the drowning world
> In chase of him . . .
> (*The Prelude*, v 135-7)

Every reader knows that 'fleet' there means *swift*; yet the pressure within that very line of both 'waters' and 'drowning'

---

[13] 'Sense in *The Prelude*', *The Structure of Complex Words* (1951), p. 290. Empson's observation that the word *sense* comes very often at the end of the line is one to which I owe a great deal.

is such as to call up that *fleet* (of ships) which the sense positively
precludes. That other sense is thereby surmised and then ruled
out, so that the total effect of the word resembles *fleet, not—*
indeed not—fleet. The adjective 'fleet' would be careless or perverse if it were not positively (rather than forgetfully or wilfully)
setting aside the other sense. Such an anti-pun is one form
which may be taken by the poet's 'disposition to be affected
more than other men by absent things as if they were present'.
Or what Wordsworth relatedly called 'The spiritual presences
of absent things' (*The Excursion*, iv 1234).

> and all
> Their hues and forms were by invisible links
> Allied to the affections.
> (*The Prelude*, i 638-40)

There on the page is such an invisible link: off the end of the
line. The line-ending can thereby be both a type of and the
instrument of all such kindly linkage.

Hartman has used the term *rites de passage*. The crossing from
one line to the next must be of particular importance to a poet
for whom crossing was so important. We think not only of
Wordsworth crossing the Alps, but also of everything which he
does with boundaries, and all which they meant to him. In
James Smith's words:

He was awake to the notion of the boundary, the imaginary line
which sets up place against place, and by crossing which, from having
been without London, he would find himself within.

> The very moment that I seem'd to know
> The threshold now is overpass'd . . .
> A weight of Ages did at once descend
> Upon my heart;
> (*The Prelude*, viii 699-704)

True boundaries are numinous, and are to be distinguished
from man-made categorising; Wordsworth uses the line-ending
here to crystallise his contempt:

> Thou art no slave
> Of that false secondary power, by which,
> In weakness, we create distinctions, then
> Deem that our puny boundaries are things

—are *things*, whereas they are only fantasies or fictions?—

> are things
> Which we perceive, and not which we have made.
> (*The Prelude*, ii 220-4)

The critic, then, will need to be alert to that stylistic potentiality, the line-ending, which furnishes a counterpart to such
a concern with boundaries. Or with borderers; not just *The
Borderers*, but much else in Wordsworth, such as the poised and
sleeping horse, 'A Borderer dwelling betwixt life and death'.
Can there be such suspended animation within a poem? Yes,
since the white space at the end of a line is such a suspension,
between linguistic life (the words) and linguistic death (*empty*
silence). One might apply (with a specific literalness which he
did not intend) F. W. Bateson's perceptive remark that for
Wordsworth 'the poetry lay *between* the words.'[14] Similarly,
John Jones has noted how Wordsworth's solitaries are 'placed
at the verge of life', and how his 'lonely buildings' are 'at the
extreme of life.'[15] Such a verge, such an extreme, has its stylistic counterpart. It too can be fostered alike by beauty and by
fear. On the one hand:

> —Ah! need I say, dear Friend, that to the brim
> My heart was full;
> (*The Prelude*, iv 340-1)

where the brim (itself the brim of the line) is delight, not peril.
On the other hand:

> To struggle, to be lost within himself
> In trepidation, from the blank abyss
> To look with bodily eyes, and be consoled.
> (*The Prelude*, vi 469-71, *1850*)

—where the sequence which leads up to abyss (which at the
end of the line opens an abyss) is fearful, so that 'and be con-
soled' comes with the force of providential surprise.

The metaphorical or mimetic possibilities are many, and
Wordsworth is fertile and various. He may take as the defining

---

[14] *Wordsworth: A Re-Interpretation* (1954), p. 38.
[15] *The Egotistical Sublime*, pp. 67, 103. Donald Wesling's chapter-title 'Images of
Exposure' might also be applied in such a way (*Wordsworth and the Adequacy of Landscape*,
1970).

term the line itself, rather than the ensuing space; and next do
the opposite:

>   Even as a shepherd on a promontory,
>   Who, lacking occupation, looks far forth
>   Into the endless sea . . .
>   (*The Prelude*, iii 546-8)

The line itself functions as a promontory, with the self-referring
word concluding it and with the punctuation circumscribing it.
Then the next line reverses the implications, with 'looks far
forth' having to look forth across the space represented by the
white space. The change from verse to prose would be the abol-
ition of the implicit metaphorical enacting: 'looks far forth into
the endless sea' lacks a dimension of enacting which operates in

>   looks far forth
>   Into the endless sea . . .

Forth has one kind of relationship to its ensuing space; *promontory* has another. A third is represented by all those words
which signify those great presences which are potent yet invisible: air, sky, space, wind, breath, echo, silence. Wordsworth
finds a metaphorical dimension in relating them to that presence
on the page which can be potent though invisible: the white
space.[16] He therefore often places them at the ends of lines; we
cannot see air or sky or space any more than we can see anything but absence at the end of the verse-line:

>   From the great Nature that exists in works
>   Of mighty Poets. Visionary Power
>   Attends upon the motions of the winds
>   Embodied in the mystery of words.
>   (*The Prelude*, v 618-21)

The varieties of visionary power are analogous, and more than
analogous; there is an effect of mysterious rhyming, with *works*,

---

[16] John Jones has said: 'Breath is also closely associated with urgent spiritual
presence. Thus he describes the thought of an absent person as being like "an *unseen*
companionship, a breath" ' (*The Egotistical Sublime*, p. 99; much of pp. 96-104 has its
bearing on my argument). I should also wish to apply David Ferry's remark: 'It is
especially moving that one of the great representatives of our human powers of
articulation should be himself a lover of silence' (*The Limits of Mortality*, 1959, p. 15).

winds and *words* ending three of the lines. And *winds* meets the invisible.

With such thoughts in mind, we may remember the best lines in *The Borderers*:

> Action is transitory—a step, a blow,
> The motion of a muscle—this way or that—
> 'Tis done, and in the after-vacancy
> We wonder at ourselves like men betrayed:
> Suffering is permanent, obscure and dark,
> And shares the nature of infinity. (Act III)

How superb is the match of sense and substance in the only line which has no concluding punctuation.

> 'Tis done, and in the after-vacancy

and there the vacancy looms, an intersection of time and the timeless, a miniature counterpart to the 'spots of time'. Of the ten instances of *vacancy* in the *Concordance*, six come at the end of the line.[17]

> What terror doth it strike into the mind
> To think of one, blind and alone, advancing
> Straight toward some precipice's airy brink!
> But, timely warned, *He* would have stayed his steps,
> Protected, say enlightened, by his ear;
> And on the very edge of vacancy
> Not more endangered than a man whose eye
> Beholds the gulf beneath.
> (*The Excursion*, vii 491-8)

The line-endings (and would that this were more often the case in *The Excursion*) are wonderfully exploited:

> To think of one, blind and alone, advancing

(—advancing into space)

> Straight toward some precipice's airy brink!

---

[17] A related, but significantly different, effect is achieved by surmising a vacancy which is to be crossed before—instead of after—the word 'vacancy':

> so wide appears
> The vacancy between me and those days,
> (*The Prelude*, ii 28-9)

—'so wide appears': and there it appears.

(—the airy brink at the airy brink)

But, timely warned, *He* would have stayed his steps,

(—with the comma staying the steps)

And on the very edge of vacancy

—with the vacancy opening before us. All this is woven through a relationship of eye to ear which is itself a lesson in 'how to read'—protected, say enlightened, by our ears. Such verse superbly practises what Coleridge superbly preached:

The reader should be carried forward, not merely or chiefly by the mechanical impulse of curiosity, or by a restless desire to arrive at the final solution; but by the pleasurable activity of mind excited by the attractions of the journey itself. Like the motion of a serpent, which the Egyptians made the emblem of intellectual power; or like the path of sound through the air; at every step he pauses and half recedes, and from the retrogressive movement collects the force which again carries him forward. (*Biographia Literaria*, ch. xiv)

The metaphorical words may refer to the line itself or to the space itself; or they may refer to what the line-ending precipitates.

Blew mimic hootings to the silent owls,
That they might answer him; and they would shout
Across the watery vale, and shout again,
Responsive to his call, with quivering peals,
And long halloos and screams, and echoes loud,
Redoubled and redoubled, concourse wild
Of jocund din; and, when a lengthened pause
Of silence came and baffled his best skill,
Then sometimes, in that silence while he hung
Listening, a gentle shock of mild surprise
Has carried far into his heart the voice
Of mountain torrents; or the visible scene
Would enter unawares into his mind,
With all its solemn imagery, its rocks,
Its woods, and that uncertain heaven, received
Into the bosom of the steady lake.
(*The Prelude*, v 373-88, *1850*)

1805 had its *pause* in the middle of the line ('That pauses of deep silence mock'd his skill'); *1850* lengthens the pause—but also removes it from simple clock-time—not only by adding the adjective 'lengthened' but by setting *pause* at the end of the line:

> and, when a lengthened pause

The *Concordance* shows how often Wordsworth places the word 'pause' so that it pauses at the brink of the line. How often, too he places his indispensable word 'hung' or 'hang' there:

> Then sometimes, in that silence while he hung

—and there is the silence before us, and he and we hang upon the brink of it. A dozen lines later, there is a literal counterpart which conveys its different sense of suspension:

> Fair is the spot, most beautiful the vale
> Where he was born; the grassy churchyard hangs
> Upon a slope above the village school,

There can be no doubt as to how much of Wordsworth's deepest concerns depended from, hung from, some such way of speaking. The inquiry into the nature of the Imagination which Wordsworth pursues in his *Preface* to *Poems*, 1815, begins with three instances which depend upon *hangs*—from Virgil, Shakespeare, and Milton: 'Here is the full strength of the imagination involved in the word *hangs*'.[18] Stephen Prickett[19] has drawn attention to 'the basic question why, for both Wordsworth and Coleridge, the most typical feature of these moments of insight is not the feeling of the Imagination at work in perception, but of its *suspension*'. The poetry itself delights in such suspensions:[20]

> Oh! when I have hung
> Above the raven's nest, by knots of grass
> And half-inch fissures in the slippery rock
> But ill sustain'd, and almost, as it seem'd,
> Suspended by the blast which blew amain,
> Shouldering the naked crag; Oh! at that time,
> While on the perilous ridge I hung alone,
> *(The Prelude*, i 341-7)[21]

[18] Milton's image of the fleet which 'Hangs in the clouds' had figured in a notable letter by Wordsworth to Sir George Beaumont, 28 August 1811.

[19] *Wordsworth and Coleridge: The Poetry of Growth* (1970), pp. 141-2.

[20] Wordsworth introduced more of them in *1850*. 'In my thoughts / There was a darkness' became 'o'er my thoughts / There hung a darkness' (i 420-1; i 393-4). 'The Moon stood naked' became 'The moon hung naked' (xiii 41; xiv 40).

[21] Donald Wesling speaks finely of the effect of *hung* here: 'it achieves the almost

There is a variety of dispositions there for the crucial words
hung, Suspended, and *hung,* and the dispositions answer to varieties of purpose. But the effect of the line-ending can be seen if
we think about that last line:

> While on the perilous ridge I hung alone,

It is not Wordsworth's intention at this point (the tone has
changed within the lines) to convey only peril; he seeks to convey also exultation, an extraordinary nonchalance of security,
and even (banal but newly important, like much of his substance) the knowledge that the young Wordsworth did not in
fact fall off. The line, therefore, although it speaks of *perilous*
and *ridge* and *hung,* does not put any of them where they could
create a frisson; each of them is safely *within* the line, not at its
extremities, and the word *hung* has a significantly different effect
from that which it had six lines before. Compare these four
different drapings of the words, the last three bogus:

(i)   While on the perilous ridge I hung alone,
(ii)   Shouldering the crag; while on the perilous
          Ridge,
(iii)   Shouldering
          The naked crag; while on the perilous ridge
          I hung alone,
(iv)   Shouldering
          The crag, while on the perilous ridge I hung
          Alone,

Granted, the wording cannot stay the same, and the rhythms
are altogether different; but we will not have a comprehensive
feeling for just what is being conveyed by

> While on the perilous ridge I hung alone,

unless we also sense how unprecipitously the line-ending is
there being used, and how easily Wordsworth could have had it
otherwise if he had wished.

Last of the important words which can act as a hinge for the
line ending—and different in kind from the others—is the
word *end* itself. This too Wordsworth frequently deploys at the

visceral quality of danger at the end of an enjambing line' (*Wordsworth and the Adequacy
of Landscape,* p. 38; see also p. 43).

end of a line. Just as the word 'beginning' finds itself charged with paradox when we hear at the end of a poem 'In my end is my beginning', so the word *end* acts upon us differently according not only to the context but also to its placing within those units which may not be units of sense—those units which constitute poetry but not prose, and which make of poetry a medium which is more totally and persistently involved in effecting something through its recurrent sense of an ending.[22] Poetry is involved, more than prose, in persistently stopping and starting—and yet it must not be a thing of stops and starts.

Once again metaphors and puns may be effected through the placing within the line. As with the bird's-nesting:

> Though mean
> My object, and inglorious, yet the end
> Was not ignoble.
>
> (*The Prelude*, i 339-41)

There the strong sense—'the aim'—is tempered, and saved from pomposity, by the play effected through the smaller sense of 'end'. Something more like a pun emerges here:

> Ah me! that all
> The terrors, all the early miseries,
> Regrets, vexations, lassitudes, that all
> The thoughts and feelings which have been infus'd
> Into my mind, should ever have made up
> The calm existence that is mine when I
> Am worthy of myself! Praise to the end!
>
> (*The Prelude*, i 355-61)

The effect of the disposition within the line ('end' at the end[23]) is to encourage us to take 'Praise to the end!' to mean 'Unending praise'. But the turn to the next line discloses a different asseveration:

> Praise to the end!
> Thanks likewise for the means!

---

[22] Geoffrey Hartman has some characteristically brilliant and arcane thoughts on beginnings and endings in his essay 'The Voice of the Shuttle', *Review of Metaphysics*, xxiii (1969). Reprinted in his *Beyond Formalism* (1970).

[23] As again seven lines later.

The result there is a severe variety of wit. But Wordsworth can elicit quite different tones, as in the touching disposition of 'in the end' (at the end of the line but not, importantly not, at the end of the verse-paragraph) within some of the most touching lines he ever wrote:[24]

> Not in Utopia, subterraneous Fields,
> Or some secreted Island, Heaven knows where,
> But in the very world which is the world
> Of all of us, the place in which, in the end,
> We find our happiness, or not at all.
>
> (*The Prelude*, x 724-8)

Within the sequence there is a delicate contrast of two kinds of line-ending.

> But in the very world which is the world

—this (in the trice before it turns before our very ears and eyes into ' . . . which is the world Of all of us') suggests the utter intransigence, as near as Wordsworth might ever get to impatience, of a tautology: with its weighty spaced insistence 'the world which is the world'. (The absence of any punctuation makes it the more appropriate that a modern vulgarism expressing something of the same feelings might be 'the world which is the world—*period*.') Then the next line deploys its ending quite differently: ending with 'in the end', and with the concluding (though not fully concluding) comma of a line which has three deliberating commas.

Yet the metaphorical possibilities of the line-ending are not limited to any particular set of words, though they may most often inhere there.

> But deadening admonitions will succeed

—we have at that stage no way of excluding from consideration the possibility that we are on the way to ' . . . will succeed in damping the spirits, etc.'. It is only when we round the corner

---

[24] The problem of tone in Wordsworth is brought home by Donald Wesling's hearing in these lines a 'jocular seriousness' (*Wordsworth and the Adequacy of Landscape*, p. 6). Nor can I agree with Mr. Wesling (p. 26) that in 'Tintern Abbey' the blank-verse lines 'in every way deny closure and pause'—not in *every* way, since this would deny the possibility of interplay between the way in which the line does indeed end and the way in which it doesn't.

that we find the neutral sense of *succeed*:

> will succeed
> And the whole beauteous Fabric seems to lack
> Foundation,
>
> *(The Prelude*, i 225-7)

Of the more dispiriting possibility which momentarily super-
vened ('will succeed in doing something unfortunate'), we
might remark:

> What might have been is an abstraction
> Remaining a perpetual possibility
> Only in a world of speculation.
>
> *(Burnt Norton)*

But it does remain that. Then after this faintly ambiguous line-
ending, the next line hinges upon a line-ending which is free of
ambiguity but which is beautifully mimetic:

> And the whole beauteous Fabric seems to lack

—waiting, we pass through a spot of time

> Foundation

—at which the foundation is found; the necessary continuance
is founded. A weirdly serene enlisting of similar feelings occurs
in the pregnant brevity which tells of the death of the young
Wordsworth's parents:

> The props of my affections were remov'd,
> And yet the building stood, as if sustain'd
> By its own spirit!
>
> *(The Prelude*, ii 294-6)

—where the sustaining is invisible but active, is indeed spiritual,
and is evoked by the invisible activity of the space.

A comparable mystery is evoked by the extraordinary line-
ending (an enjambment which takes all the time in the world
despite its necessity for proceeding apace):

> and I would stand,
> Beneath some rock, listening to sounds that are
> The ghostly language of the ancient earth,
>
> *(The Prelude*, ii 326-8)

It is not just that the sounds are the ghostly language of the
ancient earth, though that is pregnantly mysterious enough;
the basic mystery is that they exist at all, that they *are*:

> Beneath some rock, listening to sounds that are

—no other poet performs such miracles with the verb to be.

Such suggestions are transitory, but not the less telling for
that. Geoffrey Hartman praises surmises, and it is one function
of line-endings to be so delicately fertile of surmises: 'They
revive in us the capacity for the virtual, a trembling of the
imagined on the brink of the real'. That brink can be the brink
of the line-ending. Again, a perceptive comment by Herbert
Lindenberger[25] could be complemented by a consideration of
the stylistic minutiae which effect and reflect what he describes:

One can discern a certain 'brinkmanship' in which Wordsworth
engages, whereby he leads the reader to the edge of the abyss, only to
reveal the saving hand of a higher power. His image of the boy
virtually hanging from the cliff is, I think, emblematic of this habit.

What then is it which itself emblematises this emblem?

> Oh! at that time,
> While on the perilous ridge I hung alone,
> With what strange utterance did the loud dry wind
> Blow through my ears! the sky seem'd not a sky
> Of earth, and with what motion mov'd the clouds!
> (*The Prelude*, i 346-50)

Again the felicities of space, with *wind* opening into vacancy;
and with

> the sky seem'd not a sky

—it did not seem to be a sky at all, with this effect drawing
strength from the way in which *sky* is brought to the very edge,
up against that free space which is as invisible as the sky or the
wind but as existent and active. Then the sense is evolved and
dissolved, and Wordsworth is seen to have been about to say
something both more confined and less confined than that it
didn't seem to be a sky at all:

> the sky seem'd not a sky
> Of earth, and with what motion mov'd the clouds!

[25] *On Wordsworth's Prelude* (1963), p. 222.

We cannot doubt the translatable sense: that the sky did not seem to be the sky which goes with our Earth. Yet there is—at the same time as we feel the Wordsworthian sublimity which inaugurates yet another of its great lines with *Of*—something audacious to the point of apparent wilfulness about such a use of the preposition. 'A sky of earth': it cannot but sound as if the sky might be made of earth. It is not just the ambiguity of *Of* which does this, but the ambiguity of *earth*, by which although the contrast with sky does in one direction insist that earth means the Earth, another implicit contrast with sky (its airiness) suggests the sense of the element earth, the least airy of the elements. Any competent creative-writing course would at once have deleted 'seem'd not a sky / Of earth', and urged the aspiring poet to think what he was about. But Wordsworth was, as so often, about strange things. The extraordinary vision glimpsed here, of a calm vertigo, is one which delights in calling up a suggestion which it then has the power to exorcise: we are to entertain the phantasmal unimaginability of a sky of earth— to entertain it, and then with a wise relief to cleave to the other sense. Far-fetched? But less so than the supposition that Wordsworth simply did not notice how strangely misleading his wording could be or simply was unable to think of a less misleading way of putting it.

'A trembling of the imagined on the brink of the real': it is often at the brink that we shall see it happening.

> My own voice cheer'd me, and, far more, the mind's

—what this leads us to expect is something like ' . . . and, far more, the mind's own voice'. What we then meet is significantly like and unlike that.

> My own voice cheer'd me, and, far more, the mind's
> Internal echo of the imperfect sound;
>
> > (*The Prelude*, i 64-5)

The effect of the surmised sense is to make us consider the second line as in some sense a definition. What would it have meant to speak of the mind's own voice? For the mind's own voice, we are being given to understand, is in fact 'the mind's / Internal echo of the imperfect sound'. Another instance:

> The Poet, gentle creature as he is,
> Hath, like the Lover, his unruly times;
> His fits when he is neither sick nor well,
> Though no distress be near him but his own

—no distress but his own distress?—such is the expectation.
Once again it is both met and modified.

> Though no distress be near him but his own
> Unmanageable thoughts.
> (*The Prelude*, i 145-9)

For if we ask what the poet's 'own distress' would have been,
we then find it defined for us in a way which both sets the poet
among the rest of humanity in that it *is* a form of distress, and
yet distinguishes him from most of humanity in that it is a
specific form of distress: 'his own / Unmanageable thoughts'.
Such is the form that the poet's own distress would take; the
line-ending has been used to effect an exploratory definition
which is half-riddling; and there is very little poetry as great as
Wordsworth's which does not in some way tap, however sub-
terraneously, the resources of the riddle.

Surmises are doubts, but they can be happy ones. As in the
childhood pleasures of the river Derwent:

> Was it for this
> That one, the fairest of all Rivers, lov'd

—the pressure of 'fairest' is such as to make it at least possible
(I should say probable) that 'lov'd' will prove to be an epithet
for the river: 'the fairest of all Rivers, lov'd by us all with a love
deeper than etc.' Indeed, within twenty lines we are told of the
river (and the final word is well placed): 'He was a Playmate
whom we dearly lov'd.' Yet the verse-sentence evolves otherwise:

> Was it for this
> That one, the fairest of all Rivers, lov'd
> To blend his murmurs with my Nurse's song,
> (*The Prelude*, i 271-3)

Yet the momentary uncertainty, that trembling of the imagined
on the brink of the real, is itself a pointer to the lines' meaning.
For it is of the nature of the word *lov'd* that it should evince
reciprocity, just as it is of the nature of the pathetic fallacy (the
river 'lov'd to blend his murmurs') that it should succeed in

speaking the truth when it reflects feelings that are truly existent. It is because the child loved the river (as the line was at
first intimating) that it may be said that the river 'lov'd / To
blend his murmurs with my Nurse's song'. All this is blended
there in Wordsworth's song.

There is an even more piercingly charming instance a few
lines later:

> For this, didst Thou,
> O Derwent! travelling over the green Plains
> Near my 'sweet Birthplace', didst thou, beauteous Stream
> Make ceaseless music through the night and day
> Which with its steady cadence, tempering
> Our human waywardness, compos'd my thoughts

—the expectations created by 'music' and 'cadence' urge us to
take 'composed' as *fashioned* or *created*. But the sequence chooses
another emphasis:

> compos'd my thoughts
> To more than infant softness,
>   (*The Prelude*, i 276-82)

—at which we realise that the river did not so much compose
his thoughts as compose them *to* serenity. But the momentary
doubt (which would disappear in the immediate succession of
prose: 'compos'd my thoughts to . . .') precipitates the pun: it
points to what was for Wordsworth the essential relationship
between *composition* and *composure*. Just as 'music' and 'cadence'
lead mostly towards the sense of *composition*, so 'steady' and
'tempering' lead mostly towards the sense of *composure*. Wordsworth's point is the concurrence. It is, in the profoundest sense,
composure (not disturbance) which is creative, which composes.
(There is an analogous delicacy of doubt in the phrase 'make
ceaseless music', where we are happily uncertain whether the
river makes music as composer or as performer.) As John Jones
says,

It remained a cardinal principle with him that only a happy man can
write good poetry; and he attributed Coleridge's failure as a poet to
his unhappiness, because of which 'he could not afford to suffer with
those whom he saw suffer'.[26]

[26] *The Egotistical Sublime*, p. 113.

The fluidity of water and of air was for Wordsworth a type of
the perfect interrelationship. In some lines which are at once
importantly like and importantly unlike Milton, he exults in
the multifariousness of creation:

> O'er all that leaps, and runs, and shouts, and sings,
> Or beats the gladsome air, o'er all that glides
> Beneath the wave, yea, in the wave itself
> And mighty depth of waters.
>
> (The Prelude, ii 425-8)

In these lines everything turns upon what is indeed the turn:
the word *glides* at the end of the line. It beautifully takes up the
preceding 'air'—and then with the turn into the next line we
discover that *glides* is about movement through the water, not
through the air. (Again the immediateness of prose would destroy this tiny suspension: 'that glides beneath the wave'.) The
word *glides*, placed where it is, compacts the two elements without crowding them; it interfuses them, like a beautiful evocation
in Wordsworth's *Guide to the Lakes*:

and could almost have imagined that his boat was suspended in an
element as pure as air, or rather that the air and water were one.[27]

A supreme instance of such delicacy of doubt happens also to
place *hung* where Wordsworth most cared for it and with it:

> the moon to me was dear;
> For I would dream away my purposes,
> Standing to look upon her while she hung
> Midway between the hills, as if she knew

—as if she knew how much we loved her, how much we gazed
and worshipped her?

> as if she knew
> No other region; but belong'd to thee,
> Yea, appertain'd by a peculiar right
> To thee and thy grey huts, my darling Vale!
>
> (The Prelude, ii 196-202)

—and we find, with a gentle shock of mild surprise, that *knew*
was not as in *savoir* but as in *connaître*. Upon the brink of the
real, there trembled our imagining that the moon *knew*; the

---

[27] Quoted by Herbert Lindenberger, *On Wordsworth's Prelude*, p. 82.

attribution of the pathetic fallacy has seldom been made with such pathos, and the rescinding of the fallacy has seldom been made with such gentleness.

Such stylistic reaching before and after might be brought into relation with Walter Pater's words on Wordsworth's sense of past and future:

He had pondered deeply, for instance, on those strange reminiscences and forebodings, which seem to make our lives stretch before and behind us, beyond where we can see or touch anything, or trace the lines of connexion.[28]

Trace the lines, yes.

My final instance can be one where the power of Wordsworth's prepositions allies itself to the sane suggestiveness of his line-ending:

> How goodly, how exceeding fair, how pure
> From all reproach is yon etherial vault,
> And this deep Vale, its earthly counterpart,
> By which and under which we are enclosed
> To breathe in peace;
> (*Home at Grasmere* 640-4)

'By which and under which': the distinction has the scrupulous assurance and authority of Wordsworth at his finest—the poetry's distinction is in its distinctions, at once firm and serene. Then 'enclosed' is not really enclosed at all, since although it brings the line to an end it opens directly into that free space which is a 'counterpart' of all free space:

> By which and under which we are enclosed

We have only to make this line the end of its verse-sentence to find the word *enclosed* acting upon us quite differently:

> By which and under which we are enclosed.

Too total an enclosing, this would then preclude our breathing in peace; would induce just that claustrophobia, that sense of being pinioned, which Wordsworth eschews—the vault of

---

[28] 'Wordsworth' (1874), *Appreciations* (1889). Pater's words might be related to Wordsworth's mild but piercing puns on *prospect*; most notably in 'The Old Cumberland Beggar': 'one little span of earth / Is all his prospect'. (See too *The Prelude*, ii 371 and iii 229.)

heaven, after all, is such that though it does indeed enclose us,
it does so without coercion and with total freedom and airiness.
The sense of an ending is perfectly taken up within the sense of
a blending. At which point there dawns upon us the calm
splendour of the ambiguity of 'breathe in peace'. Does it mean
breathe *in peace* or *breathe in* peace? Both. Under the vault of
heaven we can breathe *in peace* because what we *breathe in* is
peace. The two meanings co-exist with perfect 'inobtrusive
sympathies'; no strain, no pressure, but an interfusion which is
limpidly and lucidly at ease. John Jones's useful phrase about
'Wordsworth's busy prepositions' would do less than justice to
this instance, which is so active and yet so unbusy.

   Such poetry both meets and makes high demands. In particular it asks that we take our time: in poetry such as Wordsworth's there is in the first place nothing more important that
we should take. In such a spirit we may recall Wordsworth's
anger: 'These people in the senseless hurry of their idle lives do
not *read* books, they merely snatch a glance at them that they
may talk about them.'[29] The obverse of his anger at such haste
of pseudo-reading is his praise for the chastening dignity of the
carver's slow art, at work upon a funeral inscription which is
committed to reticence:

The very form and substance of the monument which has received
the inscription, and the appearance of the letters, testifying with what
a slow and laborious hand they must have been engraven, might seem
to reproach the author who had given way upon this occasion to
transports of mind, or to quick turns of conflicting passion.[30]

The twentieth century is even more open to 'senseless hurry'
than was the nineteenth century. Wordsworth urges us to take
his time.

[29] Letter to Lady Beaumont, 21 May 1807.
[30] 'Essays upon Epitaphs, I' (1810); *The Prose Works of William Wordsworth*, ed.
W. J. B. Owen and Jane Worthington Smyser (1974), ii 60.

WILLIAM WORDSWORTH 2:
'A SINKING INWARD INTO OURSELVES
FROM THOUGHT TO THOUGHT'

'He has no style.' It would be a mistake simply to identify
the nineteenth-century Wordsworth with Matthew Arnold's
Wordsworth,[1] but Arnold did succeed in limning the poet with
intense recognisability. Twentieth-century criticism has mostly
been better at engaging with one half of Arnold's Wordsworth
than with the other. There has been a challenge to one aspect of
Arnold's subtle abnegation: 'The Wordsworthians are apt to
praise him for the wrong things, and to lay far too much stress
upon what they call his philosophy.' The academic study of
English literature has since seen to it that there are even more
Wordsworthians; the best of them have convincingly vindicated 'what they call his philosophy'. But the other half of Arnold's Wordsworth has proved less amenable. 'Wordsworth's
poetry, when he is at his best, is inevitable, as inevitable as
Nature herself. It might seem that Nature not only gave him
the matter for his poem, but wrote his poem for him. He has no
style.'

To the twentieth-century critic, such a way of speaking is
both defeatist and obscurantist—Arnold, we hope, must rather
have meant that Wordsworth had no 'style.' True, there is
much more by way of critical *aperçu* and local felicity than one
might think, but insights into style nevertheless remain scat-
tered and sparse in comparison with all the other varieties of
exegesis which have been devoted to Wordsworth. Hence this
attempt to marshal some related suggestions and think where
they lead.

In his fine capacious book *The Egotistical Sublime*, John Jones
suggests—one page before he comes to an end—a whole dimension of Wordsworth's stylistic achievement.

Clothed in the sunshine of the withering fern
(*The Prelude*, vi 11, *1850*)[2]

---

[1] 'Wordsworth' (1879), *Essays in Criticism*, 2nd series (1888).

[2] Quotations from *The Prelude* are of 1805 unless otherwise noted, as in the previous
essay; *The Prelude*, ed. E. de Selincourt, rev. H. Darbishire (1959).

'Clothed in sunshine' is easy: so is 'clothed in the withering fern'. But 'clothed in the sunshine of the withering fern' is odd, its oddness resting in 'of,' and the different kinds of work it has to do. One might say that the word is ambiguous; but this would be a perverse way of expressing it, since the block-impression of the phrase is clear, even without knowing its history [that is, the history of the variants]. We admit 'of' as we admit others of Wordsworth's busy prepositions: in their degree they are the stride of his thought.[3]

Mr. Jones's point is acutely vivid, and so I should like to have heard more from him—by way of an imaginative tactful unpacking—about 'the different kinds of work' which *of* is doing in that line; his point feels right and suggests much, but it doesn't perhaps help us sufficiently through the initial stages of thinking about such nuances. It could have stood a bit more spelling out; as could the general claim that Wordsworth's prepositions are 'busy' (at what, exactly?); as could the general question of the relationship between such busy prepositions and the whole Wordsworthian endeavour.

Again, there is a delicate aside by Jonathan Wordsworth in *The Music of Humanity*, his excellent study of 'The Ruined Cottage.'

She is dead,
The worm is on her cheek, and this poor hut
(103-4)

'Margaret, already dead, loses not her "vital qualities" but her humanity itself: the word "on" especially ("The worm is *on* her cheek"), reduces her almost brutally to an object.'[4] Another busy preposition; again a critic's drawing to our notice something which carries strong conviction; but again a feeling that the force, and even the full meaning, of the word *on* asks to be further pondered. One way of eliciting the further suggestiveness which Jonathan Wordsworth here divines would be to treat the clause for a moment as if it were an incomplete quotation: '. . . is on her cheek.' What would ordinarily complete such a clause is an abstract noun such as pain or grief or care: 'and care / Sat on his faded cheek' (*Paradise Lost*, i 601-2). But Margaret is dead now; if she can still be preyed upon, it is at least no longer by pain or grief or care; what is on her cheek,

---

[3] *The Egotistical Sublime* (1954), p. 206.   [4] (1969), p. 129.

the worm, is seen for precisely what it is—for good and ill—by a tacit comparison with those other ravages which had in life been on her cheek. Jonathan Wordsworth's suggestion, and it is a mark of good criticism that this should be so, is itself productive of suggestions. 'Reduces her almost brutally to an object': that *almost*, which is surprising when you look at it, needs to be seen as occasioned by the compassion at that unmentioned pain or grief or care which had earlier been on her cheek.

That Wordsworth's prepositions may be richly paradoxical is brought out, too, in another central study, David Ferry's *The Limits of Mortality*.

> Thou art a dew-drop, which the morn brings forth,
> Ill fitted to sustain unkindly shocks,
> Or to be trailed along the soiling earth;
> A gem that glitters while it lives,
> And no forewarning gives;
> But, at the touch of wrong, without a strife,
> Slips in a moment out of life.
>   ('To H.C. Six Years Old')

Does this mean he will die easily, that a child is more vulnerable to physical death than we are? Or does it mean that adulthood, maturity, is a kind of death? Both at once. . . . The maturing of the child is only the measure of its distance from that world [the world of eternity], so that the line could be reasonably construed as 'slips in a moment *into* life' without changing the feelings involved in it at all.[5]

Finally, one might cite two observations by C. C. Clarke, whose *Romantic Paradox* is a spirited inquiry into Wordsworth's meanings.

> Once again
> Do I behold these steep and lofty cliffs,
> That on a wild secluded scene impress
> Thoughts of more deep seclusion;
>   ('Tintern Abbey' 4-7)

'The formula "Thoughts of . . ." is ambiguous: a possible meaning is that the thoughts are more secluded than the secluded scene. At any rate the thoughts are not only *about* deep seclusion, they are themselves deep and secluded.'[6]

---

[5] (1959), pp. 83-4.   [6] (1962), pp. 45, 54.

> these thoughts did oft revolve
> About some centre palpable, which at once
> Incited them to motion, and control'd,
> And whatsoever shape the fit might take,
> And whencesoever it might come, I still
> At all times had a real solid world
> Of images about me;   (*The Prelude*, viii 599-605)

When therefore the metaphor of the circle ('*About* some centre. . . .')
is covertly repeated ('. . . . a real solid world Of images *about* me') the
reader tends to assume that the relationship between the images and
the self, like that between the forms and the thoughts, is not purely
external: in other words 'about me' is not interpreted simply as 'outside and independent of me' but also as 'centred upon me' and even
perhaps, in some sense, 'dependent upon me.'

Such critics as John Jones, Jonathan Wordsworth, David
Ferry, and C. C. Clarke, then, have rich and various things to
say about Wordsworth's 'busy prepositions'; but in each case
what they have to say remains a valuable aside, unrelated. I
should like to move Wordsworth's prepositions to the centre—
or rather, to suggest that they are at the centre.

If as a poet you seek the simplest and most permanent forms
of language, you are bound to give special importance to prepositions and conjunctions—those humble fundamentals, *in, up,
and, but, of*, and so on. If as a poet you are concerned above all
with relations and relationships, you are bound to give special
importance to those words which express relationships: prepositions and conjunctions. Their importance for Wordsworth
can hardly be overstated. A serious misreading is involved
when a critic can say of the boating episode (*The Prelude*, i 372-
427) that 'he stole the boat, and felt the terrifying presence of
the mountain rearing up behind him.'[7] Not behind him; in
front of him as he rowed away from it and so brought more of it
into view.

Wordsworth's poetry was to be 'important in the multiplicity
and quality of its moral relations' (*Preface* to *Lyrical Ballads*). His
commitment was to an exploration of all the most important
relationships of man: man to nature, man to family, man to
God. The humbly essential medium for all such relationships is
the preposition. Moreover, Wordsworth's demand was for 'a

---

[7] Stephen Prickett, *Coleridge and Wordsworth: The Poetry of Growth* (1970), p. 122.

more permanent, and a far more philosophical language, than that which is frequently substituted for it by Poets'; he could delight in the fact that 'the affecting parts of Chaucer are almost always expressed in language pure and universally intelligible even to this day.' There is a sense in which prepositions constitute a 'more philosophical language'; more importantly, there is a sense in which though all language changes, the language of prepositions changes strikingly less than most. In expressing the fundamental relationships of things, prepositions constitute a bedrock, subject no doubt to change but to change of a geological slowness. Old and Middle English offer even to the ignorant some foothold in some prepositions and conjunctions.

Take a famous line from 'Tintern Abbey' and imagine it as a puzzle for the compositor. 'Felt in the . . . and felt along the . . .' To be slotted in are the words *heart* and *blood*. The expected placing would give: 'Felt in the heart, and felt along the blood,' since the heart is static and the blood is diffused. Indeed elsewhere Wordsworth does give us 'along the blood.'[8] Yet Wordsworth's line—so famous by now as to be exceptionally hard to see as what it is, rather like the plot of *Hamlet*—is 'Felt in the blood, and felt along the heart.' The unobtrusive surprise of the prepositions is a matter of our being tacitly aware of how they might have been expected to figure: deploying them this way round then enables Wordsworth to challenge the presupposition that the heart is simply a place and the blood simply diffused; the relationship between the heart and its blood is seen to be more intimate, more mysterious, and more reciprocal than that. The heart has no blood that is not coming from and going to; the blood's coming and going are dependent upon the heart; and this reciprocity, like that of the 'affections sweet' can be subtly and touchingly signalled by interchanging their prepositions. Helen Darbishire picked out this line in a brief note on 'A Phrase of Wordsworth's'[9] and she mentioned some comparable uses of *along*: 'Which, like a tempest, works along the blood' (*The Prelude*, i 612); 'That flow'd along my dreams' (i 276). She was right to remark the mysterious power which 'even such a workaday word as "along" takes on' in Wordsworth. But she was reluctant to investigate the mystery,

[8] *The Prelude*, i 612.   [9] *Review of English Studies*, xxi (1945).

and said nothing of the unexpectedness of the placing of *in* and *along*, and nothing of the *blood* and *heart* themselves.

The instance is a simple one, though its workings are not. Its simplicity may serve to build up a sense of those elementary or initial stages of critical thinking about Wordsworth's prepositions which John Jones overleaped. Marshalling such *aperçus* as his may entail a rather slower exposition of what is going on. A famous instance is the crucial distinction introduced by the innocent authority of the word *in* when Wordsworth hails that spirit

> Whose dwelling is the light of setting suns,
> And the round ocean and the living air,
> And the blue sky, and in the mind of man:
> ('Tintern Abbey' 97-9)

The spirit's dwelling is light, sea, air and sky; its dwelling is in the mind of man. One has only to replace 'Whose dwelling is' by 'Which dwells in'—wording which would occlude any such distinction—to see the narrow limits within which a crucial distinction may thrive. Crucial, and mysterious, since the spirit's dwelling place *in* the mind of man remains unspecified and perhaps unspecifiable: it doesn't dwell there, it dwells in there, as if the mind of man were the darkest and deepest of continents. One is reminded of De Quincey's feeling for a great Wordsworthian moment when

> a gentle shock of mild surprise
> Has carried far into his heart the voice
> Of mountain torrents;
> (*The Prelude*, v 382-4)

'The very expression "far" by which space and its infinities are attributed to the human heart, and its capacities of reechoing the sublimities of nature, has always struck me as with a flash of sublime revelation' (*Literary Reminiscences*).

In such a case the word *in* functions explicitly, albeit strangely; that is, if you were translating the lines from 'Tintern Abbey' you would have to render the plain stated difference of sense (which is something other than a poetic suggestion) between 'Whose dwelling is *x*' and 'Whose dwelling is in *y*.' But the critic will need to deal too with suggestions and surmises. 'Three years she grew in . . .' The ordinary pressures of 'to

grow in . . .' should lead one half-consciously to expect the line
to end with qualities: 'Three years she grew in loveliness, goodness, femininity.' But the line selects a different destination:
'Three years she grew in sun and shower.' A perfectly natural
sequence; what she grew *in* was not qualities but circumstances. Perfectly natural; yet the poem's effect depends upon a
sense of the other perfectly natural sequence which the line
could well have followed.

> Footfalls echo in the memory
> Down the passage which we did not take
> Towards the door we never opened
> Into the rose-garden. My words echo
> Thus, in your mind.   (*Burnt Norton*)

Wordsworth's line echoes down a passage which it did not, in
the event, take. Yet we have no sooner put, however fleetingly,
before ourselves some such possibility as 'Three years she grew
in loveliness', than a form of the word *lovely* surfaces in the next
line:

> Three years she grew in sun and shower,
> Then Nature said, 'A lovelier flower
> On earth was never sown . . .'

Are we about to speak of the qualities in which she grew, or of
the circumstances in which she grew? The eventfulness of language makes its choice, but with quiet surprise, and with a
sense of the alternative; moreover, we are then urged back into
considering the relationship between qualities and circumstances. For is it not circumstances which foster qualities? We
have but to replace 'shower' with 'drizzle'—'Three years she
grew in sun and drizzle'—to see that 'sun and shower' aren't
just circumstances, but are there because in describing circumstances they also suggest qualities of mind. The 'sun and
shower' are not simply climatic; they suggest inner weather,
the changes and chances of this mortal life, the sunshine of happiness and the 'shower' (not yet, not for the child, the chilling
blasts of storm) of brief sadness. Such circumstances, such 'sun
and shower', naturally foster such a temperament, one which
blends sun and shower in qualities of mind and heart. In short,
the question of whether it was qualities or circumstances in

which she grew is seen to resolve itself, and dissolve itself, into reciprocity. Geoffrey Hartman has said of surmises in poetry that 'they revive in us the capacity for the virtual, a trembling of the imagined on the brink of the real.'[10]

A preposition may be a small, sturdy word, but within Wordsworth's relationships it can create a trembling of the imagined on the brink of the real. 'Though nothing can bring back the hour / Of splendour in the grass, of glory in the flower' ('Ode, Intimations of Immortality'). The characteristically Wordsworthian quality of that second line is not just a matter of its four prepositions, or of its beginning—as do so many of the great Wordsworth lines—with the word *of*. The line is saved from a merely illustrative repetition by the fact that its parallelism is subtly modified. For whereas 'splendour in' remains precisely what it states, 'glory in' cannot but be affected by the other sense, *to glory in*. So that within the line there can be heard the faint suggestion that 'nothing can bring back the hour . . . of glorying in the flower.' Whether the glory is something which is indeed within the flower or whether it is rather something which the perceiving eye works upon the flower, glorying in it—this question belongs with all those which so endlessly, and so rightly, fascinated Wordsworth: 'Creates, creator and receiver both' (*The Prelude*, ii 273). It is true (and here again one may think what it would be to translate these two lines) that there is no feasible ambiguity of syntax; Wordsworth has not created, as he might easily have done, a form of words in which *glory* might function equally and equally as either noun or verb. The syntax is such that the stated sense must be that of *glory* as a noun parallel to *splendour*. Nevertheless a surmise, created by the momentary uncertainty as to the function of *in*, has flickered: the surmise that the unit might be *glory in* rather than the units being (1) *glory*, (2) *in the flower*.

It should now be easier to see why Matthew Arnold was right (though altogether unforthcoming) in selecting as Wordsworth's 'own strong and characteristic line' the magnificent 'Of joy in widest commonalty spread.'[11] It is not just the sentiment to which Arnold might have drawn attention. Again, we have *of*

[10] *Wordsworth's Poetry 1787-1814* (1964), p. 11.
[11] From 'The Recluse'; preface to *The Excursion*.

at the head. Again, *in* is deployed with suggestiveness. For the line cannot adequately be cast, though such is indeed the main sense, as 'Of joy spread in widest commonalty.' To put it in that way would be to destroy more than the rhythm. For it would abolish the flickering suggestion of 'joy in' by which there is held momentarily before us the human need to joy in commonalty. The effect is of a superb compression which yet speaks paradoxically of the 'widest commonalty,' a compression by which the line economically but lavishly accommodates 'Of joy in widest commonalty spread in widest commonalty.' The widest commonalty is both what the joy joys in (what creates the joy) and what the joy acts upon (what the joy creates). Such joy spreads, both outwards and inwards, in the widest commonalty.

A very important class of words has not had the attention it asks. Twentieth-century criticism of Wordsworth has done much by scrutinizing some of his crucial terms. Most notable is William Empson's study of *sense* in *The Prelude*.[12] Hugh Sykes Davies[13] has mined the word *impulse*. There is C. C. Clarke's *Romantic Paradox* on the related terms *image, form*, and *shape*; he had been anticipated in some minor respects by Ellen Douglass Leyburn, whose inquiry into 'Recurrent Words in *The Prelude*'[14] singled out *earth, being, object, forms, image, presence, intercourse*, and *power*. But her belief that 'the richness of [Wordsworth's] diction goes with the richness of his thought' may be misleading unless it takes a widely imaginative view of the forms that richness may take, and in particular of the possibilities of the humblest and apparently most insignificant of words. There is nothing about prepositions in Josephine Miles's *Wordsworth and the Vocabulary of Emotion* (1942),[15] and yet it might be claimed that his prepositions are central to his vocabulary of emotion. Moreover, Lane Cooper's indispensable *Concordance* (1911, reprinted 1965) lamentably lacks them. Some of Wordsworth's most important words are therefore unrecorded in the *Concordance*: not only the forms of the verb *to be*, but also the prepositions and conjunctions. It omits *and* and *but, at, by, for, from, in,*

---

[12] *The Structure of Complex Words* (1951).
[13] 'Wordsworth and the Empirical Philosophers', in *The English Mind*, ed. Hugh Sykes Davies and George Watson (1964).
[14] *ELH*, xxvi (1949).
[15] Or in her discussion of Wordsworth in *Eras and Modes in English Poetry* (1964).

of, on, to, up, with, and so on; and it only partially lists *above, along, among,* and so on. Even those who feel that criticism (and not especially of Wordsworth) is often marred by niggling and by a lack of any sense of proportion may nevertheless feel that the attitudes of 1923 are now altogether too rough and ready: Franklyn Bliss Snyder's account of 'Wordsworth's Favorite Words'[16] was necessarily curtailing most drastically what it could hope to achieve when it announced, with round cheerfulness, that 'In compiling such a list it would seem the part of wisdom to follow the practice of the Wordsworth Concordance and omit all reference to words which were omitted entirely from the Concordance, and similarly, to omit words represented by only partial lists. In the use of *and, I, but, is,* etc., there is but little significance.' On the contrary, those four little words can be, and often are, of the greatest significance. The closing pages of *The Egotistical Sublime* (pp. 206-7) rightly insist that the Wordsworthian achievement is

an achievement shared . . . by the short words, the long words, and all the time and space of language. Shared, too, by language's humblest parts. 'And,' more frequent in Wordsworth than in any poet, is the preserver of extreme structural simplicity through hundreds of lines of *Prelude* narrative: if the ice is thin, the skating is light and swift. 'And' helps to sustain the calm elevation of *Tintern Abbey*:

> And the round ocean and the living air,
> And the blue sky, and in the mind of man . . .

By its monotony, its insistence on the particular, 'and' develops Wordsworth's expository style, in common with other words of modest function—'but,' 'thus,' 'therefore.'

A simple instance would be to contrast the changed function and attachment of *with* in *The Prelude*, i 466-7:

1805   And not a voice was idle; with the din,
         Meanwhile, the precipices rang aloud

1850   And not a voice was idle; with the din
         Smitten, the precipices rang aloud

Wordsworth was especially adept with, and committed to, the sequence by which a prepositional adverb (*up,* in *rose up*) is followed by a preposition. He sometimes pursued such se-

[16] *Journal of English and Germanic Philology*, xxii (1923).

quences to the point of an authentic gracelessness, or a graceless authenticity, and he fretted about whether the proportions
of manliness to stutter were right. In 'Michael' 455-6, the old
man after his disaster still ventures out: 'Among the rocks /
He went, and still looked up upon the sun.' The semi-stutter of
'up upon' is piercing in its combination of dignity with pre-
cariousness;[17] a lesser poet would have ironed it out, in the
interests of a simpler, more mellifluous grandeur. Wordsworth
became that lesser poet: the fine line, which had stood from
1800 to 1827, was replaced in 1832 by 'He went, and still looked
up towards the sun,' to be restlessly replaced in 1836 by 'He
went, and still looked up to sun and cloud.' But beneath the
fretting changes, the basic structure remained: verb, prepositional abverb, preposition. The best version, the earliest, is
that which most insists upon this structure by boldly juxtaposing 'up upon'.

Again and again this sequence is one of the hiding places of
his power.

> Would leave behind a dance of images
> That shall break in upon his sleep for weeks
> (The Prelude, viii 164-5)

> And, turning the mind in upon itself,
> Pored, watch'd, expected, listen'd; spread my thoughts
> And spread them with a wider creeping
> (iii 112-14)[18]

So simply lucid is Wordsworth's speech that it can constitute
a temptation: we may not pay sufficient attention to the very
words, since we are so confident of what they are saying. 'And
the whole body of the Man did seem / Like one whom I had
met with in a dream' ('Resolution and Independence'). As we
reflect upon *whom* there (*which*? does not 'one' refer back to
body rather than to *man*?), we are led to reflect upon relationships (whom/which problems) such as are central to the poem
and to the mysterious thing-like humanity of the leech-gatherer.

---

[17] Echoing an earlier pathos in 'Michael' 350-2: 'And in the open fields my life was
passed / And on the mountains; else I think that thou / Hadst been brought up upon
they Father's knees'.
[18] Donald Wesling writes excellently on the word *spread* here and its relation to
Wordsworth's verse (*Wordsworth and the Adequacy of Landscape*, 1970, pp. 18-19).

The sequence 'met with in,' with the preposition following the prepositional adverb, is firmly characteristic, with a delicately hypothetical suggestion (the hypothesis faintly advanced and rescinded) such as might, with minimal change, quietly become: 'And the whole body of the Man did seem / Like one whom I had met within a dream.'

When Wordsworth borrows, he makes the borrowing his own by assimilating it to such a sequence. In his preface, de Selincourt cites Pope, *The First Epistle of the First Book of Horace Imitated* 39-40: 'So slow th' unprofitable Moments roll, / That lock up all the Functions of my soul.' *The Prelude*, i 247-8 turns Pope to Wordsworth by creating the Wordsworthian sequence 'that now / Doth lock my functions up in blank reserve.' The *1850* revision lets that essential structure stand: 'that now / Locks every function up in blank reserve.' So it is possible to guess what it was that alerted de Selincourt (p. lxi) when he deprecated this *1850* revision:

> Catching from tufts of grass and hare-bell flowers
> Their faintest whisper to the passing breeze,
> Given out while mid-day heat oppressed the plains.

'The voice of the authentic Wordsworth is more distinctly heard in the delicate simplicity of the rejected lines:'

> Lay listening to the wild flowers and the grass,
> As they gave out their whispers to the wind.
> *(The Prelude*, vi 231-2)

He does not say in what 'the authentic Wordsworth' inheres; but one of the things which *1850* mistakenly abandons is the sequence 'gave out . . . to.' Such a sequence—strange in that it manages to be both ubiquitous and freshly potent—can be seen at work three times in a passage such as this:

> Hush'd, meanwhile,
> Was the under soul, lock'd up in such a calm,
> That not a leaf of the great nature stirr'd.
>   Yet was this deep vacation not given up
> To utter waste. Hitherto I had stood
> In my own mind remote from human life,
> At least from what we commonly so name,
> Even as a shepherd on a promontory,

> Who, lacking occupation, looks far forth
> Into the endless sea, and rather makes
> Than finds what he beholds.
>
> (*The Prelude*, iii 539-49)

At which point one may turn to the heart of Arnold's Wordsworth:

The right sort of verse to choose from Wordsworth, if we are to seize his true and most characteristic form of expression, is a line like this from *Michael*—

> 'And never lifted up a single stone.'

There is nothing subtle in it, no heightening, no study of poetic style, strictly so called, at all; yet it is expression of the highest and most truly expressive kind.

The instance is a triumphant one, and the triumph is Arnold's as well as Wordsworth's. But if the line is to be a talisman and not just a shibboleth, we need some sense of how it effects its high and true expressiveness. The immediate context says much:

> 'Tis not forgotten yet
> The pity which was then in every heart
> For the old man—and 'tis believed by all
> That many and many a day he thither went,
> And never lifted up a single stone.
>
> (462-6)

The word *single* should send us back, to see through what contrasts of singleness and multiplicity the lines evolve. *Every heart* as against *the old Man*; *all* and *many and many a day* as against *he* and *a single stone*. The focus narrows to that singleness which is loneliness and integrity; from *every* and *all* and *many and many* down to *a single stone*.

But we may approach the line from another direction if we put a question whose pseudo-rigour might justly be thought of as flippant. Given that Wordsworth's language here is that of the utmost austerity and economy, is not the word *up* redundant? Might not the line just as well be 'And never lifted a single stone'? Such a question is fatuous, but not because of an inappropriate intensity of scrutiny, not because it doesn't matter whether so small a word as *up* really earns its keep. On the contrary, the question is fatuous because the word *up* is here, for all its quietùde, intensely active. For 'Michael' is a poem which, with consummate naturalness such as never invites the suspicion of a disembodied symbolizing, sets *up* severely against *down*. Its opening is a tactful signpost:

> If from the public way you turn your steps
> Up the tumultuous brook of Green-head Ghyll,
> You will suppose that with an upright path
> Your feet must struggle; in such bold ascent
> The pastoral mountains front you, face to face.
>
> (1-5)

Up, upright, ascent: they signal. Yet at the same time the word *suppose* assures us that all is not simply as it seems, and that a *but* is imminent.

The structure of the poem, from aspiration to dignified defeat, is implicit in three echoing lines. The first sentence of the poem gives us 'Up the tumultuous brook of Green-head Ghyll'; the middle of the poem gives us, with balanced neutrality, 'Near the tumultuous brook of Green-head Ghyll' (322); the final lines give us: 'and the remains / Of the unfinished Sheep-fold may be seen / Beside the boisterous brook of Green-head Ghyll' (480-2). From *up*, via *near*, to *beside*.

The importance of the modest word *up* is evidenced in its placing: of its eleven occurrences in the poem, six are at the beginning or end of the lines. But a word like *up* derives its meaning from the contrast, implicit or explicit, with *down*. (The critic of Wordsworth must not fear, any more than did Wordsworth, the bathos of banality.) So it is at once surprising and right that the word *down* comes only twice in the poem. Indeed, there are moments when the word seems to be crying out to get into the poem and yet is fended off with a firm dexterity:

> For, as it chanced,
> Their cottage on a plot of rising ground
> Stood single, with large prospect, north and south,
> High into Easedale, up to Dunmail-Raise,
> And westward to the village near the lake
>
> (131-5)

Rising, high, and *up* are one side of all this; yet with all that

range of views, no view is *down*; instead the word *westward*
supervenes where the word *down* might have been anticipated.
And the two instances of *down*? The first has its studied neutrality; its humdrum literalness protects the poem against the
suspicion of symbolic coercion.

> Down from the ceiling, by the chimney's edge,
> That in our ancient uncouth country style
> With huge and black projection overbrowed
> Large space beneath, as duly as the light
> Of day grew dim the Housewife hung a lamp
>   (110-14)

That calm neutrality leaves everything clear for the great moment in the poem when the word *down* can figure as the sadden-
ing counterpart and contrast to all that rightly aspires:

>   'Now, fare thee well—
> When thou return'st, thou in this place wilt see
> A work which is not here: a covenant
> 'Twill be between us; but, whatever fate
> Befall thee, I shall love thee to the last,
> And bear thy memory with me to the grave.'
>   The Shepherd ended here; and Luke stooped down,
> And, as his Father had requested, laid
> The first stone of the Sheep-fold.   (412-20)

'Luke stooped down.' He was to stoop yet lower. It is that *down*
which—in the company of all which contrasts with it—informs
with pathos and gravity the small word *up* when later Michael
'thither went, / And never lifted up a single stone.'
    Many of the most memorable of Wordsworth's prose apo-
phthegms cast themselves prepositionally:

a sinking inward into ourselves from thought to thought
           ('Answer to Mathetes,' *The Friend*, 1818)

I was often unable to think of external things as having external existence, and I communed with all that I saw as something not apart
from, but inherent in, my own immaterial nature.
           (Fenwick note on the 'Immortality Ode')

Men who read from religious or moral inclinations . . . come prepared to impart so much passion to the Poet's language, that they remain unconscious how little, in fact, they receive from it.
           (Essay, 'Supplementary to the Preface,' 1815)

As for Wordsworth's critics, a cento of quotations from some of the best of them will show how natural it is for the critic's way of couching things to learn from the poet's own way. (The italics are theirs.)

Coleridge

Although Wordsworth and Goethe are not much alike, to be sure, upon the whole, yet they both have this peculiarity of utter non-sympathy with the subjects of their poetry. They are always, both of them, spectators *ab extra*—feeling *for*, but never *with*, their characters. (*Table Talk* (1835), i 61-2)

Keats

[of Milton] He did not think into the human heart, as Wordsworth has done. (Letter to Reynolds, 3 May 1818)

Clough

He is apt to wind up his short pieces with reflections upon the way in which, hereafter, he expects to reflect upon his present reflections. ('Lecture on the Poetry of Wordsworth,' *Prose Remains* (1888), p. 315)

A. C. Bradley

[In Wordsworth] the arresting feature or object is felt in some way *against* this background, or even as in some way a denial of it. (*Oxford Lectures on Poetry* (1909), p. 131)

F. R. Leavis

If these 'moments' have any significance for the critic (whose business it is to define the significance of Wordsworth's poetry), it will be established, not by dwelling upon or in them, in the hope of exploring something that lies hidden in or behind their vagueness, but by holding firmly on to that sober verse in which they are presented. (*Revaluation* (1936), p. 174)

James Smith

But is it humanly possible to carry renunciation to the point which may be necessary? It is conceivable that other things should close in to such an extent upon a creature that, if he yields to them, any inner activity left is too insignificant to be called human. ('Wordsworth: A Preliminary Survey,' *Scrutiny*, vii (1938), 51)

F. W. Bateson

[Of 'She dwelt among the untrodden ways'] The reader begins by

looking *down* at the violet, and then *up* at the star, and in the process
the two juxtaposed images form themselves into a single landscape . . .
By manipulating his words, metaphors and symbols so that they
create the illusion of cancelling each other out, he was able to suggest
a more inclusive and a more rarefied meaning than it was possible to
express directly. But the poetry lay *between* the words. (*Wordsworth:
A Re-Interpretation* (1954), pp. 33, 38)

W. W. Robson

He imposes conviction by means of that characteristic medium
through which we are made to see and judge all that Wordsworth
wishes us to see and judge. . . . Wordsworth's personal need, his
demand for reassurance, issuing in that oddly inappropriate question
['How is it that you live, and what is it you do?'], is not so much for a
reassurance *from* the old Man as for a reassurance *about* the old Man.
(1955; *Critical Essays* (1966), pp. 124, 131-2)

Hugh Sykes Davies

[On the word *impulse*] For him, it meant not an inexplicable eddy
within the human spirit, but a movement stirred in it from without.
(*The English Mind* (1964), p. 155)

Geoffrey Hartman

(1) Everything that happens on this mountain [Snowdon] is deceptive because everything leads beyond (though not away from) itself.
(2) According to Wordsworth, the imagination of a child is, like a
Romance hero, in nature but not of it.
(3) The child grows from a stage in which it walks *with* nature, to one
in which it is in search *of* nature, and finally to a crisis when nature no
longer suffices. This crisis is overcome when it is seen that Nature
itself taught the mind to be free of nature and now teaches the mind to
be free of mind and mingle with nature once more.
(4) The man who knows he has been strong *in* and *against* imagination.
(5) These spots are not only *in* time, like islands, but also creative *of*
time or of a vivifying temporal consciousness. (*Wordsworth's Poetry*
(1964), pp. 67, 75, 135, 146, 212)

Christopher Salvesen

Wordsworth is always much more aware of the *presence* of landscape,
of its surrounding influence, than of any pictorial qualities it might
have. His sense of being not merely related to it, but of being *in* it,
part of it, precludes any very objective view. (*The Landscape of Memory*
(1965), p. 69)

Donald Davie

[On two lines from 'Anecdote for Fathers': 'His head he raised—
there was in sight, / It caught his eye, he saw it plain—'] The lines
convey brilliantly how his eye flits across the weather-cock, returns to
it, and then, seeing it will do for a pretext, focuses on it. ('Dionysus in
Lyrical Ballads,' Wordsworth's Mind and Art, ed. A. W. Thomson
(1969), p. 118)

All these critics see their insights take shape prepositionally,
just as some of the best books on Wordsworth cast their titles
alike: *The Limits of Mortality, The Landscape of Memory, The Music
of Humanity.*[19] Even one critic who on this occasion stepped
from the egotistical sublime to the egotistical ridiculous found
himself ending his account of Wordsworth with the customary
turn of speech: 'Wordsworth would be a comical figure except
for the appalling fact that he has been preserved in amber (or
something) by (and with) a good many scholars and critics for
more than a century' (Yvor Winters).[20] Even Max Beerbohm's
famous caricature breathes an awareness of the Wordsworthian
prepositions: *Wordsworth in the Lake District—at cross-purposes.*
The pressure there of *in* is enough to make *at* sound as if it
ought to signify a location (at the crossroads, say); the implication is that 'at cross-purposes' is a haunt of Wordsworth—as
indeed it is. By mistitling the caricature (as 'Mr. Wordsworth
at cross-purposes in the Lake District'), Geoffrey Hartman[21]
blunts Beerbohm's point. But then how often Hartman has
shown us the fineness of Wordsworth's point. There has been
no greater poet in the two centuries since he was born, and the
best criticism does justice with as well as to him.

[19] In 1982, Jonathan Wordsworth added *The Borders of Vision.*
[20] *Forms of Discovery* (1969), p. 172.
[21] *Wordsworth's Poetry*, p. 144.

THOMAS LOVELL BEDDOES:
'A DYING START'

I

In 1849 poison achieved what the razor had failed to achieve the year before. Thomas Lovell Beddoes succeeded in killing himself. Failure seemed to have become what Beddoes was best at. True, he had started out a success: he published his first book of poems, *The Improvisatore*, in 1821 when still a freshman at Oxford, and a year later *The Brides' Tragedy* appeared to wide applause. But life withered. He published little else. His most passionately idiosyncratic enterprise, *Death's Jest-Book*, which he had drafted by 1829, was never published during his lifetime, partly because the friends to whom he sent it paltered and doubted. Self-exiled to Germany, where he went to study medicine, Beddoes had neither the amateur fame of a poet nor the professional achievement of a scientist. England seemed to him 'Cantland'; Germany pricked him into bizarrely subversive and courageous politics; neither country provided him with men or women whom he could deeply love or who could deeply love him. 'From the experiments I have made, I fear I am a non-conductor of friendship, a not-very-likeable person.'[1] Yet this non-conductor crackled with the electricity of imagination, much of it fascinatingly static. 'If my friend Death lives long enough to finish his jest-book, it will come with its strangenesses—it contains nothing else—like an electric shock among the small critics.'[2]

Critics, small and not so small, have found Beddoes very distinctly odd and very oddly distinct. One man of genius, Robert Browning, to whom Beddoes's friend Kelsall entrusted the Beddoes manuscripts, spoke out: 'the power of the man is immense & irresistible.'[3] John Heath-Stubbs, in *The Darkling Plain* (1950), is good on Beddoes and German literature and politics. But only one powerful critic has improved a high

---

[1] To T. F. Kelsall, 4 December 1825; *Works*, ed. H. W. Donner (1935), p. 610.

[2] To Kelsall, 1 April 1826; *Works*, pp. 616-17.

[3] Browning to Kelsall, 22 May 1868; *Plays and Poems of Beddoes*, ed. H. W. Donner (1950), p. lxxviii.

opinion into knowledge in a sustained and convincing way:
Northrop Frye, whose account of Beddoes in *A Study of English
Romanticism* (1968) is at once surprising and just. Anthologists,
often wiser in their generation than literary critics, have done
some justice to a poet who had no mercy on himself. So Beddoes
is known, albeit shadowily, as the crystalline voice of:

> We have bathed, where none have seen us,
> In the lake and in the fountain,
> Underneath the charmed statue
> Of the timid, bending Venus . . .[4]

As the metallic voice of 'A Crocodile'.

> Hard by the lilied Nile I saw
> A duskish river-dragon stretched along,
> The brown habergeon of his limbs enamelled
> With sanguine almandines and rainy pearl . . .

Or as the frog voice of:

> Squats on a toad-stool under a tree
> A bodiless childfull of life in the gloom,
> Crying with frog voice, 'What shall I be?
> Poor unborn ghost, for my mother killed me
> Scarcely alive in her wicked womb . . .'
>
> (III iii)

Beddoes had a soft spot for those whom literary fame treated
hardly. So he practised the sort of salvage operation which has
subsequently had to be visited upon him too. He backed a
loser, St. John Dorset, and his tragedy *Montezuma*, but there is
much that is winning about Beddoes's 'endeavour to dispel the
mists with which some unhappy fatality has obscured the poetical deserts of St. John Dorset.'[5] (For a moment those poetical
deserts sound not like what Dorset's poetry deserves, but like
its sandy wastes.)

His art is unfashionable; his productions have been not only cast
aside but the distended reputations of many of his contemporaries
who are much his inferiors, lie upon them like mountains, nevertheless poetry will out; let him remember how endless a thing hope is, &

---

[4] *Death's Jest-Book*, IV iii. All quotations are from *Death's Jest-Book* except where
stated.
[5] *Works*, p. 543.

address oblivion in the fine words of the scholar in the Merry Devil of
Edmonton:

> Yet overwhelm me with this globe of earth,
> And let a little sparrow, with her bill,
> Take but so much as she can bear away;
> That every day, thus losing of my load,
> I may again, in time, yet hope to rise.

& let us be the first sparrow in the work of his dishumation.

It is entirely characteristic of Beddoes that he should establish
his ringing confidence that 'poetry will out' by murdering the
usual confidence that 'murder will out.' For him, not only was
much poetry—most of his own poetry—about murder (in his
case, parricide laced with fratricide), but poetry itself was often
a kind of murder. He might have agreed with Wordsworth that
'We murder to dissect' but not have thought it so bad a thing.
From 'Letter to B. W. Procter':

> For death is more 'a jest' than Life, you see
> Contempt grows quick from familiarity.
> I owe this wisdom to Anatomy.

The taunting triplet depends not only on the nimbly blasé way
in which the familiar and contemptuous pun on 'quick' is bred,
but also on Anatomy's being the subtle medical training as well
as the unsubtle skeleton itself. The poet who turns 'murder will
out' into 'poetry will out' (its corpse or ghost rising reproach-
fully) is the one who gives us 'Down, Murder, down!' in *The
Brides' Tragedy* (IV i), a startling critique of *King Lear*'s 'Down,
wanton, down!'—murder in Beddoes coming on as the in-
tensest erotic experience. But then the whole of this St. John
Dorset passage is edged with Beddoes's love of Elizabethan
drama and of linguistic effrontery. 'Dishumation' is so disconcertingly alive.

Many a sparrow—including, as it happens, the scholar John
Sparrow—has engaged in the work of Beddoes's dishumation.
A poet who was obsessed with burials and exhumations, with
ghosts and with the thousand ways in which the dead won't lie
down, would have relished the grim comedy by which at intervals his art is exhumed, he being neither allowed to join the
company of the poets of his day who sheerly live on (Keats,
Shelley, Byron, Tennyson, Browning), nor allowed to rest in

peace with the rest. (1822: Beddoes, *The Brides' Tragedy*; the same year saw the publication of Bloomfield, *May Day with the Muses*; Bowles, *The Grave of the Last Saxon*; Cunningham, *Sir Marmaduke Maxwell*; and so on through a justly neglected alphabet; this from the chronological tables in the standard literary history of the period, Ian Jack's *English Literature 1815-1832*.)

One scholar gave much of his life to enforce his conviction that the achievement of Beddoes should not willingly be let die: H. W. Donner, whose assiduity created a weighty critical biography, a volume about the nineteenth-century response to Beddoes, a consummate complete edition of his works, and in 1950 an excellent substantial selection. Donner brought Beddoes's character and art to life of a sort. Yet Beddoes, like Robert Graves, knew the lugubrious truth which is buried here. In Graves's words:

> To bring the dead to life
> Is no great magic.
> Few are wholly dead:
> Blow on a dead man's embers
> And a live flame will start.

There is just one snag, for the scholar as for the necromant or the artist:

> So grant him life, but reckon
> That the grave which housed him
> May not be empty now:
> You in his spotted garments
> Shall yourself lie wrapped.

Beddoes himself knew the price that might have to be paid, and when he retold the story of Pygmalion, he brought it to an end by conceiving of the artistic creation—the metamorphosis of the stone to the statue, and then of the statue to the woman— as the artist's suicide. The poem ends with 'the sweet woman-statue' clasping the dead body which had given her life, had given her its life. Yet even here Beddoes has a last twist which is not a last twist of the knife or of the chisel, since she is 'quietly / Weeping the tears of his felicity.' Absent thee from felicity awhile. Pygmalion has joined the happier dead, and so his sacrifice is not simply what it might have seemed. The woman-statue's tears are as much the joy of congratulation as the sadness of commiseration; 'quietly / Weeping the tears of his felicity' makes a wonderfully hushed and enigmatic close, since *of* is so hauntingly suggestive. Weeping the tears of her loss: that would be nothing in comparison.

Like two other writers whose names happen to begin by chiming with Beddoes's, and who are like him in writing not only in English but also expertly in another European language, namely Beckford of *Vathek* (which influenced Beddoes) and Beckett (whose drama is invoked by Frye to illuminate Beddoes), Beddoes hankers for oblivion. From 'Death Sweet':

> Then, if the body felt, what were its sense,
> Turning to daisies gently in the grave,
> If not the soul's most delicate delight
> When it does filtrate, through the pores of thought,
> In love and the enamelled flowers of song?

That second line is pure Beddoes, and if we ask how it manages to incarnate so glidingly the life which it imagines even in the grave, one answer must be the gentle and delicate turn within the word *turning*. Its main sense is simply 'changing to,' a calm and peaceful metamorphosis so unlike the usual violences and violations of metamorphosis. But the gentle pressure of 'sense' before it, and of 'thought' after it ('the pores of thought,' incidentally, being as fine in its way as T. S. Eliot's yearning for a time when 'the intellect was immediately at the tips of the senses,'[6] the days before the dissociation of sensibility), gives to the phrase 'Turning to daisies gently' something of an exquisite social attention, turning courteously to hear their thoughts, toward them, with the perfect uncondescending politeness with which, for instance, the Mower turns to the glow-worms in Marvell's poem. Beddoes's moment—one of the great calmative evocations of the grave, and the opposite of the charnel knowledge which is usually associated with him—is the benign counterpart to what elsewhere Beddoes imagines as malign, the impatient arrival of evil conspiratorial life, turning restlessly, not restfully:

> Now see you how this dragon-egg of ours
> Swells with its ripening plot? Methinks I hear
> Snaky rebellion turning restless in it,

[6] 'Philip Massinger', *Selected Essays* (1932), 1951 edn, p. 210.

> And with its horny jaws scraping away
> The shell that hides it.   (II iv)

'Turning restless' not only as becoming restless, but also as restlessly turning. Revolution, and not just rebellion, is the word that lies curled within the shell.

It is this life, sometimes restless and sometimes restful, within Beddoes's very words, which most needs to be made manifest. Other things about him—the dark arc of his life, or the importance to literary history of his dramatic experiments— have been set down persuasively enough, but a reader of Beddoes is likely to be discontented with the way Beddoes's powers with words have been silently taken for granted by his admirers. Donner's praises are bent upon technical skill merely; and even Frye writes as if all you need to do with or for Beddoes is quote him adroitly and sympathetically. But the ways of Beddoes's words are mysterious, and a critic needs to try to show the electric shocks (of many different kinds) which give the poetry its peculiar and ghostly life. John Donne, in 'The Exstasie', has the word 'interinanimates':

> When love, with one another so
> Interinanimates two soules . . .

Webster was much possessed by death. Donne, I suppose, was such another . . . and Beddoes was yet another. It is worth stealing the word 'interinanimates' for Beddoes's art, so that it may be wrested to mean, as it did not for Donne, 'makes *in*animate' too in its interrelation, and not only 'animates.' Again like Beckett, Beddoes seeks a dark relation of life to death within his very words, an interinanimation. Since death has much to be said for it, the art itself must incorporate some proper deathward declension.

When Frye says, 'Beddoes was possessed, not so much by death, as by the idea of the identity of death and love,'[7] we hear the reverberation of that great line of Eliot's, and sure enough Eliot himself duly appears in Frye's account of Beddoes. But there is a simple juxtaposition that Frye does not exhibit. From Eliot's 'Whispers of Immortality':

---

[7] *A Study of English Romanticism* (1968), p. 52.

> Webster was much possessed by death
> And saw the skull beneath the skin;
> And breastless creatures under ground
> Leaned backward with a lipless grin.

From *Death's Jest-Book*, II iii:

> And, when the world is old and dead, the thin wit shall
> find the angel's record of man's works and deeds, and
> write with a lipless grin on the innocent first page for a
> title, 'Here begins Death's Jest-Book'.

With a lipless grin: yet Eliot's superb stanza does not make Beddoes superfluous. The internal rhymes of Beddoes's prose (*thin
. . . grin . . . innocent . . . begins*) have their own insinuating tension or torsion, different though it be from Eliot's tautened
skin/grin; and Beddoes has his characteristic flicker of the
tongue with the preposition *with*: 'and write with a lipless grin
on the innocent first page,' for a moment as if a lipless grin
('write with') were a kind of pen, a writing instrument. But
then so it is. There is a silent zeugma: the deadly title is written
with a lipless grin and a pen.

The preface to *Death's Jest-Book* was aggressively disarming:
'This is undoubtedly a very faulty [poem], nor is it intended to
be otherwise; it is offered as a specimen of what might be called
the florid Gothic in poetry, which the author desires to leave
alone and hopes therefore, probably quite superfluously, that it
will meet with no imitators.' The florid Gothic in poetry was to
be one of the many styles of which Eliot was a master. The
point is not that Eliot is an imitator of Beddoes (any more than
the poet of 'I have been one acquainted with the night' was an
imitator of the Beddoes line, 'I have been one that thought
there was a sun'), but rather that one of the things that is to
Beddoes's credit, and is also some explanation of his always
hanging by his finger-nails above literary history's *oubliette*, is
his having anticipated so many later modes. Frye invokes the
theatre of the absurd to help us see what sort of drama *Death's
Jest-Book* was or might have been. Likewise many of Beddoes's
moments are incantations to summon the spectre of an Eliot.

> Pressed from its fruit to wash Sesostris' throat,
> Or sweeten the hot palate of Cambyses . . .
> (V iv)

> Madame Sosostris, famous clairvoyante,
> Had a bad cold, nevertheless . . .

Do the things that immediately follow in *The Waste Land*, the 'drowned Phoenician Sailor' and the 'Hanged Man' and 'the horoscope,' then owe anything to the next page or two in Beddoes, with their mention of 'the drowned and the ship-wrecked,' of the need to 'put a cord round his neck and hang him up,' and of a 'horoscope'? Coincidence, perhaps, but there is a coinciding of vision too, in Beddoes's and Eliot's sense of so much of life as a grotesque and sinister farce.

Ezra Pound noticed the affinity. It was Charles Tomlinson who noticed this for me, and I am very grateful for the reference: Canto LXXX, as Mr Tomlinson points out, recalls, in Pound's Pisan captivity, a couple of phrases from Beddoes which Pound had quoted in an essay of 1913 on 'Beddoes and Chronology' ('centuries hoarded' and 'where none can speak his language') —this, in the company of Eliot.

> there is according to some authors a partial resurrection
>   of corpses
> on all souls day in Cairo
>   or perhaps all over Egypt
>   in identity but not atom for atom
> but the Saducees hardly give credence
> to Mr Eliot's version
> Partial resurrection in Cairo.
> Beddoes, I think, omits it.
>   The bone *luz*, I think was his take off
> Curious, is it not, that Mr Eliot
> has not given more time to Mr Beddoes
>   (T.L.) prince of morticians
>   where none can speak his language
> centuries hoarded
> to pull up a mass of algae
>   (and pearls)
> or the odour of eucalyptus or sea wrack

The grotesque vitality of Beddoes's phrasing has recourse to the shadowy violence of what I call the anti-pun, by which another sense of a word is called up only to be fended off. Take three seascapes. When Robert Lowell, in 'The Quaker Grave-yard in Nantucket,' speaks of how the 'dogfish barks its nose,' 'barks'—scrapes—is not a pun on the dog's noise, but, because of the pressure from 'dogfish,' it is an anti-pun. 'Barks' there does not mean both 'barks and barks', nor does it mean 'barks' (scrapes) while not meaning 'barks' (dog's noise); it means 'barks-not-barks,' the whole thing with the fending-off built in. Likewise the opening of Eliot's 'Sweeney Erect':

> Paint me a cavernous waste shore
> Cast in the unstilled Cyclades,
> Paint me the bold anfractuous rocks
> Faced by the snarled and yelping seas.

This is 'the florid Gothic in poetry,' and its manifest but impalpable violence is contained in 'snarled,' which means entangled but is then retrospectively put under pressure by 'yelping' to have something to do with the sound of snarling ('the snarling and yelping seas' would not be choppy at all in comparison); and so 'snarled' ends up, entangled, as 'snarled, not snarling.' The same source of eerie energy, of electric shock, is tapped by Beddoes in one of his seascapes, from *The Brides' Tragedy*:

> Now mercy save the peril-stricken man,
> Who 'mongst his shattered canvas sits aghast
> On the last sinking plank alone, and sees
> The congregated monsters of the deep
> For his dead messmates warring all, save one
> That leers upon him with a ravenous gaze
> And whets its iron tusks just at his feet.
>
> (III iii)

'Whets' is a grim anti-pun, under pressure from 'the deep'; grim because the tusks scarcely need to be wet with the water, and they will, all too soon, be wet with blood. The leering sense is 'whets-not-wets.' There is even a further lurking grimace in the lines; for the 'monsters of the deep' have surfaced from *King Lear* ('Humanity must perforce prey on it self, / Like monsters of the deepe'), and there in Beddoes's lines, leering horribly, is *leers*.

Beddoes likes the swell of a suggestion which may then be rebuffed or even humiliated. From *The Brides' Tragedy*:

> I cannot think
> Of that cold bed diseases make for us,
> That earthy sleep; oh! tis a dreadful thing.
>
> (*The Brides' Tragedy*, II iii)

Dreadful, but also sardonic because of the sense (*bed . . . make*) which loiters so banally in the corridor outside the lines. It is these effects which make apt an epithet that has been used of Beddoes: scary. Darkly frightening, yet colluded with, or stylized, not far from giggles. As in 'Pygmalion' (167-8):

> I breathe not aught but my own sighs for air,
> And my life's strongest is a dying start.

There we start at the word 'start,' flinching at the idea that death is a beginning and not an ending. A new start? Beddoes likes, too, such parallelisms of syntax as incite you into misreading and presumption, and he likes sound effects that set the teeth on edge. As in this fragment:

HUMBLE BEGINNINGS

> Why, Rome was naked once, a bastard smudge,
> Tumbled on straw, the den-fellow of whelps,
> Fattened on roots, and, when athirst for milk,
> He crept beneath and drank the swagging udder
> Of Tyber's brave she-wolf; and Heaven's Judea
> Was folded in a pannier.

There they are, 'Tumbled on' at the head of one line, and 'Fattened on' at the head of the next, for all the world as if they were equably parallel. There is intimated a vibrant contempt for those who would think of themselves as superior to such humble beginnings, and it can be heard in the swagging and swaggering insolence of the off-rhymes: 'udder' at the end of one line and 'Judea' at the end of the next, with 'Tyber' and 'pannier' plaiting the cadence, so that the concluding half-line is both casually tumbled or unfinished and trussed or folded. Beddoes's world-weariness is in the bone, and he continually scorns those who are merely socially world-weary.

Again, there is the life-in-death or death-in-life of the turns of phrase here:

Marry, I must either have been very sound asleep when I died, or else I died by mistake for I am sure I never intended it: or else this being dead is a quite insignificant habit when one's used to it: 'tis much easier than being alive, now I think on it: only think of the trouble one has to keep up life. One must breathe, and pass round the blood and digest and let hair, and nails, and bone and flesh grow.   (II ii)

What makes this something other than a 'quite insignificant' way of speaking is the sardonic knowledge that our hair and nails continue to grow after we have died; this, and the fact that 'pass round the blood,' though splendid as a description of the circulation of the blood, has the drunken suggestion that we are assisting at our own cannibal feast. When Beddoes writes explicitly of a cannibal feast and of the father tricked into eating his son, he has the effrontery to pun upon the word 'kid':

> 'Harpagus, hast thou salt enough,
> Hast thou broth enough to thy kid?'
> 'There's kid for child, and who has won?'
> (IV iv)

Such barbarous legends are usually—or were, within nineteenth-century poetry—given a high glaze, so that you could gaze and not be sick. Beddoes gives 'the meat and grease,' not a glaze, as in this pun on 'kid' (perfectly available, as is clear from the dictionary). No wonder his friends thought that nineteenth-century readers would not swallow him.

When the ghost of the murdered Wolfram appears to his murderer, the Duke adds insult to injury:

> Is't possible
> Thou'rt true, and worms have vomited thee up
> Upon this rind of earth?   (III iii)

'Vomited' has a sick and febrile energy: a worm seems too small for 'vomited' to be the right word, and yet the dark sense that the word is hideously right ('men have died, and worms have eaten them'—though in your case even a worm's stomach might turn) is animated by two subterranean suggestions: first, the implicit 'cast,' as both the convoluted earth thrown out by the earth-worm and as vomit; second, 'worms' as linked to 'vomited' by a twist of *vermi* (Latin: *vermis*, worm). Beddoes effects many insinuations with the word 'wormy,' and if we ask, with Keats in 'Isabella,' 'Now wherefore all this wormy circumstance?' we should be prepared to stay for an answer.

Yet the contrasting forms of life occur not only within phrases but in phrase against phrase or in mode against mode. One of the things that lifts Beddoes above his greatly gifted contemporary Thomas Hood, with the comparable love of

savage grotesquerie ('Miss Kilmansegg and Her Precious
Leg'), and indeed lifts Beddoes to the company of Browning,
another such lover of the grotesque, is Beddoes's truly com-
manding a poetry of tender solicitude, as Browning does too
but Hood does not. It may be Beddoes's savage manner that
most comes home to a modern reader. But there is an ironic
truth in what might sound like a sarcastic disclaimer by Isbrand
after his reciting of 'Squats on a toad-stool' and the ensuing
praise of it:

> I fear you flatter: 'tis perhaps a little
> Too sweet and tender, but that is the fashion;
> Besides my failing is too much sentiment.
>
> (III iii)

Isbrand, in his cynical sarcasm, means not a word of it. Not
that Beddoes's poetry was elsewhere too sweet and tender,
evincing too much sentiment; but Beddoes is as good a poet as
he is because the romantic, lyrical, and assuaging things in him
are as real in the best of his work as the antiromantic, harsh,
and feverish things. So it matters that *Death's Jest-Book* can
accommodate, so largely and reverentially for all the ironies of
the context, a song like 'We have bathed, where none have seen
us . . .' Beddoes's evocations of tenderness and awe are alive
with their own counterparts to the fiercer paradoxes of his harsher vein. He contemplates happily the meeting of the liquid
and the solid, as when the water of falling tears is imagined as
'the soft heap of drops' (*The Second Brother*, II ii). Or there is the
gentle strength of this other falling in *Torrismond*, I iii:

> Begin before another dewdrop fall
> From the soft hold of these disturbed flowers.

'Soft hold' is finely judged, as is the calm within this context of
the word 'disturbed.' Such fallings are not 'hideous ruin and
combustion down'; rather they have their chastened equanimity, as in the exquisitely simple line from the Dirge in *Death's
Jest-Book* ('We do lie beneath the grass . . .'): 'Where the snow
falls by thousands into the sea.'[8] The art is in the play, affec-

---

[8] V iv. The line is immeasurably more effective in the Dirge than in 'An Unfinished
Draft' (*Plays and Poems*, pp. 391-2), where, as 'The snow falls by thousands into the
sea', it begins and ends a ten-line fragment.

tionate and sad, of the singulars against the plural: the snow
(which is one and yet myriad) against the 'thousands' of the
unmentioned snowflakes, like the sea against the unmentioned
thousands of its water-drops, which the snowflakes, too,
become. It is like a strangely peaceful battle scene, where men
'fall by thousands'; each snowflake loses its little life. How
peaceful Beddoes makes it all may be seen if we call up a similar
experience—of snow at sea—from the sombre swell of Tennyson's *In Memoriam*: 'in the drifts that pass / To darken on the
rolling brine / That breaks the coast' (cvii).

Or take this tiny fragment, scarcely a fragment since it is as
perfectly rounded as a haiku:

> A lake
> Is a river curled and asleep like a snake.

The movement and manner of the lines (not even lines, really)
charmingly remove all danger from the snake as well as all
danger of affectation from the lovely fancy itself. Beddoes
achieves this by the interlacing which does not just rhyme
'lake' with 'snake,' but which rhymes 'lake' with '*like* a sn*ake*',
as if *lake* were the effortless curled contraction of those three
words.

For Beddoes had an excellent ear. When his words grate or
grind, that is because he wants at this point the truth of harshness, but he does not identify truth with harshness. Pygmalion
finds the beautiful fateful piece of stone in the water:

> That night his workmen wrought
> With iron under it and it was brought,
> This dripping quarry while the night was starry
> Home to the weary yearning statuary.
>
> ('Pygmalion' 94-7)

The clink of the workmen's iron against the stone (to be heard
in 'night . . . wrought . . . it . . . it . . . brought') yields to the
yearning cadences that bring home to us the poignancy of
Pygmalion's yearning. This is partly the undulation—liquid
and firm, like the water and the stone—of the rhymes, with
'quarry' internally accommodating itself to 'starry,' and then
with the crossing to 'statuary' bridged by 'weary.' Partly it is
the line-long separation of 'brought' from 'home,' so that the
line in between brings home what it is to yearn. Partly it is the

pun on 'quarry.' For the stone is Pygmalion's quarry, not only
as his stone-source but also as the living being whom he yearn-
ingly hunts, his prey. Beddoes has this pun, more fiercely, in
The Second Brother, III i:

> This is a man
> Whose state has sunk i' th' middle of his thoughts:
> And in their hilly shade, as in a vale,
> I'll build my church, making his heart the quarry.

The living and the dead are at once Beddoes's quarry, as in the
story of Pygmalion itself (especially given the outcome that
Beddoes gives it). Which is why he pursues such interinanimation within the language.

The effect is ghostly, and Beddoes speaks much of ghosts.

> For soon the floral necromant brought forth
> A wheel of amber, (such may Clotho use
> When she spins lives,) and as he turned and sung,
> The mould was cracked and shouldered up: there came
> A curved stalk, and then two leaves unfurled,
> And slow and straight between them there arose,
> Ghostlily still, again the crowned flower.
> Is it not easier to raise a man,
> Whose soul strives upward ever, than a plant,
> Whose very life stands halfway on death's road,
> Asleep and buried half?   (III iii)

The word 'Ghostlily' there creates, with its eyes open, what
William Empson once thought he had hoodwinked himself into
enjoying elsewhere, as he writes in *Seven Types of Ambiguity*:

There was a poem about strawberries in *Punch* a year or two ago,
which I caught myself liking because of a subdued pun; here what was
suggested was a powerful word, what was meant was a mere grammatical convenience:

> Queenlily June with a rose in her hair
> Moves to her prime with a languorous air . . .

I was puzzled to know why the first line seemed beautiful till I found
I was reading *Queenlily* as 'Queen Lily,' which in a child's poetry-
book style is charming: 'the lily with a rose in her hair'. . . . is a fine
Gongorism, and the alternative adverb sets the whole thing in motion
by its insistence on the verb. It is curious how if you think of the word

only as an adverb all this playful dignity, indeed the whole rhythm of the line, ebbs away into complacence and monotony.[9]

But Beddoes's 'Ghostlily' is poignant for just those reasons. Behind the uncanny but lucid adverb there is the spectral flower, the ghost-lily, just as behind the word which immediately precedes it, 'arose,' there is a ghost-rose. Floral necromancy indeed. (Two pages later we hear of a ghostly nymph who dissolves at daylight, 'Leaving behind a stalk with lilies hung'.) What in the poem from *Punch* was a fluke, and in Beddoes is elsewhere a merely casual play of the word lily against the adverbial suffix ('Of the valley-lily low, / Opening dewily and slow,' in 'The Lily of the Valley'), is here in *Death's Jest-Book* a haunting effect. As in a line from *Torrismond*, I iii: 'But the faint ghost of some dishevelled rose.'

T. S. Eliot, it will be recalled, imagined in *Little Gidding* an incantation to 'summon the spectre of a Rose'. For Beddoes, too, *spectre* is a crux, not least because it is so weirdly easy a metamorphosis of *sceptre*. Beddoes is fascinated by the powers of sceptre and of spectre and by their intertwining. 'A sceptre is smooth handling.' A spectre is less smooth handling. Kings and crowns in the vicinity of a disconcerting spectre will try in vain to convert it into a gratifying sceptre, as in 'Alpine Spirit's Song':

> Till we reach yon rocky pale
> Of the mountain crowning all,
> Slumber there by waterfall,
> Lonely like a spectre's love,
> Earth beneath, and stars above.

The murderer Duke says to his victim-ghost Wolfram:

> Then there is rebellion
> Against all kings, even Death. Murder's worn out
> And full of holes; I'll never make't the prison
> Of what I hate, again. Come with me, spectre . . .
> (III iii)

The Duke's last words, not only in the play but on this earth (not the same as his dying words, since the play ends a few lines

[9] (1930), 1947 edn, p. 65.

later with Wolfram taking him 'still alive, into the world o' th'
dead'), are of *crown* and *spectre*:

> Torwald, the crown is yours; I reign no more,
> But when, thou spectre, is thy vengeance o'er!

Never, because the spectre is the vengeance of the sceptre.
Like Wolfram, Beddoes might say:

> I have a fascination in my words,
> A magnet in my look, which drags you downwards,
> From hope and life.   (IV ii)

The fascination of Beddoes's words is clearly not the end of the
matter. Frye offered a profound tip about the dramatic monologue, for the 1820's, when Beddoes flowered and soured, were
on the brink of discovering or inventing this, the most inaugurative of nineteenth-century poetic kinds, the dramatic monologue of Tennyson and of Browning in the 1830s. There were
extraordinary possibilities held out by Beddoes (few of them
realized, but all of them sufficiently there to be truly tantaliz-
ing) as to the silent interlocutor, the presence which speaks
volumes but is silent. Such as the dog whom (not which) Beddoes addresses in one of his most affectionately charming
poems—addresses in the knowledge that the dog cannot reply
but is master of its own profound and daily language:

TO TARTAR, A TERRIER BEAUTY

> Snowdrop of dogs, with ear of brownest dye,
> Like the last orphan leaf of naked tree
> Which shudders in bleak autumn; though by thee,
> Of hearing careless and untutored eye,
> Not understood articulate speech of men,
> Nor marked the artificial mind of books,
> —The mortal's voice eternized by the pen,—
> Yet hast thou thought and language all unknown
> To Babel's scholars; oft intensest looks,
> Long scrutiny o'er some dark-veined stone
> Dost thou bestow, learning dead mysteries
> Of the world's birth-day, oft in eager tone
> With quick-tailed fellows bandiest prompt replies,
> Solicitudes canine, four-footed amities.

Such a four-footed silent interlocutor is at home in the dramatic monologue, and gives Beddoes one of his triumphs as well as giving us some sense of his having lived as a poet just before his time. In his last letter Beddoes wrote: 'I am food for *what I am good* for—worms,' with a characteristic retrospective contraction of '*for* what I am g*ood*' into *food*. He wrote in the postscript: 'I ought to have been among other things a good poet.'[10] More exactly, more justly, he ought to have seen that he had been among other things a good poet.

II

Beddoes knew that there was something wrong with the drama of his day, but he was not sure whether it was sleep or death. 'Say what you will—I am convinced the man who is to awaken the drama must be a bold trampling fellow—no creeper into worm-holes—no reviser even—however good'.[11] The burly noisiness of 'trampling' is good, as who should say 'Rise and shine'; it rouses what would otherwise be the drowsy cliché of awakening the drama from its dormouse dormancy. But as soon as Beddoes, the poet of wormy circumstance, slides on to 'no creeper into worm-holes', death takes over from sleep, and the next sentence is naturally this: 'These reanimations are vampire-cold'. But then again death is after all not the end of the matter in the world of Beddoes, and a macabre revival is possible even though it would not be as great as a new begetting. The worm in the grave is kin to the worm in the page, and Beddoes glides at once from vampires to ghosts:

Such ghosts as Marloe, Webster &c are better dramatists, better poets, I dare say, than any contemporary of ours—but they are ghosts— the worm is in their pages—& we want to see something that our great grand-sires did not know. With the greatest reverence for all the antiquities of the drama, I still think that we had better beget than revive—attempt to give the literature of this age an idiosyncrasy & spirit of its own, & only raise a ghost to gaze on, not to live with—just now the drama is a haunted ruin.

A spirit of its own, and not just a ghost.

He writhed. He could write, dedicating *The Brides' Tragedy*, 'the following scenes were written, as you well know, exclusively

---

[10] To R. Phillips, 26 January 1849; *Works*, p. 683.
[11] To Kelsall, 11 January 1825; *Works*, p. 595.

for the closet', but he himself well knew that he would like
to come out of the closet, and he challenged those who pre-
tended otherwise to themselves: 'You are, I think, disinclined
to the stage: now I confess that I think this is the highest aim of
the dramatist, & I should be very desirous to get on it. To look
down on it is a piece of impertinence as long as one chooses to
write in the form of a play, and is generally the result of a consciousness of one's own inability to produce anything striking
& affecting in that way'.[12] The characteristic life of Beddoes'
prose is there in the relation of 'highest' and 'get on it' to 'look
down on it', and then of them all to literally looking down—not
with godlike impertinence but from the 'gods'—on to the stage.

He had a very penetrating apprehension of drama, and two
in particular of his critical forays ought to have classic standing.
One is the long letter to Kelsall in 1831 about dramatic illusion,
the publicizing self-attentions of actors, the use of masks on the
stage, the price paid for the pause between acts, and the functions and force of comedy within tragedy. Beddoes sees that the
playbill notoriety of actors makes for a reversal of roles ('Othello
& Richard & Rosenkranz are here obliged to play Claremont &
Kean, instead of the reverse'), and he wants the actors' names
withheld, since the actor, 'deprived of his private name & existence, must feel more convinced of the reality of his 5-act life,
would be liberated from the shackles of timidity & the temptations of individual vanity'.[13] A century later, an heir of Beddoes, T. S. Eliot, was to underline the point: 'the ideal actor
for a poetic drama is the actor *with no personal vanity*'.[14]

The other classic appraisal by Beddoes is his earlier letter, in
1825, about the doctor and the dramatist:

Again, even as a dramatist, I cannot help thinking that the study of
anat[y], phisiol-, psych-, & anthropol-ogy applied to and illustrated by
history, biography and works of imagination is that w[h] is most likely
to assist one in producing correct and masterly delineations of the
passions: great light w[d] be thrown on Shakespeare by the commen-
taries of a person so educated. The studies then of the dramatist &
physician are closely, almost inseparably, allied; the application alone

[12] To Kelsall, 27 February 1829; *Works*, p. 640.
[13] 10 January 1831; *Works*, pp. 651-4.
[14] '*The Duchess of Malfi* at the Lyric: and Poetic Drama', *Art & Letters*, iii (1919-20),
39.

is different; but is it impossible for the same man to combine these two professions, in some degree at least? The science of psychology, & mental varieties, has long been used by physicians, in conjunction with the corresponding corporeal knowledge, for the investigation & removal of immaterial causes of disease; it still remains for some one to exhibit the sum of his experience in mental pathology & therapeutics, not in a cold technical dead description, but a living semiotical display, a series of anthropological experiments, developed for the purpose of ascertaining some important psychical principle— i.e. a tragedy. Thus far to show you that my studies, pursued as I pledge myself to pursue them, are not hostile, but rather favourable to the development of a germ w^h I w^d fain believe within me. You will say, 'this may be theoretically true, but no such physician has ever yet appeared'. I shall have great satisfaction in contradicting you, as Dr. Johnson did the man who denied motion.[15]

This great satisfaction was denied to Beddoes; no play of his was truly a play. But the truth of his understanding of this profound affinity was to be vindicated; vindicated, in many 'a living semiotical display' so living as to make the word 'semiotical' seem a cold technical dead description, and so unostentatious as to make the word 'display' weigh much less than a play, in the plays of Anton Chekhov.

From the start, Beddoes's readers knew that it was Beddoes's readers that they wished to be, not his audience. 'If Mr. Beddoes would write a poem instead of a play, we have no doubt that he would realize all the expectations which this brilliant first performance has excited'.[16] Yet even there the word 'performance' seems to acknowledge that Beddoes's powers stood in some relation to the dramatic. Next year, Beddoes peered lugubriously into the future: 'If I were the literary weatherguesser for 1825 I would safely prognosticate fog, rain, blight in due succession for its dullard months'.[17] In 1840, he was still something of a literary weather-guesser, and was lecturing—to an audience that was more certainly few than fit—on 'The History, Past and Present, and the Hopes of Future Dramatic Poetry of the Caucasian Race in Europe'.[18] But between 1825 and 1840, something had happened to dramatic poetry which

[15] To Kelsall, 4 December 1825; *Works*, pp. 608-11.
[16] *The Album*, May 1823; *Plays and Poems*, p. lxxiii.
[17] To Kelsall, 25 August 1824; *Works*, p. 589.
[18] *Plays and Poems*, p. lxii.

would forever change its history and its hopes: the dramatic monologue.

Beddoes had not prognosticated this, and he had not conceived of it when he insisted that in drama 'we had better beget than revive'. He was essentially a poet of the 1820s, thwarted then and thereafter by his friends' misguided caution, by his willed exile, and by his embitterment; his art is at once precocious and retarded, and not only because *Death's Jest-Book* languished unpublished, forever exercising him and never being exorcized. So the great inauguration in the 1830s—the discovery or invention of the dramatic monologue independently by Browning and Tennyson—passed him by, or overtook him perhaps along the road he was taking. For he had an intuitive sense of the power to be felt in the true tension of the dramatic monologue, the presence and the pressure of the silent interlocutor.

To speak of a silent interlocutor is already to acknowledge something strange or paradoxical, though anybody who has seen the shrouded figure in Beckett's *Not I* raising his arms in a gesture of helpless compassion while the illuminated mouth flickers on like mad, a pulsing polyp, will know what it is for silence to speak. In the best book (far and away) on the dramatic monologue, *The Poetry of Experience* (1957), Robert Langbaum brought out how much the silent interlocutor contributes, in force and in nuance, to the tension of such Browning poems as 'Andrea del Sarto' and 'My Last Duchess'. The wife whose silence may be that of the wronger or the wronged, or any proportion of the one to the other; the envoy who may lack power, both personal and hierarchical, but who does have to be wooed even by a Duke: these constitute the living ground against which a forceful figure takes shape and is himself. Some critics have spoken as if the silent interlocutor were a convenience merely, scarcely rising even to a convention. But it is the mark of a true poet that what would be mere convention in others is validated in the art, so that recourse to the word 'convention' is just what the poems do not ask. The art of the dramatic monologue begins in an acute sense of the circumstances in which strong speech meets strong silence. *The Ring and the Book*, that extraordinary sequence of dramatic monologues, is among other things an answer to the question, in what setting are scrutinized people most allowed their full say? The answer is, in court.

A wife, Andrea del Sarto's, who no longer has anything to reply, which is not to say that she has nothing to say for herself; an envoy whose deferential silence is at one with his keeping what is after all not his own counsel: these are interlocutors though they do not say a word, and so is the God who all night does not say a word in reply to the man who has made it impossible for his loved Porphyria, in whose company he in a way still is, ever to say another word.

T. S. Eliot knew that stringency is the ally not the enemy of the artist: 'A form, when it is merely tolerated, becomes an abuse. Tolerate the stage aside and the soliloquy, and they are intolerable; make them a strict rule of the game, and they are a support'.[19] Tolerate the fact that a dramatic monologue is a dialogue in which only one party speaks, and it is intolerable; make it a strict rule of the game, and you can feel the tension and the responsible revelatory economy of the form. When people say that a convention has broken down, often what they mean is that something has broken down and revealed that all we have got is a convention.

'Browning wrote dull plays, but invented the dramatic monologue', said Eliot, half-wonderingly. Beddoes wrote not dull plays but hectic shivered ones; he did not invent the dramatic monologue, but he was alive to its essential pressures, the silent interlocutor. Eliot pondered 'The Three Voices of Poetry':

The first voice is the voice of the poet talking to himself—or to nobody. The second is the voice of the poet addressing an audience, whether large or small. The third is the voice of the poet when he attempts to create a dramatic character speaking in verse; when he is saying, not what he would say in his own person, but only what he can say within the limits of one imaginary character addressing another imaginary character.

It is in this Eliot essay that the voice of Beddoes is unexpectedly but aptly heard, Beddoes himself hearing one of his eeriest imagined voices. 'What you start from', said Eliot,[20]

---

[19] *Dial,* lxxi (1921), 215. *Athenaeum,* 14 May 1920.
[20] (1953); *On Poetry and Poets* (1975), pp. 89, 97-8.

is nothing so definite as an emotion, in any ordinary sense; it is still more certainly not an idea; it is—to adapt two lines of Beddoes to a different meaning—a

> bodiless childful of life in the gloom
> Crying with frog voice, 'what shall I be?'

But with what voice could you reply to a question asked by a frog voice? What would you have to be, to answer its question, 'What shall I be?' What interlocution is possible?

> Squats on a toad-stool under a tree
> A bodiless childfull of life in the gloom,
> Crying with frog voice, 'What shall I be?
> Poor unborn ghost, for my mother killed me
> Scarcely alive in her wicked womb . . .'

The frog voice strikes a chill; fortunately, the dog voice casts a warmth. So the tenderness of 'To Tartar, a Terrier Beauty' is in the love which ruefully knows itself to be excluded from the dog voices. Tartar

> oft in eager tone
> With quick-tailed fellows bandiest prompt replies,
> Solicitudes canine, four-footed amities.

The poem's tone, just as it takes all possibilities of insolence out of the word 'bandiest' (a dog won't bandy words with you), is full of solicitude and amity. The poem has quick-eyed love, but not because the speaker is a quick-tailed fellow of the dog. (Lovely of Beddoes to take mild advantage of the human sense of 'fellow', too.) The poem, for all its pathos, has to stand on its own two feet. Perhaps, like many a human being, the poet is closer in solicitude and amity to this four-footed creature to whom he can't exactly speak (though tones of voice will work wonders) than to any fellow biped, but he still has to acknowledge that the dog and he are not on all fours. In its poignancy, waggish comedy and singularity, the poem is a feat.

Beddoes's scholar, H. W. Donner, was right in his sense of where, as a play, *Death's Jest-Book* goes wrong: 'All the characters seem to declaim into the void, and none answer the others'.[21] But the power of Beddoes's best poems or best passages is just that: the void being truly a void (of fear or pathos),

---

[21] *Plays and Poems*, p. xl.

and the unutterability of an answer being as audible as a gong. Likewise, when Edmund Blunden turned upon Beddoes the word which had been used of Coleridge's conversation, 'monopollylogues',[22] this could have caught the successes as well as the failings. Beddoes imagined circumstances in which there would be a kind of dialogue where nevertheless one party would have a monopoly of speaking and might speak like Poor Poll. Beddoes wrote non-plays, but invented the dramatic monopollylogue.

For Northrop Frye, 'perhaps Beddoes' real form, so far as it was dramatic, was less the stage-play than the kind of near-death monologue represented by Browning's *Bishop Orders His Tomb*, Eliot's *Gerontion*, or Tennyson's *Ulysses*'.[23] The trouble is that any such form in Beddoes is much less clear than is the impulse, which is why his art was as often frustrating for him as it is for us. The exceptional person who was Beddoes never did assuredly find the form for his force; I am thinking of Frye's words:

The exceptional person is exceptionally isolated, and may in himself be a force for exceptional good or evil: as Isbrand says to himself when plotting revenge:

> Art thou alone? Why, so should be
> Creators and destroyers.   (I i)

It is the presence of a silent interlocutor which may most convey what it is to be isolated. For it is not simply that creators and destroyers should be alone, but that Beddoes as a creator needs to convey the particular sense of being alone which comes from the company of the actively silent. 'A feeling of being cut off', says Frye,[24] and the feeling is heartfelt when a voice addresses ears that do not hear or mouths that do not answer. The word 'alone' is at its most powerful in Beddoes when a man is not exactly alone:

> Now mercy save the peril-stricken man,
> Who 'mongst his shattered canvas sits aghast
> On the last sinking plank alone, and sees

[22] *Votive Tablets* (1931), pp. 294-6; *Plays and Poems*, p. lxxxiii.
[23] *A Study of English Romanticism*, pp. 67, 74.
[24] *A Study of English Romanticism*, p. 83.

> The congregated monsters of the deep
> For his dead messmates warring all, save one
> That leers upon him with a ravenous gaze
> And whets its iron tusks just at his feet.
>
> (*The Brides' Tragedy*, III iii)

Alone? Would that he were. For he is still in the company of his
messmates, dead though they are; and he is in the company of
the monsters of the deep, the congregation of whom is sardonically at odds with a prayer for mercy. The man may pray for
mercy, but there will not be much point in his asking for it
exactly, from the shark (is it?) which has its eye on him and is
so silently interlocuting.

> And the shark looked on with a sneer
> At his yearning desire and agony.
>
> ('The Old Ghost')

The creative fire will ignite when the artist is alone, but Beddoes makes this idea itself catch fire by his realizing what it is
for the artist to feel alone, that is, his being alone with the un-
speaking. So it is that Pygmalion fashions his silent statue.

> He stole unseen into the meadow's air
> And fed on sight of summer—till the life
> Was too abundant in him and so rife
> With light creative he went in alone
> And poured it warm upon the growing stone.
> The magic chisel thrust and gashed and swept
> Flying and manifold; no cloud e'er wept
> So fast, so thick, so light upon the close
> Of shapeless green it meant to make a rose—
> And as insensibly out of a stick
> Dead in the winter-time, the dew-drops quick
> And the thin sun-beams and the airy shower
> Raise and unwrap a many-leaved flower
> And then a fruit—So from the barren stock
> Of the deer-shading formless valley-rock,
> This close stone-bud, he, quiet as the air,
> Had shaped a lady wonderfully fair.
>
> (106-22)

It is a great work of erotic shaping, itself both flying and manifold (amazing epithets for the rigour of a chisel), with the perils
of 'too abundant' and 'rife' converted into the purely creative

(the syntax too is manifold, so that it is not clear at first whether the words 'and so rife' mean '*and so* rife' or 'and *so rife*'); with the frank eroticism of 'poured it warm' and 'thrust and gashed' tempered by its not being dwelt upon but at once followed by the life of great nature; with the possible sentimentalities of the organic likenings stilled by the chastely wintry description that is given to what nature has to work upon ('the close / Of shapeless green', and 'a stick / Dead in the winter-time'): all these coming to rest in the quiet conjunction, within one line, of the sculptor and the sculpture which has now flowered under his hands into art and which will later flower under his hands from art into life: 'This close stone-bud, he, quiet as the air . . .'. This wonderfully plays the stone's weight and solidity against the air's lightness and fluidity, with the bud as the mediator. And is it the sculptor or the sculpture which is 'quiet as the air'? Throughout the lines, what is magically yet naturally unwrapped is the creative energy of the word 'alone':

> and so rife
> With light creative he went in alone
> And poured it warm upon the growing stone.

There is, for Beddoes, no such thing as a thing that is alone.

> All round and through the spaces of creation,
> No hiding-place of the least air, or earth,
> Or sea, invisible, untrod, unrained on,
> Contains a thing alone.
>
> (*The Second Brother*, I ii)

But the overpowering sensation in his work is that of feeling alone, and it is enforced by the company of silence. The dead may speak once they have matured into ghosts, but the dead can be so newly dead as to seem asleep. Any talk in the company of the dead should be chastened; Beddoes's father wrote fiercely about unchaste talk in the company of the dead:

It is not possible to conceive emotions more opposite than those excited by the aspect of a dead body, and by licentious conversation; or even by the jests, from which, unfortunately, many persons of reflection, and, in other respects, of decent conduct, do not restrain themselves in the presence of boys. No power would afterwards be able to deprive the ideas, impressed by such a sight, of their serious complection.[25]

[25] H. W. Donner, *Thomas Lovell Beddoes: The Making of a Poet* (1935), p. 49.

The boy Beddoes was to become the author of *Death's Jest-Book*, and was to show himself one of those persons of reflection who nevertheless bring jests and licentious conversation into the company of corpses. Three of his best poems are haunted by the same act of contemplation, as a ghost gazes at his newly dead corpse and at the opportunity it gives for children's ghosts to play at hide-and-seek in its holes ('Dream of Dying', 'Lines Written at Geneva', and *Death's Jest-Book*, V iv). The fledgling adult ghost has as yet no voice with which to rebuke the ghost-children who are both younger and older than he. Beddoes, who imagined that human ghosts eat the ghosts of animals, even spared a thought for the problems raised for ghosts, and for interlocution, by historical linguistics and spook-speak:

> Thou art so silent, lady; and I utter
> Shadows of words, like to an ancient ghost,
> Arisen out of hoary centuries
> Where none can speak his language.
>
> (I ii)

'These lines are as beautiful as anything he has written', said Ezra Pound, 'but they bring us directly to the question: Can a man write poetry in a purely archaic dialect? Presumably he can, and Beddoes has done so; but would not this poetry, his poetry be more effective, would not its effectiveness be much more lasting if he had used a real speech instead of a language which may have been used on the early Victorian stage, but certainly had no existence in the life of his era?'[26]

The plays try openly to set the speaker against the unreplying. Lenora in *The Brides' Tragedy* (III v) takes her murdered daughter in her lap and sings a lullaby to her. (The dead are reduced to a speechlessness which is like infancy; Beddoes is drawn to lullabies because they move towards the silence of an interlocutor.) Then Lenora speaks to her husband, only to find that he is not asleep or deaf but dead. Yet in the actual or acted scenes of the plays, as against their songs or their fantasies, Beddoes was seldom able to achieve either the proper preposterousness of his curdled comedy or the delicate transparency of

---

[26] 'Beddoes and Chronology' (1913); *Selected Prose 1909-1965*, ed. William Cookson (1973), p. 351.

his pathos. Imagining an answer: this remains the nub of the
matter, but in scenes like that of Lenora, or the earlier scene
(III i) in which everybody tries to wrest words from stonily
silent Hesperus (after more than fifty lines of their all soliciting
him in vain, a clock strikes and he is moved to exit with the
words 'The hour is come'), the pressure of the unanswering is
farcical or melodramatic. Whereas a mere memo by Beddoes to
himself can imagine a death's jest of interlocution:

MEM. When I write to Bourne to begin with telling him that I have
been dead a fortnight—make my will and say a fine angel wanting to
visit Earth pulled on my carcase for a pair of breeches & now inhabits
D. Court.[27]

What would count as a reply by Bourne to that comedy? But
then what would count as a reply to the pastoral peace of the
Dirge, 'We do lie beneath the grass'? When Beddoes writes a
dirge, it is sung by the dead, not the living, but either way we
are in the presence of something which is at once a monologue
and a dialogue.

'Who breaks my death?' (III iii) asks the aggrieved and conjured ghost, where we mortals might say 'Who breaks my
sleep?' The frustrations and rewards of talking to a corpse or a
sleeper, the sheer imaginative oddity of it all, give the dramatic
tension to many of Beddoes's best things, always on the brink
of the dramatic monologue proper. Perhaps his sense of these
alienations was fed by the death of his father when he was only
five and by the separation from his mother, and likewise by his
exile in Germany where he must have been more than usually
conscious of what it was for the speakers in a conversation to be
on different planes. He delights in those extremities of the
telephonic which try to imagine exchanging words with a frog
voice or a dog; or with the silent jaws and throat of a crocodile,
peopled with its young and its parasites; or with a statue; or
with a tree:

> Here thou at morn shalt see
> Spring's dryad-wakening whisper call the tree
> And move it to green answers.
> ('Letter to B. W. Procter')

[27] *Works*, p. 520.

You will not *hear* a whisper or a call or an answer, you will see
them in their effects, a triumph of silent utterance.

For power is not simply with the talker, and there may be
crevices and crevasses not just between what is said but within
it, as Beddoes brings out by his deft use of the preposition 'in':
'There were deep hollows / And pauses in their talk' (*The
Second Brother*, I ii).

'This talking is a pitiful invention' (I ii). Beddoes did not
quite arrive at the great invention of verse-talking, the dramatic
monologue. But his work remains full of resources unexhaus-
ted, of possibilities which could yet bud no less successfully
than Robert Lowell's great stroke in 'Under the Dentist',
where what you know of the silent interlocutor is that his
mouth is open but he cannot speak. Only a poet of eldritch
talents, alive to the cutting edge of the dramatic monologue,
would have been able to imagine the relations of speech to
silence as tellingly as Beddoes does.

HYMN

And many voices marshalled in one hymn
Wound through the night, whose still, translucent moments
Lay on each side their breath; and the hymn passed
Its long, harmonious populace of words
Between the silvery silences, as when
The slaves of Egypt, like a wind between
The head and trunk of a dismembered king
On a strewn plank, with blood and footsteps sealed,
Vallied the unaccustomed sea.

What voice could answer the voice of such a hymn? What
divine interlocutor could this hymn move from silence? The
worshippers are as alienated from the god they worship as were
the Jews from the Egyptians, though to speak of the Jews as
'the slaves of Egypt' is grimly to compact the two nations, to
press them to fly apart. Such a poem has a miraculous impunity, and its severed head still speaks.

A.E. HOUSMAN:
THE NATURE OF HIS POETRY

Housman thought that literary critics were even rarer than poets or saints, so he would not have been surprised that we are hard put to say why we like or dislike his poems. His admirers usually offer little more than pious generalities, and his detractors say 'adolescent'—a word used by critics as different as Edmund Wilson, George Orwell, Cyril Connolly, R. P. Blackmur, and Conrad Aiken. There is an excellent annotated bibliography of early writings on Housman which is by R. W. Stallman,[1] who not surprisingly found it necessary to include a section on that famous difficulty, 'The Problem of Belief.' After speaking of Housman's pessimism, he summarised the critical groupings:

On the ground of these beliefs his poetry is evaluated thus: (1) The poetry is adversely criticised or rejected on the ground that *his beliefs*, being adolescent, unsound, or without a final standard of value, *interpose obstacles to the enjoyment or appreciation of the poetry*; (2) the poetry is discredited on the ground that *his beliefs*, being agnostic or un-Christian, *are discreditable beliefs*; (3) the poetry, *with his beliefs abstracted*, is valued apart from and in spite of these beliefs; (4) the poetry is valued *because of the beliefs*; the poetry, however pessimistic his beliefs, is 'good medicine,' an anodyne for the wounds of life.

But there is an odd omission; everyone seems to take it for granted that Housman's poems unwaveringly endorse the pessimistic beliefs which they assert. To me his poems are remarkable for the ways in which rhythm and style temper or mitigate or criticise what in bald paraphrase the poem would be saying. Rhythm and style never abolish the beliefs, and this for the good reason that the beliefs (the urge to pessimism, the need to strike a strong pose) are not abolishable—we can call them adolescent or childish or puerile or immature only if we also concede that there has never been a man adult enough not to feel some magnetic pull from them, some wish to succumb to them, some uncertainty as to whether they are temptations or aspirations.

[1] *P.M.L.A..*, lx (1945), 463-502.

Housman has often been compared to a child, and not always by those who dislike his poems. A. F. Allison: 'It is the attitude of the child whose party has been spoilt'.[2] Randall Jarrell: 'It has more than a suspicion of the child's *when I'm dead, then they'll be sorry*'.[3] His poems often assert positions that are inadequate in ways suggested by calling them adolescent—inadequate not as utterly alien to our experience, or wilfully thought-up, but in the sense that we ought not to be in one mind about them, and should fear that they might be sirens. There are usually three reactions to this adolescence of attitude. We may say that what a poem asserts, its attitudes or beliefs, has no bearing on its poetic quality. Here we might call up Housman, who seems at times (but only at times) to be saying this in *The Name and Nature of Poetry*. Or we may say that a poem's beliefs are inseparable from its quality, and that his poems suffer because of the childishness of what they say. Such is the opinion of the most articulate of his detractors. Or we may agree that the beliefs of a poem are inseparable from its quality, but argue that the relationship between belief and the final total meaning may be strange and oblique. This is to argue that in the best of Housman's poems, the childishness of what is said is part of the effect, but only part, and is absorbed to produce something fine and true—though often something that is, quite legitimately, in two minds. Clearly this does not apply to many of his most attractive and simple poems; these I rate less highly not because they are simple but because they are not profound.

A straightforward example. In paraphrase, the poem 'I to my perils' says that if you look on the black side you will never be disappointed. Childish, in the narrow sense that it expresses an attitude commoner in children than in adults. Taking an exam at 16, one said 'I'm sure I've failed.' Childish, too, in the larger sense, that later on one couldn't but see how little use it actually was in the face of troubles—indeed, one had a reluctant sense of that all along. On the other hand, it is also an inextinguishable attitude; I have not met a man so mature as never to glance wistfully towards it as a possible bolt-hole from what is intolerable. There is no reason why a poem shouldn't express the attitude, but, yes, there would be something un-

---

[2] *R.E.S.*, xix (1943), 279.

[3] *Kenyon Review* (1939); reprinted in *Kipling, Auden & Co.* (1980), pp. 20-8.

thinkingly shallow about a poem which found this advice
adequate to the troubles of life. But if we go from paraphrase to
the poem itself, we find something different.

> I to my perils
>   Of cheat and charmer
>   Came clad in armour
>   By stars benign.
> Hope lies to mortals
>   And most believe her,
>   But man's deceiver
>   Was never mine.
>
> The thoughts of others
>   Were light and fleeting,
>   Of lovers' meeting
>   Or luck or fame.
> Mine were of trouble,
>   And mine were steady,
>   So I was ready
>   When trouble came.
>   (*More Poems*, vi)

The poem says a dour glum cramping thing, but how does it
say it? With gaiety and wit that are, if you like, utterly inappropriate. Instead of the 'steady' tramp of military fortitude, there
is the exquisite interlacing of a dance; instead of granite rhymes,
there is a supple effrontery and insouciance that links 'charmer'
and 'armour', and in so doing opposes something to the simple
sturdiness, the indurated hopelessness, of armour. It says that
'The thoughts of others / Were light and fleeting' while 'Mine
were of trouble,' but whatever the poem may say (in its natural
human wish to find armour for itself, to find steadiness), this
cannot be the case. The movement itself is light and fleeting,
and not just in the lines about others. Just how much difference
the movement makes to what in the end is *said*, can be seen
when Edmund Wilson, in his excellent essay (in *The Triple
Thinkers*), quotes these lines but prints them as prose, as a
parenthetical gloss on a pessimistic bit of Housman's prose.
Housman in this poem may have tried to be a philosopher, but
cheerfulness was breaking in. That the poem is not resting
smugly in shallow pessimism is borne out by its emphatic
closing words: 'When trouble came.' The Biblical figure who

endured all that life could inflict, but who was sustained by
something other than a habit of looking on the black side,
would have retorted harshly. 'Job curseth the day of his birth'
(chapter iii)—a chapter which ends emphatically: 'I was not in
safety, neither had I rest, neither was I quiet; yet trouble came.'
If Housman (as Norman Marlow[4] noted) tacitly invokes Job, it
is not because he thinks he has found a moral stance which
could cope unrepiningly with all that Job suffered, but because
he knows he has not. Housman's position may be inadequate,
but it would be ignoble only if he thought it was adequate.

It would not do to claim this as a subtle poem, but it shows
the tug of contraries which so often makes for the profoundest
of Housman. And it is not adolescent. Louis MacNeice was
rebuked in *Scrutiny*[5] for saying that 'Housman uses his tripping
measures to express the profoundest pessimism'—'as though,'
objected Mr. Mellers, 'as though the vulgar lilt weren't a comment on the pessimism's profundity.' Clearly Mr. Mellers took
the lilt as a 'comment' on the pessimism only in a derogatory
sense. Not in the true sense that the movement of many of
Housman's poems comments on, and alters, what they say.
We must not support Housman's provocative rearguard action:
'Poetry is not the thing said but a way of saying it.' Yet the
'way' is legitimately part of the total effect, and many of his
poems show *what is said* teasingly at odds with *how it is said*. His
sense of decorum is a larger one than that which oppresses a lot
of contemporary verse, where we find that the rhythm and
movement simply say again in their own medium what the
diction too is saying. A violent expressiveness can become as
tedious as a thrice-told tale; told once by the words themselves,
again by a violence of crowded or jammed rhythms, and a third
time by brutal changes of line-length or stanza form.

It might be objected that Housman left us a clear statement
in *The Name and Nature of Poetry*. He said categorically that
'meaning is of the intellect, poetry is not.' So how can it be of
any use to explore his meaning? But: (i) critics as unlike as
II. W. Garrod and Cleanth Brooks have agreed that many of
Housman's best effects cannot be encompassed by his theory
(as in Wordsworth); (ii) the theory itself is confused and self-

[4] *A. E. Housman: Scholar and Poet* (1958), pp. 112-5.   [5] *Scrutiny*, ix (1941), 383.

contradictory; (iii) the contrarieties which underlie many of the best of Housman's poems are not so much intellectual as emotional, and Housman certainly did not ask that poetry should be emotionally simple or single-minded. (Nor are his detailed criticisms of his brother's poems easy to reconcile with the abdication of intellect in poetry.) Note, for example, the word 'vibration' when he says that the function of poetry is 'to set up in the reader's sense a vibration corresponding to what was felt by the writer.' There 'vibration' does not seem to be simply a loose word for 'feeling.' Vibration may be oscillation, moving to and fro like a pendulum. Of bad 18th-century verse he complained that 'it could not express human feelings with a variety and delicacy answering to their own.' His account of Collins, Cowper, and Blake is not unthinkably far from saying that the force of their work came from a war within the poems; these three poets were not altogether mad, 'but elements of their nature were more or less insurgent against the centralised tyranny of the intellect, and their brains were not thrones on which the great usurper could sit secure.'

Such contrarieties characterise many of his examples in the lecture. When he wished to commend diction and movement, why did he choose (good though it is) a stanza by Daniel?

> Come, worthy Greek, Ulysses, come,
>   Possess these shores with me:
> The winds and seas are troublesome,
>   And here we may be free.
> Here may we sit and view their toil
>   That travail in the deep,
> And joy the day in mirth the while,
>   And spend the night in sleep.

But the effectiveness of this stanza comes not just from its diction and movement but from a fact unmentioned by Housman: that the Siren speaks to Ulysses. The speaker is disowned or resisted even while we read and are attracted; the movement may be free and mirthful, but the whole sense of the lines is not so, and the movement of Ulysses's reply is significantly harsher. Like the best of Spenser, the emotional effect of Daniel's lines is not simple, and they did not come to Housman's mind just because of their fluent diction and movement.

From 'Ode to the Cuckoo,' which was either written by John

Logan or stolen (why?) by him from Michael Bruce, Housman
quoted:

> Sweet bird, thy bower is ever green,
>   Thy sky is ever clear;
> Thou hast no sorrow in thy song,
>   No winter in thy year.

'A tinge of emotion,' said Housman. But once again the effect
comes from something implied but not stated, an emotion
running counter to the explicitly stated joy which the poem
celebrates. The effect of 'thy . . . thy . . . thou . . . thy . . . thy'
is to set up a keen unspoken sense of what, for others than the
migrating cuckoo, is harshly true. There is, as it were, a counter-
pointed stress: '*Thou* hast no sorrow in *thy* song.' The verse
may speak of '*no* sorrow' and '*no* winter,' but its effect is to
leave sorrow and winter undissolved; the mood, on the verge of
self-pity, is emotionally various. The stanza is the only good
one in a poor poem; but if we put it back in context we find that
implicit in it (and finely so) is all that the surrounding stanzas
so miserably spell out:

> What time the pea puts on the bloom
>   Thou fliest thy vocal vale,
> An annual guest in other lands,
>   Another Spring to hail.

> Sweet bird! thy bower is ever green,
>   Thy sky is ever clear;
> Thou hast no sorrow in thy song,
>   No winter in thy year!

> O could I fly, I'd fly with thee!
>   We'd make, with joyful wing,
> Our annual visit o'er the globe,
>   Companions of the Spring.

All those unattainable aspirations poorly spelled out in 'O
could I fly, I'd fly with thee,' all the chafing at the fact that
even in speaking of the cuckoo's joy one could not but invoke
sorrow—all these were contained in the stanza Housman
quoted. He liked it, not because it was 'tinged with emotion,'
but because it was tinged with conflicting emotions.

The same is true of Housman's highest example, once again
a phrasing which is touchingly simple and yet assaulted by

feelings which deny it:

> *Duncane* is in his Grave:
> After Lifes fitful Fever, he sleepes well.

These lines would hardly be the same if they were spoken by a
pious old man reconciled to death, and not by Macbeth, guiltily
jealous of Duncan still, even now; guiltily exonerating himself
too (Duncan is now better off); on the verge of self-pity, fitful
and feverous and yet creating a momentary and precarious
peace in thinking of a death which nevertheless he will defy to
the utmost. The lines are an oasis in Macbeth's speech—but
a delusion or a sudden understanding?

> But let the frame of things dis-joynt,
> Both the Worlds suffer,
> Ere we will eate our Meale in feare, and sleepe
> In the affliction of these terrible Dreames,
> That shake us Nightly: Better be with the dead,
> Whom we, to gayne our peace, have sent to peace,
> Than on the torture of the Minde to lye
> In restlesse extasie.
> *Duncane* is in his Grave:
> After Lifes fitfull Fever, he sleepes well,
> Treason has done his worst: nor Steele, nor Poyson,
> Mallice domestique, forraine Levie, nothing,
> Can touch him further.   (III ii)

'*He* sleepes well'; it is hardly right to return to 'Thou hast no
sorrow in *thy* song,' but here too it will have been the swelling
of self-pity that drew Housman's attention. That, and the conflict lying behind the simple lines, a conflict made hideously
explicit when Macbeth speaks of gaining peace, and when he
utters words that are, literally speaking, nonsensical: when he
says that the world may fall *before* he will suffer that which he
already suffers, 'these terrible Dreames.'

In defending his position, Housman was willing to say that
Shakespeare sometimes wrote nonsense. But once again his
example is of a certain kind of emotional undercurrent:

Even Shakespeare, who had so much to say, would sometimes pour
out his loveliest poetry in saying nothing.

> Take O take those lips away
> That so sweetly were forsworn,

> And those eyes, the break of day,
>   Lights that do mislead the morn;
> But my kisses bring again,
>   bring again,
> Seals of love, but seal'd in vain,
>   seal'd in vain.

That is nonsense; but it is ravishing poetry.

Housman does not say that the lines are meaningless; non-sense is a different thing. In one important way this song is nonsense; how can you bring kisses back again? The force of the song comes from the fact that the powerful undertow of its feeling is so much at odds with what it is asserting (much as the force of Tennyson's 'Ulysses' comes from the contrast between the robust sentiments and the slow-wheeling verse). The song may say that the false lover must 'Take O take those lips away,' but somehow it doesn't turn out like that; the sorrowing repetitions show us an attachment that is still very much alive, refusing to accept that the false lover is false and ought to send back the kisses much as a gentleman sends back old love-letters. The context of the song (*Measure for Measure*, IV i) brings out very clearly these double feelings. It is sung at Mariana's insti-gation; she still loves Angelo although he falsely broke his promise to her. The song *purports* to be addressed to a woman; part of its force comes from this transference, a wishful turning of the tables which makes the woman the powerful one who is pleaded with. The Duke had said to Isabella in III i: 'This fore-named Maid hath yet in her the continuance of her first affec-tion: his unjust unkindenesse (that in all reason should have quenched her love) hath (like an impediment in the Current) made it more violent and unruly.' This is in the current of Housman, whose poems again and again show the continuance of emotions which should in all reason have been quenched, so that it is the impediment itself which results in the force of feeling. We never hear all of Mariana's song (many of Housman's best poems are fragments), because the Duke en-ters, disguised as a friar, and Mariana dismisses the boy who has sung it:

> Breake off thy song, and haste thee quick away,
> Here comes a man of comfort, whose advice
> Hath often still'd my brawling discontent.

> I cry you mercie, Sir, and well could wish
> You had not found me here so musicall.
> Let me excuse me, and beleeve me so,
> My mirth it much displeas'd, but pleas'd my woe.
> *Duke*: 'Tis good; though Musick oft hath such a charme
> To make bad, good; and good provoake to harme.

It was just this power that drew Housman, the power of music
radically to change what is said. To make bad good, and 'nonsense' sense? The sequence of Mariana's words suggests that
she will no longer need the song *because* 'Here comes a man of
comfort . . .'; and when she speaks of '*brawling* discontent' we
return to the stream unruly because of impediments. She has to
apologise for the song, and the Duke does not accept the simple
plea that it will have made her feel appropriately sad. The
'charm' of the song is as much magic as delight; will it bring
Angelo back even while it urges him (her) to go? 'His unjust
unkindenesse (that in all reason should have quenched her
love)'—what the song presents is the co-existence of that love
with a keen sense of that unkindness, and yet with the sexes
reversed. The combination touched Housman.

It was a tug of this kind, against the explicit meaning, of
which Housman spoke in the most famous passage of his
lecture:

In these six simple words of Milton—

> Nymphs and shepherds, dance no more—

what is it that can draw tears, as I know it can, to the eyes of more
readers than one? What in the world is there to cry about? Why have
the mere words the physical effect of pathos when the sense of the
passage is blithe and gay? I can only say, because they are poetry, and
find their way to something in man which is obscure and latent.

Housman is well aware that there is nothing to cry about, and
that the sense is blithe and gay. He simply says that there is
also a strong counterfeeling of sadness. F. W. Bateson attacked
vigorously:

The pathos of Milton's six simple words obviously derives for
Housman from the last two of them. As Shenstone had pointed out
in the middle of the eighteenth century, 'the words "no more" have
a singular pathos; reminding us at once of past pleasure, and the
future exclusion of it.' But Milton's injunction to the nymphs and

shepherds was not, in fact, to stop dancing, but to 'dance no more /
By sandy *Ladons* Lillied banks.' The nymphs were only to transfer
their dances from Arcadia to Harefield in Middlesex. . . . Housman's
tears came from taking Milton's line out of its context and giving it
a meaning it was never intended to have. By misreading Milton he
has created what is essentially his own private poem.[6]

Housman's 'own private poem,' not surprisingly, resembles
his own poems. But somehow the Shenstone passage seems
slightly to support Housman, and one thinks of Tennyson's 'So
sad, so fresh the days that are no more' or of his early poem 'O
sad *No more*! O sweet *No more*!' In the song from Arcades,
Milton does after all leave us with that momentary hesitation
(at least on the brink of pathos) which comes from having the
line end at 'no more'—there is a feeling that the line *could* be
sad though delightfully it turns out not to be. Certainly the
main sense is gay, but is there something of an undertow, just
as there is in the 'Nativity Ode' when 'The Nimphs in twilight
shade of tangled thickets mourn'? 'Twilight' (with its associations of sad beauty) is found too in the song, in conjunction
with nymphs; indeed the song concedes that to move one's
home even on such a noble occasion cannot be achieved without
some sadness to someone (one reason why it is a great compliment to the Countess of Derby):

> Nymphs and Shepherds dance no more
>   By sandy *Ladons* Lillied banks.
> On old *Lycæus* or *Cyllene* hoar,
>   Trip no more in twilight ranks,
> Though *Erymanth* your loss deplore,
>   A better soyl shall give ye thanks . . .

Housman was certainly over-sensitive to the pathos, and he
leaves the impression that it obliterates the explicit joy of the
lines. But some pathos there is ('Though *Erymanth* your loss
deplore'). Once again one of his examples is characterised by
conflicting emotions, as on this occasion he expressly noted:
'Why have the mere words the physical effect of pathos when
the sense of the passage is blithe and gay?'
    Housman took provocativeness to the point of silliness when
he called the song from *Measure for Measure* 'nonsense,' but this

---

[6] *English Poetry: A Critical Introduction* (1950), pp. 15-16.

would be less absurd if we connected it with 'nonsense-verse.'
Nonsense-verse is not meaningless, and the sense of it matters;
its emotional force comes from the disparity between the absurd-
ity or falsity of what is said and the emotional truth of what is
felt. The childishness or cruelty is combined with a jauntiness,
wit, and aplomb of style and movement. John Wain, speaking
of the great difficulty which many 19th-century poets had in
breaking free of responsibilities and saying what was in their
minds, strikingly juxtaposed Hopkins and the nonsense-poets.
He quoted Edward Lear:

> There was an old man who screamed out
> Whenever they knocked him about . . .

'A modern writer might well begin a poem in this way, but he
would not pretend that he was doing it to amuse the children'.[7]

Housman wrote a good deal of nonsense verse; Laurence
Housman included twelve examples in *A.E.H.*, and three more
were separately reprinted. H. W. Garrod took the view that
'the nonsense verse was well worth having—who had believed,
else, that Housman had it in him either to be happy or to
write nonsense?' But were Carroll and Lear happy? Much of
Housman's serious verse uses a method—of indirections, disparities, and emotional cross-currents—that is at its clearest in
nonsense-verse. What is said is not what is meant, but something is certainly meant. (Often one cannot but think that a
Freudian thing is meant.) When you met an old man 'whose
nerves had given way,' you 'attended to his wants': by putting
his head into the ants' nest, tying his hands, and filling his
mouth with hay:

> He could not squeal distinctly,
>   And his arms would not go round;
> Yet he did not leave off making
>   A discontented sound.

What more natural at this than mild irritation?

> And I said 'When old men's nerves give way,
>   How hard they are to please!'

Such a poem is not an allegory, but how long is it since madness

---

[7] 'Gerard Manley Hopkins' (1959); *Essays on Literature and Ideas* (1963), pp. 117-9.

was treated in such a way? How and why was Wilde punished? 'Oh they're taking him to prison for the colour of his hair'— this poem is in a way the greatest of Housman's nonsense-verses, moving out into a larger lunacy. 'The Crocodile, *or* Public Decency' shows us how children, made ashamed of nakedness, sacrifice themselves when the crocodile calls:

> 'Come, awful infant, come and be
> Dressed, if in nothing else in me.'

Such poems—and there are many more—are not lacking in personal feelings; their force comes from the fact that no man could have had a more rigid sense of Public Decency than had Housman, even though in one vital respect it oppressed his deepest feelings.

Both the nonsense-verse, then, and *The Name and Nature of Poetry* offer evidence that contrarieties and disparities of feeling fascinated Housman. In many of his more strangely powerful poems, the force comes from what is submerged, 'obscure and latent,' so it is not surprising that he was fond of that particular kind of pun or anti-pun which creates its double meaning by invoking but excluding. When Milton described something in Paradise as 'wanton,' his meaning did not just forget about the fallen sense of the word; it invoked it but excluded it, so that Eve's hair was 'wanton (not *wanton*).' As the man waited to be hanged in Housman's 'Eight O'Clock,' he 'heard the steeple / Sprinkle the quarters on the morning town.' 'Morning (not mourning)': the town does not mourn.

> The diamond tears adorning
> Thy low mound on the lea,
> Those are the tears of morning,
> That weeps, but not for thee.
> (*Last Poems*, xxvii)

'Morning (not mourning).' George Herbert, in 'The Sonne,' had applauded the English language:

> How neatly doe we give one onely name
> To parents issue and the sunnes bright starre!

Housman, more lugubriously but no more absurdly, relished the conflict between morning and mourning. When the nettle dances on the grave, 'It nods and curtseys and recovers.'

'Recovers,' as a term in dancing; the dead man does not recover in this or any (unspoken) sense. 'Curtseys,' as part of the dance; but the curtsey is hardly a courtesy—indeed to dance on a grave is traditionally the extreme discourtesy.

Housman's sure feeling for a subterranean link comes out in the finest such unspoken pun, in the magnificent and solitary reflection:

> When the bells justle in the tower
>   The hollow night amid,
> Then on my tongue the taste is sour
>   Of all I ever did.
>
> (*Additional Poems*, ix)

When Laurence Housman printed this, he gave the alternative reading 'Then to my heart the thought is sour.' Without 'tongue' and 'taste,' nothing is left. This is not just because an immediacy of detail is lost. The uncanny connection between the sound of bells and the sour taste depends on 'tongue.' Bells have tongues. Emily Dickinson, a poet greater than Housman but not different in kind, begins a poem:

> It was not Death, for I stood up,
>   And all the Dead, lie down—
> It was not Night, for all the Bells
>   Put out their Tongues, for Noon.

Housman was not punning; he would have been perfectly happy if the obscure force of his stanza (which he never published, though it is one of the best things he ever wrote) had come home without any sense of the bizarre surrealist connection between the bells and the taste. 'Surrealist' may go too far, but the first (unauthorised) printing of these lines (1930) bore the title: 'A Fragment preserved by oral tradition and said to have been composed by A. E. Housman in a dream.' And what is the sourest taste of all?

> Instead of sweets, his ample palate took
> Savour of poisonous brass and metal sick.
>   (Keats, *Hyperion*, i 188-9.)

What is easily the best discussion of Housman, that by Randall Jarrell in the *Kenyon Review* (1939), brings out clearly and wittily the antagonisms in two poems: 'Crossing alone the nighted ferry,' with its love sliding over into contempt and self-contempt, so that two poems occupy the same space; and 'It nods and curtseys and recovers,' where the beautiful syntactical ambiguity of *of* (as in the murder-story *Murder of My Aunt*, where it turns out that the aunt does the murdering) suggests that if a man kills himself for love, it is too for love of the grave: 'The lover of the grave, the lover / That hanged himself for love.' Jarrell deals deftly with those who would murmur 'adolescent':

Nor is this a silly adolescent pessimism peculiar to Housman, as so many critics assure you. It is better to be dead than alive, best of all never to have been born—said a poet approvingly advertised as seeing life steadily and seeing it whole. . . . The attitude is obviously inadequate and just as obviously important.

But certainly a full-scale defence of Housman would have to reply in detail to the important charges of 'failure of specification' and of 'violence to common experience' that were brought by John Crowe Ransom[8] and by F. R. Leavis.[9] Ransom attacked 'With rue my heart is laden,' partly on the grounds that one of its images 'runs counter to the ironic intention'— but elsewhere Housman made good use of such running counter. Leavis's extremely forceful remarks on 'Wake: the silver dusk returning' depend on our being certain that Housman has simply blundered into 'insensitive falsity' and is not *using* it.

My final example is one of Housman's best poems. Yet it does apparently take up an attitude that is silly or absurd. In 'Tell me not here, it needs not saying,' William Empson noticed the way in which each penultimate line breaks into Alcaics, and then offered a superb insight into how the poem works:

I think the poem is wonderfully beautiful. But a secret gimmick may well be needed in it to overcome our resistances, because the thought must be about the silliest or most self-centred that has ever been expressed about Nature. Housman is offended with the scenery, when he pays a visit to his native place, because it does not remember the great man; this is very rude of it. But he has described it as a lover, so in a way the poem is only consistent to become jealous at the end. Perhaps the sentiment has more truth than one might think. . . . many English painters really are in love with the scenery of England,

and nothing else, so they had much better give up their theoretical tiff
with Nature and get back to painting it. The last verse of the poem,
driving home the moral, is no longer tenderly hesitant and therefore
has given up the Alcaic metre.[10]

Housman's attitude, which would be little more than silly if
concerned only with Nature, turns into a curious kind of jealousy if it deals too with love of a woman. The poem is magnificent as natural description; Housman's eye and ear were never
more alert. But this straightforward, respectable and explicit
feeling is entwined with a remarkable erotic force. Not that the
poem is 'really' erotic and not about Nature; it is about both.
Housman, with disconcerting literalness, really does write
about his mistress Nature as if she were his mistress. Hence the
peculiar force derived from casting the poem in the form of a
monologue from an old cast-off lover to the young man who
has succeeded him. You need not tell *me* about her, 'for she and
I were long acquainted.' So that the act of resigning (a resigna-
tion stated, but still showing 'the continuance of [his] first
affection') is fraught with an intensity hard to understand if we
think only of Nature:

> Possess, as I possessed a season,
> The countries I resign.

Housman is taking seriously two conventions that are usually
trifled with: that Nature is like a mistress, and that loving
a mistress is like loving Nature (the long vogue for poems which
describe love-making in topographical terms). There is the contrast between the unhurried rhythm and the momentary flash
of bitterness in 'a season,' and there is the complete propriety
of 'Possess,' emphatically placed and repeated. The enchantress
was not just distantly *heard* on the new-mown grass or under the
trees.

> On acres of the seeded grasses
> The changing burnish heaves . . .

Are we to remember how Tennyson brings together love and
Nature in 'Locksley Hall'?

---

[10] *British Journal of Aesthetics*, ii (1962), 40-1.

> In the Spring a livelier iris changes on the burnish'd dove;
> In the Spring a young man's fancy lightly turns to thoughts of love.

It is not just of Nature as *like* a mistress that we think when we hear how

> full of shade the pillared forest
> Would murmur and be mine.

The poem is not a code, and we cannot go through it looking for point-by-point correspondences. What we have is the co-existence of powerful love for Nature with powerful erotic feelings. It is in the last stanza that the bitterness makes itself heard; the poet is still in love with something he knows is literally heartless and witless (no substitute for the love of people, though people are even worse when *they* are heartless or witless). Lurking behind this attack on the faithless promiscuity of Nature is the traditional image for a promiscuous woman as 'the wide world's common place,' or 'the bay where all men ride.' Bitterness, perversity, and self-reproach are all fused by lyrical grace into a poem unique in the language. 'What tune the enchantress plays'—no wonder Housman remembered that stanza from Daniel's 'Ulysses and the Siren':

> Come, worthy Greek, Ulysses, come,
> Possess these shores with me . . .

As the Duke said in *Measure for Measure*, 'Musick oft hath such a charme / To make bad, good; and good provoake to harme.'

WILLIAM EMPSON:
THE IMAGES AND THE STORY

I

Empson might not disapprove of one's pondering a poem of
his in terms of its story, since he has always stuck up for story
as one of the great things about literature. Obviously so, one
would have hoped, for a novel or a play. Of Virginia Woolf,
Empson remarked that 'the impressionist method, the attempt
to convey directly your own attitude to things, how you connect
one thing with another, is in a sense fallacious; it tries to substitute for telling a story, as the main centre of interest, what is
in fact one of the byproducts of telling a story'.[1] Which drew
him to Shakespeare: 'Even those delicate interconnections on
which the impressionist method depends . . . need a story to
make them intelligible, and even if Shakespeare (since I have
dragged him in) could afford to abandon himself to these
delicious correspondences he had first to get a strong and obvious
story which would be effective on the stage.'

Some of Empson's most valuable vigilance has been in defence of story, seeing in real terms the situation out of which a
person speaks. There is his salutary parenthesis about Lear
which questions the status of imagery as Maynard Mack conceives it: 'he has now escaped from the ''the incessant conflict expressed by the images of the play'' (not by the *story*, of
course)'.[2] There is yet another of the odd things about Hamlet:
'Here as elsewhere he gives a curious effect, also not unknown
among his critics, of losing all interest for what has happened in
the story; but it is more impressive in him than in them'.[3] Or
there is the attack, which he has launched twice, on D. A.
Traversi's incomprehension of Perdita's flower-speech: 'I think
that this critical belief comes solely from being too proud to
attend to the story'.[4]

[1] *Scrutinies II* (1931), pp. 214-5.
[2] *Essays in Criticism*, xvii (1967), 100.
[3] *Sewanee Review*, lxi (1953), 39.
[4] *British Journal of Aesthetics*, ii (1962), 52; also *Times Literary Supplement*, 23 April
1964.

True, Empson's attending to the story sometimes comes to resemble a private detective dutifully making smoke without fire; his piece on *The Spanish Tragedy*[5] hunts gamely for its unscotched quarry ('I think the point was obvious at the time, so obvious that it did not get stated in the text . . . I think, then, that the play could be produced so as to make pretty clear to the audience that Andrea had been murdered for love, but I admit that it is peculiar for the text never to say it . . . ['Correction'] I thus lose the one bit of the text which appeared to tell the secret. But Lodovico would have been unlikely to tell it anyhow, so this does not refute the theory'). Empty-handed. But never empty-hearted; witness the ebullient generosity of his reading of Joyce's *Ulysses*, which believes in a magnanimous outcome for the story ('that Stephen *did* go to bed with Molly, very soon after the one day of the book'), and furthermore trusts that in the life of Joyce, and of all concerned, the outcome had been all the liberation that one could hope: 'I think it equally likely that the original Bloom couple did have a son as a result of this incident, a son by Bloom, who will now be about fifty, and that is why Joyce always felt such glee about the whole affair.'[6]

Story, properly widened to include an apprehension of a real situation, is crucial too to Empson's criticism of poetry. *Milton's God* is in large part the reconstruction of a story which Empson glimpses in the interstices; he complains of Grant McColley's approach that 'this view lets you off attending to the story, and anything which does that ends by making you feel the poetry is bad'.[7] Likewise the poetry of Marvell, Empson has twice maintained, has been shrunk by critics: 'To imagine this personal situation helps you to make human sense of the paradoxes of the poem';[8] 'Literary critics nowadays I think lose the impact of the poem because they refuse to look at it in this real way'.[9] Empson delights in the zest of story (' *The Passionate Pilgrim* . . .

[5] *Nimbus*, iii (1956), 16-29. Reprinted in *Elizabethan Drama: Modern Essays in Criticism*, ed. Ralph J. Kaufman (1961).

[6] *Kenyon Review*, xviii (1956), 26-52, incorporating a B.B.C. talk of 1954. Reprinted in *A James Joyce Miscellany: Third Series* ed. Marvin Magalaner (1962), pp. 129, 140.

[7] *Milton's God* (1961), p. 99.

[8] *Essays in Criticism*, iii (1953), 116.

[9] *British Journal of Aesthetics*, ii (1962), 49.

starts with two genuine sonnets (138 and 144 in *Sonnets*) each of them implying plenty of story');[10] and he deplores the narrow-minded squandering done by critics who throw away both a delight and a comprehension. Of 'Sailing to Byzantium', which F. A. C. Wilson misread as sailing *to* Ireland, Empson remarks: 'The effect of the mistake is that Mr Wilson ignores the "story", the actual human situation which the poet is describing with much humour and good sense'.[11] Likewise, in a later essay, of 'Byzantium': 'One would like to have more story in the poem here'.[12]

This sense of and for story is at work in Empson's criticism of the poet who means most to Empson's poems: Donne. 'The idea that the story needs explaining away is itself what needs explanation'.[13] Of 'The Expiration': 'So far they are merely lovers with feelings that drag them into conflict; but then he began inventing a larger and more Byronic story'.[14] Of 'Aire and Angels': 'One needs to get the story of the poem clear'; the story in this case, it seems, is of the strong silent type: 'Between the two verses we are to assume he gets to bed with her'.[15]

And the story in Empson's own poems? On general grounds it is unlikely that poems as good as his best would derive and create all their energies from those philosophical problems and pains, that siege of contrary ideas, which critics have rightly seen the poems as engaging with; certainly that siege is crucial to them, but the question for the critic—as it was for the poet—is that of the relation between such a siege and an 'actual human situation'. What is it about the two things—this contrariety and that situation—which precipitates the one thing, the poem? Riddling in so many ways, the poems are openly secretive, publicly so as poems, not privately as autobiography. One remembers Empson's remark about Hamlet: 'he successfully kept a secret by displaying he had got one'.[16]

One approach to the story in Empson's case is by first reconsidering the famous reverberation of his contrarieties, his

[10] *Shakespeare: Narrative Poems* (1968), p. xxvii.
[11] *Review of English Literature*, i (1960), 51.
[12] *Essays Presented to Amy G. Stock* (1965), p. 22.
[13] *Critical Quarterly*, viii (1966), 279.
[14] *Just So Much Honor*, ed. P. A. Fiore (1972), p. 113.
[15] *Kenyon Review*, xix (1957), 383.
[16] *Sewanee Review*, lxi (1953), 27.

'cymbal of clash', and then asking of the contrarieties what
'actual human situation' it is that they converge upon. Even
with 'Bacchus', story is very much to the point; first, in that
Empson's notes (too handily notorious) are primarily concerned
to make clear the story which the poem tells; and second, in
that the poem itself is concerned to progress from its initial
story, a story which is allegory, to its conclusive story, a story
which is an 'actual human situation'. The final twenty lines of
the poem, which marry exultation and despair, give the ascen-
dancy to the human story; in the simple words of Empson's
note on the record, 'The poem then turns to an actual lady feeling what it has tried to describe.' But it is not only the poem
which gains in dignity and humanity when story is respected;
the same is true of a critical apprehension. Since Empson's
poems are known to be alive with significances (and sometimes
stillborn with them, as is 'Plenum and Vacuum'), and Empson's
criticism likewise, a critic is liable to be hypnotized by meaning—wrongly because exclusively, or wrongly because meaning in poetry finds itself too narrowly conceived. In 'Aubade',
after the earthquake: 'Then I said The Garden? Laughing she
said No.' No critical apprehension can come to anything much
here which is not grounded upon the story, upon the fact that
'The Garden?' in the first place, in the actual human situation,
means 'Is it safer to be out in the garden or inside the house
when an earthquake has started?'

The year before he published 'Aubade', Empson made an
essential point about obscurity in poetry when defending
W. H. Auden against some strictures from David Daiches:

The following line from Auden's *Orators* is quoted as 'free association',
therefore demonstrably bad or rather null. It seems to me plain
realism.

      Well?
      As a matter of fact the farm was in Pembrokeshire.

We are told that though the separate lines of the poem have isolated
prose meanings they are only connected by Auden's memory or subconsciousness, so cannot make poetry. But if you get the general
context, of a man making a shameful confession, this creaking pretence of ease and nervous jerk into irrelevance is no kind of breach
with 'meaning', whether with poetry or not; nor is it 'obscure'. It is
a piece of horrible photography, and I remember shuddering as I first

set eyes on it. But of course if a critic goes on expecting Pembrokeshire
to symbolize something he is likely to get irritated. Often indeed
when a poem goes on living in your mind, demanding to be re-read,
you do not so much penetrate what at first seemed its obscurities as
forget them; they turn out to be irrelevant. The critic therefore cannot come in and demonstrate that a poem is bad because it has no
meaning—obviously, in the first place, because he may merely not
know the meaning, but he can say it is too hard to know; yet there
may be an answer to this too—that he is wrong to expect a meaning at
the point he has chosen.[17]

What liberates Empson's criticism here—and Auden's line—is
the respect for story. So the hope is that to ask about the story
in Empson's poems will help with their meaning, not only in
making clearer at some points what their meaning is, but also
in making clearer at others why it is not exactly meaning that
we should be expecting.

II

'Like involves maintaining oneself between contradictions that
can't be solved by analysis; e.g. those of philosophy, which
apply to all creatures, and the religious one about man being
both animal and divine.' Empson's note to 'Bacchus' is well
known, and known to widen out to take in a great many of his
other poems; among them 'Arachne', which sets out life's contradictions with gruesome neatness; 'Aubade', with its antithetical refrains; and 'Let it go', where 'The contradictions
cover such a range'. Empson has always been explicit about
contradiction and conflict as the foundation of his poems—a
true foundation for them because so for all poems and, wider
yet, because of what life is. 'To take real pleasure in verse' is to
feel 'so straddling a commotion and so broad a calm'.[18] This is
what we value in poems: 'That all these good qualities should
be brought together is a normal part of a good poem; indeed, it
is a main part of the value of a poem, because they are so hard
to bring together in life'. It is what we value in myths, where
'incompatibles are joined'.[19] And in goddesses: Venus in

[17] *Criterion*, xv (1936), 519.
[18] *Seven Types of Ambiguity* (1930), 1947 edn, pp. xv, 114.
[19] *The Structure of Complex Words* (1951), p. 242.

Shakespeare's poem remains somehow cool and calmly good, and 'the suggestion that the rowdy and lustful Venus keeps all these qualities makes her a goddess because she resolves the contradictions of normal life'.[20]

Such is the *raison d'être* of ambiguity, Empson's first book of criticism; of pastoral and irony, his second; and of complex words, his third, where for instance 'the honest man in achieving normality reconciles a contradiction'.[21] What is true of the arts is simply true of people: 'Indeed the way in which a person lives by these vaguely conceived opposites is the most important thing about his make-up; the way in which opposites can be stated so as to satisfy a wide variety of people, for a great number of degrees of interpretation, is the most important thing about the communication of the arts'.[22]

Yet there are two further dimensions of contradiction which man must accommodate to brace him. The first we glimpse in an uncharacteristic hesitancy ('it may be . . . '), when Empson remarks that 'it may be that the human mind can recognize actually incommensurable values, and that the chief human value is to stand up between them'.[23] One would have thought it plain that for Empson this is indeed the chief human value. Why then his hesitancy? Because he is aware of this further dimension of contradiction: that one should reject absolutes and even primacies, and should then accord an absolute status or a primacy to doing so. T. S. Eliot remarked: 'we can always accuse the pragmatist of believing his own doctrine in a sense which is not pragmatic but absolute—in other words, of eating his cake and having it too'.[24] Similarly Empson saw that I. A. Richards was involved in some such straddling but that this was inevitable. Of Beauty in *The Foundations of Aesthetics* (by Richards, Ogden, and Wood), Empson says, reviewing the book's reissue:

There is an inherent tug between the tentative solution of the problem, offered in the last chapter, and the theory of Multiple Definition presented before. This is inherently concerned to say that in such

[20] *Criterion*, xiv (1935), 485.
[21] *Complex Words*, p. 196.
[22] *Seven Types*, p. 221.
[23] *Complex Words*, p. 421.
[24] *New Statesman*, 29 December 1917.

cases one should tabulate the sixteen or more meanings of the term in question and expect nothing further. What you have gained by your tabulation is that you can no longer be deceived—never again will an argument by an aesthetician prevent you from appreciating something unusual but good, or force you into admiring a narrow type of mysticism. But if the last chapter gives the answer, and furthermore if all the deluded aestheticians were actually fumbling after this solution, so that they would be convinced once they had been given it, then the whole position is quite different. All their sentences are simply wrong even from their own point of view, and they could be made to see it, had we but world enough and time. This fundamental ambivalence of course makes the book more interesting. But after the lapse of a generation one ought to be able to form some kind of view about which side holds the field, whether the Multiple Definition theory or the Synaesthesis theory has survived. If they both survive for ever they are only another of those tedious pairs of frustrated Kilkenny cats, like Aristotle and Plato.

The extreme brevity and caution, not to say timidity, of the final chapter puts the weight in favour of the Multiple Definition technique. But I have long been inclined to believe that the Ogden-Richards programme really did say what Beauty is, though of course only in a rough, tentative manner. If so, it is rather embarrassing for them; they are left with an Absolute Beauty on their hands, a baby which they never expected to have the trouble of bringing up. For that matter when Professor Richards wrote *The Principles of Literary Criticism*, not long after, he felt he needed to put in a chapter which in effect saddled him with an Absolute Goodness, an even more unwelcome baby. It is a familiar paradox; any serious attempt at establishing a relativity turns out to establish an absolute; in the case of Einstein the velocity of light, and I understand a good deal more by this time.[25]

There remains a further vista. For Empson—in poetry and in prose—insists not only that we must stand up between incommensurable values, but also that we must move, act, do something. The refusal to act or to decide, however rich its contemplation of complexity, is an act of indecision; prolonged, it can have no end but paralysis and neurosis. So among our other contradictions not the least is the tug between a reflective duty and a practical one. Empson's consciousness that 'life involves maintaining oneself between contradictions' is tensed against a further antithesis: that maintaining oneself is not

[25] *Hudson Review*, ii (1949), 95.

enough in life. Hence his claim about the casket-scene in *The Merchant of Venice*: 'What the allegory meant to Shakespeare was probably something rather different from the Christian interpretation; I think it was that you ought to accept the actualities of life courageously even if rather unscrupulously, and not try to gloss over its contradictions and the depths that lie under your feet'.[26]

III

Empson has always written with poignancy and urgency about decisions. His poem 'Doctrinal Point', as he says, 'yearns to be always sure what to do' (record-notes):

> Magnolias, for instance, when in bud,
> Are right in doing anything they can think of;
> Free by predestination in the blood,
> Saved by their own sap, shed for themselves,
> Their texture can impose their architecture;
> Their sapient matter is always already informed.
>
> Whether they burgeon, massed wax flames, or flare
> Plump spaced-out saints, in their gross prime, at prayer,
> Or leave the sooted branches bare
> To sag at tip from a sole blossom there
> They know no act that will not make them fair.

'High Dive', his most cryptic and elaborated conception of what decision is, knows that 'One would be ashamed to walk down; the proper thing is to take a decisive action whose results are incalculable' (record-notes).

The shadowy, the complex, the inherited, the assumed, all play a part in decision. Hence Empson's view of 'the main business of a novelist':

By the very structure of the sentences, we are made to know what it felt like for the heroine to make up her mind. Of course in itself this is not new; it is the main business of a novelist to show his reader, by slow accumulations, all the elements and proportions of a decision, so that the reader knows how the character felt about it; but Mrs Woolf, so as to be much more immediately illuminating, can show how they are at the back of a decision at the moment it is taken.[27]

---

[26] *Complex Words*, p. 124.   [27] *Scrutinies II*, pp. 210-11.

What sustains and invigorates *The Structure of Complex Words* is Empson's justified confidence that such verbal complexities are intimately involved in everyday decision: 'A man tends finally to make up his mind, in a practical question of human relations, much more in terms of these vague rich intimate words than in the clear words of his official language'.[28] When Empson lets drop the word *decide* in writing of King Lear, it enforces respect and humanity: '"O sides, you are too tough" implies that an explosion, even perhaps of madness, would be a relief, but as the insults sharpen he becomes wary and decides not to let them send him mad'. A sense of Ezra Pound's personal tragedy, as well as of his misguided aesthetic, informs Empson's remark that 'the way his mind decides for him is rather too much above his own head'.[29]

There is in Empson a deep sympathy for those confronted with decision, as when he says of *Ulysses*:

All this background seems fussy and pedantic until you realize that it builds up the terrible refusal to choose, done by Stephen in the Question-and-Answer chapter . . . The chapter certainly need not be taken to mean that Stephen will never accept; surely the chief point of it is that in real life he couldn't decide, at such a peculiarly exhausting moment.[30]

To remind ourselves of what, for Empson, it is that Stephen was having to decide, is a direct route to Empson's poems and to a contrariety they embody. For Stephen is deciding whether or not to sleep with Molly Bloom and (consequentially) whether to free Bloom to father a son. In Empson's poems, as in the life of any sensitive person, the fear of a commitment to love is entwined with the fear of that most daunting and exhilarating of all human commitments, the begetting of a new life. As Empson said à propos of Imagery (in a sentence, incidentally, which speaks of 'the variety of life and the decisiveness of the immediate judgments upon it'), what is to be deduced from a poem is 'usually a very plain fact of life'.[31] The plainest fact of life must be the facts of life. A great many of Empson's poems

[28] pp. 158, 133.
[29] *British Journal of Aesthetics*, ii (1962), 50.
[30] *A James Joyce Miscellany*, p. 133.
[31] *British Journal of Aesthetics*, ii (1962), 50.

seem to me to comprise within their story or situation a sense of
this most incalculable of high dives, the getting of children. But
let me first quote one of Empson's most fervid responses to
a man's decision:

Donne really does intend to boast about his marriage; you can impute
bad motives to him, or lies, and you are within the field of human
probability, but if you say he insinuated a 'bitter irony' into the
middle of this fighting and defiant praise of the most decisive action
of his life you are mistaking him for some other author.[32]

A glory of Donne is the intensity alike of his uniqueness and
of his commonalty; it is splendidly true that his marriage was
specially courageous, and yet true too that for many people the
most decisive action of their lives is their marriage. Unless it is
their getting a child. For that act is even more awe-inspiring; of
all decisions it is the most grandly simple and extensive, in
being a decision to create a life which will itself then make
decisions; in being so supremely irrevocable (even more so
than the act of marrying); and in that its status as a decision—
is it a decision, exactly?—is so insinuatingly in doubt. One
could always feel that, with so much uncertainty about it, the
steely responsibility of a decision need never quite make itself
felt; the lap, that of the gods. Contraception has complicated
and intensified all this, in that it patently heightens decision.
Of Othello's jealousy, Empson has said: 'it seems to me that
Othello's principles about the matter were all wrong, let alone
the way he applied them. The advent of contraceptives has
taken a lot of strain off the topic'.[33] But contraception has not
simply taken strain off the decision to have children, as against
the decision not to have them; on the contrary, it has in some
respects intensified the strain, in that it has made choice (decision, and responsibility unignorably entered upon) more
manifestly part of the act of love. Nothing ever simply reduces
strain all round, and one need not be in any way unappreciative
of contraception in maintaining that it does nothing to lessen,
and something to heighten, certain strains inseparable from
this grave decision. Most people's lives have at some point
been haunted and thrilled by this gravest of responsibilities,
albeit in imagination or in anticipation; not many poems recog-

<hr/>

[32] *Just So Much Honor*, p. 124.   [33] *Complex Words*, p. 245.

WILLIAM EMPSON   189

nize this but Empson's poems do, sometimes being truly fearful and at other times truly robust.

                            IV

For anybody, begetting a child is a high and deep decision. But
for those who believe certain things of life it involves maintaining oneself between contradictions. It is not rare for people to
believe that the world, or the world now, is such that children
should not be brought into it; it is uncommon, though by no
means unheard of, for people to act upon this belief, and on
principle to have no children; more usual is for people both to
acknowledge the force of a grim truth and yet also to have children because of what seems a different duty and delight. In so
far as they involve such feelings Empson's poems are not a bit
abstruse or idiosyncratic. But such feelings did press with
further force in his case. For it is not just the conditions of
modern life (rectifiable perhaps?, the would-be parent may ask
faintly), but the very conditions of life which have seemed tragic
to Empson. To anybody convinced of how much pain, waste,
loss, and despair there is in life, it must be always be a question;
believing life to be so, why create a child to endure it?

    Granted, Empson's crucially sombre word *waste* can some-
times leave room for an accompanying delight, as when he says
of Virginia Woolf that 'her images, glittering and searching as
they are, spreading out their wealth of feeling, as if spilt, in the
mind, give one just that sense of waste that is given by life
itself'.[34] But elsewhere the sad weight of Empson's words is
such as to make it a real question whether life is a gift we should'
give. 'The waste remains, the waste remains and kills.'

It is only in degree that any improvement of society could prevent
wastage of human powers; the waste even in a fortunate life, the
isolation even of a life rich in intimacy, cannot but be felt deeply, and
is the central feeling of tragedy.[35]

'Isolation' and 'intimacy' there hint at that creation, the family,
which both fosters what is good and protective in life and also
furthers life which cannot be protected. A child, then, can be
the bleakest reminder of the loss inherent in life:

[34] *Scrutinies II*, p. 216.   [35] *Some Versions of Pastoral* (1935), pp. 5, 260-1.

It [a Romantic and Victorian feeling about children] depends on a feeling . . . that no way of building up character, no intellectual system, can bring out all that is inherent in the human spirit, and therefore that there is more in the child than any man has been able to keep.

It is natural that the most ringing and yet most secure expression of such feelings in Empson should embody one of life's contradictions: 'The feeling that life is essentially inadequate to the human spirit, and yet that a good life must avoid saying so, is naturally at home with most versions of pastoral'.[36] Naturally at home too with Empson, the very prose makes that clear; and yet implicated in parenthood's decision. For if life is essentially inadequate to the human spirit, should we blithely create new human spirits? And if we should, must it not be with the same consciousness of an unappeasable other principle, unappeased but overruled, which informs our other decisions in life?

There is no doubt about the gaiety and buoyancy that are also strong in Empson. But the darkness is no less deep than they are. Of *Measure for Measure* he says (and it is patently true to his own beliefs) that it includes 'the idea that one must not act on these absolutes prematurely. Even granting that the conditions of life are inherently repulsive, a man makes himself actually more repulsive by acting on this truth'.[37] The paradox and the straddling make clear that what is at stake is close to Empson's heart, and 'Even granting . . . ' is not a mere granting, a purely concessive entertaining of a supposition totally at odds with Empson's own sense of life. (Nor does it comprise the major part of his sense of life.) Empson has, after all, reprinted from his first book of poems that translation from *The Fire Sermon* which now stands as the full-page epigraph to his *Collected Poems*; it is true that he urged Allan Rodway not to make so much of it, but his way of doing so was scrupulous and therefore revelatory:

The Fire Sermon itself is unlike most of Buddhism, and leaves Christianity far behind, in maintaining that all existence as such, even in the highest heaven, is inherently evil. Such is the great interest of it . . . But, all the same, when I mention fire in my verse I mean it to have the usual confused background of ideas, not (as Mr Rodway

[36] *Some Versions*, p. 114.   [37] *Complex Words*, p. 284.

thinks) the specific and raging dogma of the Fire Sermon. I can be sure of this because, though I probably never thought about the Fire Sermon when writing or revising, I had already decided that I thought its doctrine wrong, though fascinating and in a way intelligible. You might say that it is present as one extreme of the range of human thought, because the poetry often tries to take the position 'what I am saying is admitted to be true, though people look at it in so many different ways'; but even so it is pretty remote, and not appealed to.[38]

If all existence is inherently evil, we should think twice about bringing anything into existence.

Moreover Empson has drawn attention to some such tug in two poets who particularly matter to him. Of Rochester's 'Satire on Man', he has said: 'One cannot help regarding it less as a general truth than as a source of evidence about the deep dissatisfaction or resentment with the world which drove him to his death'.[39] Of Dylan Thomas: 'You must realise that he was a very witty man, with a very keen though not at all poisoned recognition that the world contains horror as well as delight; his chief power as a stylist is to convey a sickened loathing which somehow (within the phrase) enforces a welcome for the eternal necessities of the world'.[40] Much of that strange loathing and welcoming is directed by Thomas to thinking about begetting, and one remembers Empson's comment on 'Before I knocked and flesh let enter': 'Jesus by choosing virginity ended an immense series of births, betraying the purpose of the creator which his mother had obeyed; but he did not end it for Dylan Thomas'.[41]

Empson's recognition of the world is likewise 'not at all poisoned'. But it is styptic; think of the terms in which he ends his essay on *Hamlet*:

The eventual question is whether you can put up with the final Hamlet, a person who frequently appears in the modern world under various disguises, whether by Shakespeare's fault or no. I would always sympathize with anyone who says, like Hugh Kingsmill, that he can't put up with Hamlet at all. But I am afraid it is within hail of

[38] *Essays in Criticism*, vi (1956), 481-2.
[39] *New Statesman*, 28 November 1953.
[40] *New Statesman*, 15 May 1954.
[41] *Listener*, 28 October 1971.

the more painful question whether you can put up with yourself and
the race of man.[42]

A real question for Empson and not just a final flourish; a question then which must ask us why we wish to further the race
of man.

Yet I can't help being aware that Empson is likely to repudi-
ate this bit at least; I must say why I think this may be so,
especially as it bears on his having given up writing poetry since
1951 (and very little in the ten years before that).

The various tensions and contradictions involved in begetting were not only one of the important subjects but one of the
important sources of energy for his poems. An enabling tension
was that between the ordinary human wish to beget life and the
equally ordinary sense that life is too dark and bleak a gift. But
this tension has progressively slackened for Empson. In the first
place, for good personal reasons—it is after all a tension more
likely to precede than to follow parenthood, and Empson's giving up writing poetry dates more or less (the later poems are
important but very few) from his marriage in 1941 and his
becoming a father in the following years. In the second place,
because of a shift of belief. Empson no longer has quite the
same sense of life; or, more specifically, the main thrust of his
writing since 1951 has been against those 'neo-Christians' who
peddle a wilfully gloomy and lowminded account of this life.
The necessity to dissociate himself from such monkishness has
increasingly made Empson put his stress where he had not previously put it. His earlier semi-acknowledgment that 'life is
essentially inadequate to the human spirit' could too easily be
wrested to give comfort (that is, a gratifying comfortlessness) to
the enemy.

In 1949 Empson could still feel that the holy enemy was 'holy
optimism', as when he objected to R. B. Heilman's 'evasive
pietistic technique' at work on one of 'the key sentences of the
play [King Lear] expressing despair':

> When we are borne, we cry that we are come
> To this great stage of Fooles.

Empson insisted that 'the main statement is very plain and says
that life on earth is an evil. To twist it round into a bit of holy

---

[42] *Sewanee Review*, lxi (1953), 205.

optimism seems to me to falsify the play'.[43] Lear's words are a key sentence in more than one way, since they seize upon the idea that the baby at the moment of its birth is uniquely able to testify to the wrong that has been done to it in having been born. As Empson said elsewhere: 'To the Freudian, indeed, it is the human infant to whose desires this life is essentially inadequate; King Lear found a mystical pathos in the fact that the human infant, alone among the young of the creatures, is subject to impotent fits of fury'.[44]

Still, in 1949 'holy optimism' shocked Empson; since then, it has been holy pessimism which he has set himself to challenge. 'Modern critics tend to assume both (a) that it isn't artistic to preach any doctrine and (b) that the only high-minded doctrine to preach is despair and contempt for the world'.[45] (What Empson's poems do with despair is not preach it—but few poems have made more, and so variously, of the word.) *Tom Jones* possesses its secret: 'Actually, the modern critic does know what kind of thing the secret is; but he has been badgered by neoclassicism and neo-Christianity and what not, whereas the secret is humanist, liberal, materialist, recommending happiness on earth.' No more than Fielding are we to concur with the Old Man of the Hill, 'who thanks God he has renounced so lunatic a world'. In the same vein, of *When We Dead Awaken*: 'there is nothing in the play to show that Ibsen isn't being "mystical", in the sense of simply praising the double suicide as a means of getting to a less nasty world'.[46]

It is on these grounds that Empson repudiates Maynard Mack's view of *King Lear*: 'Shakespeare's audience too would want to know what the saint will do next, after his daughter is killed; how the story will go on. It makes one realize the peculiarity of the assumptions of Professor Mack; who, as he only wants to hear a monk telling the audience to be monks, will not admit that there is any story at all'.[47] When Mack speaks of the play as a 'metaphor, or myth, about the human condition', Empson swoops: 'What the metaphor recommends, so far as we can gather, is becoming a monk or a yogi, on the ground

[43] *Kenyon Review*, xi (1949), 350.
[44] *Some Versions*, p. 249.
[45] *Kenyon Review*, xx (1958), 217.
[46] *A James Joyce Miscellany*, p. 143.
[47] *Essays in Criticism*, xvii (1967), 102.

that the world is inherently inadequate for us.' Yet aren't those last words, offered for our scorn, perilously close to what had once been offered for our chastened acceptance: that 'life is essentially inadequate to the human spirit'?

In 1964 Empson repudiated the slander that he had in one particular way slandered God the Father: 'I did not say he was bad because he created the world, and I think that idea a disgusting one. It is petulant snootiness to say "The world is not good enough for me"; the world is glorious beyond all telling, and far too good for any of us'.[48] The energy and generosity of that are fine (and they know their enemy), but they manifest an energy of a very different kind, and of a very different direction, from that which centrally animated Empson's poems, delighted though the poems are too by the rich oddity of the world.

In suggesting that Empson's poems found power and truth in the tug between a sense of life's darkness (which would sway us not to bring children into life) and a sense of the deep right wish to propagate, I am not implying any neurosis or personal predicament in the poet; it is ordinary to feel some such tug, and in so far as these poems feel a more than ordinary tug that is because of a public—perfectly discussable—commitment to certain beliefs, and in particular to beliefs about where we stand: between contradictions. Again, in stressing a shift, at least in emphasis, in Empson's sense of the world, at one with his crusade against neo-Christianity, I am not implying that he was ever much of a monk, or that he has modified his views for combative purposes, but simply pointing out that the new energies and emphases are very different—a fact which (whether as chicken or as egg) is likely to have something to do with Empson's stopping writing poetry. The holy and the monkish are certainly part of this shrubbery of ideas, for Empson as for most people. Take his words about Philip II: 'One could hardly say that he got Portugal by marriage; he got it because the more direct male heirs of that house had become too holy to produce children'.[49] Or this: 'A monk oughtn't to have a baby, but somebody else has to have babies, if only to keep up the supply of monks'.[50] Or Empson's deploring the critic who finds

[48] *Critical Quarterly*, vi (1964), 83.
[49] *Elizabethan Drama*, ed. Kaufman, p. 67.
[50] *Critical Quarterly*, vi (1964), 83.

'The Ancient Mariner' 'a spiritual allegory in which the neo-
phyte (the Guest) is gradually beaten down until he attains ''a
thorough acceptance of spiritual values'', and after that, of
course, he can't breed'.[51]

V

The many dismaying parenthoods in the story of Oedipus have
long been important to Empson: witness his poem 'Four Legs,
Three Legs, Two Legs', or the play which he wrote as an under-
graduate, *Three Stories*, of which *Granta* in 1927 spoke with a
graceless ambiguity: 'He had achieved an almost complete mas-
tery of his Oedipus complex, and used it for very intelligent
purposes.' His criticism too has surged with it, most obviously
on *Hamlet*:

A feeling that this hero is allowed to act in a peculiar way which is yet
somehow familiar, because one has been tempted to do it oneself, is
surely part of the essence of the story. There is a clear contrast with
Oedipus, who had no Oedipus Complex. He had not wanted to kill
his father and marry his mother, even 'unconsciously'; if he came to
recognize that he had wanted it, that would weaken his bleak surprise
at learning he had done it.[52]

But more important than the Oedipus Complex is ordinary
parenthood, more simply fearful and strange. Empson's criticism has always been especially vivid, imaginative and central
when it contemplates parenthood, its responsibilities and the
world's. He thinks with humanity about those who are thinking about it; his rebuke to D. A. Traversi focuses upon Perdita's
cool courage in using the word *breed*:

> No more than were I painted, I would wish
> This youth should say 'twer well: and onely therefore
> Desire to breed by me.
> *(The Winter's Tale*, IV iv)

All the talk about the flowers, which Mr Traversi finds symbolic, was
unlikely to hit an audience with any shock. What did do that was the
word *breed* used coolly by a young virgin. It would sound shameless if

[51] *Coleridge's Verse: A Selection* (1972), p. 77.
[52] *Sewanee Review*, lxi (1953), 202.

she were less fiercely virtuous; but somehow the effect of being so
farmyard is to appear very aristocratic.[53]

He delights in her virgin generosity and pluck, and he had
manifested a comparable zest when it suddenly came to him that
Tennyson was making a practical point about the high snow-
pure barrenness of virginity in *The Princess*:

When I was ski-ing recently I found myself reciting that Love is of the
valleys:

'nor cares to walk
With Death and Morning on the silver horns',

and suddenly realized that that grand lyric comes from *The Princess*. It
means that the girls won't get husbands if they go to college, and if
you start from there all the description fits in.[54]

There is, once more, his reading of *Ulysses*:

Bloom is described, with startling literary power so that there is no
doubt about it, as having a very specific neurosis: the death of his
infant son ten years before gave him a horror of the business of having a child so that he can't try to have another one. At the same time
he longs to have a son, and so does Molly . . . He feels that if he could
plant on her a lover he was fond of, who would even take his advice
instead of jeering at him, he could even now have this son himself by
his wife . . . To be sure, the novel does not ask you to believe that
Bloom *did* have a son, but it does expect you to believe that on this
day Bloom is getting a real opportunity to produce a son; the problem
as it is shown to you is not trivial.[55]

Such is the largeness of a story; it is characteristic too of
Empson that he should submit himself to a detail of wording, as
in his question about the first sentence of Dylan Thomas's 'A
Refusal to Mourn the Death, by Fire, of a Child in London';
Empson ponders 'the distinction between *making* and *fathering*;
perhaps the construction of *mankind* is a special process, as in
Genesis'.[56] A special process for mankind, certainly; the difference between the birth of a child and that of a flower or a leaf
is seen with cool responsible pathos in a ballad:

---

[53] *Times Literary Supplement*, 23 April 1964; similarly, *British Journal of Aesthetics*, ii
(1962), 51-2.

[54] *Criterion*, xvii (1937), 128.

[55] *A James Joyce Miscellany*, pp. 132, 134.

[56] *Strand Magazine* (March 1947), 60-4. Reprinted in *Modern Poetry*, ed. John
Hollander (1968), p. 244.

> She leaned her back against a thorn
> (Fine flowers in the valley)
> And there she has her young child born
> (And the green leaves they grow rarely).

'The effect of the contrast is not simple; perhaps it says "Life went on, and in a way this seems a cruel indifference to her suffering, but it lets us put the tragedy in its place, as we do when we sing about it for pleasure" '.[57]

Parenthood, though, is more than—though seldom less than —giving birth. I think of Empson's insistence that when one ponders the soldier's question before the dead Cleopatra, 'Is this well done?', 'one must remember that by choosing this death she destroys her children only to avoid a hurt to her pride'.[58] Or his response to *Paradise Lost*, where he exults in what the poetry intimates ('Nor where *Abassin* Kings thir issue Guard': 'all the references to guarding children remind us that children were the result of the fall');[59] but where he excoriates Milton's God for withholding from Adam and Eve a clear warning that their posterity would suffer the results of the Fall. Or there is Empson's discussion of 'The Phoenix and Turtle', which asks us to recall the story, the human situation, of Sir John Salisbury, a story of progeny: 'The subsequent poems all deal with Salisbury's domestic life, wife or child being mentioned every time, so that Shakespeare's poem acts as a watershed'.[60] Shakespeare's poem, moreover, is about a principled abstention from parenthood: 'Oddly enough Shakespeare manages to work the same reflection [as Jonson] into his mood of total praise; the reproduction of the Phoenix, he surmises, has only failed because of the married chastity of the couple':

> Leaving no posteritie,
> 'Twas not their infirmitie,
> It was married Chastitie.

A scarcely less mysterious abstention from parenthood is the subject of many of Shakespeare's Sonnets, among them some which most engaged Empson early in *Seven Types of Ambiguity*.

> Which eyes not yet created shall ore-read . . .
> (Sonnet 81)

[57] *Complex Words*, pp. 347-8.
[59] *Some Versions*, p. 174.
[58] *Some Versions*, pp. 233-4.
[60] *Shakespeare: Narrative Poems*, p. xliii.

These shadows of his perfection were once to have been his children,
but Shakespeare's partly scoptophile desire to see him settled in love
has by now been with a painful irony thwarted or over-satisfied , and
they are now no more than those who read his praise.[61]

Empson's exploration of these Sonnets does justice to both
pulls here: first a recognition of a natural trepidation at the prospect of parenthood, which paraphases 'To give away your selfe,
keeps your selfe still' (Sonnet 16) as 'you are not less yourself
because you have had children'—indeed not, but the idea is
not at all thought to be a mad one, and has its undeniable mag-
netism; but second a recognition that we too, like Shakespeare,
would have to call upon an Irish bull (with its genially mysterious self-enfoldedness) to assert the purpose of the creator:
'You had a Father, let your Son say so' (Sonnet 13).

   Again, there is a special urgency in Empson's challenge to
L. C. Knights (delivered twice), since it manifests the meeting
of a central plea to respect story with a most bitter childlessness.

The great question 'How many children had Lady Macbeth?' had
better be fitted in here. The question cannot be regarded as merely
farcical, as one might say, 'Who wants children anyhow?' Macbeth is
far more concerned to found a royal line than to be king himself; he
howls on and on against the threat that his descendants will be sup-
planted by Banquo's. When Lady Macbeth says she would kill her
child she is felt to be ridiculous as well as devilish, because without a
child the main purpose would be defeated. But the murdered or the
helpless child comes echoing back into the play all through (as Mr
Cleanth Brooks pointed out); it is the one thing strong enough to
defeat Macbeth and the whole philosophy he has adopted. In the
story, however, we are left in doubt whether the Macbeths have any
children; it would be symbolically appropriate if they hadn't, but
Macbeth's talk would be absurd unless they have, as perhaps it is;
and there the matter is left. It is the only crux in the play, I think,
which need be regarded as a radical dramatic ambiguity.[62]

In one of his most striking speeches, Macbeth implies that he has in-
curred Hell for the sake of his family, sacrificing himself to found a
dynasty ('To make *them* Kings? The sons of Banquo, Kings?'). He is
the last person to have thought it didn't matter whether he had a son
or not.[63]

[61] *Seven Types*, pp. 53-4, 56, 52.
[62] *Kenyon Review*, xiv (1952), 91.
[63] *Critical Quarterly*, vii (1965), 285.

Such is childlessness as nemesis. Empson has been no less vivid about the opposite terror, parenthood as nemesis: 'There are times when Lear maintains that vengeance is the due of all parenthood, however licit'.

> Is it the fashion, that discarded Fathers,
> Should have thus little mercy on their flesh:
> Judicious punishment, 'twas this flesh begot
> Those Pelicane Daughters.

'He starts saying this as soon as he is mad; it is treated as a signal to the audience that he is now mad.'[64] It is Empson's sanity which rightly insists that we know Lear to be mad to consider parenthood so; but the poignancy of Lear's words, and of Empson's comment, is a matter of yet finding the hideous sentiment appallingly magnetic. As with Edgar:

> The Gods are just, and of our pleasant vices
> Make instruments to plague us:
> The dark and vitious place where thee he got,
> Cost him his eyes.

'And the thrill of Edgar's remark, sure enough, is to imply: "He begot a monster by it; yourself who betrayed him to torture and death." ' An implication and a thrill to be resisted. The critical mind which responds so deeply and truly to such imaginings is not one which can invariably contemplate begetting with equanimity.

At the other extreme, relatedly so, is Empson's Alice. Many have thought this essay his best sustained criticism of a single work. If it is so, that may be because Empson's tart affection, sympathy, and respect for Alice are so truly matched by a deep comprehension of Lewis Carroll's bachelorhood, incorporating a dismay at most children which is by no means abolished by a delight in a special child. Empson's prose rises to a delicious hyperbole of such dismayed distaste, with the prose not shrinking at all at its imagined shrinking:

One need not read Dodgson's satirical verses against babies to see how much he would dislike a child wallowing in its tears in real life. The fondness of small girls for doing this has to be faced early in attempting to prefer them, possibly to small boys, certainly to grown-ups;

[64] *Essays in Criticism*, xvii (1967), 98.

to a man idealising children as free from the falsity of a rich emotional life their displays of emotion must be particularly disconcerting. The celibate may be forced to observe them, on the floor of a railway carriage for example, after a storm of fury, dabbling in their ooze; covertly snuggling against mamma while each still pretends to ignore the other.[65]

Empson is no celibate, but he is invigoratingly free from condescension towards celibates because he is not lordlily free from their dismays.

It may be objected that I am making too much of those things in Empson's criticism which respond strongly to parenthood, in that any critic who has much interest in life is likely to have something to say on so important a matter. In fact it would be very difficult to assemble worthwhile *aperçus* on parenthood and begetting from many a distinguished critic, and in any case Empson's sensibility and conscience have here been exceptionally moved. Let me quote two paragraphs from a poetry review in 1931; the humanity, lucidity, and courtesy with which the first poet is dispraised and the second praised have a lot to do with story, with what is at issue in the respective poems: two versions of parenthood and of other-worldliness.

Mr Robinson Jeffers, like Mr Galsworthy, often seems to write from his conscience rather than his sensibility. He chooses painful subjects, one may suspect, less because he feels strongly about them than because he feels it shameful not to feel strongly about them; because one cannot be comfortable and unimaginative, with the world as it is. You may honour this feeling very much and yet say it does not produce good writing; it gives an air of poking at the reader, or trying to catch him on the raw, and it tends to falsify a dramatic issue. At the crisis of the 'Loving Shepherdess' the hero nearly remembers that her life could be saved by a Caesarean operation: he can't quite think of it, and the word Caesar, thus suggested, becomes a vision of human and then heavenly glory, which is described very finely and apparently justifies his failure to help her. For a moment this may seem the soul of tragedy, but next moment it seems cock-eyed. He had remembered enough to tell her to go to a clinic, anyway; I speak under correction about visions, but I don't believe he would have had a vision just then if he had not been a shamefully self-centred person.

'Marina' seems to me one of Mr Eliot's very good poems; better than

---

[65] *Some Versions*, p. 272.

anything in 'Ash-Wednesday'. The dramatic power of his symbolism is here in full strength, and the ideas involved have almost the range of interest, the full orchestra, of the 'Waste Land'. One main reason for this is the balance maintained between otherworldliness and humanism; the essence of the poem is the vision of an order, a spiritual state, which he can conceive and cannot enter, but it is not made clear whether he conceives an order in this world to be known by a later generation (like Moses on Pisgah) or the life in heaven which is to be obtained after death (like Dante). One might at first think the second only was meant, but Marina, after all, was a real daughter; is now at sea, like himself, rather than already in the Promised Land; and is to live 'in a world of time beyond me', which can scarcely be a description of Heaven. At any rate, the humanist meaning is used at every point as a symbol of the otherworldly one; this seems the main point to insist on in a brief notice because it is the main cause of the richness of the total effect. In either case the theme is the peril and brevity of such vision.[66]

VI

It was always clear that Empson's poems were graced by Donne, and he has been explicit about it more than once:

In the twenties, when my eyes were opening, it was usual for critics to consider that Donne in his earlier poetry held broad and enlightened views on church and state, that he was influenced by the recent great scientific discoveries, and that he used the theme of freedom in love partly as a vehicle for these ideas . . . I was imitating this Donne, the poet as so conceived, in my own verse at the time with love and wonder, and I have never in later years come across any good reason for the universal change of opinion about him at the start of the thirties.[67]

For Empson, and for his poems, Donne's love-poems embody a defiance of church and state, an adventurous freedom brought home by 'making the idea of the inhabited planet a symbol of the lovers' independence from the world'.[68] Hence Empson's title 'Donne the Space Man'. Or, twenty years earlier:

[66] *Nation and Athenaeum*, 21 February 1931.
[67] *Just So Much Honor*, p. 95; similarly, *Kenyon Review*, xix (1957), 337-99, and *Critical Quarterly*, viii (1966), 255-6.
[68] *Sewanee Review*, lxiii (1955), 477.

The idea that you can get right away to America, that human affairs
are not organised round one centrally right authority (e.g. the Pope)
is directly compared to the new idea that there are other worlds like
this one, so that the inhabitants of each can live in their own way.[69]

My argument about Empson's poems does not entail a consideration of just how much truth there is in this view of
Donne; but it entails some other questions. If Donne's poems
celebrate freedom and independence, do they limit that to independence from church and state? Or do they in some way recognize those other threats or limitations upon the freedom and
independence of young lovers, those involved in parenthood,
both in our being children and in our perhaps begetting them?
After all, 'one centrally right authority' may be that of the
family from which we depend (often at one with church and
state but not to be escaped by escaping those); an inherent ob-
stacle to young lovers' simply being able to 'live in their own
way' is the family, both that to which we belong and that which
may come to belong to us.

Praising Donne, Empson spoke of 'that secret largeness of
outlook which is his fascination'.[70] Some of that secret largeness is to be divined in the particular way in which the poems
celebrate young love's freedom from parenthood, young love
seen at a moment when it has the right, for now, to be free from
responsibilities to its heirs. Donne's best poems are rich in the
way Empson suggests, with a buoyancy of freedom; yet they
feel quite without sentimentality, whereas there would be sentimentality in a presentation of young love as naturally, always,
everywhere, for ever independent of all which family brings as
dependence. ('All my perfumes, I give most willingly / To'
embalme thy fathers corse; What? will hee die?')

In Donne's poems there is a marked absence of such depen-
dences; absence, in that they seldom directly figure; marked, in
that they persistently surface as metaphors or ways of speaking.
Young love is presented as possessing a season; or its deserved
weightlessness is made real to us (and made a recognition of the
realities of life) by the fact that as it floats so little clogged by
gravity we see it accoutred with what would ordinarily be
weight. Accoutred with metaphors. Donne's poems do not feel

[69] *Some Versions*, p. 75.   [70] *Some Versions*, p. 84.

irresponsible, they feel non-responsible—but responsibly so, honouring a season when anything else would be too glum a gravity. Donne's poems repeatedly move us to a recognition of responsibilities inseparable from love, those of parenthood; responsibilities, though, which young love should not as yet confront but which no one should imagine not to exist.

J. B. Broadbent has said of Donne that 'he has to wriggle, joke, argue himself out of the dead end, the shut bedroom, whence, like Mellors' cottage, history and children, as well as wives and busybodies, are excluded'.[71] But a consciousness of exclusion, the sense that a door is shut which cannot, should not, always stay so: this is very different from an ignorance or an ignoring. Children, wives: can they not continually be heard in Donne outside that shut door? They make their presence felt—as metaphors or figures, yes, but not forbidden to call up the real and the literal.

As a man Donne was to have ample reason to be exceptionally aware of his family, his in both directions: the greatness of his mother's family behind her, her three marriages, his five siblings; and in due course his intrepid marriage, his nine children and two others stillborn (in Empson's words, 'gradually killing his wife by giving her a child every year'[72]); eventually the death of his mother in her eighties, two months before his own death.

The curious weight of the early poems, though, at one with their weightlessness, is partly a matter of their intimation that 'the right true end of love' is not, as young lovers should be forgiven (liked, even) for supposing, making love but making life. An intimation recurrently to be glimpsed in metaphors, asides, or details of the story.

> But since my soule, whose child love is,
> Takes limmes of flesh, and else could nothing doe,
> More subtile than the parent is,
> Love must not be, but take a body too.
>
> ('Aire and Angels')

At one extreme there are the bitterly unreal realities of 'The Curse', with its 'if he had not / Himself incestuously an heire begot', and 'His sonnes, which none of his may bee', and its

---

[71] *Poetic Love* (1964), p. 224.   [72] *Kenyon Review*, xix (1957), 345.

'stepdames'. At the other extreme there are the children, agog,
who appear in 'Farewell to Love' as part of a metaphor which
tells how lovers sadly tire of their treat; the children hot for
gingerbread grow into those riddling lines, so variously punctuated, which tell how

> that other curse of being short,
> And onely for a minute, made to be
> Eager, desires to raise posterity.

The desire to raise posterity is—in bidding farewell to love—
made explicit; elsewhere some sense of it animates poems as
different as 'The Good-morrow' ('were we not wean'd till
then? / But suck'd on countrey pleasures, childishly?'), and
'The Indifferent' ('Will it not serve your turn to do, as did your
mothers?'). True, the getting with child in 'Song' is 'Get with
child a mandrake roote'; true, the midwife in 'To his Mistris
Going to Bed' is an audacity of metaphor:

> Then since I may knowe,
> As liberally as to a midwife showe
> Thy selfe.

What is 'begot' in 'The Will' is love, and in 'A Nocturnall
upon S. Lucies Day' it is the poet ('I am re-begot'); what the
lovers 'produce' in 'A Lecture upon the Shadow' is two shadows, and the infants that grow are 'our infant loves'; what is
'pregnant' in 'Loves Alchymie' is the alchemist's pot, and in
'A Valediction: of Weeping' his loved one's tears:

> For thy face coines them, and thy stampe they beare,
> And by this Mintage they are something worth,
> For thus they bee
> Pregnant of thee.

Yet is it not the case that these last lines, and the others too, depend for their liberating force upon invoking, even while resisting, the idea of that more usual pregnancy, that usual way in
which a woman coins those miniatures which bear her stamp?

It is this tacit sense, so humane, of what begetting truly is
that seems to me to hold Donne's poetry together, ranging as it
does from, say, 'The Flea' to 'The Exstasie'. For what gives
'The Flea' a bounding lightness and not just a levity is the

notion that the flea is like a child of their love:

> Mee it suck'd first, and now sucks thee,
> And in this flea, our two bloods mingled bee . . .
> And pamper'd swells with one blood made of two . . .
>
> Oh stay, three lives in one flea spare,
> Where wee almost, nay more than maryed are:
>   This flea is you and I, and this
> Our mariage bed, and mariage temple is;
>   Though parents grudge, and you, w'are met,
> And cloysterd in these living walls of Jet.

That the flea is in a way their baby informs even the diminutive
horror when it is murdered in its miniature innocence of blood.
Vaster but related, 'The Exstasie' insinuates through its metaphors a world not metaphorical:

> Where, like a pillow on a bed,
>   A Pregnant banke swel'd up . . .
>
> And pictures in our eyes to get
>   Was all our propagation . . .
>
> When love, with one another so
>   Interinanimates two soules,
> That abler soule, which thence doth flow,
>   Defects of loneliness controules . . .
>
> As our blood labours to beget
>   Spirits, as like soules as it can,
> Because such fingers need to knit
>   That subtile knot, which makes us man . . .

The point is not that such metaphors give away what the poem
is *really* up to; rather, that the poem's meaning is the relation
between the metaphorical sense and the literal world from
which they are drawn. It speaks beautifully, not slightly, of the
soul; but 'that abler soule' which flows from interinanimation,
and which controls 'defects of loneliness', is estimated truly by
being seen against the ordinary child of love, a child who controls the defects of loneliness in another manner. It is the literal
meaning which, never belittling soul, yet protects the poem (in
Donne's great words elsewhere) 'From thinking us all soule'.

   The love-poems of Donne, then, to which the young Empson
responded, seem to me alive with thought and feeling about

begetting and posterity and about the relation between a true
worldliness and a true unworldliness; alive in a way which was
to create such a life in Empson's own poems. Empson's criticism of Donne has spoken of the ordinarily biographical things
about Donne: his need to 'feed his wife and children'; 'if she
is dead, there is nothing to keep him out of the Church any
longer, and (though the thought is not fit for verse) money will
have to be got hold of for all those children'.[73] But for my purposes the emphasis is different; and when Empson remarks
gruffly that 'Donne says nothing in verse about his children
because he found them merely a nuisance, but this didn't keep
him from being devoted to his wife; I expect Blake and D. H.
Lawrence would have felt the same, if they had not been
spared', I need to urge the claims of a different angle: not why
Donne says nothing in verse about his children, but whether
he says anything about the thought of childing—a thought
superbly fit for verse.

   'The separate planet stood for freedom'.[74] But Empson and
his poems are aware that freedom is an equivocal matter; his
note on *free* in 'Sonnet' says he 'was trying to give the word the
impact of a contradiction; as in "Letter IV"', where it probably
doesn't come off either'. In 'Letter IV' it is used of the stars
and the music of the spheres, and one of the most important
implications of the space-travel metaphor concerns a responsibility inseparable from the freedom it attests. Freed from the
claims of church and state (and of one's parents too), the lovers
must enter upon a special responsibility; to be upon a new
planet is to take all the responsibility for posterity there. It is
therefore of great importance that Empson should have said of
Adam and Eve before the Fall that 'they indeed are the type
case of lovers on a separate planet'[75]—they, the father and
mother of mankind. It is the grandeur of this responsibility
(any lover ought to feel some such grandeur and awe, as if
henceforth a new series of births will begin) which leads Empson to use a word like *colonise* ('When he colonises such a planet
with a pair of lovers'[76]). It is this too which lends depth to

[73] *Critical Quarterly*, viii (1966), 274-5.
[74] *Kenyon Review*, xi (1949), 587.
[75] *Kenyon Review*, xix (1957), 366.
[76] *Critical Quarterly*, viii (1966), 255.

Empson's feeling for the line in 'The Good-morrow', 'Let us possess one world, each hath one, and is one':

The sound requires it to be said slowly, with religious awe, as each party sinks into the eye of the other; it is a space-landing. Then there is a pause for realization, and the next verse begins in a hushed voice but with a curiously practical tone: 'You know, there's a lot of evidence; we really are on a separate planet'.[77]

For the curious practicalities of life on a separate planet have much to do with creating a posterity and a society from scratch. One kind of loneliness is epitomized in the lovers' each being a planet; of the 'Valediction: of Weeping', Empson says that 'now he sees another aspect of space-travel—if they become separated, the gulfs between them are absolute. He sees her with a terrible clarity falling away from him on her tiny planet';[78] 'Once the lovers are separated they are absolutely separated, so great is the isolation of these starry habitations'.[79] But there is also the possibility of a different isolation, alone together the two of them upon what is insufficiently a habitation. It is such a loneliness which Empson glimpses when he brings Donne back to earth:

It is from this background that he was keenly, even if sardonically, interested in the theology of the separate planet—from fairly early, though he did not come to feel he was actually planted on one till he realized the full effects of his runaway marriage. By the time he took Anglican Orders I imagine he was thankful to get back from the interplanetary spaces, which are inherently lonely and ill-provided.

An odd and compelling angle, then, upon the responsibilities of and for parenthood is implicit in this metaphor of newly inhabited planets which Empson drew from Donne. That Empson sensed this is clear not only from that remark about Adam and Eve but also from the beginning and the end of 'Donne the Space Man'.[80] It ends with a discussion of 'A Nocturnall upon S. Lucies Day' which twines together childbirth, the separate planet, and Empson's own poems:

He [J. B. Leishman] deduces that 'The Nocturnal' was written in Paris on the night of the 13th December 1611; Donne was there with

---

[77] *Kenyon Review*, xix (1957), 360.   [78] *Critical Quarterly*, viii (1966), 264-5.
[79] *Kenyon Review*, xix (1957), 372.   [80] *Kenyon Review*, xix (1957), 337-99.

the Drury family, and anxious about his wife's coming child-birth
(Izaac Walton says he knew by telepathy that not the wife but the
child was dead, and so it was, but one can well believe there was a certain amount of confusion). As a young man I snatched at any chance
to hear wisdom drop from Mr T. S. Eliot, and he once remarked that
the test of a true poet is that he writes about experiences before they
have happened to him; I felt I had once passed this test, though I forget now in which poem. The doctrine makes one very doubtful of any
dating of poems by internal evidence, and I should think it might be
true of Donne . . . But still, the only definite reason for supposing that
Donne refers to a separate planet in 'The Nocturnal' is that he does it
so often in other poems, sometimes obviously, but often so vaguely
that we are only sure of it because the poem becomes better if we
recognize it.

As for the start of 'Donne the Space Man', it is so clear in the
connections it weaves, and so weird in the double-duty which it
asks—on the one page—the word *kids* to do, that it is incontro-
vertible evidence that, in responding to Donne, Empson responded to a special responsibility and *élan* about begetting that
were implicit in the loved metaphor:

Donne, then, from a fairly early age, was interested in getting to
another planet much as the kids are nowadays; he brought the idea
into practically all his best love-poems, with the sentiment which it
still carries of adventurous freedom . . . No reasonable man, I readily
agree, would want space travel as such; because he wants to know, in
any proposal for travel, whether he would go farther and fare worse.
A son of my own at about the age of twelve, keen on space travel like
the rest of them, saw the goat having kids and was enough impressed
to say 'It's better than space travel'. It is indeed absolutely or meta-
physically better, because it is coming out of the nowhere into here;
and I was so pleased to see the human mind beginning its work that I
felt as much impressed as he had done at seeing the birth of the kids.
One does not particularly want, then, to have Donne keen on space
travel unless he had a serious reason for it.

VII

The complex of thinking and feeling involved in begetting—
man's desire to raise posterity—is 'the right handle to take hold
of the bundle', or at any rate a right handle, in considering
Empson's poems. Sometimes explicit; sometimes like Donne's

planets, an implicit part of that 'secret largeness of outlook' which Empson shares with Donne, and so part of the poem's richness—richness having been defined in a powerful paren-thesis by Empson: 'the sense of richness (readiness for argu-ment not pursued)'.[81] As to the tacit, there is some reassurance in Empson's fine exploration of the fact that 'Every one of [Hamlet's] soliloquies . . . contains a shock for the audience, apart from what it says, in what it doesn't say'.[82]

Ian Hamilton has complained that the inaugurating percep-tion in an Empson poem is seldom chosen 'because it can dis-cover something of an important experience that the poet has already had'.[83] Indeed no; the usual thing is for an Empson poem to be about an experience not yet had (one half-feared and half not); in so far as the poem embodies an experience, it is usually the experience of not yet having had such-and-such an experience. Empson has said that since 1951 or so 'the motives which made me want to write had I suppose largely disappeared. I didn't feel I had to do it anyway. I think many people actually feel they've got to go on, because it's the only way they can support their wife and children or something'.[84] Empson's marriage and parenthood have effected a shift of motives, partly because much in his poems had obscurely to do with parenthood. (On such happy yet disconcerting losses, see his poem 'Success'.) He does not re-make other poets in his own image, but one of the endeavours he has engaged with—proving that Marvell did marry—matters in part because the marriage, in Empson's view, is involved in Marvell's giving up poetry and becoming a different kind of writer. This has at least some relation to Empson's own career.

Love and war make up much of Marvell, as of Empson. His *Poems* were published in 1935, and *The Gathering Storm* in 1940. He has pungently repudiated one particular accusation:

The idea that Empson lost his nerve with the second volume has always seemed to me very unreasonable. The first book, you see, is

---

[81] *Some Versions*, p. 145; also p. 100: '. . . as often happens to poets, who tend to make their lives a situation they have already written about'.(Cp. Eliot's remark on p. 208 above.)

[82] *Sewanee Review*, lxi (1953), 26.   [83] *the Review*, Nos 6 and 7 (1963), 37.

[84] *the Review*, Nos 6 and 7 (1963), 26. This interview was reprinted in *The Modern Poet*, ed. Ian Hamilton (1968).

about the young man feeling frightened, frightened of women, frightened of jobs, frightened of everything, not knowing what he could
possibly do. The second book is all about politics, saying we're going
to have this second world war and we mustn't get too frightened about
it. Well, dear me, if you call the first brave and the second cowardly it
seems to me that you haven't the faintest idea of what the poems are
about.[85]

Both volumes are brave in their way; and one remembers
'Courage means Running', with its laconic confidence: 'Usual
for a man / Of Bunyan's courage to respect fear'. But what
yokes the two volumes is the fact that the approach of a world
war lends a further gravity to the decision whether or not to
beget children. (Incidentally, I think it touching and noble of
Empson to have given to his two sons—among their middle
names—the names of the two Allied victories which coincided
with their birth.)

'Just a Smack at Auden' makes the yoking clear; true, it
mocks the funk of those who are apocalyptically, with ripe
relish, 'waiting for the end', but its mockery is not at all directed at the idea that the fears are farcical. An ironical poem,
yes, but 'an irony has no point unless it is true, in some degree,
in both senses'.[86]

> Shall I send a wire, boys? What is there to send?
> All are under fire, boys, waiting for the end.
> Shall I turn a sire, boys? Shall I choose a friend?
> The fat is in the pyre, boys, waiting for the end.

'Shall I turn a sire, boys?': it is a scorching question, and of the
three *Shall I*'s here, the only one which needed to be clad in the
asbestos of whimsical wording. To speak of fatherhood as to
'turn a sire' is to intimate a distaste for those who let such a
question be mainly a matter of ministering to their finicking
self-importance, but that does not deny that the question is indeed important, too important to be left to fluttering apocalyp-
ticists. 'The fat is in the pyre': any life is already in the funeral
flames. The impulses are contradictory even in this hosing-
down poem, but then Empson's attitude to the approaching
war was rightly compacted of contradictory impulses: people
needed to be made truly, and not falsely, afraid. There is such

[85] *the Review*, Nos 6 and 7 (1963), 29.   [86] *Some Versions*, p. 56.

a thing as false insecurity as well as false security. Usual for a man of Empson's courage to respect fear. Think of his superb laying-bare of Dryden's 'Charge, charge, 'tis too late to retreat' ('Song for St Cecilia's Day'):

It is curious on the face of it that one should represent, in a mood of such heroic simplicity, a reckless excitement, a feverish and exalted eagerness for battle, by saying (in the most prominent part of the stanza from the point of view of final effect) that we can't get out of the battle now and must go through with it as best we can . . . Evidently the thought that it is no good running away is an important ingredient of military enthusiasm . . . Horses, in a way very like this, display mettle by a continual expression of timidity.[87]

But it is Auden that Empson's poem (good-humouredly enough, in his case) is just a smack at, and one should recall Empson's first exploration of Auden. His 'Note on "Paid on Both Sides"' deals, after all, with a work which imagines love within a feud tantamount to civil war. John Nower, whose father has been killed in the feud, is in love with Anne from the enemy family; John has to decide whether to plunge upon marriage, and whether to escape (emigrate) with or without her. He tries to straddle it all—but he has Anne's brother shot as a spy. His decision to do so precipitated from Empson the most elaborate analysis that he has ever made of a decision:

He has the spy shot partly to tie his own hands, since he will evade the decision if he can make peace impossible, partly (the other way round) because it will make peace difficult, so that the attempt, if he chooses to make it, will expose him to more risk (for this seems to make it more generous), partly from a self-contempt which, in search of relief, turns outwards, and lights on the man who seems likest to himself, for he too is half a spy in his own camp; partly because he must kill part of himself in coming to either decision about the marriage, so that it seems a first step, or a revenge, to kill by an irrelevant decision the man likest him (for whom he must at the moment, from the point of view which still excites horror in him, feel most sympathy), partly because only by making a decision on some associated matter can he string himself up to know his own mind on the matter in question, partly because what is in his own mind makes him feel ashamed and guilty among his supporters, so that he mistakenly thinks it necessary for his own safety to prove to them he is wholeheartedly on their side.[88]

[87] *Seven Types*, p. 198.   [88] *Experiment*, No. 7 (1931), 60.

What matters to my argument is the way in which the decision which here so fascinates Empson is entwined with marriage, family, and parenthood within what is in effect war. Given war's world it seems impossible either to create marriage here or to flee and create it elsewhere. Moreover Empson saw that Auden was implying a further relation: 'John, the hero of the play, is born prematurely from shock, after the death by ambush of his father'; 'And yet it is precisely the painfulness and dangerousness of these expulsive forces that make it possible for him to give birth to a decision.'

That was in 1931, but Empson has never lost interest in this cluster of feelings and moral concerns. The three examples in 'Argufying in Poetry'[89] run from Yeats's 'Byzantium', described as 'a fascinating bit of science fiction', via a love-complaint by Wyatt, to 'Letter to Anne Ridler', in which 'the young G. S. Fraser, on the troopship taking him to Africa, considered why men allow themselves to be conscripted':

> Or freedom, say, from family love and strife
> And all the female mystery of a room
> That half supports and half imprisons us
> May drive a man from father, mother, wife
> And every soft reminder of the womb.

The reasons why Empson finds this 'magnificent' are among the reasons why his own poems are magnificent.

'And every soft reminder of the womb': a world of war gives special pain and pathos to the question 'Shall I turn a sire?' Which recalls that the first Shakespeare play to be discussed by Empson in terms of its plot was *Troilus and Cressida* (1932 and 1935). 'Certainly the play is not interested in marriage so much as in the prior idea of loyalty, but it was to the interest of these lovers to marry so as to have a claim against being separated'.[90] Yet it is the father's claim not to be separated from his daughter that determines the tragedy. (It is in speaking of *Troilus and Cressida* that Empson provides the best summary of what one feels about those of his poems which do not come off: 'Much of the language of *Troilus,* I think, is a failure; it makes puzzles which even if they can be unravelled cannot be felt as poetry'.)

[89] *Listener,* 22 August 1963.   [90] *Some Versions,* pp. 35, 41.

'To marry so as to have a claim against being separated': this cannot but call up Empson's best and contemporaneous poem, 'Aubade'. The best because it has plenty of story; because it fuses, as no other poem does, the two principled preoccupations (of bold commitment and of shrewd good sense); because it marries the love-poems and the war-poems; and because it deserves the praise which Empson gave to Swinburne's best poem, 'The Leper': 'a story where both characters are humane, and indeed behave better than they think; Swinburne nowhere else (that I have read him) succeeds in imagining two people'.[91]

'Aubade' is about the sexual situation. When I was in Japan, from 1931 to 1934, it was usual for the old hand in the English colony to warn the young man: don't you go and marry a Japanese because we're going to be at war with Japan within ten years; you'll have awful trouble if you marry a Japanese, and this is what the poem is about . . . It just says 'All right, we can't marry, we must expect to separate'.[92]

> A bedshift flight to a Far Eastern sky.
> Only the same war on a stonger toe.
> The heart of standing is you cannot fly.
>
> Tell me more quickly what I lost by this,
> Or tell me with less drama what they miss
> Who call no die a god for a good throw,
> Who say after two aliens had one kiss
> It seemed the best thing to be up and go.

The piercing pathos of that penultimate line is achieved by its being so parenthetical; the sentence sweeps pitilessly on past the words 'after two aliens had one kiss' and simply swallows them up. But the force of the understatement springs from those largest and most ordinary things that should follow a kiss: marriage, children. The two people will never become that three or more which is a new world, an inhabited planet; the bleak stoical arithmetic of 'two aliens . . . one kiss' divides, not multiplies. What is so expansive in the poem is not only its largeness of moral feeling (the decent expendiency of 'up and go' never either demeaning or truckling to the tragic dignity of 'the heart of standing'), but its strange power of heartening: 'Up was the heartening and the strong reply.' It celebrates an

[91] *Complex Words*, p. 78.   [92] *the Review*, Nos 6 and 7 (1963), 29-30.

experience, and a mutuality, yet a great part of that experience
was a sense of future experiences not to be had here. In its way
a 'Valediction: forbidding Mourning', its personal fervour and
generosity are at one with its sense that in times of war such
a loss is simply to be expected.

VIII

'To an Old Lady' is rightly revered. The dignity with which it
conceives of another's dignity; its calm refusal either to melo-
dramatize or to sentimentalize the great gulf it contemplates;
its ability to withhold and yet not to grudge: these make the
most serious use of the spacemanship which Empson learnt
from Donne.

TO AN OLD LADY

Ripeness is all; her in her cooling planet
Revere; do not presume to think her wasted.
Project her no projectile, plan nor man it;
Gods cool in turn, by the sun long outlasted.

Our earth alone given no name of god
Gives, too, no hold for such a leap to aid her;
Landing, you break some palace and seem odd;
Bees sting their need, the keeper's queen invader.

No, to your telescope; spy out the land;
Watch while her ritual is still to see,
Still stand her temples emptying in the sand
Whose waves o'erthrew their crumbled tracery;

Still stand uncalled-on her soul's appanage;
Much social detail whose successor fades,
Wit used to run a house and to play Bridge,
And tragic fervour, to dismiss her maids.

Years her precession do not throw from gear.
She reads a compass certain of her pole;
Confident, finds no confines on her sphere,
Whose failing crops are in her sole control.

Stars how much further from me fill my night.
Strange that she too should be inaccessible,
Who shares my sun. He curtains her from sight,
And but in darkness is she visible.

The last stanza soars; the second stanza does something more

disconcerting, it leaps. We should be sufficiently surprised by
the line 'Bees sting their need, the keeper's queen invader' to
ask with some urgency what it is up to. For one thing, it is the
only moment in the poem when the planetary metaphor is
replaced by quite a different figure; elsewhere the planet fades
(for instance, the fourth stanza), but nowhere else is it abruptly
and totally replaced by an altogether alien metaphor. Why the
brusqueness? Moreover the train of thought is odd. The first
two lines of the stanza follow on naturally enough, making
their crucial point about systems of belief. You cannot get to
her planet; (and then, with something of a shrug, a diverting
concession) and even if you could, you would only do damage
as well as make a fool of yourself.[93] But then there is this odd
leap into a further *and even*: and even an invader of the highest
authority, the grandest of ladies, and absolutely essential to the
place, the queen-bee, finds herself stung for her pains. The line
is a bizarre moment of uncalled-for aggression, not only in
being about aggression but in the way it behaves in the poem;
it is itself an invader, and we have to ask what sting, what
need, makes it suddenly insist upon making its presence felt.
Simply, what are we to make of this reminder that there is a
way of life (the bees whom we are so often asked to admire; see
Empson's large response to 'The singing masons building roofs
of gold'[94]), a way of life so suspicious of any invasion that it
will kill the only means it has of reproduction? What, in short,
has the threat to reproduction to do with the poem?

For a start, the poem beautifully uses a question which is
bound to be felt in any poem 'to an old lady' that insists 'do not
presume to think her wasted'. We are not to think of her as an
old maid; but we are positively not to think of her so—that is,
the matter is to arise. Such is the most immediately presump-
tuous way in which people are prone to presume that an old
lady's life is wasted; a presumption from which Empson is

[93] A magnificent bit of Empson's Englishness, 'and seem odd'. As in his remarks on
Donne's marriage: 'He couldn't have been certain when he did this that it would
break his career, because it wouldn't have done if the father hadn't behaved foolishly;
the father first insisted on having Donne sacked and then found he had better try to
have him reinstated, which Egerton refused on the very English ground that the fuss
about the matter had been sufficiently ridiculous already' (*Kenyon Review*, xix, 1957,
345).
[94] *Seven Types*, pp. 112-3.

always challengingly free, as in the implied rebuke in *Seven Types*: 'The object of life, after all, is not to understand things, but to maintain one's defences and equilibrium and live as well as one can; it is not only maiden aunts who are placed like this.'[95] (The poem's use of *maids* as meaning servants plays its part as a negative implication, 'what you imply but to exclude', in the words of 'Letter V'.) Certainly it is part of the point of the metaphor 'appanage' that it should call up its literal sense too: provision made for younger children. Likewise of 'successor', again a metaphor but again not to be narrowly conceived as to the way in which it works upon us (quietly strengthened as it is by Empson's putting *whose* instead of 'of which the'). Moreover, what is not metaphor at all, but story—'Wit used to run a house'—invokes a family and a household rather than a solitary life. Empson's subject is the solitariness not of the solitary life, but of the unsolitary one, 'the isolation even of a life rich in intimacy'. That the bees and their propagation have something really to do with the poem seems to me confirmed by the happiness which Empson felt at the reception of the poem by the old lady herself: 'My mother, but when she came across it in print she luckily thought it meant her own mother, thus showing that it tells a general truth' (record-notes). This was the right thing to be delighted about, but the general truth then includes a sense of a vista, of parents' parents and of children's children. The general truth is about parenthood, not about a friend's or an acquaintance's distance from us. Empson in the record-notes has paraphrased '. . . Who shares my sun' as 'though isolated we shared a system closer than the great minds in books', and the system in question is a family. It is natural to think of the solar system as a family. So that when Empson says without qualification ' "Sun" not "son" is meant', his comment should be resisted or amplified. The literal sense of son would ruckle the line; but I don't think that all suggestion of son can be or should be eliminated, even if the proper way to put it is to say that the phrase means *sun-not-son* rather than means *sun*, not *son*. The effect of the word 'share' is to make it even harder altogether to preclude an intimation of the family; and it is inherently improbable that

95 p. 247.

a man who so honours Donne and whose own poems can speak of Lucifer as 'Sun's Son' could imagine that all trace of *son* could so easily be vetoed.

The point matters because the succession (appanage, successor) of grandmother, mother, son is part of what creates as well as of what created the poem. The poem is warm with family feeling (strangely, given its recognition of cooling and of inevitable distance), and family there has to include not only progenitors but also the absent descendants. One aspect of the proper (and public) self-consciousness of the poem is its sense that no life can simply be thought of as wasted which has brought a new life into the world, and that this bears upon those who have not, or not yet, done so. At which point we should ask about that calmly surprising opening, which so ripens in the poem, and which so utterly earns the right to its audacious appropriation of great Shakespeare: 'Ripeness is all'. The first words of this poem to an old lady are those in which a son offers comfort to a parent. It is an odd comfort, not only in that Gloucester could never in certain respects be comforted by it; what he can say is what the old lady might say of her poem, 'And that's true too', a dignified austerity of comfort. But we need to remember just how Edgar thought it best to comfort his father: by recalling the birth which we were given as well as the death approaching us. The ripeness is that of gestation as much as of moribundity:

> Men must endure
> Their going hence, even as their comming hither,
> Ripenesse is all.

The range of Empson's poem is a matter of its taking within itself a sense of the coming hither as well as of the going hence. It sees the paradox of any family, that the very light which it shares makes for a daily invisibility. 'And but in darkness is she visible': the darkness is that of a night-time realization, of sadness or despair or memory, and also of the shadow of death. The poem has its cool light, and its source is revealed when for a moment it flashes into fieriness, stung by need.

The infinite spaces precipitate a multiplicity of feelings.

> You were amused to find you too could fear
> 'The eternal silence of the infinite spaces'.
>   ('Letter I')

Amusement and fear meet in the love-poems.

Although, as a matter of fact, most of them turned out to be love poems about boy being too afraid of girl to tell her anything, the simple desire to think of something rather like Donne was the basic impulse. But I think my few good ones are all on the basis of express-ing an unresolved conflict.[96]

Of 'The Ants', the first poem in the *Collected Poems*, Empson has said: 'It is a love-poem with the author afraid of the woman' (record-notes). But we need to distinguish fears: it will not do just to assume that every boy is afraid of a girl since anybody fears rebuff and any other body can be dangerous—both true, but only part of what haunts Empson's poems. What we should (women included) fear in women is their power to bring forth life, a power which is both mysteriously generous and unper-turbed by scruple. In 'The Ants' the woman is thought of as a tree of life, teeming not just with leaves but with the parasi-tical greenfly and with the ants parasitical upon the greenfly. The ants, with sinister care, protect the greenfly so as to live, via them, upon the tree's life.

THE ANTS

We tunnel through your noonday out to you.
We carry our tube's narrow darkness there
Where, nostrum-plastered, with prepared air,
With old men running and trains whining through

We ants may tap your aphids for your dew.
You may not wish their sucking or our care;
Our all-but freedom, too, your branch must bear,
High as roots' depth in earth, all earth to view.

No, by too much this station the air nears.
How small a chink lets in how dire a foe.
What though the garden in one glance appears?

Winter will come and all her leaves will go.
We do not know what skeleton endures.
Carry at least her parasites below.

I don't want to linger over this poem, mainly because I am still unhelpfully perplexed by it, though moved; but there is special force in Empson's note: 'The ants build mud galleries into trees

[96] *the Review*, Nos 6 and 7 (1963), 34-5.

WILLIAM EMPSON   219

to protect the greenfly they get sugar from, and keep them
warm in the nest during winter'. A travesty of a warm nest;
and of the strange activity of the womb. There is a sense of
what the grandest parasites are; there is the aphids' 'sucking',
and in the association of 'branch' with 'bear' a feeling that any
woman is a family tree. This is indeed what women must bear,
and it is very different from man's 'all-but freedom'. And in
the admonition 'How small a chink lets in how dire a foe' there
is the sharpest sense of begetting—rightly thought of as an inti-
midating prospect, and with the fear braced against unmanli-
ness or panic by that humour and coolness of archaism with
which the poems outfrown indignity, as in 'Shall I turn a sire?'

'Invitation to Juno' ponders the centaur bred by Ixion from
the delusive cloud substituted for Juno (an act of begetting for
which he was as punished as if he had had the real goddess);
and of the 'gennets for germans' which 'sprang not from
Othello'. It asks: are all attempts at 'inheriting two life-periods'
doomed?

> Courage. Weren't strips of heart culture seen
> Of late mating two periodicities?
> Could not Professor Charles Darwin
> Graft annual upon perennial trees?

The name Darwin is called upon because it so stands for a
great family—a family can in its way inherit two life-periods.
But being about a transcendent act of breeding doesn't here
make for a good poem. It admonishes: 'Courage.' But there is
not enough fear for it to mean more than cheer up. That is
because no woman—no sense of woman—is allowed into it;
Juno, or rather the cloud that simulated her, lurks only in the
title, and the poem grants all its room to males: Lucretius, Dr
Johnson, Othello, Ixion, and Charles Darwin. Like a club; Invitation to Athenaeum. The point is not the presence of ideas but
the absence of that human situation which makes a poem convince our nerves. Another poem of 1928 shows the difference.

VALUE IS IN ACTIVITY

Celestial sphere, an acid green canvas hollow,
His circus that exhibits him, the juggler
Tosses, an apple that four others follow,
Nor heeds, not eating it, the central smuggler.

> Nor heeds if the core be brown with maggots' raven,
> Dwarf seeds unnavelled a last frost has scolded,
> Mites that their high narrow echoing cavern
> Invites forward, or with close brown pips, green folded.
>
> Some beetles (the tupped females can worm out)
> Massed in their halls of knowingly chewed splinter
> Eat faster than the treasured fungi sprout
> And stave off suffocation until winter.

The maggot, the seed, the mite, the pip; out to the apple, and then to the juggler, to the circus-tent, and to the world; and then swoop in again, back down to the beetles within the world. As to its metaphysics, the poem was well scrutinized by Martin Dodsworth;[97] the metaphors tense the metaphysics. As in 'To an Old Lady' there is a sudden, and similar, fierceness: 'Some beetles (the tupped females can worm out) . . .' The very parentheticalness is a jolt, an eruptive energy which might splinter the poem if the brackets did not pinion its arms; and 'tupped' is like no other word in the poem. For among the 'Inhabitants' who at first gave the poem its title, there with 'the central smuggler', the maggots, the dwarf seeds, the mites, and the 'close brown pips', are the future beetles with which the tupped females teem—and which make it a good thing for male beetles that the females 'worm out'. Many feelings play over such a notion; it is with affection as well as perturbation that we may think of an embryo as a 'central smuggler'. How sharply and oddly 'dwarf seeds unnavelled' invites us forward to think of birth, and then 'scolded' sees them as children. How quiescent the 'close brown pips, green folded', with future apples folded within those folded pips. Pips and seeds are reproduction as much as 'tupped', a word which certainly must not be allowed to domineer, and yet which must be allowed to be—as was 'Bees sting their need . . .'—the jolt which shakes the kaleidoscopic poem so that we see its pattern.

The title, 'Value is in Activity', would suggest (as well as Aristotle on happiness) that value and activity can especially be seen in the value and activity of perpetuating life.

>   We gain
> Truth, to put it sanely, by gift of pleasure
> And courage . . .
>   ('Courage means Running')

[97] *the Review*, Nos 6 and 7 (1963), 8-10.

Truth, and life too; the act of begetting is the gift which marries pleasure and courage. The act of begetting is a type case of activity, not just because it makes possible great vistas of others' activity ('Cradle within cradle', in the words of Yeats which appear in Empson's epigraph to 'Autumn on Nan-Yueh'), but also because in its irrevocable decisiveness it most violates that other deep wish of ours, to foresee. 'High Dive' is Empson's elaboration of the necessity to act. The idea of the poem is 'that one must go from the godlike state of contemplation even when attained either into action which cannot wholly foresee its consequences or into a fixed condition, due to fear, which does not give real knowledge and leads to neurosis' (Notes). The poem, exceptionally hard to construe, sees the type case of an 'action which cannot wholly foresee its consequences' as the act of begetting. Action is not here limited to such an act, and moreover any attempt to write about activity would inevitably find itself using words which invoke begetting. Yet the poem goes further than a poem would be obliged to, or advised to, unless it wished to invoke begetting. It is characteristic too of Empson, as of Donne, that his metaphors are not reduced to blank obedience but are allowed to ask for themselves a larger presence. So that when the attained contemplation, from the diving-board, is given as

> I Sanctus brood thereover,
> Inform *in posse* the tank's triple infinite,

we should see this brooding as indeed like that of the Holy Ghost, intent upon the creation of life (rather than intent upon some action or other). Likewise when, within this same sentence, the ripples are seen as 'maggots', and when in the next sentence they 'rut or retract', we should not ignore the teeming life of maggots, or the sexual suggestions of 'rut or retract' (though the main sense is 'form ruts or draw back'). We are told that their ripples are 'Thicker than water'—a phrase which insists upon the human family, and which Empson emphasizes by enclosing it (needlessly, otherwise) in quotation marks, alone in the poem. (The proverb is important in 'Bacchus', too:

> Making a brew thicker than blood, being brine,
> Being the mother water which was first made blood,
> All living blood, and whatever blood makes wine.

Empson's note says: ' "Blood is thicker than water", but blood connects us with near relations, as the phrase is used, and this with all life'.) The water will 'clot . . . unless . . .'; will clot into the inactivity of neurosis, here invoked in the line 'These doves undriven that coo, Ark neuroses'. It is a baffling phrase; the only sense that I can make of it is to think that the animals that went in two by two are likely to have suffered from the neuroses consequent upon the whole survival of their kind being now dependent upon their power to propagate; and one of the poor doves saw its only mate sent forth three times, not even to return the last time (*Genesis*, viii 12.) The responsibility would make propagation a weighty enough matter to foster any number of 'Ark neuroses' ('Sitting two and two, boys, waiting for the end').

Now the two stanzas that particularly matter. The water will clot unless one

> Unchart the second, the obstetric, chooses,
> Leaves isle equation by not frozen ford,
> And, to break scent, under foamed new phusis
> Dives to receive in memory reward.

> Fall to them, Lucifer, Sun's Son. Splash high
> Jezebel. Throw her down. They feast, I flee
> Her poised tired head and eye
> Whose skull pike-high mirrors and waits for me.

Unless one chooses the second alternative, an 'unchart' because it leads to the uncharted but is a way out; and it is 'obstetric', it brings to birth. In bringing to birth, one 'leaves isle equation by not frozen ford'; the isle equation is that of believing that man is an island ('Each of us enisled, boys, waiting for the end'; and Empson has observed that 'most of the later sayings of Donne still famous are also a renunciation of separateness; as in "no man is an island; he is a piece of the Continent, a part of the Main" [98]). The 'not frozen ford' by which one leaves the paralysing equation is in human terms love, and the act of love, and the woman's obstetric act. Any act can be disastrous; Lucifer's fall was (yet he is 'Sun's Son', not man's son), and so was Jezebel's. The dive into life can be the dive into death. Lucifer falls; Jezebel is thrown down. That we are

to recollect the very words of *II Kings*, ix 30 is clear from *tired*,
which mostly means 'attired' (and is pronounced by Empson
on the record as a disyllable, as is 'poised'): 'And she painted
her face, and tired her head, and looked out at a window'.
Then since 'Throw her down' gives the exact words of Jehu's
order, we should remember just who they were who received
the command: 'And there looked out to him two or three
eunuchs. And he said, Throw her down. So they threw her
down'.

'High Dive' is too secret, too racked, a poem, but its preoccupations are crucial to Empson. In the same way, we should
not leave flat the terms in which 'Dissatisfaction with Metaphysics' chooses to speak:

> Whose hearth is cold, and all his wives undone.
>
> Adam and Eve breed still their dotted line,
> Repeated incest, a plain series.

The same with 'Earth has Shrunk in the Wash', which Empson
has summed up as 'Civilized refinement cutting one off from
other people' (Notes): 'Space-travel compared to neurotic isolation and the dangers of the increase of power' (record-notes).
It ends:

> One daily tortures the poor Christ anew
> (On every planet moderately true)
> But has much more to do,
> And can so much entail here,
> Daily brings rabbits to a new Australia,
> New unforeseen, new cataclysmic failure,
>
> And cannot tell. He who all answers brings
> May (ever in the great taskmaster's eye)
> Dowser be of his candle as of springs,
> And pump the valley with the tunnel dry.

The rabbits brought to a new Australia are an unwished-for
colonization and a teeming mischief; 'entail' is free to revert to
its oldest sense, to settle an estate in succession; and the
'unforeseen' becomes particularly a matter of the unforeseeable
effects of procreation. 'Dowser' is, as Empson says in the
Notes, 'a pun on putting out a light and smelling out water';
that the same word can bring forth the waters of life and can

put out the candle of life is the centre of the poem's puzzlement.
'And cannot tell'.

Again, the best stanza of another flawed heterogeneous
poem, 'Letter IV' (Empson is dissatisfied with it), is its opening, which imagines a grotesque birth and then a grotesque
kind of parturition; at once heroic and mock-heroic—the child
cicada a tiny Childe Roland—like many of the begettings, love-
tunnellings and brave acts of building which most move Empson:

> Hatched in a rasping darkness of dry sand
> The child cicada some brave root discovers:
> Sucks with dumb mouth while his long climb is planned
> That high must tunnel through the dust that smothers:
> Parturient with urine from this lover
> Coheres from chaos, only to evade,
> An ordered Nature his own waste has made,
> And builds his mortared Babel from the incumbent shade.

No one else's love-poem would set itself such a long climb; the
triumph of life is seen as a triumph over the inevitable waste,
using waste instead of denying it. 'Bacchus' too celebrates birth:
'The laughing god born of a startling answer'; 'Incestuous
Chaos will breed permanent', and so too must Order, or it will
leave the world to Chaos. Chaos or nothingness—'Four Legs,
Three Legs, Two Legs' is disturbed by 'The delta zero':
Oedipus 'short-circuited life by keeping it all in the family'
(Notes).

I believe that almost all of Empson's poems have to do with
the way in which we do or do not short-circuit life. Even 'This
Last Pain', the poem in which Empson devoted the most of his
energies to drawing abstractions taut, needed to begin with a
grim repudiation implicit in the application of the word *fathers*:

> This last pain for the damned the Fathers found:
> 'They knew the bliss with which they were not crowned.'

The poem needed too at its centre the deep pun on 'conceivable':

> 'What is conceivable can happen too',
> Said Wittgenstein, who had not dreamt of you;

You there being as wide as the world; any *you*, including those not yet conceived, or you, gentle reader ('Which eyes not yet created shall ore-read'), as undreamt of by me the poet as by Wittgenstein. Any individual human being is conceived and yet inconceivable. The poem needs this pun not only because of its tension between an intangible idea and a tangible person, but also because the pun is then itself in tension with the end of the poem:

> Feign then what's by a decent tact believed
> And act that state is only so conceived,
>   And build an edifice of form
>   For house where phantoms may keep warm.

> Imagine then, by miracle, with me,
> (Ambiguous gifts, as what gods give must be)
>   What could not possibly be there,
>   And learn a style from a despair.

What keeps warm the poem's ending, what fleshes its phantoms and abstractions, is the robust return in 'so conceived'; the act of imagining, of so conceiving, is as odd, as trusting, as precarious and as implicated in hope, as the act of conceiving life. 'Ambiguous gifts, as what gods give must be': of such gifts, the most 'by miracle' is the gift of life.

Last of the more covert instances is the end of 'Your Teeth are Ivory Towers'. Like many of Empson's endings, it soars and broods:

>   He who tries
> Talk must always plot and then sustain,
> Talk to himself until the star replies,

> Or in despair that it could speak again
> Assume what answers any wits have found
> In evening dress on rafts upon the main,
> Not therefore uneventful or soon drowned.

The delicate stoical wit of this gains from our being alive to a great many aspects of the brave doomed life on the raft, but we need particularly to sense that the raft cannot but short-circuit life; what it most epitomizes is not only certain death but the impossibility of furthering life. 'Not therefore uneventful or soon drowned'—but the greatest eventfulness of all is out of the question. Many readers of Empson's poems have found the feeling of this ending to be quite different from any other in Empson, and

the shape of the ending is unique in his work. In all of his other
poems in *terza rima*, the end of the poem returns to its beginning;
a cycle is completed. Indeed they usually invoke some such cir-
cularity or return. 'Arachne', with its bubbles, sends back its last
rhyme to its first pair; 'The Scales', with its tunnels, likewise;
'Reflection from Rochester', with its search for a pattern, is
doubly concluded, sending back its last pair to its first pair; and
'Courage means Running', its last rhyme to its first pair. Alone
of the *terza rima* poems, 'Your Teeth are Ivory Towers' short-
circuits the life of its verse-form; it leaves its final rhyming not
fully consummated, no third rhyme ever forthcoming to grace
the conjunction of 'found' and 'drowned'.

IX

For the rest, I want to end by doing the lavish thing, and quote in
sequence ten of Empson's poems which are among his best,
remarking briefly why I think they too are animated by these
concerns.

CAMPING OUT

And now she cleans her teeth into the lake:
Gives it (God's grace) for her own bounty's sake
What morning's pale and the crisp mist debars:
Its glass of the divine (that Will could break)
Restores, beyond Nature: or lets Heaven take
(Itself being dimmed) her pattern, who half awake
Milks between rocks a straddled sky of stars.

Soap tension the star pattern magnifies.
Smoothly Madonna through-assumes the skies
Whose vaults are opened to achieve the Lord.
No, it is we soaring explore galaxies,
Our bullet boat light's speed by thousands flies.
Who moves so among stars their frame unties;
See where they blur, and die, and are outsoared.

The ordinary dawn turns out to have its feat of creation; for our
own bounty's sake we are to share the lavish relaxation of 'her
own bounty's sake' and its power of vivifying. The stars have
faded from the lake, but her toothpaste re-creates them, and as
they fly apart it is as if we were flying towards them. The poem
is Empson's most exuberant evocation of a delight in creative

multiplicity; the creation of those mimic stars (and the evening and the morning were the fourth day) is at one with a full sense of a tenderly human erotic generosity: 'who half awake / Milks between rocks a straddled sky of stars'. Just as Empson has always been fascinated by the idea that any man can become a Christ (the idea occurs throughout his criticism), so here my lady can become Madonna. The vaults of the skies which 'are opened to achieve the Lord' are open to the achievement of a fecundating glory (reminiscent of Tennyson's 'St Agnes' Eve' in its erotic fervour but triumphantly secular). The Madonna's body went to heaven without bodily decay; 'through-assumes' incorporates the way in which any woman's body can in love assume as much, both because an ecstasy makes physical decay at once unthinkable and insignificant, and because the creation of any new life, whether by a Madonna or not, confutes decay. The jet-like boost which 'Madonna' gives is powered by the delighted implication that for a virgin to conceive is nowhere near as grand and jubilant a thing as for a woman to do so. The 'bullet boat light's speed' ('The toothpaste specks as they go apart on the water look like approaching a constellation at more than the speed of light'; record-notes) includes an evocation of the moment of conception. Then in the last two lines, which Empson has summarized as 'a great enough ecstasy makes the common world unreal' (Notes), there is an extraordinary combination of triumph with chastening gravity, since 'are outsoared' suggests both a diminution and a something else's victory. 'Who moves so among stars their frame unties': the impulse of the line is thrilled yet sober, responsible, and admonitory. Nothing here smoothly 'makes the common world unreal' in any airy way, for the claims of the common world are supremely there in the wish to create a pattern of stars that will not blur and die and be outsoared. The feeling of vigilance in the closing lines creates what Empson found in 'The Good-morrow': religious awe, a hushed voice wonderfully implicated in the curiously practical. I realize that these impulses are not presented as the self-evident subject of 'Camping Out', but then one of the challenges of all Empson's poems (one of the ways by which they move you to make human sense of them) is that they are proudly unostentatious about their subjects. Welcoming but wary, they are open secrets.

'Camping Out' is not a poem about camping out, or about toothpaste specks; but camping out and space-travel are both modes of lovers' freedom. The poem makes courteous use of its toothpaste specks rather as Marvell's 'The Mower to the Glo-worms' is courteous to its friendly helpful glowworms. It is only by seeing that the adventure and pathos of begetting are in the poem's air that we can grasp how it earns its buoyancy and grave calm; or grasp how Empson is here moved to a love-poem which so exhilaratingly casts out fear; casts it out, not denies its existence; a fear that would be natural to a bullet boat at the speed of light as to the creation of a new inhabitant of the starry habitations.

It is fecundity in 'Camping Out'; in 'Letter II', it is destruct-ive barrenness. 'The young couple are merely curious about each other, therefore they lose interest in whatever they think they have found out; a nagging process' (record-notes).

LETTER II

Searching the cave gallery of your face
My torch meets fresco after fresco ravishes
Rebegets me; it crumbles each; no trace
Stays to remind me what each heaven lavishes.

How judge their triumph, these primeval stocks,
When to the sketchbook nought but this remains,
A gleam where jellyfish have died on rocks,
Bare canvas that the golden frame disdains?

Glancing, walk on; there are portraits yet, untried,
Unbleached; the process, do not hope to change.
Let us mark in general terms their wealth, how wide
Their sense of character, their styles, their range.

Only walk on; the greater part have gone;
Whom lust, nor cash, nor habit join, are cold;
The sands are shifting as you walk; walk on,
The new is an emptier darkness than the old.

Crossing and doubling, many-fingered, hounded,
Those desperate stars, those worms dying in flower
Ashed paper holds, nose-sailing, search their bounded
Darkness for a last acre to devour.

The barrenness is brought alive to us precisely as *not* creating new portraits, merely using the old ones up; and the central metaphor of the portrait deserves, once more, not to be dwindled into being slackly exchangeable with many another way of putting it. The effect within the poem is to intimate that there have been ancestors. Ancestors first appear in the poem as available to condescension, the disconcerting lordliness of tone in 'these primeval stocks' ('the early race that made the pictures'; Notes). But then, after 'the golden frame', they change, as by evolution and history, and what was a cave gallery becomes an ancestral gallery of family 'portraits' ('how wide / Their sense of character, their styles'). True, as in Marvell's 'The Gallery' each such picture is in the first place conceived of as a facet of the lover's character; but the effect of the metaphor is to suggest a short-circuiting, a line of ancestors coming to an end. Such is the taunting sadness of 'fresco after fresco' (Italian, *fresh*) as each fresh apprehension crumbles. The sight of each fresco 'ravishes / Rebegets me', but the ravishing only re-begets him and is no begetting. The Notes by Empson say: 'They have a ground in common only so long as there is something new to find out about each other.' Indeed, the whole poem is a penetrating and shaming evocation of this particular form of *égoïsme à deux*; two is the number, two only, no created other to create the newly unforeseeably interesting. The drastic shift of manner and tone in 'Whom lust, nor cash, nor habit join, are cold' (there is nothing else that is hortatory, let alone so lavishly and Gallicly sententious, in the poem) should challenge us to ponder what it really is that joins and warms lovers; lust, cash, and habit are a determinedly low-minded trio, especially as we should have expected a high-minded admonition, and to find it low is to be aware of other possibilities for the list. 'What each heaven lavishes' is only some facet of her; not a lavishness beyond the one or the two of them. The two are contrasted with the many portraits, and with the stars, the flickering flames, and the tendrils of smoke (like the smoke from sophistication's cigarettes) that spill many-fingered from the fearful torch. The immense series of births is curtailed; the lovers' inability to create anything newly of interest to each other is implicit in their condescension towards the past and their blankness towards the future. What gleams is not life, since it is killingly out of its element: 'A gleam where jellyfish have died on rocks'. 'No trace / Stays to remind me'. It is this

short-circuiting of life which furnishes one of the senses in
which 'The new is an emptier darkness than the old'. The force
of the final stanza, which with effortless surprise moves up and
out, 'nose-sailing', into a rich surrealism of style quite new to
the poem, is in its travesty of fecundity; neither its 'crossing'
nor its 'doubling' can urge the generative sense of those words;
and its many fingers, its 'desperate stars, those worms dying in
flower', have the bizarre vitality of death. Of Milton's Death,
to whom 'nose-sailing' is a grim guide; Death scenting his victims even before they become such:

> So saying, with delight he snuff'd the smell
> Of mortal change on Earth. As when a flock
> Of ravenous Fowl, through many a League remote,
> Against the day of Battel, to a Field,
> Where Armies lie encampt, come flying, lur'd
> With sent of living Carcasses design'd
> For death, the following day, in bloodie fight.
> So sented the grim Feature, and upturn'd
> His Nostril wide into the murkie Air.
>
> (*Paradise Lost*, x 272-80)

'Camping Out' experiences a delighted creating; 'Letter II',
a sterility which is a travesty of vitality (a vitality associated
with art-work and with worms). 'Arachne' fears the pride
which thinks it can create on its own, the one of it, not even the
two of them.

ARACHNE

> Twixt devil and deep sea, man hacks his caves;
> Birth, death; one, many; what is true, and seems;
> Earth's vast hot iron, cold space's empty waves:
>
> King spider, walks the velvet roof of streams:
> Must bird and fish, must god and beast avoid:
> Dance, like nine angels, on pin-point extremes.
>
> His gleaming bubble between void and void,
> Tribe-membrane, that by mutual tension stands,
> Earth's surface film, is at a breath destroyed.
>
> Bubbles gleam brightest with least depth of lands
> But two is least can with full tension strain,
> Two molecules; one, and the film disbands.

> We two suffice. But oh beware, whose vain
> Hydroptic soap my meagre water saves.
> Male spiders must not be too early slain.

It is the pounce within the final pounce which so unpredictably wrests the poem, and which we need to tremble at if we are 'to make human sense of the paradoxes of the poem'. It is disconcerting enough when in the last stanza the poem is suddenly seen to be a love-poem. 'We two suffice.' The peremptory chill of that sentence is not only that a 'we' suddenly asserts itself where there has as yet been no I or you, but also that this three-word sentence (the barest of sufficiencies) follows upon sentences which have been fifty, twenty-one, and twenty-four words long. The poem had seemed to be serenely braced, a dazzling act of abstraction-acrobatics, itself walking the velvet roof and dancing on pin-point extremes. Then the last stanza converts all those extremes into a silky, thoughtful counter-threat, designed to meet a thoughtless threat. At first, in simply insisting that we two need each other, since neither soap nor water can alone create the bubble; and then with the altogether unexpected leap which takes the earlier 'Birth, death' with nothing like the earlier calm: 'Male spiders must not be too early slain.' For all its cold courtesy (akin to the counter-threats in Shakespeare's Sonnets), it is a weird and violent end. We had not been much thinking about the title 'Arachne'; had come gradually to forget it squatting over the poem; and then she is what the poem finally, superbly uncalled-for, drives at. The 'King spider' who is 'man' (and there is, one now realizes, a trick with 'man', as in 'Invitation to Juno', that man's world of a poem) is the counterpart and rival to Arachne, 'a queen spider and disastrously proud' (Notes). For the last line enters upon a different dimension of threat and fear: that a woman can be so predatorily proud as not just to destroy life but to preclude it. The female spider who jumps that gun, and the proud Arachne who challenged the goddess, hanged herself in despair, and was changed into a spider: these coalesce. The sudden pounce of the last line calls up the eruption into 'To an Old Lady' of 'Bees sting their need . . .', with its same wilful perilous precluding of a life-series. Is it only the accident of their having become famous as the epigraph to Robert Lowell's

'To Speak of Woe that is in Marriage' that makes one remember those words of Schopenhauer? 'It is the future generation that presses into being by means of these exuberant feelings and supersensible soap bubbles of ours.'

Empson does not read 'Arachne' on the record:

I left it out because I'd come to think that it was in rather bad taste. It's boy being afraid of girl, as usual, but it's boy being too rude to girl. I thought it had rather a nasty feeling, that's why I left it out.[99]

One sees what he means, and 'Arachne' will always be a poem that one changes one's mind about. But its fierceness is true and deep, and the end—just because it is a meticulous slow-paced warning—includes its own plea for something other than pride all round. There is another poem in which a man might be considered too rude to a woman, one which has, on and off, a rather nasty feeling, and one about which Empson has written with passion: Donne's 'The Apparition', with its chillingly torrid conclusion:

> and since my love is spent,
> I'had rather thou shouldst painfully repent,
> Than by my threatnings rest still innocent.

Just as Donne's ending with *innocent* (and not with *repent*) holds open, imperiously but magnanimously, the door to something else, so Empson's threatenings, 'Male spiders must not be too early slain', incorporate some intimation that it is even now not too late. Even so, a central source of energy in 'Arachne' is the full tension of feelings about begetting, and it is worth remembering where 'hydroptic' comes from. In Donne, it evokes the death-bed in a poem which Empson is not alone in thinking of as enshrining Donne's fears for his wife's child-bed:

> The generall balme th' hydroptic earth hath drunk,
> Whither, as to the beds-feet, life is shrunke,
> Dead and enterr'd.
>> ('A Nocturnall upon S. Lucies Day')

It sums up, too, the fierce father in 'The Perfume': 'By thy Hydroptique father catechiz'd'.

'The Scales' is a catechism by a figure not only fatherly but

[99] *the Review*, Nos 6 and 7 (1963), 27.

also avuncular. This girl, should she be patted (small, child-like, a miniature landscape like that of a sand-castle), or is she a grander adventurous landscape? 'The Scales'—'in the sense of the first estimate of size which decides what kind of tool to use; an excuse to a woman for not showing enough love' (record-notes).

THE SCALES

The proper scale would pat you on the head
But Alice showed her pup Ulysses' bough
Well from behind a thistle, wise with dread;

And though your gulf-sprung mountains I allow
(Snow-puppy curves, rose-solemn dado band)
Charming for nurse, I am not nurse just now.

Why pat or stride them, when the train will land
Me high, through climbing tunnels, at your side,
And careful fingers meet through castle sand.

Claim slyly rather that the tunnels hide
Solomon's gems, white vistas, preserved kings,
By jackal sandhole to your air flung wide.

Say (she suspects) to sea Nile only brings
Delta and indecision, who instead
Far back up country does enormous things.

The right and usual commentary on this poem which speaks of Alice is Empson's essay on Lewis Carroll:

A desire to include all sexuality in the girl child, the least obviously sexed of human creatures, the one that keeps its sex in the safest place, was an important part of their fascination for him. He is partly imagining himself as the girl-child (with these comforting character-istics) partly as its father (these together make *it* a father) partly as its lover—so it might be a mother—but then of course it is clever and detached enough to do everything for itself.[100]

'So it might be a mother': this is what vibrates the delicious perplexity of scale, the gravity and tremor, in those lines about 'nurse', and this is what animates the ample triumph of the poem's concluding lines, which are at once the most casual of gestures (vaguely across a continent) and the most princely of admonitions. Still, 'an excuse to a woman for not showing

[100] *Some Versions*, p. 273.

enough love'? The lurking presence of an excuse is to be sensed
in a most marked absence from those last lines; delta and indecision at the mouth of the Nile, yes, and enormous things far
back up country. But is there nothing between? There is the
great fecundating power of the Nile, neither indecision nor
those vaguely enormous things but the one superbly decisive
(decisive for Egypt) enormous thing which is the life of Egypt
and which epitomizes the mysteries of the genial powers of life.
From 'castle sand' to 'jackal sandhole' to the Nile: the shift is
not just into grandeur but into the lifegiving. As in 'the fructu-
ant marsh' in that poem by Empson which begins 'Egyptian
banks . . .', and as in the line about the Sphinx in 'Four Legs,
Three Legs, Two Legs': 'Behind, Sahara, before Nile and
man', on which Empson comments: 'I have never seen anything in print about how dramatically she is placed between the
desert and the sown' (Notes). 'The Scales' does not speak of
the Nile's most real power, its most enormous thing, but far
back up country the poem knows of it, and is itself fecundated
by its implication, in suggesting a possible motherhood in the
girl ('so it might be a mother') from which for now the speaker,
preferring an excuse, averts his perplexed eyes. Not showing
enough love, perhaps, but with the tenderest of affection and
indeed a great sense of why love is the grandest of the enormous
things.

'Homage to the British Museum' may seem altogether remote from any such concerns. Its subject, clearly enough (it is
Empson's most gruffly lucid and humorous poem), is modern
man's all-but-paralysing consciousness of the range and variety
of beliefs alive in the world; it is aware of the paradox that
would grant an absolute status, a supremacy, to its own large
relativism. (Empson says of Fielding: 'he does not find relativism alarming, because he feels that to understand codes other
than your own is likely to make your judgments better'.[101])
Aware, too, that the only way out of this paradox is through
good-humour, a repeated willingness to admit (admission as
paradoxically the way out), and a quizzical freedom from
fluster.

[101] *Kenyon Review*, xx (1958), 231.

HOMAGE TO THE BRITISH MUSEUM

There is a Supreme God in the ethnological section;
A hollow toad shape, faced with a blank shield.
He needs his belly to include the Pantheon,
Which is inserted through a hole behind.
At the navel, at the points formally stressed, at the organs of
    sense,
Lice glue themselves, dolls, local deities,
His smooth wood creeps with all the creeds of the world.

Attending there let us absorb the cultures of nations
And dissolve into our judgment all their codes.
Then, being clogged with a natural hesitation
(People are continually asking one the way out),
Let us stand here and admit that we have no road.
Being everything, let us admit that is to be something,
Or give ourselves the benefit of the doubt;
Let us offer our pinch of dust all to this God,
And grant his reign over the entire building.

Yet even here what has moved Empson to speak with such
largeness of mind is the largeness of begetting. It is not only
that this 'Supreme God' is Tangaroa, the sea god, in the act of
creating the other gods and man; he is seen as wonderfully able
to do all the creating all by himself, and so to absorb the powers
of womanhood within his manhood. He shows that we can imagine, though we cannot enter, a world in which it is not any
longer true that

> two is least can with full tension strain,
> Two molecules; one, and the film disbands.

He alone has the right to think that he can create it all alone; he
possesses the true pride of which Empson's Arachne was the
travesty. 'A desire to include all sexuality . . .', 'clever and
detached enough to do everything for itself': Alice too belongs
to this odd family of Arachne and the supreme god and the
phoenix-like tree of 'Note on Local Flora'.

The supreme god's face is a blank shield, still to receive lin-
eage and arms. His belly is a comical womb, an unaggressive
Wooden Horse—'He needs his belly to include the Pantheon',
not as we need ours. His 'navel' is even more delightful a super-
erogation than those of Adam and Eve. We are from the first

line in the world of mock-heroic (often, as in Dryden and Pope, a world of primal acts of creation), but there is no demeaning. That this should be so is a consequence of the shrewd calm with which the poem contemplates the greatest-ever act of begetting; one is one and yet not all alone.

The world of 'Note on Local Flora' is mock-heroic too, and it again celebrates an extraordinary begetting, not in the backward vista but in the forward.

NOTE ON LOCAL FLORA

> There is a tree native in Turkestan,
> Or further east towards the Tree of Heaven,
> Whose hard cold cones, not being wards to time,
> Will leave their mother only for good cause;
> Will ripen only in a forest fire;
> Wait, to be fathered as was Bacchus once,
> Through men's long lives, that image of time's end.
> I knew the Phoenix was a vegetable.
> So Semele desired her deity
> As this in Kew thirsts for the Red Dawn.

The poem is itself a hard cold cone which then miraculously ripens. The buoyant snap of the eighth line—'I knew the Phoenix was a vegetable'—is that of a ripened conclusion (though it importantly does not conclude the poem); the poem's first sentence had ripened through seven lines to bring this triumphant jauntiness to birth. Manifestly the poem is, among other things, a policital *aperçu*; but this does not alter the fact that what animates it, what makes it ripen in the mind (ripeness is all), is its relief as it contemplates this apocalyptic begetting. Miraculous, in that the cones are already gestating ('Will leave their mother only for good cause') but somehow have not yet been fathered ('Wait, to be fathered as was Bacchus once'); and in that what Donne called 'the phoenix riddle' is solved, newly solved and yet one had always dimly known that must be it. The tree is not to feel any pain; yet the last two lines of the poem are chastening (as so often in an Empson poem), for they expand from the previous line's single succinctness into a graver tone and a larger movement, and they bring before us not just the fathering of Bacchus but the woman who was destroyed in bringing into the world 'The laughing god born of a startling answer' (Empson's 'Bacchus'). Semele, burnt to destruction by the god she loved, reminds the poem of the pangs of birth and of the terribly unforeseen; Kew is securely and therefore insecurely within the real world; 'thirsts' stands in an oddly challenging relation to Bacchus; and the Red Dawn is something from which only this extraordinary tree (not native here, remember, though 'local flora') can have no impulse whatsoever to flinch. It would be wrong to darken this invigorating poem, but the crisp weight of its joking is a matter of its knowing the usual gravity of birth; indeed it is invigorating just because it speaks from Kew and not from Turkestan. The gaiety of 'Note on Local Flora' and of 'Homage to the British Museum', like the joy of 'Camping Out', derives its pungent force from appropriating to itself these lavish grotesqueries of begetting (the phoenix tree, the all-creating god, the Madonna); the gaiety banishes the usual anxieties and trepidation that are involved in begetting—banishes them, which is not the same as ignoring them; they put in a spectral appearance so that they can be exorcised. 'Note on Local Flora'—the mother as a mysterious tree—is in its way an exorcism of the darker mysteries involved in the woman as tree in 'The Ants'. In 'The World's End', there is Empson's feeling for 'the gulf that lies so snugly curled', possibilities of independence and freedom, conceivabilities which lie like embryos never to be given birth there 'Where nameless Somethings in their causes sleep'.

For the tree, fire is a thirsted-for begetting. In 'Missing Dates', 'The complete fire is death.' It is a poem about life as a long day's dying and about inevitable waste; what reinforces the feeling that it is the grimmest of Empson's three villanelles is the way in which the two refrains—'Slowly the poison the whole blood stream fills', and 'The waste remains, the waste remains and kills'—manifest the same impulse, oppressively at one, whereas they stand at something of an angle to each other in 'Villanelle' ('It is the pain, it is the pain, endures', and 'Poise of my hands reminded me of yours'), as in 'Reflection from Anita Loos' ('No man is sure he does not need to climb', and '"A girl can't go on laughing all the time"').

MISSING DATES

Slowly the poison the whole blood stream fills.
It is not the effort nor the failure tires.
The waste remains, the waste remains and kills.

It is not your system or clear sight that mills
Down small to the consequence a life requires;
Slowly the poison the whole blood stream fills.

They bled an old dog dry yet the exchange rills
Of young dog blood gave but a month's desires.
The waste remains, the waste remains and kills.

It is the Chinese tombs and the slag hills
Usurp the soil, and not the soil retires.
Slowly the poison the whole blood stream fills.

Not to have fire is to be a skin that shrills.
The complete fire is death. From partial fires
The waste remains, the waste remains and kills.

It is the poems you have lost, the ills
From missing dates, at which the heart expires.
Slowly the poison the whole blood stream fills.
The waste remains, the waste remains and kills.

When he reads this poem and speaks of it, Empson usually denies that 'missing dates' had for him any real connection with the true, the frustratedly amatory, meaning of the phrase; he was using it only to mean appointments that fell through, opportunities missed. Yet it is impossible to feel that when 'the poems' suddenly surface at the end they can really be thought of as carrying most of the gravity of the poem. I like the oddity of their sudden intervention, but it is important that they should seem so desolatingly much smaller than the dark intimations of this poem itself. For the pull towards death, towards a sense of waste and death in life, is very much a matter of feeling so many possibilities of life unbegotten. 'The consequence a life requires' has to include some sense of the many things consequence can be (the act of most consequence which a life requires is to perpetuate the sequence of life). The old dog who gets the young dog's blood gets a cruel parody of begetting (the generations the wrong way round, moreover), as 'a month's desires' suggests—and how long is a month to a dog? The waste-tombs of ancient death and the waste-mounds of modern life between them leave no room for that soil which should be the ground of present life, new life. Yet I don't think that 'Missing Dates' is clear to itself about the consequence this poem requires. Perhaps because it is the poem which most raises to a glare the two focuses (upon life as dark and upon life as the creation of light); perhaps because it so completely lacks a sense of anybody or anything else addressed, whether a tree, a general audience or a person—it self-communes as no other poem of Empson's does, its *you* a desolating vacancy; perhaps because it allows so little room to Empson's humour, whether sardonic or affectionate; perhaps because its refrains concur as hammer-blows rather than converging as pincers: at any rate I find that it presents a mind troubled like a fountain stirred, and the poem itself sees not the bottom of it. 'Or tell me with less drama . . .'

Of 'The Teasers' one is fearful of saying anything at all because of the high scorn which Empson let play upon G. S. Fraser:

When dear old George Fraser says it was all against being horrified by women when they're menstruating, and offering my person to all the women in the world and so forth, I was much shocked. I don't entertain these shocking sentiments at all, do you see? Absolutely nothing to do with what is in my mind; I wouldn't even have thought it was in George's mind.[102]

THE TEASERS

Not but they die, the teasers and the dreams,
Not but they die,
                    and tell the careful flood
To give them what they clamour for and why.

You could not fancy where they rip to blood,
You could not fancy
                    nor that mud
I have heard speak that will not cake or dry.

Our claims to act appear so small to these,
Our claims to act
                    colder lunacies
That cheat the love, the moment, the small fact.

[102] *the Review*, Nos 6 and 7 (1963), 28.

Make no escape because they flash and die,
Make no escape
                    build up your love,
Leave what you die for and be safe to die.

Empson has insisted that the four stanzas which make up 'The
Teasers' were salvaged from a long poem and that they cannot
really be made sense of. It is clearly an erotic poem; 'the careful
flood' (at once cautious, full of unforeseen cares, and both destructive and creative—the Nile's flood as well as Noah's)
creates life, 'what they clamour for' ('the clamour of life' is a
prominent phrase in Empson's 'Ignorance of Death'); the fantasies of life are no more evanescent than our love-hopes and
our acts of love, and yet this should move us not to escape but
to build. The last stanza sees begetting as the true recourse
which is not falsely an escape; sees it as the way 'to build up
your love', and as the paradox: 'Leave what you die for and be
safe to die.' *Leave* both as quit and as leave behind you when
you go; what we all die for—whether in terms of ideals or of the
hungry generations—is our progeny, and it is only in doing so
that we can 'be safe to die'. 'To give away your selfe, keeps
your selfe still': that was the line from Shakespeare's Sonnet 16
which Empson paraphrased as 'you are not less yourself because
you have had children'.

'Safe': the word is at home in 'Thanks for a Wedding Present', one of the very few poems in the *Collected Poems* that are
later than the 1940 volume.

THANKS FOR A WEDDING PRESENT

[It was a compass on a necklace with the poem:
Magnetic Powers cannot harm your House
Since Beauty, Wit and Love its walls de-Gauss.
And if, when nights are dark, your feet should stray
By chance or instinct to the Load *of Hay*
With me drink deep and on th'uncharted track
Let my Magnetic Power guide you back.]

She bears your gift as one safe to return
      From longer journeys asking braver fuel
            Than a poor needle losing itself an hour

Within a *Load of Hay* needs heart to learn.
      She wears the birth of physics as a jewel
            And of the maritime empires as a flower.

I think this a lovely poem and am surprised that it never gets mentioned. What is especially fine in it is that it carries out its delicate double-duty so unassumingly: it needs to incorporate gratitude to the giver within a larger gratitude to the woman who has given so much larger a gift: herself; and this without slighting the wedding present and its friendly love. Likewise it needs to praise the wedding present and more vastly to praise the woman (and moreover without self-congratulation); and this it does by letting us feel that it is not only the compass, but the wearer, who is delighted in as a jewel and as a flower. The serenity and safety of the poem derive from the tact and secret largeness with which it includes a sense of what the right true end of love in marriage is. The poem has two sentences only, one beginning 'She bears your gift', and the other 'She wears the birth'; the parallelism, the internal rhyme, and the words 'bear' and 'birth' all ask us to feel something of a future such as we are usually guided to glimpse in an epithalamium. The dignity of the poem is achieved by its compacting so much of what had always been the preoccupations of Empson's poems: the compass; safety and yet adventurous 'longer journeys asking braver fuel'; physics; the maritime empires. But just as the giver's verses had spoken of 'your House' (and in so doing could not but suggest, as it were, a royal house), so the birth of physics and of the maritime empires, those past discoveries of richness, should be felt as indeed births. The poem's climax, they expand to a full sense of the human situation, and of future births as rich.

   The last four poems in the *Collected Poems* are 'Let it go' (which is 'about stopping writing poetry'; record-notes); 'Thanks for a Wedding Present'; 'Sonnet' (published 1942, on 'the cultures of man'); and—translated in 1951 and published in 1952—'Chinese Ballad'. I think it sheer grace that 'Thanks for a Wedding Present' and 'Chinese Ballad' should form the points that they do in the arc of Empson's poetry. 'The bit of a *Chinese Ballad*, about resistance to the Japanese, is direct translation; I felt that it achieved without effort the metaphysical poetry which we struggled to write when I was young' (record-notes).

CHINESE BALLAD

Now he has seen the girl Hsiang-Hsiang,
    Now back to the guerrilla band;
And she goes with him down the vale
    And pauses at the strand.

The mud is yellow, deep, and thick,
    And their feet stick, where the stream turns.
'Make me two models out of this,
    That clutches as it yearns.

'Make one of me and one of you,
    And both shall be alive.
Were there no magic in the dolls
    The children could not thrive.

'When you have made them smash them back:
    They yet shall live again.
Again make dolls of you and me
    But mix them grain by grain.

'So your flesh shall be part of mine
    And part of mine be yours.
Brother and sister we shall be
    Whose unity endures.

'Always the sister doll will cry,
    Made in these careful ways,
Cry on and on, Come back to me,
    Come back, in a few days.'

Love in time of war, with the poignancy of what war does to
parenthood; the intrepid journey; the respect for courage and
for decision; the fording of the river (which had once been
'Leaves isle equation by not frozen ford') and its unobtrusive
paradox about the right choice ('He crosses the stream where
it turns because it is wider therefore shallower there', Notes);
the pathos of the utterly disparate time-scales ('Cry on and on,
Come back to me, / Come back, in a few days'); and at its
heart symbolic begetting of dolls (how different from those
'dolls' on the 'Supreme God'), of two people, an act of self-
begetting, offering a magical reassurance and an unmagical
epitome of faithfulness, and which recalls the children begotten
by the ordinary magic of birth: all this, the fullness of the poem's
respect for what it contemplates, is achieved because the subject
so fully reconciles so much in Empson's thinking and feeling.

He took no liberties, and it is altogether right that the only point on which he needs to say anything should be this: 'I added the bit about children, but I understand that is only like working a footnote into the text, because the term specifically means dolls for children' (Notes). What is created is what is honoured: an assurance that though life may be essentially inadequate to the human spirit, the human spirit is essentially adequate to life.

Empson has said that when he finished *The Structure of Complex Words* he felt *Nunc dimittis*.[103] Fortunately he was not so possessed by the feeling as to write no further criticism. But given the particular kind of conclusive triumph which 'Chinese Ballad' is, there is a simple dignity, clear-sighted and touching, in its having been Empson's *Nunc dimittis* as a poet.

[103] *Mandrake*, ii (1955-6), 447-8.

STEVIE SMITH:
THE ART OF SINKING IN POETRY

Fausse-naïve: an odd turn, but Philip Larkin[1] devised it as a route into the world of Stevie Smith. All its quirks are right for this truly quirky poet: its feminizing, its Anglo-French, and its paradox. For the first question to ask about the poems of Stevie Smith is, can she possibly be as ingenuous as she sounds? An ingénue is of interest only if you can't be entirely sure. A few critics raise the question and show that it need not be nailed down. If critics 'portray her often as a naïve writer,' says Michael Schmidt, 'this reveals the success with which she projected the mock-innocence of her public image.'[2] But her writing depends upon its being always in question to what degree her innocence *is* mock-innocence. She disliked 'the false-simple' (which she associated with Nazism) as much as she liked 'the childish delight in a daily use of colour and form, the naïveté that has in it something of innocence'.[3] Not that innocence is a simple thing. In the words of 'The Last Turn of the Screw': 'Some children are born innocent, some achieve it'. And some have it thrust upon them? In her novel *The Holiday*, she permitted herself a risqué joke by allusion to a low paper, yet she did so in schoolgirl French: 'As the sunlight saturates my flesh and bones I feel I should like it to go on for a long time (comme disait Ingenuous Isabel dans le Pink 'Un d'autrefois).'[4] To speak in this way of Ingenuous Isabel must be to leave the question of Ingenuous Stevie or Disingenuous Stevie teasingly unresolved.

When she deprecated the political animus of *Murder in the Cathedral*, she went for an unexpected double charge that it was both childish and disingenuous:

This does not seem a constructive political opinion, it seems rather childish, as if he thought men did not sometimes have to govern, as if he thought that by the act of governing they became at once not men

[1] *New Statesman*, 28 September 1962; *Required Writing* (1983), p. 153.
[2] *An Introduction to Fifty Modern British Poets* (1979), p. 200.
[3] *The Holiday* (1949), 1979 edn, pp. 143-4. *Over the Frontier* (1938), 1980 edn, p. 271.
[4] *The Holiday*, p. 149.

but monsters. It is a disingenuous and not uncommon thought, it is one aspect of the arrogance of art and the arrogance of highminded-ness divorced from power, it is something one should not put up with.[5]

The word 'disingenuous' turns up in 'Private Means is Dead', an early poem partly about the language's being eager to doff its civilian clothes and don its uniform. 'Major Portion / Is a disingenuous person.' Others in this monstrous regiment of men are Private Means, Major Operation, the Generals Collapse Debility Panic and Uproar, and a disguised figure (unseen but not unheard), 'The crux and Colonel / Of the whole matter.' Yet the crux and kernel of the poem must be acknowledged, namely the Shakespearean allusion:

> Captive Good, attending Captain Ill
> Can tell us quite a lot about the Captain, if he will.

For Shakespeare's Sonnet 66 was never far from her thoughts: 'Tyr'd with all these for restfull death I cry'. Many of her best poems cry for restful death: 'Come Death' (the early poem, and also her very last, which used the title again), 'Tender Only to One,' 'The Bottle of Aspirins,' 'The Hostage,' 'My heart goes out,' 'Thoughts about the Person from Porlock,' and 'Why do I think of Death as a friend?' In *The Holiday* there is a telling moment: 'And I smile at Basil and I say: Tired of all these, for restful death I cry, as to behold desert a beggar born.'[6]

> And simple-Truth miscalde Simplicitie,
> And captive-good attending Captaine ill.

Miscalled simplicity? She was not simple-minded, and speaking to her friend Kay Dick, she declined to be assimilated to Phèdre: 'She's much simpler than I am . . . I'm straightforward but I'm not simple.'[7] As she put it in 'Phèdre':

> Yes, I should like poor honourable simple sweet prim Phèdre
> To be happy. One would have to be pretty simple
> To be happy with a prig like Hippolytus,
> But she was simple.

[5] 'History or Poetic Drama?' (1958), reprinted in *Me Again* (1981), p. 148.
[6] *The Holiday*, p. 17.
[7] Kay Dick, *Ivy and Stevie* (1971), p. 49.

Still, whether or not this was the simple biographical truth, it is
not the truth that the poems promulgate.

MAGNA EST VERITAS

> With my looks I am bound to look simple or fast I would
>   rather look simple
> So I wear a tall hat on the back of my head that is
>   rather a temple
> And I walk rather queerly and comb my long hair
> And people say, Don't bother about her.
> So in my time I have picked up a good many facts,
> Rather more than the people do who wear smart hats
> And I do not deceive because I am rather simple too
> And although I collect facts I do not always know
>   what they amount to.
> I regard them as a contribution to almighty Truth,
>   magna est veritas et praevalebit,
> Agreeing with that Latin writer, Great is Truth and
>   will prevail in a bit.

Simple truth, or affectation? The odd gait of the lines ('And
I walk rather queerly'); the queer freedom suddenly to lop their
lolloping, so that the lines can lope and pace; the off-rhyming,
off-hand but also a bit off its head; the straight gaze and
straight face which can then move from one kind of inspired
inane rhyming ('too' with 'to') into another kind: 'et praevale-
bit' with 'and will prevail in a bit': these constitute the art of a
poem which will not let on how artless or artful it is being.

Stevie Smith once produced an anthology of children's
verse, *The Batsford Book of Children's Verse* (1970), which was sold
in America without 'children' in the title. But then who but she
would have prefaced such a collection by giving these lines by
Shelley as just the thing for children?

> His big tears, for he wept well,
> Turned to mill-stones as they fell;
>
> And the little children, who
> Round his feet played to and fro,
> Thinking every tear a gem
> Had their brains knocked out by them.

None of the things that come together in her poems is in itself
unusual, but the combination is unique. The accents are those

of a child; yet the poems are continually allusive, alive with literary echoes as no child's utterance is. The accents are those of a child, and at the same time of a patient instructor of a child. The poems sound like child's-play, but are inimitable. In their memories of nursery rhyme and of fairy tale, in their lisping and lilting, they are a child's eye view; yet children don't write poems which matter except as that diminished thing, poems-by-children. Helen Vendler pointed out a paradox:

All poetry deserving of the name has been written by people who have passed through puberty. On the other hand, there are some aspects of poetry—notably, originality of perception and spontaneity of language—which appear frequently in the speech and writing of children, but which are so dishearteningly killed off by life and schooling that a way with words is one of the rarest of adult talents.[8]

This is a paradox which Stevie Smith's poems not only embody but also attend to, albeit cryptically.

'WHAT IS SHE WRITING? PERHAPS IT WILL BE GOOD'

What is she writing? Perhaps it will be good,
The young girl laughs: 'I am in love'.
But the older girl is serious: 'Not now, perhaps later.'
Still the young girl teases: 'What's the matter?
To lose everything! A waste of time!'
But now the older one is quite silent,
Writing, writing, and perhaps it will be good.
Really neither girl is a fool.

When the child-prodigy Minou Drouet burst upon French life with her poems, Jean Cocteau stood firm. 'All eight-year-olds have genius—except Minou Drouet.' Yet really neither girl is a fool. Stevie Smith played the fool; and she held this high-spirited modesty in tension with a higher spirit.

Behind her simplest work is a very unsimple tradition: *The Praise of Folly*. The account of Erasmus' book given by William Empson, in *The Structure of Complex Words*, suits Stevie Smith and her proclivity to use the word 'fool' widely and discriminatingly. 'We could indeed say,' says Empson, 'that the simpleton is innocent and natural; this sums up most of the conception.'[9]

---

[8] *New York Review of Books*, 24 November 1977.
[9] *The Structure of Complex Words* (1951), pp. 106-7.

Stevie Smith was a natural. 'Simpletons, children, madmen of various sorts, saints': these are the types who throng forward with a claim to Erasmus' invaluable folly, and they are the types who populate her poems. One novelty here is that the poet, the Fool, is a woman. After all, the Fool is most often a man. Stevie Smith is still further seen as Fool (as well as minstrel) in her extraordinarily funny account, all piercing simplicity (in Kay Dick's *Ivy and Stevie*[10]), of her audience with the Queen in Buckingham Palace, when she received the Queen's Gold Medal for poetry in 1969.

Among her many subjects, Stevie Smith had two great ones, children and death. Her excellent perturbed critiques of Christianity—doubly perturbed in that, as she said, she was always in danger of falling into belief[11]—are essentially death-poems: they believe eternal life to be a threat and not a promise, and not only when it takes the form of eternal torment.

Yet children and death sit oddly together. The usual thing is to say that children cannot imagine death. Stevie Smith insists that she for one could and did. At the age of about eight, she realized that if life were more than she could bear, she could decide not to bear it. 'Life lay in our hands.'[12] No doubt she was precocious, but her art has the disturbing power to suggest that in this matter too we sentimentalize children. They have intimations of mortality; they should be educated, she says, explicitly in the feasibility and—on occasion—propriety of suicide. Her anthology of children's verse, or rather of verse for children, offers not only Spenser's Despair and Shakespeare's 'Fear no more the heat of the sun,' but also the dark old consolation that it is better to be dead than alive, best of all never to have been born. 'From *Oedipus Coloneus* (Sophocles)':

> *Chorus:*   Not to be born at all
> Is best, far best that can befall,
> Next best, when born, with least delay
> To trace the backward way.

A riddling consolation. Perhaps it is not that children are more

---

[10] pp. 51-2.

[11] 'The Necessity of Not Believing', *Gemini*, 2:1 (1958), 19-32.

[12] Preface to *The Batsford Book of Children's Verse.* Also *Novel on Yellow Paper* (1936), 1951 edn, pp. 135-7.

like adults than is generally assumed in that both can imagine death, but in that neither can. (Though it is the adult who can imagine the unimaginability of death.) *Imagination Dead Imagine*, intones the greatest of these modern writers who are grateful, as Stevie Smith was, to believe that there is no such thing as eternal life. When Samuel Beckett, in *Murphy*, refers darkly to 'the next best thing to never being born', we know where we are. As we do when Stevie Smith issues a simple remonstrance: 'There are some human beings who do not wish for eternal life.' [13]

The crucial critical question is the same for her as for Beckett. Since each subscribes to the belief that life is not simply a good thing or death simply a bad thing, what sort of life should there be in their words? The young Beckett could praise the words of James Joyce because 'they are alive', they are not 'abstracted to death.' [14] But Beckett became a great writer once he realized that it does not make sense to use the word 'life' approvingly of words, and 'death' disapprovingly, if you do not yourself happily approve of life and disapprove of death. The very words must incarnate the acknowledgement, a relationship of life to death, as they did when Robert Lowell fashioned wording glad to be suddenly cut short: 'All's well that ends.' Less curt, more sidling, Stevie Smith works towards the same end: 'But all good things come to an end, and the same goes for all bad things'. [15] Death is the nothing that supremely ends all bad things, and her language will bring a spectral life to what is usually a moribund turn of phrase:

When I was talking to Harley at the Ministry one day about my poems, he said, I am rather disturbed about this death feeling in your poems.

Oh, I said, that is nothing, that death feeling, it is absolutely nothing. [16]

For 'that death feeling' is not only one's feelings about death, but also there being no feeling once dead, and 'absolutely nothing' is not only a social sootheing but 'the vision of *positive*

---

[13] With a sketch reproduced in *New Directions*, Nos 7-8 and 10-11 (1975), 19.

[14] *Our Exagmination Round His Factification* . . . (1929), pp. 15-16.

[15] *Novel on Yellow Paper*, p. 155.

[16] *The Holiday*, p. 62.

annihilation' (in the words of Beckett).[17] Absolutely, that is
what death is: nothing. 'Be absolute for death', in the words of
the Duke in *Measure for Measure*. 'Why do I think of death as a
friend?': there is no question about the answer.

So Stevie Smith, like Beckett, uses clichés; they are phrases
which are dead but won't lie down. From *The Holiday*:

> I said to my cousin on another occasion when we had gone horse-
> back riding together: Do you like Death?
> Caz said: He is nothing to write home about.[18]

Beckett is a writer who did wonders with this cliché, nothing to
write home about: see his story, *The End*.

Again like Beckett, she uses literary allusions to catch a paradox of life and death, of life in death or death in life.

Tennyson: Deep as first love, and wild with all regret;
              O Death in Life, the days that are no more.
                             ('Tears, Idle Tears')

Beckett: 'O Death in Life,' vociferated Belacqua, 'the days that are no
           more.'[19]

Stevie Smith: I think of my poems as my kiddo, and no doubt but
           Tennyson felt that way too, 'Deep as first love and wild
           with all regret, Oh death in Life the days that are no
           more.'[20]

THE DEATH SENTENCE

Cold as No Plea,
Yet wild with all negation,
Weeping I come
To my heart's destination,
To my last bed
Between th'unhallowed boards—
The Law allows it
And the Court awards.

For all its articulations, 'The Death Sentence' is one sentence,
and it is more merciful than the poem called 'The Commuted
Sentence,' next in the *Collected Poems*, which opens:

[17] To Joseph Hone; Deirdre Bair, *Samuel Beckett* (1978), p. 254.
[18] p. 151.
[19] 'Love and Lethe', *More Pricks than Kicks* (1934), p. 133.
[20] *Novel on Yellow Paper*, p. 23.

Shut me not alive away
From the light of every day
Hang me rather by the neck to die
Against a morning sky.

'The Death Sentence' begins in Tennyson, and in the eerie
death in life of a phrase torn from its original life; it echoes her
own very short 'Quand on n'a pas ce que l'on aime, il faut
aimer ce que l'on a—':

Cold as no love, and wild with all negation—
Oh Death in Life, the lack of animation.

And it ends in Shakespeare, in Portia's acquiescence in the
law's severity of justice. (Stevie Smith wrote in *The Holiday*,
'And I thought that Shakespeare had caught in a phrase the
cruelty and blindness of the world and of history, "the law
allows it, and the court awards."')[21] Her lineation in the poem
breaks the backs of both the Tennyson and the Shakespeare
lines and then does not put them out of their misery. Such ways
with words are a counterpart to the explicit death in life in a
characteristic poem, 'Under Wrong Trees':

Under wrong trees
Walked the zombies

Yet her most distinctive ways are with rhythm and rhyme.
From her early 'Death Came to Me':

For underneath the superscription lurked I knew
With pulse quickening and the blood thickening
For fear in every vein the deadly strychnine.

The sequence 'quickening,' 'thickening,' 'strychnine,' makes
for a killing rhyme, like a killing joke, especially given what it is
to quicken. Such rhyming is both youthful and deathwards,
and it illuminates a paradox which she herself acknowledged:
'I'm astonished the young like my poems. They're rather melancholy on the whole . . . I say to them, I can't see what you
see in them, because on the whole they're a bit deathwards in
their wish.'[22] But poems which are deathwards in their wish
must be deathwards in their words, too, even if they also need

[21] p. 130.   [22] *Ivy and Stevie*, p. 48.

to be sufficiently alive for their death-wish to impinge. 'Oh
Death in Life, the lack of animation.'

In rhythm and rhyme she found her deathwards animation
most vividly and memorially. 'A Dream of Comparison,'
which is about a conversation between Eve and Mary, turning
on whether death is unimaginable and undesirable, ends like
this:

> They walked by the estuary,
> Eve and the Virgin Mary,
> And they talked until nightfall,
> But the difference between them was radical.

The rhymes pole-axe the poles of the argument. These are
'Simpsonian rhymes,' to use the term wielded by C. S. Lewis
(after the scholar who first diagnosed the disease). In his *English
Literature in the Sixteenth Century*, Lewis is eloquent about these
extraordinary rhymes—extraordinary in that we can't now see
how it was that good and even great poets were happy to
rhyme, for instance, 'on the second syllable of a disyllabic word
where metre forbids that syllable to carry the stress.'[23] Here,
however, is Stevie Smith's achievement, since she apprehended that this 'metrical phenomenon distressing to the modern ear' may be perfect for distress signals. It is also a deadly or
deathly thing to do, and a poet who was happy about death
would be happy sometimes to rhyme so. 'The Murderer' ends:

> She was not like other girls—rather diffident,
> And that is how we had an accident.

What a diffident accident a rhyme may be—and no less lethal
for that. A rhyme might be expected to be a coupling which will
rise as an arch; in her poems, it is a couple which leaves all in
rubble—itself a rhyme to which she turned and turned:

> Thus spake the awful aging couple
> Whose heart the years had turned to rubble.
> ('Advice to Young Children')

> They were a precious couple,
> And let the people feed on straw and rubble.
> ('Après la Politique, la Haine des Bourbons')

[23] (1954), pp. 478-9.

> Banausic, he called them banausic,
> A villainous banausic couple.
> He turned to blow on his love for his father
> And found it rubble.   ('Easy')

Such rhyming reaches its high point in the nadir of a dyslec-
tic rhyme like this, about a bust of mother:

> Upon its plinth
> It beholds the zenith
> Of my success on the pianoforte.

This is from a poem called 'The Virtuoso'; it is itself a piece of
virtuosity in *The Art of Sinking in Poetry*.

The third Class remains, of the *Diminishing* Figures: And first, The
ANTICLIMAX, where the second Line drops quite short of the first, than
which nothing creates greater Surprize.

At other times this Figure operates in a larger Extent; and when the
gentle Reader is in Expectation of some great Image, he either finds it
surprizingly *imperfect*, or is presented with something very *low*, or
quite *ridiculous*. A Surprize resembling that of a curious Person in a
Cabinet of antique Statues, who beholds on the Pedestal the Names of
Homer, or *Cato*; but looking up, finds *Homer* without a Head, and
nothing to be seen of *Cato* but his privy Member.   (ch. xi)

Poetry is tempted to say, lo and behold. The art of sinking in
poetry presents 'something very *low*' to a reader 'who beholds
on the Pedestal the Names of *Homer*, or of *Cato*'.

> Upon its plinth
> It beholds the zenith
> Of my success on the pianoforte.

Much of this classic Augustan essay in mock-criticism (1727)
is germane to Stevie Smith. She cultivated the art of sinking,
the stone of bathos falling through the waters of pathos.

The Taste of the *Bathos* is implanted by Nature itself in the Soul of
Man; 'till perverted by Custom or Example he is taught, or rather
compell'd, to relish the *Sublime*. Accordingly, we see the unprejudiced
Minds of Children delight only in such Productions, and in such
Images, as our true modern Writers set before them. I have observ'd
how fast the general Taste is returning to this first Simplicity and
Innocence.   (ch. ii)

There is the Anticlimax. There is the Infantine: 'This is when a
Poet grows so very simple, as to think and talk like a Child'.
There is the Inanity, or Nothingness. There is the Mixture of
Figures:

> Its principal Beauty is when it gives an Idea just opposite to what it
> seem'd meant to describe. Thus an ingenious Artist painting the
> *Spring*, talks of a *Snow* of Blossoms, and thereby raises an unexpected
> Picture of *Winter*.   (ch. x)

But an artist both ingenuous and ingenious may raise a true art
of sinking on just such a foundation.

> The churchyard pales are black against the night
> And snow hung here seems doubly white.
> ('Night-Time in the Cemetery')

Stevie Smith's choice of the noun 'pales' for the black railings
has an inspired perversity: an anti-pun, it gives an idea just opposite to what it seemed meant to describe, and it pales into
significance.

All these are the figures of speech for someone who, in the
words of the Augustan mocker, has 'a mind to be simple'.
Stevie Smith's mind to be simple was subtle with all of them,
and with rhythms and rhymes.

'Is there not an Art of *Diving* as well as of *Flying*?' The art of
sinking in poetry reaches one of its high (and low) points in her
most famous poem.

NOT WAVING BUT DROWNING

Nobody heard him, the dead man,
But still he lay moaning:
I was much further out than you thought
And not waving but drowning.

Poor chap, he always loved larking
And now he's dead
It must have been too cold for him his heart gave way,
They said.

Oh, no no no, it was too cold always
(Still the dead one lay moaning)
I was much too far out all my life
And not waving but drowning.

It is literally about sinking, and its laughter is submarine and profound. Submarine, in the way in which the nouns 'wave' and 'waves' are forever fended off within the poem and yet are what tacitly corroborates the antithesis of 'not waving but drowning'; the likelihood of which is clear from 'Death's Ostracism,' where 'he will call the waves to friend,' and from 'Mrs Arbuthnot':

> Crying: I should write a poem,
> Can I look a wave in the face
> If I do not write a poem about a sea-wave,
> Putting the words in place.

Profound, in that the dead man has not been allowed to die, truly to die.

In her poem about a Roman family, 'Tenuous and Precarious,' 'There was my brother Spurious, / Spurious Posthumous.' Spurious Posthumous, because it may be that there is something spurious about the fear—or the hope—that anybody will ever be allowed to become really posthumous; and Spurious Posthumous for the more worldly reasons. There has been something spurious about Stevie Smith's posthumous reputation. In the years since her death in 1971, she has been co-opted into a feminism for which she felt some sympathy but also some distaste; she deplored 'the flag-wavers of both sexes,' and might have thought that they were not only waving but drowning. She has been playwritten as 'Stevie,' her poems and her nature cropped so that she might be plausibly rendered on stage and screen by Glenda Jackson. She has been adapted for a staged anthology. Still, these years have seen the reprinting of her novels, which matters; the publication of a Penguin *Selected Poems*, and of an excellent selection of poetry and prose (by Hermione Lee), which matters more; and the publication of the *Collected Poems*, which matters most. If we are to honour her this side idolatry, the reservations need not only be about her drawings (which are too cute, as Larkin thought), but about the price paid for her unmistakability, her idiosyncrasy. Larkin said of some of the less good poems that 'one could never forget when reading one that this was a *Stevie Smith* poem.'[24] Yet how good of Stevie Smith to have written so many poems that one could simply never forget.

ROBERT LOWELL:
'THE WAR OF WORDS'

Robert Lowell died at sixty. Ten years earlier, his autumnal fame at fifty had been itchy on his shoulders:

> I, fifty, humbled with the years' gold garbage,
> dead laurel grizzling my back like spines of hay.
>
> ('Mexico')

That was prickly; 'humbled' was proud, and 'gold garbage' and 'dead laurel' impatiently writhed at the poetical trappings, the laurels and gold garb. 'Grizzling' was not a snivel but the threat of an ageing bear-hug. Nothing violent happens in the lines, but you feel the pressure of the possibility. The poem's first line, leading into those two, was 'The difficulties, the impossibilities . . . '; the sonnet went on to imagine the Aztecs and human sacrifice; and its last line saw a clock with 'the hand a knife-edge pressed against the future'. Violence, yet not quite or not yet.

Violence was Lowell's essential subject, terrible in its variety (of time, of place, of motive, of nature) and terrible in not changing.

> Nothing underneath the sun
> Has bettered, Uncle, since the scaffolds flamed
> On butchered Troy . . .
>
> ('The Death of the Sheriff')

From his earliest poems to the last, he was preoccupied with violence. The national violence that is war, in poems about Napoleon, the Somme, Alexander, Hitler, Hamburg, the American Civil War, Mussolini, the Cuban missile crisis. The supra-national violence that is myth, in poems about the Gorgon, Odysseus, Clytemnestra. The civic violence that is persecution (of the Jews, among others), or revolution (the French, among others), or martyrdom, or massacre of innocents (and not only of *the* innocents). The social violence that is assassination, or the law's injustices, Al Capone's lawlessness, and the policemen who manage 'The Pacification of Columbia' and who are the other half of the reason why Central Park at night spells danger. The machine-age violence that is a car crash. The Mammonist violence that is greedy exploitation and ecological havoc. The domestic violence that is nagging or infidelity or battering or murder or incest or the war between children and parents. The personal or psychic violence that is nightmare or madness or suicide. Lowell wrote poems on all of these and more. There is not a kind of violence, a time and a place for it, that he did not imagine on our behalf. We are all tilling some Egyptian desert:

> Think of them, afraid of violence,
> afraid of anything, timid as sheep
> hidden in some casual, protective crevice,
> held twelve dynasties to a burning-glass,
> pressed to the levelled sandbreast of the Sphinx—
> what were once identities simplified
> to a single, indignant, collusive grin.
>
> ('Sheep')

'I am against violence; if I were still Calvinist I would call it *the* hell-fire'.[1] And at once we are aware, as Lowell was, of the problems and paradoxes. For you do not have to go along with the lavish dilution of the word 'violent' (like that of the word 'obscene') to acknowledge that the burning-glass of hell-fire is a violent doctrine, violent in its extremity and in its inflictions.

So we have to ask how Lowell manages to avoid, if he does, the 'collusive grin'. For this is the nemesis that lies in wait for all imaginings of violence, even or especially the denunciations of violence: that to imagine it may be to collude with it and to minister to it.

Lowell, like any man, does sometimes fall victim to a plea-sure in vividly realizing the plight of a victim.

> 1790
> (FROM THE MEMOIRS OF GENERAL THIEBAULT)
> On Maundy Thursday when the King and Queen
> Had washed and wiped the chosen poor and fed
> Them from a boisterous wooden platter; here
> We stood in forage-caps upon the green:
> Green guardsmen of the Nation and its head.
> The King walked out into the biting air,

---

[1] *the Review*, No. 26 (1971), 21.

Two gentlemen went with him; as they neared
Our middle gate, we stood aside for welcome;
A stone's throw lay between us when they cleared
Two horse-shoe flights of steps and crossed the Place Vendôme.

"What a dog's life it is to be a king",
I grumbled and unslung my gun; the chaff
And cinders whipped me and began to sting.
I heard our Monarch's Breughel-peasant laugh
Exploding, as a spaniel mucked with tar
Cut by his Highness' ankles on the double-quick
To fetch its stamping mistress. Louis smashed
Its backbone with a backstroke of his stick:
Slouching a little more than usual, he splashed
As boyish as a stallion to the Champ de Mars.

This early poem does not just acknowledge nemesis, it gloats.
For the coincidence of a turn of phrase—'What a dog's life it is
to be a King'—patly serves the poet's turn, and turns the poem
into too happy a satire of circumstance, thought up by the spirit
ironical. The royal gratuitous violence—

> Louis smashed
> Its backbone with a backstroke of his stick:

is effected with effortlessly casual mimicry, but the very effortlessness is then morally disconcerting, the *tour de force* a backstroke of a stick. What a dog's life it is to be a king; and ah what
a dog's death it will be. The poem does an undoglike thing: it
purrs.

But then was not Lowell famous for the violence of his ways
with language, with poetic forms, with writer-reader understandings? And how can there be an art which preaches non-
violence and practises violence? 'They sing of peace, and preach
despair', the hymns of New England; and the next lines of
'Waking Early Sunday Morning' are a very equivocal acknowledgment:

> yet they gave darkness some control,
> and left a loophole for the soul.

Control over darkness, or by it? Or is the point that unless you
grant that darkness will exercise some control over you, you
will never truly be able to exercise control over it? To rhyme on
the word *control* may be at once to assert a poet's controlling

prerogative and to admit how frighteningly dependent upon contingency and coincidence a poet may be.

That Lowell was himself a poet who gave darkness some control, in both senses, is clear enough from the poems which speak with pain of mental disturbance and inner rebellion, bizarrely sloganed as peace:

> the same six words repeating on a disk:
> marching for peace with paranoia marching,
> marching for peace with paranoia marching . . .
> ('Stairwell')

Peace with honour? But it would be impertinent to mention the violence and non-violence within Lowell's own person were it not the subject of some of his best poems, poems like 'Waking in the Blue':

> We are all old-timers,
> each of us holds a locked razor.

—the poem, by the time it ends like this, has unlocked many things, but, as its steadiness makes clear, it does not unlock any razor for murder or suicide. Or there is 'Skunk Hour', which Lowell managed to calm down from its first-draft gratuitousness; 'I found the bleak personal violence repellent'.[2]

When Lowell was forty, he remembered his imprisonment during the war, in his late twenties, not as a pacifist but as a conscientious objector.

MEMORIES OF WEST STREET AND LEPKE

> Only teaching on Tuesday, book-worming
> in pyjamas fresh from the washer each morning,
> I hog a whole house on Boston's
> 'hardly passionate Marlborough Street',
> where even the man
> scavenging filth in the back alley trash cans,
> has two children, a beach wagon, a helpmate,
> and is 'a young Republican'.
> I have a nine months' daughter,
> young enough to be my granddaughter.
> Like the sun she rises in her flame-flamingo infants' wear.

---

[2] (1964); *Robert Lowell*, ed. Thomas Parkinson (1968), p. 133.

These are the tranquillized *Fifties*,
and I am forty. Ought I to regret my seedtime?
I was a fire-breathing Catholic C.O.,
and made my manic statement,
telling off the state and president, and then
sat waiting sentence in the bull pen
beside a negro boy with curlicues
of marijuana in his hair.

Given a year,
I walked on the roof of the West Street Jail, a short
enclosure like my school soccer court,
and saw the Hudson River once a day
through sooty clothesline entanglements
and bleaching khaki tenements.

Strolling, I yammered metaphysics with Abramowitz,
a jaundice-yellow ('it's really tan')
and fly-weight pacifist,
so vegetarian,
he wore rope shoes and preferred fallen fruit.
He tried to convert Bioff and Brown,
the Hollywood pimps, to his diet.
Hairy, muscular, suburban,
wearing chocolate double-breasted suits,
they blew their tops and beat him black and blue.

I was so out of things, I'd never heard
of the Jehovah's Witnesses.
'Are you a C.O.?' I asked a fellow jailbird.
'No,' he answered, 'I'm a J.W.'
He taught me the hospital 'tuck',
and pointed out the T-shirted back
of *Murder Incorporated's* Czar Lepke,
there piling towels on a rack,
or dawdling off to his little segregated cell full
of things forbidden the common man:
a portable radio, a dresser, two toy American
flags tied together with a ribbon of Easter palm.
Flabby, bald, lobotomized,
he drifted in a sheepish calm,
where no agonizing reappraisal
jarred his concentration on the electric chair—
hanging like an oasis in his air
of lost connections . . .

Violence is there, but it is calmed by pathos and by comedy as well as by wit. The Fifties are tranquillized, not tranquil; Lowell may have said in a late poem, 'Suburban Surf', that 'A false calm is the best calm', but we are not simply to agree. 'I was a fire-breathing Catholic C.O.': this acknowledges that the militant assertion of peacefulness may be as aggressive in motivation and in manner as any other assertion, and yet the line does not demean, with any ingratiating retrospective self-disparagement, the moral and political decision which Lowell took during the war: to go to prison, not as a pacifist (Lowell, who had volunteered for the Navy, later gave unforgettable expression to the conviction that 'the one thing worse than war is massacre'), but as a conscientious objector, objecting to the saturation bombing of Hamburg and to the Allied insistence on unconditional surrender. Lowell had indeed come to deprecate the manner of his public letter to President Roosevelt, with its miscalculated appeal to the family traditions of which Lowell could not be so simple an heir—

You will understand how painful such a decision is for an American whose family traditions, like your own, have always found their fulfillment in maintaining, through responsible participation in both civil and military services, our country's freedom and honor—[3]

> and made my manic statement,
> telling off the state and president,

but there is nothing in 'Memories of West Street and Lepke' which takes the line of retreating, with cadging unpriggishness, from a principle acted upon and stood by. Lowell does not confuse the principled peace which he gratefully wins for himself in this poem with either the principled un-peace of Abramowitz, the 'fly-weight pacifist', a vegetarian preferring not even to pluck fruit, or with the unprincipled peace of the gangster Lepke: 'Flabby, bald, lobotomized, / he drifted in a sheepish calm'.

Lowell thought hard, and felt deeply, about violence. His own life (born 1917) was contemporary with that of the words 'non-violence' and 'non-violent' (both born 1920, fathered by—and mothered by—Gandhi). The last half-century has tried to make imaginable an opposite of violence and an alternative to it; has tried to create 'the principle and practice of

[3] Quoted in Philip Cooper, *The Autobiographical Myth of Robert Lowell* (1970), p. 24.

abstaining from the use of violence'. The attempt is admirable
in its aspiration; grim in its recognition that our century stands
in hideous need of such a word and concept; inspiring in that it
has at least partially succeeded in bringing to birth and to life
such a word; and dispiriting in that it has succeeded only
partially—'non-violent' and 'non-violence' do *not* sit peace-
fully at home within either the American or the English language,
and there is about the words an air of strain and so of cant such
as precipitated this citation in the *H-N* Supplement (1976) to
the *Oxford English Dictionary*, from Mary McCarthy's *Birds of
America*: 'Peter replied non-violently. "It's for my mother."'

A less brittle sense of the fragility of 'non-violent' is alive in
Lowell's sonnet 'Non-Violent':

> In the sick days of the code duello,
> any quick killer could have called you out—
> a million Spanish war dead, ninetenths murdered—
> *Viva la guerra civile, viva la muerte!*
> As boys we never fell in the hole to China—
> few of us fell in wars, our unnegotiable
> flag still floating the seven seas like a bond . . .
> Better fight to keep love, or milk bottles made of glass,
> than go pluming as crusaders from left to right . . .
> in the war of words, the lung of infinitude.
> I must either be Christian or non-violent,
> past history is immobile in our committed hands,
> till Death drops his white marble scythe—Brother,
> one skeleton among our skeletons.

To ponder 'the war of words' is to be led toward one of the
ways in which Lowell elicits a life within his words which is at
once a war (with its recognition that there is violence, actual or
potential, everywhere) and a peace or at least a truce: a recognition that it will not do to yield to, or minister to, such violence. 'The life of a Wit is a warfare upon earth', said Pope.[4]
But there can be a conscientious objection to that too, and 'the
war of words' must not be war-mongering and word-mongering.

The imagination can create a benign and uncollusive apprehension of violence, a non-violence that has the positive power
which the term 'non-violence' so sadly lacks. But 'I must either
be Christian or non-violent': this is not a sarcasm, it is a worth-

---

[4] Preface to *Works* (1717).

while irony, since it is not a single reversal but a thought which is differently true in two senses. Lowell's conversions, first within Christianity into Roman Catholicism, and then into not being a Christian, are at one with his feeling the glory and the peril, the lure, of idealism, 'pluming as crusaders'.

'Violence and idealism have some occult connection',[5] he said in conversation with A. Alvarez. It is a connection which Bob Dylan caught in his song 'Love Minus Zero / No Limit':

> My love, she speaks like silence,
> Without ideals or violence.

Lowell, like Dylan, knows that the difficulty comes when you need something more than silence and must speak. The rhyme of 'silence' and 'violence' is at once forced and easy enough, and it is a rhyme which Lowell needed in his translation of Racine's *Phèdre*; Lowell gives a greater strain to the rhyme than Dylan does, by insisting metrically (Dylan did the opposite) on the extra syllable in 'violence':

> Lady, if you must weep, weep for your silence
> that filled your days and mine with violence.
>
> (I iii)

But violence can take a larger stage. In the 1960s, Lowell mingled an old relief and a new dismay at the thought of the new 'non-violent' non-idealist flattening:

I don't meet people who are violently anti-Russian very often. That doesn't seem to be the air.

Alvarez: They still exist, though.

They exist, but they don't exist very much in the intellectual world. While in the thirties everybody was taking sides on something, usually very violently—violent conversions, violent Marxist positions, violent new deal, violent anti-new deal—things couldn't be more different now. The terrible danger now is of the great impersonal bureaucratic machinery rolling over everything and flattening our humanity.[6]

Yet Lowell was not only a post-war poet (his first volume came out in 1944), he was altogether an American poet. He himself speculated on a phenomenon which has long struck

[5] *Encounter*, xxiv (1965), 41.   [6] *the Review*, No. 8 (1963), 39-40.

Americans and others: the paradox and the power of violence in American life. No wonder Concord is so important a place, and the subject—the site and the situation—of one of Lowell's early militant poems. The Civil War; the massacre of the Indians, and the lynching of blacks; the assassination of Presidents, and of trade-unionists; the lunatic mass-murders, the gangsterism, and the police; the war machine; the violence of so many American energies in the arts, and in rhetoric; the political and religious animosities: these have some counterpart in every country, but there has long been an appalling propensity to violence in American life—appalling and paradoxical, as Lowell himself brought out in the most famous of his early poems, 'The Quaker Graveyard in Nantucket'. That it should have been Quakers who treated whales, and men, so: this is a central perturbation in the poem (as it was in Nixon's Watergate times that it should have been Quakers who furnished a 'praetorian guard'). Some of the entanglements of violence and non-violence are occult in the poem, as in the fact that Lowell's poem about whaling is explicitly in memory of a cousin who died, not in the peacetime slaughter that is whaling, but in the slaughter of the Second World War—and yet that the cousin went down with his ship not in combat but because of an explosion in harbour. 'For Warren Winslow, Dead at Sea'.

Lowell's sense of violence and of 'the war of words' is evident in the first sentence of his poem, which uses the word 'violently' but has just previously tranquillized it by using it of the sea's 'breaking' (when the sea breaks violently, it can be mercifully intransitive—it breaks, it does not necessarily break anything); and Lowell then calms the word again, but sinisterly, by following it at once with the image of night as a hostile convoy. There is no collision, though the sense of one is called up to be made ghostly:

> A brackish reach of shoal off Madaket,—
> The sea was still breaking violently and night
> Had steamed into our North Atlantic Fleet,
> When the drowned sailor clutched the drag-net.

Our fleet did not steam into the night; the night steamed into our fleet. There is no impact—except of the words.

When he was asked about the violence of the U.S.A., Lowell

spoke of an idealistic crusading history, a nation 'founded on a declaration', but he admitted, too, that there is no knowing.

I don't know where it comes from—whether it's the American genius, or just the chaos of our schools and that young people are badly brought up—but I think it has something to do with both the idealism and the power of the country. Other things are boring for these young people, and violence isn't boring.[7]

Yet Lowell as a poet stood in a tense relation to boredom—how could he create non-violent excitements that would not be incitements? 'The remorseless, amplified harangues for peace'. 'America's ghastly innocence' is not necessarily the more harmless for being innocent, despite what the word 'innocence' should mean. The first poem in *History* ended with this fear of and for Lowell himself:

> As in our Bibles, white-faced, predatory,
> the beautiful, mist-drunken hunter's moon ascends—
> a child could give it a face: two holes, two holes,
> my eyes, my mouth, between them a skull's no-nose—
> O there's a terrifying innocence in my face
> drenched with the silver salvage of the mornfrost.
>
> ('History')

These lines manifest one of Lowell's central poetic insights and practices, by way of recognizing violence while escaping it—and yet not escaping it into mere fatigue ('We have talked our extinction to death'). The practice, which you may call a technique in the spirit of T. S. Eliot's remark that we cannot say at what point technique begins or where it ends, is that of inviting a word or a sense which is then fended off. If it were both invited and allowed in, there would be a collision with the other sense of the word; but if no such possibility of collision were ever even conceivable, life would be being travestied into sentimentality in the poems. (Lowell wrote lovingly of guinea-pigs—'little pacific things'—but he had no impulse to see or treat men as guinea-pigs.) The practice is a variety of pun, but it is an anti-pun; whereas in a pun there are two senses which either get along or quarrel, in an anti-pun there is only one sense admitted but there is another sense denied admission. So

[7] *Encounter*, xxiv (1965), 41-2.

the response is not 'this means x' (with the possibility even of its meaning y being no part of your response), but 'this-means-x-and-doesn't-mean-y', all hyphenated. All poets do some such thing sometimes; but it is a trademark or hallmark of this poet. 'Drenched with the silver salvage of the mornfrost' depends for its force upon calling up the idea of the silver salver, a salver which is suggested (and not only by *silver salv*- but by the fact that the sentence is all about the sight and shape of the moon) but is then rescinded or repudiated. 'The silver *salvage* of the *morn*frost'—the moonlight spectrally batheing the face—gains its territory by fighting off the silver *salver* of the *moon*. The 'silver salvage' is remote from the 'gold garbage' of Poesy, but Lowell (preternaturally 'predatory') will have remembered two lines in Keats: 'The lustrous salvers in the moonlight gleam', and 'With all my jewelled salvers, silver and gold.'[8]

'The silver salvage of the mornfrost' means intensely by meaning the whole thing including its exclusion: 'this, and not that'. There is no collision, since what is not granted admission is not there to be collided with or colluded with, any more than you can collide with a ghost. A 'terrifying innocence' is at work. Harm, though, is incipient. 'Nor nocent yet', in the words which Milton bends upon the sleeping snake whom Satan will possess.

William Empson said that 'the pleasure in style is continually to be explained by just such a releasing and knotted duality, where those who have been wedded in the argument are bedded together in the phrase'.[9] But the pleasure, or pertinent displeasure, in Lowell's style is to be explained by the breakdown of such wedding and bedding. The senses of the words are divorced, and one of them is now acknowledged to be living elsewhere. Lowell in 1947 quoted William Carlos Williams: 'The language / is divorced from their minds'. He quoted, too, Williams's mourning over the bud, 'perfect / in juice and substance but divorced, divorced / from its fellows, fallen low'. Lowell commented: 'This is the tragedy of Paterson, what the poem is really about. It is the divorce of modern life,

---

[8] 'The Eve of St. Agnes', xxxii; *Otho*, I i.
[9] *Seven Types of Ambiguity* (1930), 1947 edn., p. 132.

of intellect and sensibility, spirit and matter'.[10] Williams's 'divorced, divorced' became Lowell's:

> a Jonah—O divorced, divorced
> from the whale-fat of post-war London!
> ('Ford Madox Ford')

But divorce may indeed be 'post-war'. There may be worse things than divorce. Separation may put an end to wars. Lowell is a poet of divorce, not only in that his poems so often contemplate marital misery, and toll out the word 'divorce', and not only in that they mourn 'the divorce of modern life', but also in that they grimly put in a good word for that not simply bad thing divorce. Instead of 'the war of the words', there is the divorce of words.

'In the Lowell country', Marjorie Perloff has said, 'objects never touch gently; there is always a head-on collision'.[11] But often in a Lowell poem there are not two realized presences which can collide; in the absence of one of the terms, the collision remains a perpetual possibility only in a world of speculation. 'In a day when poets long to be irresistible forces, he is an immovable object', said Lowell's best critic, Randall Jarrell.[12] Lowell may have yearned to be both, but he knew what a collision there would then be, and so he allowed only one of his meanings a collidable reality.

The unreality of the other half of the anti-pun is similar to the known (admitted, intended) unreality of Lowell's cliché-hyperboles. Phrases in Lowell like 'hit the streets', or 'strike for shore', or 'clashing colours' or 'clashing outfits', at once evoke a potential violence (they have a violence of expression and a hardened unfeelingness, such as we hear by now in a cliché like 'a sickening thud') and also are phantasmal, precipitating no real pain of violence—it is streets that are hit, not people, and colours that clash, not people. So those critics of Lowell are right who feel a disconcerting unreality in his violence of expression, but wrong when they make this an accusation against the poetry. 'She thundered on the keyboard of her dummy

---

[10] *Sewanee Review*, 1v (1947); *William Carlos Williams*, ed. Charles Tomlinson (1972), p. 161.

[11] *The Poetic Art of Robert Lowell* (1973), p. 17.

[12] *Poetry and the Age* (1953), 1955 edn., p. 194.

piano':[13] this thunders on neither a real piano nor a dummy
one, and itself constitutes a strange art of the shadowily unimaginable or inaudible. The unreality is sometimes an evocation
of an absent reality, imaginable but not here fully imagined;
and the point of this is to escape the very collusion with violence,
the 'collusive grin', of which hostile critics have accused him.
It is an accusation which American literature has often invited;
Hazlitt's criticism of the American Gothic novelist Charles
Brockden Brown, a hundred and fifty years ago, is justly a criticism because Brockden Brown's writing does not *contain* its own
violence: 'His works . . . are full (to disease) of imagination—
but it is forced, violent, and shocking. This is to be expected, we
apprehend, in attempts of this kind in a country like America,
where there is, generally speaking, no *natural imagination*. The
mind must be excited by overstraining, by pulleys and levers'.[14]
Lowell's bombardments are different:

> it's enough to wake without old fears,
> and watch the needle-fire of the first light
> bombarding off your eyelids harmlessly.
> ('Overhanging Cloud')

The poem which reminds us that 'the one thing worse than
war is massacre' is about social Darwinism and its ruthlessness.
It is called 'Struggle of Non-Existence', a title which holds off
its adversary at arm's length, the 'struggle of existence', and
refuses to allow it a combative presence or existence within the
poem. Like all poets, Lowell was sensitive to such potent absences; a late poem, 'Logan Airport, Boston', can say 'Your
absence is presence', and we know what pressure this has and is
about. Lowell's poems are always alive with these vigorous spectral combats, at once violent (they disturb) and non-violent (one
sense of the words cannot strangle itself). So a characteristic
response to Lowell's phrasing has always been to wonder for a
second if you are misreading it or if perhaps there is a misprint.

> In the grandiloquent lettering on Mother's coffin,
> *Lowell* had been mispelled LOVEL.
> ('Sailing Home from Rapallo')

[13] 'My Last Afternoon with Uncle Devereux Winslow'.
[14] *Edinburgh Review*, October 1829; *Collected Works*, ed. A. R. Waller and Arnold
Glover, x (1904), 311.

The early poems are muscular with these ripples of solicited misconstruction; Lowell was young then, and the staving-off of violence was more aggressive, manifesting more possibility of violence itself, than in his later achievements. 'Where the heel-headed dogfish barks its nose': the *dog*fish *barks*? No, but the head of the one sense of 'barks' is bruised by the heel of the other sense. 'The corpse was bloodless, a botch of reds and whites'; *bloodless* seeps into *botch* and blotches it. The waves rolled forward: 'And blue-lung'd combers lumbered to the kill'—*lunged*? No, but 'lung'd' craves to become 'lunged' ('lumbered to the kill') and then is refused.[15] (Saying aloud these phrases of Lowell's does of course remove some of these intended flickers of warring possibilities.)

The characteristic early or middle poem by Lowell has such a combative fending-off. The referee in the ring needs to be pugnacious in his very peace-keeping within ruled and stylized combat. The anti-sense or misconstruction plays its part in a violence-acknowledging non-violence.

> Hussar and cuirassier and grenadier
> Ascend the tombstone steppes to Russia.
> ('Napoleon Crosses the Beresina')

—there the flatness of the *steppes* fights against the rebellious uprising ('Ascend the tombstone steppes') of phantasmal *steps*.

> The lifers file into the hall,
> According to their houses—twos
> Of laundered denim. On the wall
> A coloured fairy tinkles blues
> And titters by the balustrade;
> Canaries beat their bars and scream.
> ('In the Cage')

For a moment a black homosexual is glimpsed—thanks to 'denim' and 'blues'—as if 'coloured' meant *coloured*. (Lowell's small act of Civil Rights non-violence may be one of the things which gave the euphemism 'coloured' a bad name.)

> Wallowing in this bloody sty
> I cast for fish that pleased my eye.
> ('The Drunken Fisherman')

[15] These three instances are from 'The Quaker Graveyard in Nantucket'.

The language squinnies at you; *sty* is so bloodshot as to look like the stye of an eye, and *cast* wavers into a squint. 'The groined eyeballs of my sin' ('France') are *eye*balls, for all their being groined. 'Walden's fished-out perch' ('Concord') is a place, not a fish, and so is indeed 'fished-out'.

> and snatched away his crucifix
> And rolled his body like a log to Styx.
> ('The Soldier')

Styx, not sticks, for this doomed log.

Or there is the candle which is 'pin-beaded' ('Thanksgiving's Over'), though the words four lines earlier in the poem, 'poor numskull', cannot but call up what is then fended off, 'pin-headed' ('pin-head' is a powerful Lowell word elsewhere). There is a description of Hermes and his wand, 'His caduceus shadow-bowing behind him'.[16] Shadow-bowing like an archer's *bow* or like a respectful *bow*? Either way it flickers like a misprint for 'shadow-boxing', called up and held off—the perfect image for that combative non-combatancy of Lowell's which yet is not rigged but is an imaginative attempt at an uncollusive imagining of violence. In 'Winter in Dunbarton', 'Belle, the cat' is her name, not the injunction 'bell the cat'; the cat ('predatory, the beautiful') is tamed by her name, not by a warning bell hung around her neck.

Lowell created some characteristic effects of '*x* not *y*' within the translations in *Near the Ocean*. There are the old men in his translation of Juvenal, 'The Vanity of Human Wishes':

> another's spoonfed: listen,
> they yawn like baby swallows for their swill!

—where 'swallows' as birds is not exactly in *conflict* with 'spoonfed. . . . yawn. . . . swill' although the greedy sense cannot but yawn. Or notice how 'escaping . . . limping . . . running' all make you want *fleet* to be *feet* (fleet of foot, too) in this translation of Horace:

> and with a single ship, and scarcely
> escaping from your limping fleet, on fire,
> Cleopatra, with Caesar running on the wind.
> ('Cleopatra')

---

[16] 'Orpheus, Eurydice and Hermes' (from Rilke).

But there can be no actual conflict, in this war-scene, because *fleet* fights by sea and *feet* by land (and it was this misgeneralship which cost Cleopatra her life). Again, Horace's *pallida mors*—pale death—finds itself translated by Lowell, in 'Spring', as 'bloodless death', where the sardonic force of the phrase is the shadowy combat between the two senses of 'bloodless': death is bloodless, not—indeed not—bloodless. Or there is the vibrant sexual frustration in Juvenal's lines about men wronged by the women whom they rejected:

> But beauty never hurts the good! Go ask
> Bellerophon, go ask Hippolytus.
> Chastity couldn't save their lives from Phaedra,
> or Sthenoboea, faithful wives, then scorned
> lovers screwed on to murder by their shame.

Screwed, not screwed: that is the frustration which precipitated the murderous violence; and yet 'screwed' is not a pun, it is an anti-pun, a phantasmal violence.

But Lowell grew older, and his sense of how to deal with combat and violence somewhat calmed. In *Life Studies*, his turning-point, the extraordinary autobiographical prose of '91 Revere Street' was devoted largely to the paradoxes of his father's life in the Navy and at home, mostly both at once. Lowell as a child loved toy-soldiers, he tells us; and his father is loved as a toy-sailor. Most of '91 Revere Street' should be read as an affectionate (not scornful or cutting) evocation of the absurdities and decencies of a civilized military world. 'As a civilian he kept his high sense of form, his humour, his accuracy, but this accuracy was henceforth unimportant, recreational, *hors de combat*'. *Hors de combat* is the right Lowell phrase for a violence acknowledged but not invited in.

In the very first poem in Lowell's first British volume, *Poems 1938-1949*, 'The Exile's Return', the liberating soldiers 'ground arms'. Lowell later came to distrust even the violence with which arms may be grounded—the violence of the command and of the butts hitting the ground. His last poetry was an attempt to advance non-violence by a less violent staving-off or holding at arm's length or coming between the combatants. So 'the war of words' was replaced by something of a truce, a contrariety of ideas now expressing the old eschewed combat in terms of a sentiment not a wording. 'Our rust the colour of the chameleon':[17] there no words fight, even spectrally, but the imagined *idea* of the chameleon's colours is in combat with something absent: the imagined other colours of the chameleon when elsewhere. The effect is less immediate than that of 'clashing colours', but this denial of immediacy is not a failure of energy; it is, in the continuing world of violence, a new form of mediation.

In what was to prove Lowell's final volume, *Day by Day*, the poem called 'The Day' begins with a new sense of the *hors de combat*, depending less upon a contrariety of phrasing or diction and more upon the image of a harmlessness of violence:

> It's amazing
> the day is still here
> like lightning on an open field,
> terra firma and transient
> swimming in variation,
> fresh as when man first broke
> like the crocus all over the earth.

'Broke', but like a flower bursting up and open, not like a destruction or a fracture or a disease: 'like lightning', but 'on an open field'. There is an openness of violent non-violence about the very idea. The line 'terra firma and transient' encourages the Latin language and the English to sit together at the negotiating table, and to accept the paradox of the earth as both 'firma' and 'transient'. 'Like lightning on an open field': no harm done, but with a sense of relief which knows what harm is:

> as if in the end,
> in the marriage with nothingness,
> we could ever escape
> being absolutely safe.

Lowell's attempt to create a positive non-violence, something which didn't feel like a non-, was taking new and more gentle forms and words. The threatening story could not change. It is the old old story, 'the Ahab story of having to murder evil: and you may murder all the good with it if it gets desperate enough to struggle.'[18]

17 'Our Afterlife: 1'.   18 *Encounter*, xxiv (1965), 42.

> Where the heel-headed dogfish barks its nose
> On Ahab's void and forehead.

Lowell sought to wage peace within 'the war of words'. His art of conscientious objection was at one with his sense of 'family traditions', for the Lowell family crest incorporated a non-violent recognition of violence, in the pointed form of 'a dexter hand couped at the wrist grasping three pointless darts'.

PHILIP LARKIN:
'LIKE SOMETHING ALMOST BEING SAID'

'The whole frame of the poem', said Donne, 'is a beating out of
a piece of gold, but the last clause is as the impression of the
stamp, and that is it that makes it current.' Larkin's endings
are finely judged, and so he proved a just judge of a poet—
Emily Dickinson—who, like Donne, inaugurated poems magnificently: 'Only rarely, however, did she bring a poem to a
successful conclusion: the amazing riches of originality offered
by the index of her first lines is belied on the page . . . Too often
the poem expires in a teased-out and breathless obscurity.'[1]
Larkin's poems do not expire. 'An Arundel Tomb' ends its
volume, *The Whitsun Weddings*, and ends consummately.

AN ARUNDEL TOMB

Side by side, their faces blurred,
The earl and countess lie in stone,
Their proper habits vaguely shown
As jointed armour, stiffened pleat,
And that faint hint of the absurd—
The little dogs under their feet.

Such plainness of the pre-baroque
Hardly involves the eye, until
It meets his left-hand gauntlet, still
Clasped empty in the other; and
One sees, with a sharp tender shock,
His hand withdrawn, holding her hand.

They would not think to lie so long.
Such faithfulness in effigy
Was just a detail friends would see:
A sculptor's sweet commissioned grace
Thrown off in helping to prolong
The Latin names around the base.

They would not guess how early in
Their supine stationary voyage
The air would change to soundless damage,
Turn the old tenantry away;

---

[1] *New Statesman*, 13 March 1970; *Required Writing* (1983), p. 194.

How soon succeeding eyes begin
To look, not read. Rigidly they
Persisted, linked, through lengths and breadths
Of time. Snow fell, undated. Light
Each summer thronged the glass. A bright
Litter of birdcalls strewed the same
Bone-riddled ground. And up the paths
The endless altered people came,

Washing at their identity.
Now, helpless in the hollow of
An unarmorial age, a trough
Of smoke in slow suspended skeins
Above their scrap of history,
Only an attitude remains:

Time has transfigured them into
Untruth. The stone fidelity
They hardly meant has come to be
Their final blazon, and to prove
Our almost-instinct almost true:
What will survive of us is love.

It is hard to say just where the ending begins. Not with the
last line, which is ushered in by a colon. Not with the last sentence, which begins in mid-line, in the second line of the last
stanza, and which anyway is an elucidation of the riddling half-
a-dozen words which precede it. Not with the last stanza,
which might well (less well) have been self-contained but is
ushered in by its colon. Yet if you work back within the penultimate stanza, you find that again the sentence-shape is
played against the stanza-shape: this sentence too begins in the
stanza's second line, and it begins with 'Now', intimating a
retrospect as well as a prospect. But if you work still further
back, you find that the previous sentence begins with 'And'.
And this would not provide the marked inauguration of an
ending . . . The poem speaks of prolonging, and is itself a
tender prolongation. No stiffened pleats, no rigid persistence.
In short, you cannot abbreviate the poem if you want to speak
of its finality. Nevertheless:

Time has transfigured them into
Untruth. The stone fidelity
They hardly meant has come to be

> Their final blazon, and to prove
> Our almost-instinct almost true:
> What will survive of us is love.

Love, not art, though it is art which tells us so.
The very last line has the apophthegmatic weight of classical
art. Yet Larkin combines what in less good poets prove incom-
patible: the understandings both of classicism and of romanticism. It is a matter of tone, but the printed page, or rather the
printed page of my discursive prose, is crude in its notation of
intonations; it cannot but harden intimations into what Beckett,
in *Company*, calls imperations: 'Same flat tone at all times. For
its affirmations. For its negations. For its interrogations. For its
exclamations. For its imperations. Same flat tone.' Still, to put
it simply, Larkin's last line has at least two different possibilities of intonation. If you lay more weight on 'survive', you hear
a classical asseveration—'What will *survive* of us is love'. Classical because what is meant by the less stressed 'us', taken in
passing, is humanity at large, the largest community of all men
and women; classical because of the transcending of individuality within commonalty. But the weight could, with equal propriety, be distributed differently; the words might be heard
with more of their weight and salience devoted to 'us'—'What
will survive of *us* is love'. This would be the weight of romantic
apprehension; 'us', not as the unstressed and properly undif-
ferentiated mankind, but as a particular 'us', here and now,
moved not just personally but individually, particular visitors
to a tomb or particular contemplators of one such visitor.
Romanticism's pathos of self-attention, its grounded pity
for itself, always risks self-pity and soft warmth; classicism's
stoicism, its grounded grief at the human lot, always risks
frostiness. What Larkin achieves is an extraordinary comple-
mentarity; a classical pronouncement is protected against a
carven coldness by the ghostly presence of an arching counterthrust, a romantic swell of feeling; and the romantic swell
is protected against a melting self-solicitude by the bracing
counterthrust of a classical impersonality. The classical intonation for the line says something *sotto voce*: 'What will survive—
and not just mount, shine, evaporate, and fall—of us is love'.
The romantic intonation says something different *sotto voce*:

'What will survive of us—of us too, ordinary modern people in
an unarmorial age, uncommemorated by aristocratic art or by
a Latin inscription—is love'.

Nothing could be more effortlessly direct than such a line as
'What will survive of us is love' (there is nothing disingenuous
about the poem's introducing it with a colon), and yet the line
is an axis, with two directions. The dignity and pathos of this
line which opens out at the end of 'An Arundel Tomb' flow
from its being strictly ineffable; you cannot simultaneously
utter both of these intonations, though in uttering it—or in
hearing it with an inner ear—with one of the intonations, you
should comprehend that it might be otherwise uttered. If you
were to stress both 'survive' and 'us', the line would not survive the plethora; and if you were to stress neither, the line
would not survive the inanition. The line's compactness is that
two lines, identical in wording but not in intonation, occupy
exactly the same space.

> Nature that hateth emptiness,
> Allows of penetration less.
> ('An Horatian Ode')

The penetration of Marvell's poetry was at one with its
duality of wit, and there is a sombre wit in Larkin's line, wit as
most comprehensively defined by T. S. Eliot in speaking of
Marvell: 'It involves, probably, a recognition, implicit in the
expression of every experience, of other kinds of experience
which are possible.' The dignity of such wit comes from its conceding that the possibilities cannot all be made simultaneously
explicit and yet that the magnanimous imagination can grant
their existence; the pathos comes from the acknowledgement
that we can entertain the thought of such a universal realm but
cannot enter the realm itself.

> The trees are coming into leaf
> Like something almost being said.
> ('The Trees')

There is many a way in which things may almost be said.
Absences, as in Larkin's poem of that title, make themselves
felt; and 'Maiden Name' ends with a line the obvious rhyme
for which has not been granted but left unsounded, silently
wedded: 'With your depreciating luggage laden'. As with so

much of Larkin, the art is a version of pastoral, an apprehension of poignant contraries. The last line of 'An Arundel Tomb' functions as in an inscription itself, lucid and gnomic, an oracular and honourable equivocation, its possibilities equally voiced. Like the Latin inscription spoken of within the poem, it entails some contrariety of looking and reading. The earl and countess would not have imagined the swift decay of the international language of commemoration: 'How soon succeeding eyes begin / To look, not read'.

Larkin's classical temper shows its mettle when he deplores modernism, whether in jazz, poetry, or painting: 'I dislike such things not because they are new, but because they are irresponsible exploitations of technique in contradiction of human life as we know it. This is my essential criticism of modernism, whether perpetrated by Parker, Pound or Picasso: it helps us neither to enjoy nor endure.'[2] Dr. Johnson compacted classicism into the confidence that men more often require to be reminded than informed, and it was Dr. Johnson of whom Larkin reminded us when he said that modernism 'helps us neither to enjoy nor endure'. 'The only end of writing is to enable the readers better to enjoy life or better to endure it.' Yet though Larkin's convictions are classical, his impulses are romantic; as in a great deal of romantic poetry, self-pity is a central concern and has to be watched lest it become the dominant impulse. The argument about Larkin is essentially as to whether his poems are given up to self-pity or given to a scrutiny of self-pity and in particular to an alert refusal of easy disparaging definitions of it. If we should love our neighbour as ourselves, why should we not be permitted to feel as sorry for ourselves as for our neighbour?

The objection to Shelley's torrid cry, 'I fall upon the thorns of life! I bleed!', is that it would sound coolly unconcerned if it were transposed to the third person plural: 'They fall upon the thorns of life! They bleed!' *Tiens*. Whereas the triumph of Larkin's ending to 'Afternoons' is that, though it is specifically about the young mothers and has no *œillade* of mirrored self-attention, it yet would not be an embarrassing or self-pitying reflection if it were turned to the first person.

---

[2] *All What Jazz* (1970), p. 17.

Their beauty has thickened.
Something is pushing them
To the side of their own lives.

To grow old is to be pushed to the side of your own life; something pushes all of us there, yet the somethings are different. The life to which you have given birth, a child, is a manifest and embodied something which pushes you to the side of your own life. But then your poem might push you there too. There is no sense of grievance or of being victimized, simply a flat fidelity. So if we were to transpose it into either a large commonalty, with 'them' meaning not only young mothers but all of us, the poem's way of speaking would be large enough to accommodate this; or if we were to imagine the 'them' contracted into any single one of us—'Something is pushing me / To the side of my own life'—Larkin's way of speaking would be strict enough, calm enough, to acknowledge the pity of it. The poetry is in the pity, for oneself no less than for others.

> *Poor soul,*
> They whisper at their own distress.
> ('Ambulances')

At, not *to*, though it is to their distress that they are moved to whisper.

Larkin's responsible control of tone includes the delegation of responsibility. In responses begin responsibilities, and the recognition, implicit in the expression of every experience, of other kinds of experience which are possible, informs Larkin's belief that for his poetry of lyric meditation the proper medium is the printed page, since there the words are not pressed to the either/or of utterance. The poet who wrote 'The Importance of Elsewhere' is alive to the importance of elsehow—a word from elsewhen which should not have been let die. Wittgenstein's duck/rabbit cannot simultaneously be seen as a duck and as a rabbit, however fast we click our focusing; yet it can be known to be also the other even while it is being seen as the one. What is a perceptual or philosophical trick or flick becomes in Larkin this version of pastoral. Hence Larkin's greatest soft sell, when he did his best to discourage prospective purchasers of his recording of *The Whitsun Weddings*; the form which solicited your order included Larkin's rumbling comedy:

And what you gain on the sound you lose on the sense: think of all the mishearings, the 'their' and 'there' confusions, the submergence of rhyme, the disappearance of stanza-shape, even the comfort of knowing how far you are from the end!

For the sense of nearing a destination, something which is apprehended by sight quite differently from hearing, and which itself arrives at one of Larkin's great destinations, the end of 'The Whitsun Weddings': this sense is more than a comfort; it is a shaping spirit of imagination. Indeed, it is one of the paradoxes and strengths of his art that it is at once diversely idiomatic and yet in some crucial respects cannot be voiced at all. When a poetry-speaker on the B.B.C. ushers in a poem by saying '1914', you sympathize, since some title has to be given and he couldn't say 'MCMXIV'. Yet how much of the sense of loss is lost. How long the continuity was with ancient wars and with immemorial commemoration; how sharp is the passing of an era. 'Never such innocence again'.

Tact is necessary but insufficient, since there may still be an irreducible other sounding. The movement of a poem like 'Going, Going' ('Gone' has not gone, but will come soon, sadly) is one which gives a particular hinged stress to these lines:

> For the first time I feel somehow
> That it isn't going to last.

For the stress has to go, delicately, on 'isn't', not exactly where it would have gone if the lines had not been anticipated within the poem. 'That it *isn't*—contrary to what I had once thought—going to last'. For thirty lines earlier, the poem had kicked off with: 'I thought it would last my time'; and we find that we needed to carry responsibly and lastingly forward the memory of that launching, that attractive and good-humoured irresponsibility, so that this might brace the later moment with a salutary recognition, now that the crucial word 'last' (coming for the second time) demands the strongly conceded stress on 'isn't':

> For the first time I feel somehow
> That it isn't going to last.

The poem is going to.

It is a corollary that the moment at which a Larkin poem

loses hold is likely to be one when a reader cannot make sense and sensibility of the relation between repetition and intonation. As, for me, just before the end of 'The Whitsun Weddings'. The newly-weds watched the landscape:

> —and none
> Thought of the others they would never meet
> Or how their lives would all contain this hour.
> I thought of London spread out in the sun,
> Its postal districts packed like squares of wheat:

I don't know how the man knows that none of them thought those things (and yet this itself doesn't seem to be up for scrutiny within the poem), and my unease is accentuated by my not being able to hear the relation between 'none thought' and 'I thought'. None thought this whereas I thought it, or whereas I thought something quite other? If there is no stress placed upon 'I' in 'I thought', the hinge turns idly; but if 'I' is at all stressed, what depends from the hinge? Pronouns, especially in their both contrasting and assimilating 'I' and others, are asked to take such weight in Larkin's poems that any factitious relationship (none thought / I thought?) does real damage.

The very structure of a poem like 'Mr Bleaney' turns upon the decision as to the precise degree of stress and precisely where to lay it. Once the speaker (so to speak) takes Mr Bleaney's place, the shape of the poem is simple: 'I know his habits' (this and that), and 'their yearly frame' (this, that, and the other):

> But if he stood and watched the frigid wind
> Tousling the clouds, lay on the fusty bed
> Telling himself that this was home, and grinned,
> And shivered, without shaking off the dread
>
> That how we live measures our own nature,
> And at his age having no more to show
> Than one hired box should make him pretty sure
> He warranted no better, I don't know.

But if he stood, as I do, and . . .: the plot of the poem asks some stress on *he*; and yet it is a stress that becomes increasingly and illuminatingly difficult to maintain with grace and exactitude as the final eight-line sentence rolls on. 'Telling *him*self'—as I tell *my*self: the antithesis-cum-assimilation may still be pointed up by the voice, but by the time we reach 'at his age', and 'make him pretty sure', and 'he warranted', the contrastive *I* has been dissolved to wan wistlessness. At which point 'I' makes itself heard: 'I don't know'. But to accentuate this other arch of the structure (I know his habits, but these things I *don't* know) by coming down unignorably on 'don't' would be as coarsening as it would be to slight this structural turn.

Without the contrast furnished by 'I know his habits', there would be at the end a more mild puzzlement, equalizing the stresses within 'I don't know'; and this puzzlement must not be sacrificed to the more urgent fears (was he just like me? am I just like him?), since these last eight lines subtly twine an ordinary wondering and a morbid anxiety. Is the speaker imputing his own sensitivities and anxieties to Mr Bleaney, or is he acknowledging a true fellow-feeling? Any act of imagination risks the accusation that it is just an imputing of oneself, a sort of anthropomorphism, but then is this accusation too an unimaginative imputation? 'I don't know.' You must stress to some degree all three of those concluding words; yet you mustn't treat 'don't' as if it were not an unpriceable pivot. But then nor must you slight the first of persons, 'I', or the searching verb 'know'. 'Mr Bleaney' is one of Larkin's best poems, and it is natural that it should come to its consummation of 'incomplete unrest' with those three words: the pronoun which so often marks the crucial turn or takes the crucial stress in his poetry; the colloquial negative 'don't'; and the admission as to doubtful knowledge.

'Know' can function similarly at the start of a poem, as with 'Ignorance', where the first words might advance naturally towards a stress on nothing—'Strange to know *nothing*'—only then to be retrospectively reconsidered because of being followed by 'never to be sure / Of what is true or right or real'. For the succession asks that there be a stronger stress on 'know' than you could have known at the time:

> Strange to know nothing, never to be sure
> Of what is true or right or real,
> But forced to qualify *or so I feel*. . . .

An equal stress on 'I' and 'feel'?

The start of 'Toads' offers a pronominal prospect which is likewise qualified as the poem moves on:

> Why should I let the toad *work*
> Squat on my life?

The general aggrievedness, which is at first all there is to go on, would stress 'should'—'Why *should* I?'. But it then turns out, as things continue, that there is a particular aggrievedness instead or as well, which means: 'Why should *I*, who am no fool, let the toad work squat on *my* life?' You can feel these challenging undulations of tone, idiomatic and yet unspeakable, in a stanza like this:

> Their nippers have got bare feet,
> Their unspeakable wives
> Are skinny as whippets—and yet
> No one actually *starves*.

This needs both the tone of matter-of-fact reportage, without argumentative stresses until the last word, and the pitching upon 'have' and 'Are' which will bring out the concessive combativeness: 'True, their nippers *have* got bare feet, and their unspeakable wives *are*—oh yes—skinny as whippets—and yet . . .'. Larkin's accents are audible either as equable or as elbowing.

'Unspeakable': the negative prefix matters to Larkin for what it cannot but call up, and an unspoken but not unheard melody is one of his honest insinuations. The negative prefix may be markedly absent, as when Larkin musically imagines 'Mute glorious Storyvilles' ('For Sidney Bechet'), challenging us to sound the mute prefix *in*—or at least not to succumb to merely hitting upon 'glorious' as if this would make music or sense. Allusion like this (double or triple, since it plays upon Gray as well as upon Milton: 'Some mute inglorious Milton here may rest') always invites at least two effects of intonation: the voice must use its pitch so that it gives one kind of salience to the words that have been carried over unchanged, and it must use its stress so that it gives a different kind of salience to the words that have been changed and that therefore constitute the narrative of the matter. The opening of Edmund Blunden's best poem, 'Report on Experience', would not be sounded in the same way if it were not that the Psalmist were audible.

> I have been young, and now am not too old,
> And I have seen the righteous forsaken . . .

'I have been young, and now am old: and yet saw I never the
righteous forsaken . . .' So the tones of Blunden's lines must be
something like this:

> '*I* have been young, and now am' *not too* 'old',
> And I *have* 'seen the righteous forsaken' . . .

A characteristic Larkin turn of phrase like 'the wind's incomplete unrest' ('Talking in Bed'[3]) alludes to the easy restful-
ness of the phrase 'a complete rest'—a phrase newly completed
unrestfully. But uttering this—saying the words, as against
imagining them—is not as easy as it sounds. If you stress the
negative prefixes, '*in*complete *un*rest', you reduce the effect to
that of a dig in the ribs; but if you don't stress them at all, you
cut free from the tacit down-to-earth idiom which touchingly
tethers the high fancy. Again, it is commonplace to meet a
welcome, and easily said, but how do you say 'Meet a vast
unwelcome' ('First Sight')? It asks a stress small enough to be
no strain. Or there is the negative prefix at the very end of
'Spring': 'Their visions mountain-clear, their needs immodest'.
Our modest needs are one thing; our immodest needs would be
something other than quite other, since immodest isn't exactly
the opposite of modest. Yet the alighting upon the negative
prefix must be delicate—must meet the modest needs of such
exact art. Likewise with the felicity which ends a poem ('Wild
Oats') with the line 'Unlucky charms, perhaps'. To stress the
prefix would be to smirk, and to ignore it would be to wear a
vacant look. Larkin's art is varying and almost invariably
lovely, and a phrase like 'Unvariably lovely there' ('Lines on a
Young Lady's Photograph Album') depends on 'unvariably'
being a variation of the usual 'invariably', from which it differs
as minutely and substantially as does T. S. Eliot's 'unsubstantial' ('Are become unsubstantial', in 'Marina') from 'in-
substantial'. Larkin's too is a poetry in which things both great
and small shine substantially expressed.

---

[3] The whole poem may be found on p. 387.

GEOFFREY HILL 1:
'THE TONGUE'S ATROCITIES'

A principled distrust of the imagination is nothing new. One triumph of the imagination is that it can be aware of the perils of the imagination, the aggrandisements, covert indulgences, and specious claims which it may incite. Great art is often about the limits of what we should hope for even from the greatest of art, and among the many things which the imagination can realize on our behalf, one such is the limits of the sympathetic imagination.

A poem by Geoffrey Hill speaks of 'The tongue's atrocities' ('History as Poetry'), compacting or colluding the atrocities of which the tongue must speak, with the atrocities which—unless it is graced with unusually creative vigilance—it is all too likely to commit when it speaks of atrocities. For atrocity may get flattened down into the casually 'atrocious', or it may get fattened up into that debased form of imagination which is prurience. So the general burden of the imagination's self-scrutiny presses particularly upon all such art as contemplates (in both senses) atrocities.

In his literary criticism, Geoffrey Hill has worried at this, as when he praised the poetry with which Ben Jonson both fleshes and cauterizes the atrocities of imperial Rome: 'Jonson's qualifications worry the verse into dogs-teeth of virtuous self-mistrust';[1] and again when Hill praised the 'terrible beauty' of Yeats's 'Easter 1916': 'the tune of a mind distrustful yet envious, mistrusting the abstraction, mistrusting its own mistrust'.[2] This subject of much of Hill's criticism is the impulse of much of his poetry. 'Annunciations: I' is about art as connoisseurship (for its creators as much as for its audiences or critics—Hill never makes a complacent distinction between the likes of him and the likes of us). 'The Humanist' and 'The Imaginative Life' are both impelled by virtuous self-mistrust; 'The

---

[1] (1960); *The Lords of Limit* (1984), p. 53.
[2] ' "The Conscious Mind's Intelligible Structure": A Debate', *Agenda*, 9:4-10:1 (1971-2), 23.

Martyrdom of Saint Sebastian' bends its attention upon the
glazing of the martyr's pains.

The act of imagining, and of inscribing in words, can so
easily claim 'too much or too little'. The prose-poem which
uses those words, 'Offa's Sword' (*Mercian Hymns*), ponders the
great gift brought to Offa: 'The Frankish gift, two-edged, regaled with slaughter'. Regaled, with its regalia (and *regalo* means
a gift); but 'regaled with slaughter' opens up a grim fissure—
the poem uses the word 'fissured'—between the barbaric opu-
lence and the jaded prurience: regaled with good stories, with
Christmas fare (the poem speaks of 'Christ's mass'), and with
deliciously domesticated slaughter. 'Two-edged'.

But let me quote Hill's most explicit imagining of prurience
as imagination's dark double, 'Offa's Journey to Rome':

> At Pavia, a visitation of some sorrow. Boethius'
> dungeon. He shut his eyes, gave rise to a tower
> out of the earth. He willed the instruments of
> violence to break upon meditation. Iron buckles
> gagged; flesh leaked rennet over them; the men
> stooped, disentangled the body.

> He wiped his lips and hands. He strolled back to the
> car, with discreet souvenirs for consolation and
> philosophy. He set in motion the furtherance of
> his journey. To watch the Tiber foaming out
> much blood.

See how 'gave rise to' is redeemed from its heartless officialese;
and how the very instruments of imprisonment ought to have
vomited (to have gagged in gagging him); and how the body
becomes that of an unweaned calf, its rennet curdling; and how
the poem itself honourably fears the feasting prurience of all
such imaginings: 'He wiped his lips and hands'. Can we remember such things without reducing them to discreet sou-
venirs? Is even God above such diseased imaginings? God,
'voyeur of sacrifice'. But it is characteristic of Hill to have de-
italicised the word 'voyeur' when he reprinted that poem after
its first publication ('Locust Songs')[3]—who are the English to
imply that voyeurism is foreign to them? A comment by Hill on
'Annunciations: II' might stand as an epigraph to all such

[3] *Stand*, 5:2 (1961); then *King Log* (1968).

poems of his: 'But I want the poem to have this dubious end; because I feel dubious; and the whole business is dubious'.[4]

Yet upon this ancient dubiety, which is not a failure of nerve but an acknowledgment of what a success of nerve might be, there has been urged in the last forty years a unique and hideous modern intensification. The Nazi extermination-camps are a horror which has been felt to dwarf all art and to paralyse all utterance. There would be something suspect about anybody who felt nothing of the impulse which voiced itself in George Steiner as 'The world of Auschwitz lies outside speech as it lies outside reason'.[5] But then this very impulse can uglily become a routine, a mannerism, or a cliché. There is something oppressively to-be-expected about beginning a book on *The Holocaust and the Literary Imagination* (1975)[6] with a chapter entitled 'In the Beginning Was the Silence', with its epigraph from Beckett: 'Speech is a desecration of silence', and with the first sentence invoking Adorno's cry that to write poetry after Auschwitz is barbaric. A poet may feel that not only is Auschwitz unspeakable but that this fear itself has become unsayable, so much said as scarcely to be accessible to feeling. There press upon all these grim doubts and realities both a harsh unignorability and a smoothly righteous triteness.

Geoffrey Hill was born in 1932. He is in my judgment the best of those English poets who entered into adult consciousness in the post-war, not the pre-war or the war-time, world. Poets just older than Hill—Philip Larkin, say—were in possession of a conscious experienced public conscience when the news and then the newsreels of Belsen and Auschwitz disclosed the atrocities. A poet of exactly Hill's age did not yet possess any such experienced conscience; Hill was thirteen in 1945, and he belongs to the generation whose awakening to the atrocity of adult life was an awakening to this unparalleled atrocity. It is true that no Englishman had ever before known anything like those newsreels, those photographs, those histories; but Englishmen older than Hill did not have this atrocity as their first introduction to atrocity. Hill wrote his first poems in the late 1940's; mercifully, there is every reason to believe that the

[4] In *The Penguin Book of Contemporary Verse*, ed. Kenneth Allott (2nd edn, 1962), p. 393.
[5] *Language and Silence* (1967), p. 146.   [6] By Lawrence L. Langer (1975).

poems were not bent upon the Nazi holocaust. But since then,
he has written the deepest and truest poems on that holocaust:
'September Song', and 'Ovid in the Third Reich', as well as
a few other poems on this atrocity which are honourable, fierce
and grave: 'Two Formal Elegies', 'Domaine Public', and section IV in 'Of Commerce and Society':

> Statesmen have known visions. And, not alone,
> Artistic men prod dead men from their stone:
> Some of us have heard the dead speak:
> The dead are my obsession this week
>
> But may be lifted away. In summer
> Thunder may strike, or, as a tremor
> Of remote adjustment, pass on the far side
> From us: however deified and defied
>
> By those it does strike. Many have died. Auschwitz,
> Its furnace chambers and lime pits
> Half-erased, is half-dead; a fable
> Unbelievable in fatted marble.
>
> There is, at times, some need to demonstrate
> Jehovah's touchy methods, that create
> The connoisseur of blood, the smitten man.
> At times it seems not common to explain.

The dignified force of Hill's poetry on such atrocity is a matter
of his grasping that the atrocity both is and is not unique, and
that it presents to the imagination a challenge which likewise
both is and is not unique. Hill does not permit the Jews' sufferings to be separated from or aloof from the other hideous
sufferings which fill the air of the past and the present. It is
characteristic of him that he should not countenance the well-
meant but misguided turn which would monopolize the word
'holocaust' for the sufferings of the Jews. He does not withhold
the word from the Jews (though not in the dangerous form 'the
Holocaust'), and this not least because he feels dismay at the
unjustly retributive irony of the word's etymology and its religious allegiance: 'A sacrifice wholly consumed by fire; a whole
burnt offering'. But he would support neither monopoly nor
pedantry, and he says of the Battle of Towton (Palm Sunday,
1461): 'In the accounts of the contemporary chroniclers it was
a holocaust'.[7]

[7] From the Essay accompanying 'Funeral Music', *King Log*.

This poem, 'Statesmen have known visions . . . ', is a poem
which knows what it is up against. Its pained rhythms resist
both a facile self-exculpation and a facile self-inculpation. 'The
dead are my obsession this week': the rhythm is at once strong
and strained, and it protects the groundedly sardonic against
the ingratiatingly self-deprecating. It is doubly styptic. As is
the turn which first grimly shrivels 'deified' down into 'defied'
and then shrivels them both down to 'died'. 'Many have died'.
'Deified' into 'defied' is a genuine but precarious movement of
the imagination; so the subsequent pared-down 'died' rightly
does not disown it, but does place and weigh it. Against that
laconic shrivelling root-simplicity is set the grossly burgeoning
unimaginability of Auschwitz, with the very sounds moving
from delicacy ('a fable') into the fattened slabs of monumental
evil:

> a fable
> Unbelievable in fatted marble.

For '*fa*tted mar*ble*' is a distending of the word 'fable' into a
sleek stoniness; and 'fatted' is the ancient sacrifice. To 'pass
on the far side' may at the time be well-judged but may also
later be harshly judged. The poem is forced to ask, at least,
about the relation between the Jews and their God:

> There is, at times, some need to demonstrate
> Jehovah's touchy methods, that create
> The connoisseur of blood, the smitten man.
> At times it seems not common to explain.

For 'the smitten man' is a thrust at one of those moments when
the God of the Jews moves in an appallingly mysterious way:

And a certain man of the sons of the prophets said unto his neighbour
in the word of the Lord, Smite me, I pray thee. And the man refused
to smite him. Then said he unto him, Because thou hast not obeyed
the voice of the Lord, behold, as soon as thou art departed from me,
a lion shall slay thee. And as soon as he was departed from him, a lion
found him, and slew him. Then he found another man, and said,
Smite me, I pray thee. And the man smote him, so that in smiting he
wounded him. (*I Kings*, xx 37).[8]

---

[8] Mr Brian Oxley drew my attention to *I Kings*, xx 37.

'At times it seems not common to explain'. Which is not to say
that the poem asks us to accept the cliché, the common explanation. For the 'unbelievable' is also the unexplainable, and
the world of Hill's poem is completely different from the world
of George Steiner's prose with its explanation of why all this
befell the Jews: 'the blackmail of perfection' which the Jews
three times visited upon Western life: the intolerable idealisms
of, first, monotheism; then Christian adjuration; then messianic
socialism. 'When it turned on the Jew, Christianity and European civilization turned on the incarnation—albeit an incarnation often wayward and unaware—of its own best hopes'.[9]

> Statesmen have known visions. And, not alone,
> Artistic men prod dead men from their stone.

Hill has pronounced

TWO FORMAL ELEGIES

For the Jews in Europe

I

Knowing the dead, and how some are disposed:
Subdued under rubble, water, in sand graves,
In clenched cinders not yielding their abused
Bodies and bonds to those whom war's chance saves
Without the law: we grasp, roughly, the song.
Arrogant acceptance from which song derives
Is bedded with their blood, makes flourish young
Roots in ashes. The wilderness revives,

Deceives with sweetness harshness. Still beneath
Live skin stone breathes, about which fires but play,
Fierce heart that is the iced brain's to command
To judgment—(studied reflex, contained breath)—
Their best of worlds since, on the ordained day,
This world went spinning from Jehovah's hand.

II

For all that must be gone through, their long death
Documented and safe, we have enough
Witnesses (our world being witness-proof).
The sea flickers, roars, in its wide hearth.

[9] *In Bluebeard's Castle* (1971), p. 41.

Here, yearly, the pushing midlanders stand
To warm themselves; men, brawny with life,
Women who expect life. They relieve
Their thickening bodies, settle on scraped sand.

Is it good to remind them, on a brief screen,
Of what they have witnessed and not seen?
(Deaths of the city that persistently dies . . .?)
To put up stones ensures some sacrifice.
Sufficient men confer, carry their weight.
(At whose door does the sacrifice stand or start?)

The first poem, which begins with the dangerous word 'Knowing', knows that our comprehension of it will have to be a matter
of grasping it, with some of the urgent haste of such seizing.
Like its creator, 'we grasp, roughly, the song'. *Roughly* as
untenderly (how else can we resist the solicitations of a false
tenderness—'Knowing the dead'? But, like Hill, we never did
know them as people known to us; and a sense of threat swells
within that other dark meaning of 'knowing the dead. . . . '—and
what they are capable of). But *roughly*, too, as approximately
(to hope for more than an honourable approximation in such
a case would be dishonourable hubris).

There is an angry vibration in this response to the outraged
dead. Life, bristling against injustice, quivers in the restive
play upon *disposed*: 'Knowing the dead, and how some are disposed'—a disposition of mind, or the disposal of a body? Likewise in *subdued*: 'Subdued under rubble'—a crushed body, or
a quietly stoical mind? The quivering of life is there again in
the bitter archaism of 'war's chance': 'those whom war's chance
saves'. For where in the world of technologized extermination
is there even a memory of what was once true and poignant:
'The chance of war / Is equal and the slayer oft is slain' (*The
Iliad*)?[10] There is the old sense of outrage felt yet once more, in
the mingled gratitude to and warning to Voltaire: 'Their best
of worlds'. There is the simultaneous delight and fear in 'This
world went spinning from Jehovah's hand': spinning effortlessly
into its ordained arc, or spinning away for ever from his hand?

In the second poem, there is the same glowering intensity
alive to the terrible questions which ask what good it can do
even to think on these things, truly knowing that it may well do

---

[10] *Iliad*, xviii 388; Bryant's translation (1870).

ill. 'For all that must be gone through': for all which, or—with
the known acknowledged *that* as either shouldered or shrugged
off—'For all that must be gone through'. Gone through, as
endured, or as wearisomely enumerated? How hostile the
relation is between 'witness' and 'proof', held apart and together by their hyphen: 'witness-proof', and then between
'witness-proof' and fireproof or foolproof. What are we proofed
in, armoured in, that we think we can witness, let alone bear
witness to, such happenings? The 'midlanders', after all, are
English tourists as well as Mediterranean natives. With the last
line of the second poem, there ignites the fierceness which was
smouldering in the first poem. For 'Without the law' had not
forgotten Kipling's 'Recessional':

> Such boastings as the Gentiles use,
>   Or lesser breeds without the Law—
> Lord God of Hosts, be with us yet,
> Lest we forget—lest we forget!

No tremor passes through Kipling's line: 'Still stands Thine
ancient sacrifice'. Hill's final line has the tremor of genuine
interrogation: '(At whose door does the sacrifice stand or
start?)' 'The guilt of blood is at your door', wrote Tennyson.
And *start* is a last twist: jump in shock (as against the stolid
stand), or learn to begin? Hill, who says in another poem about
the dead that 'Some, finally, learn to begin' ('The Distant Fury
of Battle'), ends this poem with a sudden 'start'; he has brought
us to the point at which we may indeed start.

These are poems which carry their weight, and they are substantially resistant, so there remain many serious questions as
to how to construe and what to make of them. But I wish to
move to a consideration which then bears on others of Hill's
poems, a consideration which becomes manifest in the revisions
which Hill made to this poem after its first publication. As
originally published,[11] it had within brackets the dedication
'(For the Jews of Europe)', and the second poem then ended
with an extraordinary tour-de-force: of the last four lines, not
only the first and the last were each within brackets, but so too
were the second and the third. The poem ended with four successive lines each within brackets. Hill was right to think that

---

[11] *Paris Review*, No. 21, Spring-Summer 1959.

his is a poetic gift which must be profoundly and variously alive to what simple brackets can do. He had been wrong to think that he could command to favourable judgment a concatenation of four lines, each bracketed, without his poem's indurating itself into mannerism and self-attention, a sequence of self-containednesses such as then seals the poem into self-congratulation. By removing the brackets from both the antepenultimate and the penultimate lines, he not only removed the oppression of paralysing self-consciousness, but also tautened the arc of the poem. For, unlike the first poem, the second has at last gravitated to couplets; against which there is now played a beautiful and complementary chiasmus, *a/b/b/a*, in the sombre punctuation alone. Of the last four lines, the first and second, and then the third and fourth, rhyme together, but it is the second and third, and then the first and fourth, which punctuate together. The tensions of the last four lines now dispose themselves differently; less disruptedly, less fracturedly, and more finally, since chiasmus comprises an arc.

Brackets are a way of containing things and feelings, in both of the senses of containing: including and restraining. It is then a true sense of the metaphorical power even of ordinary punctuation which led Hill to have, as the only parenthesis within the first poem, the words '—(studied reflex, contained breath)—'. The parenthesis holds the breadth of the dead; we hold our breath, and contain ourselves, even as the speaking poet does, with his syntax suspended and his rhythm tensed (a steadying of the voice is necessary in 'contained breath', with its minute resistance to the iambic movement), so that, at once trained and spontaneous—'(studied reflex, contained breath)'—, the lines may 'command to judgment . . . Their best of worlds'.

There is a different kind of metaphorical life in the parenthesis in the second poem: '(our world being witness-proof)'. For here the brackets suggest the corrupt separateness of which contained breath is the pure counterpart; the brackets now act as a kind of proof or armour against all penetrative imagination, with *our world* fortified in blasé imperviousness by its brackets, unlike their open hope, 'Their best of worlds', 'This world'. The two other bracketings (two from what, as I have said, had been four) embody a move from one kind of musing, a brooding upon a paradox such as may be religious or religiose, musing into the truth-gathering or the wool-gathering of three dots: '(Deaths of the city that persistently dies . . . ?)'—a move from this kind of musing into something much sharper in sound and sense, a 'perplexed persistence', a baffled indictment: '(At whose door does the sacrifice stand or start?)'[12] Yet the end is at once curt and muted—muted by the inevitably receding or *recessional* quality of brackets as we read them.

But 'read them' is equivocal. Eyes and ears? Although our inner ear may divine a tone from such brackets, may sense a lowering of the timbre or pitch or tone or note or simply loudness, one of the important things about brackets is that they belong with those signs of punctuation which the voice cannot sufficiently utter. Hill's poetry makes weighty and delicate use of this very fact. Hugh Kenner has pointed out that you cannot say a footnote or an asterisk; I disagree with him about parentheses.

The footnote's relation to the passage from which it depends is established wholly by visual and typographic means, and will typically defeat all efforts of the speaking voice to clarify it without visual aid. Parentheses, like commas, tell the voice what to do: an asterisk tells the voice that it can do nothing. You cannot read a passage of prose aloud, interpolating the footnotes, and make the subordination of the footnotes clear, and keep the whole sounding natural. The language has forsaken a vocal milieu, and a context of oral communication between persons, and commenced to take advantage of the expressive possibilities of technological space.[13]

This is entirely true of the footnote and the asterisk; perhaps the auditory imagination, when the eye reads such punctuation, hears something, calls up some tone to itself for what it is apprehending, but this auditory imagination is essentially private. You could not, in the manner of French dictation at school, read aloud such punctuation and elicit accurate transcriptions from your hearers, any more than you could of T. S. Eliot's spacing-punctuation in *The Waste Land*. The eye can here allow to enter its consciousness what the tongue cannot then utter.

---

[12] With the bracketed 'door', compare the gates in 'Solomon's Mines', bracketed: '(Let the hewn gates clash to)'; and the bracketed 'citadels' in the house of 'Asmodeus'. T. S. Eliot shut his poem about himself with the bracketed line: '(Whether his mouth be open or shut)'.

[13] *Flaubert, Joyce and Beckett: The Stoic Comedians* (1964), pp. 39-40.

But Kenner is wrong to set up the contrast: 'Parentheses, like commas,[14] tell the voice what to do: an asterisk tells the voice that it can do nothing'. For though a parenthesis is a syntactical unit, and of course the voice can make such a thing clear, a parenthesis is a syntactical unit which may be qualified by very different punctuations. *Parenthesis*: 'An explanatory or qualifying word, clause, or sentence inserted into a passage with which it has not necessarily any grammatical connexion, and from which it is usually marked off by round or square brackets, dashes, or commas' (*OED*). We use the word parenthesis both for the unit and for one of the many ways of indicating it, and the voice is not able to make adequately clear (adequate in both delicacy and clarity) whether the parenthesis is bracketed off, comma'd off, or dashed off. (Even apart from the fact that the voice cannot utter a square as against a round bracket.)[15] For although it may be true that such punctuation as is markedly durational may be uttered (a full stop is likely, though only likely, to mean a longer pause than a comma), the thing about brackets is that they are not essentially an indicator of duration. They indicate a relationship which may or may not have a durational dimension, and they speak to the eye and not to the ear. A poet who has a strong sense both of all that the voice can do and of all that it cannot, a poet who knows that the timing within a poem both is and is not a matter of tempo,[16] will be a poet who seizes upon the particular power of the bracket to incarnate something which commands a sense of the difference between what can be printedly read and what can be said.

It is Hill's 'September Song' which most fully realizes, in both senses, how much a simple point of punctuation may weigh.

[14] A sharp piece of punctuation, and heir to Dryden's:

> Yet this I Prophesy; Thou shalt be seen,
> (Tho' with some short Parenthesis between:)
> High on the Throne of Wit;
>   ('To Mr Congreve')

[15] Much of the comedy of Laurence Sterne's punctuation is the play of the speaking voice against the typographical notation.

[16] Hill has written of the 'timed and weighed' impropriety in Robert Lowell (*Essays in Criticism*, xiii, 1963, 188-97), and of the 'timed and placed' repetition in Jon Silkin (*Poetry and Audience*, 9:12, 1962, 5).

SEPTEMBER SONG
born 19.6.32—deported 24.9.42

Undesirable you may have been, untouchable
you were not. Not forgotten
or passed over at the proper time.

As estimated, you died. Things marched,
sufficient, to that end.
Just so much Zyklon and leather, patented
terror, so many routine cries.

(I have made
an elegy for myself it
is true)

September fattens on vines. Roses
flake from the wall. The smoke
of harmless fires drifts to my eyes.

This is plenty. This is more than enough.

It is a poem which has elicited from Jon Silkin a sustained critical meditation, which I shall quote in its entirety:

A concentration camp victim. Even the 'play' in the subtitle 'born
19.6.32—deported 24.9.42' where the natural event of the birth is
placed, simply, beside the human and murderous 'deported' as if the
latter were of the same order and inevitability for the victim; which,
in some senses, it was—even here, the zeugmatic wit is fully employed. The irony of conjuncted meanings between 'undesirable'
(touching on both sexual desire and racism) and 'untouchable',
which exploits a similar ambiguity but reverses the emphases, is
unusually dense *and* simple. The confrontation is direct and unavoid-
able, and this directness is brought to bear on the reader not only by
the vocabulary, but by the balancing directness of the syntax. This
stanza contains one of Hill's dangerous words—dangerous because of
its too-frequent use, and because these words sometimes unleash
(though not here) a too evident irony:

Not forgotten
or passed over at the proper time.

'Proper' brings together the idea of bureaucratically correct 'as
calculated' by the logistics of the 'final solution' and the particular
camp's timetable; it also contrasts the idea of the mathematically
'correct' with the morally intolerable. It touches, too, on the distinction between what is morally right, and what is conventionally
acceptable, and incidentally brings to bear on the whole the way in

which the conventionally acceptable is often used to cloak the morally unacceptable. One of Hill's grim jokes, deployed in such a way that the laughter is precisely proportionate to the needs of ironic exposure. It is when the irony is in excess of the situation that the wit becomes mannered. But here it does not. So the poem continues, remorselessly.

> As estimated, you died. Things marched,
> sufficient, to that end.

One feels the little quibbling movement in

> As estimated, you died.

as, without wishing to verbalise it, Hill points to the disturbing contrast between the well-functioning time-table and what it achieved. 'Things marched' has the tread of pompous authority, immediately, in the next line, qualified by the painfully accurate recognition that just so much energy was needed, and released, for the extermination. 'Sufficient' implies economy, but it also implies a conscious qualification of the heavy, pompous tread of authority. The quiet function of unpretentious machinery fulfilled its programme, perhaps *more* lethally. One also notices here how the lineation gauges, exactly, the flow and retraction of meaning and impulse, and how this exact rhythmical flow is so much a part of the sensuous delivery of response and evaluation. It is speech articulated, but the lineation provides, via the convention of verse line-ending, a formal control of rhythm, and of sense emphasis, by locking with, or breaking, the syntactical flow. Thus in the third stanza the syntax is broken by the lineation exactly at those parts at which the confession, as it were, of the poem's (partial) source is most painful:

> (I have made
> an elegy for myself it
> is true)

The slightly awkward break after 'it' not only forces the reading speed down to a word-by-word pace, in itself an approximation to the pain of the confession, but emphasises the whole idea. By placing emphasis on the unspecifying pronoun, Hill is able to say two things: that the elegy was made for himself (at least, in part) since in mourning another one is also commiserating with one's own condition.

> When we chant
> 'Ora, ora pro nobis' it is not
> Seraphs who descend to pity but ourselves.
> ('Funeral Music:5')

But 'it' may also refer to the whole event; I have made an elegy for myself, as we all do, but I have also made an elegy on a 'true' event.

True imaginatively, true in detailed fact; both for someone other than myself. Thus he is able to point to the difficulty of the poet, who wishes, for a variety of reasons, to approach the monstrousness of such events, but has compunction about doing so. He tactfully touches for instance on the overweening ambition of the poet who hitches his talent to this powerful subject, thereby giving his work an impetus it *may* not be fully entitled to, since, only the victim, herself, would be entitled to derive this kind of 'benefit'. But he also modestly pleads, I think, with 'it / is true' that whatever the reasons for his writing such an elegy, a proper regard for the victim, a true and unambitious feeling, was present and used.[17]

Silkin's sense of the poem is scrupulous and touching. The poem is indeed 'dense *and* simple'; so I should add that, for instance, the awful weight upon

> Not forgotten
> or passed over at the proper time

is instinct not only with the bitter reversal of the Passover (with its further flickering reminder that innocent Egyptians and not just guilty ones were smitten with the loss of their first-born), but also with the petty grievance of promotion denied: 'passed over'. Similar vibrations stir in the dehumanizing militaristic bureaucracy of 'Things marched', and in the tiny dubiety of 'Just so much . . .', where 'Just' is both the casually murderous 'Merely' and the meticulously murderous 'Precisely'. 'Zyklon' is then, in every sense, a word from—a wafting of poison gas from—a completely different world from that of everything else in the poem, unutterably alien and not just foreign; ugly; imperious (Hill had originally given it only a lower-case z, which too much lowered its hateful rank)—a word (is it a *word*, even?) which did not have this 'patented' sense until our time, scarcely belongs in the English language, and which is now for ever doomed to the detestation of one immediate association. There it is, capitalized, in this poem which has no name for the dead child. Then there is the sickening glissade from *leather* to *patented*, and the awful possibility of fatigued exasperation in 'so many routine cries'. Routine cries, to the camp's officials; can a poem raise itself above a routine cry?

---

[17] 'The Poetry of Geoffrey Hill', in *British Poetry since 1960*, ed. Michael Schmidt and Grevel Lindop (1972), pp. 145-7. Reprinted by kind permission of Jon Silkin.

The poem moves through from two groupings (they can't be called stanzas) which are 'you', through two which are 'I' and 'my', to a bleak curt shaping (one line only) which is neither 'you' nor 'I'. 'This is plenty. This is more than enough'. This? This, as the smiling month of September, a mockery of that September in 1942, which itself had mocked the month of the Jewish New Year and of the Day of Atonement. The anger at the month is unjust, casting-about for a scapegoat: 'September fattens on vines'—again the basking fatness, being fattened for the kill, a fertilising richness. But then there is the other 'This'—This, as the attempt to speak of it (it, the further 'This,' the happening itself). Bitter at the ineffectuality of even its own best efforts, and so dismissing them curtly and yet with the reluctance of repetition: 'This is plenty. This is more than enough'. Plenty, as gratitude to nature's foison, but also as brusque slang; 'more than enough', as needing to end in something more English, an unillusioned understatement. The last line pounces, and yet its cadence doesn't fall into the trap which waits for the separate finality of that old reassurance, the clinching iambic pentameter. Partly this is a matter of the delicacy which which it both is and is not preceded by an iambic pentameter: 'The smoke / of harmless fires drifts to my eyes'. That is not one line, but one and a half; the cadence drifts across, and then what had been drifting suddenly clenches itself. Yet not into anything easily clinching, since the one line is both one and two in its structure: 'This is plenty. This is more than enough'. Behind the poet's pinched self-scrutiny, having to bite back, we should poignantly hear the age-old open-hearted fierce gratitude with which the Jews thank their God at Passover:

If he had brought us forth out of Egypt but had not executed judgments upon the Egyptians, it would have been enough.
If he had executed judgments upon the Egyptians, but had not executed judgments upon their gods, it would have been enough.
If he had executed judgments upon their gods, but had not slain their first-born, it would have been enough.
If he had slain their first-born, but had not bestowed their wealth on us, it would have been enough.
If he had bestowed their wealth on us, but had not divided the sea for us, it would have been enough . . . [18]

[18] I owe this point to Miss Aloma Halter and to Mrs. Nita Mandel.

Jon Silkin feels, and helps us feel, the central gravity of the
three lines

> (I have made
> an elegy for myself it
> is true)

But I believe that it is crucial to them that they are in brackets.
For it is this, and not their tone or syntax alone, which gives
them that unique feeling of being at once a crux and an aside,
at once an inescapable honourable admission and something
which the poem may then honourably pass over. It is the
brackets which embody the essential discrimination between
the right and the wrong kind of detachment. Hopkins may tell
his autumnal griever that she is grieving not for Goldengrove
but for herself: 'It is Margaret you mourn for'. Hill acknowledges that he mourns for himself, but he refuses to make the
total concession which would evacuate the whole matter; he
does not say that he has made an elegy only for himself; and 'it is
true'—which is unsayably punctuated so that only the eye can
sense its utterance—is not only the concession, and not only an
insistence that the deportation indeed happened, but also a
quietly confident insistence that the elegy itself is true.

For its truth is partly that it embodies the truth that what happened was unspeakable, and at the heart of the poem is this
moment of something that is perfectly lucid but unspeakable,
unsayable. A man may write of it, and that is not nothing, but
he cannot *speak* of it, any more than you can speak those brackets.
If you know that there are brackets there, you can strain to hear
them; and the eye may be deeply moved by the way in which
the brackets lower the words within them down into silent
depths. But they intimate an irreducible recalcitrance, of the
kind which any true poem on such atrocities ought to intimate.
'The tongue's atrocities': but these bracketed words protect
themselves against the tongue and its arts.

I have quoted Silkin on Hill; let me return the compliments
by quoting some earlier criticism, Hill on Silkin, a passage
which evokes something of the sense which a profound parenthesis may make within a poem:

He is able to make his words hover and brood, often by re-iteration
within and across the short line. The total effect is a curious amalgam

of the forthright and the tentative. It is like a man facing his accusers; or like a man giving lessons in elementary logic; or like a man repeating to himself instructions for personal survival. The diffidence makes Silkin a 'man of his age', though his self-questioning is quite without the 'pawkiness' that can be so irritating in, say Philip Larkin or John Wain.[19]

Hill's parenthesis—bracketed parenthesis—in 'September Song' incorporates a true diffidence, an amalgam of the confessedly central with the proportionedly peripheral, 'a curious amalgam of the forthright and the tentative'. For the poet who used those words also said this:

> Language *contains* everything you want—history, sociology, economics: it is a kind of drama of human destiny. One thinks how it has been used and exploited in the past, politically and theologically. Its forthrightness and treachery are a drama of the honesty of man himself. Language reveals life.[20]

The forthright and the treacherous; the forthright and the tentative: these struggle in an art that tries to '*contain* everything'. '(Studied reflex, contained breath)'.

Yet this poet who knows about treachery, who knows that his line 'Our God scatters corruption' means both 'Our God puts corruption to flight' and 'Our God disseminates corruption',[21] is someone who knows that any device of language is an axis, not a direction. The very thing which may do such-and-such may do its opposite. So it must be added that, though it is true that the unsayableness of a typographical sign like a bracket may truly embody a recognition of the morally, spiritually and politically unspeakable, it is no less true that this very unspeakableness may choose exactly the same form: a voiceless and dehumanized 'language', denying the warm humanity of the voice and steeling its cold eye. What Kenner calls 'the expressive possibilities of technological space' have their appalling possibilities, in the technology for instance of extermination. So it is important that Hill's 'September Song' should incorporate both edges of this two-edged recognition, as it does in

---

[19] 'The Poetry of Jon Silkin', *Poetry and Audience*, 9:12 (1962), 7.

[20] Hill, as reported in *The Illustrated London News*, 20 August 1966.

[21] In *The Penguin Book of Contemporary Verse*, p. 392.

the italicised sub-heading (dedication? epigraph? subtitle?):

born 19.6.32—deported 24.9.42

For it is not only that though you may be able to say some italics (simply emphatic ones), you cannot say these; it is also that you can scarcely, without a terrible dehumanized bureaucratic numerateness, say '19.6.32' or '24.9.42'. A brutal official haste and economy lop off the centuries. The month in '24.9.42' can scarcely be felt to be the same month as September. 9 is unsayable (you may be saying *nine*); it is international, but with internationalism's anonymity and inhumanity; it is hatefully congruent with the calm hideous substitution of 'deported' for 'died' in the flat item. But then 'deported' amounted to 'died', and we are contemplating a repulsive travesty of the inscription on a memorial-stone. The effect is the counterpart, in its summoning up of professionalized dishonour, to Philip Larkin's title 'MCMXIV'. I cannot say MCMXIV; yet I cannot think it right of the B.B.C., in a reading of Larkin's poems, to say the title as '1914'. For what Larkin intimated, through those unsayable ancient numerals, was at once a continuity with age-old wars and a unique disjunction—both such as make 1914 the meeting of two eras. Larkin uses roman numerals for a departed honour; Hill uses modern numerals for a new dishonour. Moreover he made here a minute change to the punctuation after first publication;[22] instead of a bureaucrat's semi-colon, a stonemason's dash. The eye takes it in; in despairing of adequately, sufficiently, uttering it, the imagination creates something out of its own despair.

(I have made
an elegy for myself it
is true)

For within the brackets there lurks another decent equivocation, another curious amalgam of the centrally forthright and the tangentially personal. I should like to come at it by way of one of the most moving entries in Dr Johnson's annals and prayers:

Oct. 18. 1767 Sunday. Yesterday, Oct. 17 at about ten in the morning

---

[22] *Stand*, 8:4 (1967); then *King Log*.

I took my leave for ever of my dear old Friend Catherine Chambers, who came to live with my Mother about 1724, and has been but little parted from us since. She buried my Father, my Brother, and my Mother. She is now fifty eight years old.

I desired all to withdraw, then told her that we were to part for ever, that as Christians we should part with prayer, and that I would, if she was willing, say a short prayer beside her. She expressed great desire to hear me, and held up her poor hands, as she lay in bed, with great fervour, while I prayed, kneeling by her, nearly in the following words.

Almighty and most merciful Father, whose loving kindness is over all thy works, behold, visit, and relieve this thy Servant who is grieved with sickness. Grant that the sense of her weakness may add strength to her faith, and seriousness to her Repentance. And grant that by the help of thy Holy Spirit after the pains and labours of this short life, we may all obtain everlasting happiness through Jesus Christ, our Lord, for whose sake hear our Prayers. Amen.

Our Father.

I then kissed her. She told me that to part was the greatest pain that she had ever felt, and that she hoped we should meet again in a better place. I expressed with swelled eyes and great emotion of tenderness the same hopes. We kissed and parted, I humbly hope, to meet again, and to part no more.

Nowhere do these moving words mention something which is at once properly central to Johnson's feelings and yet at the same time tangential to any such feelings: the fact that Johnson, like his dying Kitty Chambers, 'is now fifty eight years old'. 'After the pains and labours of this short life . . .': all human life is short, but it may feel the more short when you kneel beside someone of your own age who is dying. As Johnson composed his words and as he set them down (just a month after his 58th birthday), he must have thought of something which he did not mention, and his thoughts swell tacitly within his affecting prayer. And Geoffrey Hill, who was born in 1932, must he not have thought of something which he did not mention, when he wrote the simple evil headstone *born 19.6.32—deported 29.9.42*? Something at once central to his feelings and yet adventitious, tangential?

> (I have made
> an elegy for myself it
> is true)

It is the brackets, with the heart in hiding, which here 'come as near as may be to the impossible ideal of a silent eloquence',[23] and which make possible a mingling of the candid and the covert which is 'the true voice of feeling' partly because it acknowledges that some true feelings cannot exactly be voiced. Hill has noted, with good-natured scorn, that 'Henry Adams, it is true, remarked that "Beyond a doubt, silence is best"'.[24] But, for Hill, there are few truths which are beyond a doubt, and even the word *beyond* has its equivocation:

> so we bear witness,
> Despite ourselves, to what is beyond us,
> ('Funeral Music: 8')

Beyond us? Serenely out of our sphere, or exasperatingly out of our comprehension?—it's beyond me. But brackets may hint at something which is beyond us, but not beyond us; they can be at once tentative and forthright, a moment of silent eloquence and of 'contained breath'.

> But we are commanded
> To rise, when, in silence
> I would compose my voice.
> ('Men are a Mockery of Angels')

George Steiner must be speaking a truth when he says that 'the ineffable lies beyond the frontiers of the word',[25] but it may still be decent for a poet to seek the impossible ideal of a worded ineffability. What is 'beyond the frontiers' may be glimpsed in that special beyond/within which is parenthesis, a voice subdued to a kind of silence. T. S. Eliot allows us to hear this, when he encloses his paradox of silence and speech within the murmuring shell of brackets:

> At nightfall, in the rigging and the aerial,
> Is a voice descanting (though not to the ear,
> The murmuring shell of time, and not in any language)
> 'Fare forward, you who think that you are voyaging;'
> (*The Dry Salvages*)

Hill, in his early poems, often drew upon this sense of the privi-

[23] Donald Davie, *Articulate Energy* (1955), p. 25: 'As Miss Rosemond Tuve has said so well'.
[24] (1972-3); *The Lords of Limit*, p. 84.   [25] *Language and Silence*, p. 30.

leged paradoxicality of brackets, in their relation to silence. It could be an open juxtaposition, as in his beautiful early poem, published but uncollected, 'Summer Night':[26]

> The air yields to the nudging owl
> Stressing the dark with its long call
> Over the coppice and the pool:
> Silence has stirred inside this shell.
>
> The dark creaks like an empty house:
> (There is nothing, over the white fields, amiss)
> Though like the air the untroubled water flows,
> Time stands upon its toes.
>
> Overhead move the tense stars
> Stripping off such disguise
> As 'this will be' and 'this was.'
> There is not another moment to lose.

Silence, the shell, and the eerie security of the parenthesis: it may owe something to Eliot, but it earns enough to repay the debt. The end of another early uncollected poem, 'An Ark on the Flood',[27] owes too much to Melville, but even here there is life stirring within the collocation of 'ears . . . sound . . . mouths . . . silent' and the elegiac brackets:

> But Ishmael's ears are crippled to that sound,
> (O starry mouths amid the oozes drowned)
> The harp hangs silent from the windless tree.

Sometimes, even in tragic poems by Hill, the impulse seems to me to harden into mere mannerism, and there floats up the Rev. Dr. Edmund Law:

According to Paley, the Bishop was once impatient at the slowness of his Carlisle printer. ' "Why does not my book make its appearance?" said he to the printer. "My Lord, I am extremely sorry; but we have been obliged to send to Glasgow for a pound of parentheses" '.[28]

I feel a disproportionate mannerism, for instance, throughout 'A Prayer to the Sun', particularly at the moment when the parenthesis

[26] *The Isis*, 19 November 1952.
[27] *The Isis*, 10 March 1954; reprinted in *Oxford Poetry 1954*.
[28] Boswell's *Life of Johnson*, ed. G. B. Hill and L. F. Powell (1934-50), iii 402 n.l.

                              (Hell is
                              silent)

offers something which sounds flatly inured and impervious.
There is more of a living cadence in the relation of the succeeding brackets (about 'mystery') to the way in which men 'Still
leave much carefully unsaid', in the early uncollected poem
'For Isaac Rosenberg'.[29] Or in the later poem about another
poet, 'Old Poet with Distant Admirers', with its final laconic
deepening, from 'silence' to 'mouth' to 'death-songs' and then
to the muted and altogether final parenthesis, at once tremu-
lous and offhand:

                              If
          I knew the exact coin for tribute,
          Defeat might be bought, processional

          Silence gesture its tokens of earth
          At my mouth: as in the great death-songs
          Of Propertius (although he died young).

Or there are the only brackets in the whole of the sequence
Mercian Hymns, sealing the lips at the end of XXIV:

     Itinerant through numerous domains, of his lord's
        retinue, to Compostela. Then home for a lifetime
        amid West Mercia this master-mason as I envisage
        him, intent to pester upon tympanum and chancel-
        arch his moody testament, confusing warrior with
        lion, dragon-coils, tendrils of the stony vine.

     Where best to stand? Easter sunrays catch the ob-
        lique face of Adam scrumping through leaves; pale
        spree of evangelists and, there, a cross Christ
        mumming child Adam out of Hell

     ('Et exspecto resurrectionem mortuorum' dust in the
        eyes, on clawing wings, and lips)

The lips are sealed by the dust and by the brackets, somewhat as
all sounds are muffled in the silent art-work which is masonry.[30]
The shaping spirit of one imagination cannot be translated into

---

[29] *The Isis*, 20 February 1952; reprinted in *The Fantasy Poets, Number Eleven: Geoffrey Hill* (1952).

[30] Seamus Heaney has a fine account of this poem, in 'Englands of the Mind', *Preoccupations* (1980), pp. 159-61.

the dimensions of another, any more than Latin can breathe within exactly the same world as what precedes it. Yet how creatively Hill translates into his religious art-world—'(. . . dust in the eyes, on clawing wings, and lips)'—the very different impulse of Eliot's evocation of a pagan art-world: '(Another hid his eyes behind his wing)'.

The maturing of Hill's achievement in an art of the parenthesis—a maturing technical and human, for as Eliot knew, we cannot say at what point technique begins or where it ends—comes with Hill's remarkable rotations of what Eliot had sensed as the life lived within the contained breath and silent eloquence of brackets. Perhaps the crucial moment was the grim turning of the tables upon Eliot, in the opening of Hill's 'Solomon's Mines':

> Anything to have done!
> (The eagle flagged to the sun)

—an allusion, presumably, to the wings which folded themselves around Eliot's notorious parenthesis in *Ash-Wednesday*:

> (Why should the agèd eagle stretch its wings?)

—itself a strange sibling to that parenthesis of elegant pagan prurience in *The Waste Land*:

> The Chair she sat in, like a burnished throne,
> Glowed on the marble, where the glass
> Held up by standards wrought with fruited vines
> From which a golden Cupidon peeped out
> (Another hid his eyes behind his wing)
> Doubled the flames of sevenbranched candelabra . . .

Certainly by the time of his poem 'Doctor Faustus', Hill had learnt, probably from Eliot, the various effects which a poet can gain from rhyming a word with its bracketed self, so that the rhyme is not truly a *rhyme*, and yet is gruesomely perfect, and yet is on a different plane or in a different dimension. In the first poem of 'Doctor Faustus', 'The Emperor's Clothes', there is no nakedness, and no candid child's voice to be heard:

> There is no-one
> Afraid or overheard, no loud
> Voice (though innocently loud).

How oddly that second *loud* ends the poem, played against the brackets' pressure towards a feeling for the *sotto voce*. The insidious impalpability recalls one of Eliot's greatest triumphs, the astonishing play of the cadences and the sense against the punctuation's demands, in *The Waste Land*:

> Only
> There is shadow under this red rock,
> (Come in under the shadow of this red rock),
> And I will show you something different from either
> Your shadow at morning striding behind you
> Or your shadow at evening rising to meet you;
> I will show you fear in a handful of dust.

The ear registers no disturbance, but the eye should be disturbed by its being so 'different' from the ear. For if there is one thing which would be thought to be stable, it is that if bracketed words are removed, there will be no stumble but an unbroken syntactical stride. Puttenham said of the parenthesis: 'when ye will seeme, for larger information or some other purpose, to peece or graffe in the middest of your tale an unnecessary parcel of speach, which neverthelesse may be thence without any detriment to the rest'.[31] Johnson defined a parenthesis as 'A sentence so included in another sentence, as that it may be taken out without injuring the sense of that which encloses it: commonly marked thus ( )'. So that when you exclude such 'intercluding' ('Parenthesis, an intercluding . . .'), your stride can pick up where it left off. Yet what happens if we exclude Eliot's intercluded parenthesis?

> Only
> There is shadow under this red rock,
> And I will show you something different . . .

The sense is so precarious as to sound deranged; so a reader is pressed to let the words '(Come in under the shadow of this red rock)' come in, or come out from the shadow of their brackets, in order that there may then be the sane sequence: 'Come in under the shadow . . . And I will show you'. It is a revolutionary moment in English poetry, in the mildness of its violence. Such a parenthesis deepens the meaning of Puttenham's defini-

---

[31] *The Arte of English Poesie* (1589), III xiii.

tion of a parenthesis as 'your first figure of tollerable disorder'. Eliot had not arrived at this eerie profundity in his original version of these lines, in 'The Death of St. Narcissus', where the sequence 'Come . . . And I will show you . . .' was not imperilled by any brackets.

I spoke of the broken syntactical stride not only because Eliot here speaks of 'striding', but also because there is a relation between these junctions and disjunctions and certain rhythmical triumphs which have fascinated Hill. Of the movement within Wordsworth's 'Ode: Intimations of Immortality', a movement from the 'weighed acknowledgment of custom's pressure':

> Heavy as frost, and deep almost as life!

to the 'fresh time-signature' of

> O joy! that in our embers
> Is something that doth live . . .

Hill has said:

Crudely stated, the difference is between being 'in' stride and 'out of' stride. The 'magical change' [quoting Hopkins] in the 'Immortality' Ode is perhaps the greatest moment in nineteenth-century English poetry; but in choosing this term one is suggesting restriction as well as potency. The recognition and the strategy to match the recognition—the cessation of 'stride', the moment of disjuncture, the picking up of fresh 'stride'—were of their very nature inimitable; they were of, and for, that moment.[32]

It is a creative disjuncture which Hill—like Eliot—effects, among other ways, through the imaginative use of mere brackets, such as give a different signature which is not exactly a matter of rhythm, or of timing, or of syntax, but a ghostlier demarcation.

In the essay from which I have quoted, 'Redeeming the Time', Hill considers the ways in which a particular passage by George Eliot suffers from having 'excluded the antiphonal voice of the heckler'; Hill imagines the heckler's interjections, and naturally intercludes them in brackets; and he is moved to quote what is for him (he alludes to it elsewhere) a crucial text

[32] (1972-3); *The Lords of Limit*, p. 97.

from one of Coleridge's letters:

Of parentheses I may be too fond, and will be on my guard in this respect. But I am certain that no work of impassioned and eloquent reasoning ever did or could subsist without them. They are the *drama* of reason, and present the thought growing, instead of a mere *Hortus siccus.* (28 January 1810, to Thomas Poole).

Hill remarks: 'He surely foresaw the obligation to enact the drama of reason within the texture of one's own work, since nothing else would serve. His parentheses are antiphons of vital challenge'. Now it is evident that for Coleridge a parenthesis need not be something in brackets, and Hill is aware of the range and variety of the parenthetical. Yet one of the most obvious, and subtlest, forms of the parenthesis is simple brackets, and Hill is, as it happens, an especially keen observer of what other writers have done with brackets.

The bizarre scene in Jonson's *Catiline* is an awkward case for me, since it is not clear to me how an actress utters *brackets* exactly, but still the instance is potent enough, and Hill dourly delights in it:

> *Sempronia.* I ha'beene writing all this night (and am
> So very weary) unto all the *tribes,*
> And *centuries,* for their voyces, to helpe Catiline
> In his election. We shall make him *Consul,*
> I hope, amongst us . . . *Fulvia.* Who stands beside?
> (Give me some wine, and poulder for my teeth.
>
> *Sempronia.* Here's a good pearle in troth! *Fulvia.* A pretty one.
>
> *Sempronia.* A very orient one!) There are competitors . . .
>
> (II i)

On which Hill comments: 'The derangement is here stressed by the abrupt parenthesis of womanish trivia, chatter about pearls and dentrifice'.[33]

It is not only the 'parenthesis' there, but the word 'abrupt' which points towards one of Hill's convictions. For him, Hopkins is preeminently the poet of—in Hopkins's phrase—'abrupt self', where *abrupt* is used 'both for a very technical thing and for a very spiritual or psychological thing';[34] and the abrupt-

---

[33] *The Lords of Limit,* p. 43.
[34] Hill, interviewed by Hallam Tennyson (1977), for a B.B.C. programme on Hopkins.

ness manifests itself in movements of disjunction and junction such as brackets may encompass, as when Hopkins's power is for Hill eloquently realized in the final line of 'Carrion Comfort': '(my God!) my God'.[35]

Or there is this praise of Keith Douglas, and in particular of the poem 'Adams':

In it, Douglas swings abruptly from a description of the bird to the evocation of a (supposed) acquaintance, a dominating personality:

> Adams is like a bird;
> alert (high on his pinnacle of air
> he does not hear you, someone said).

Hill's bracketed '(supposed)' may remind us of the title of one of his best religious poems, 'To the (Supposed) Patron', wittily turning upon the God of love what the devout love-versifying seventeenth-century cleric was obliged to say of his loved one: 'To his (supposed) Mistresse'. What Hill responds to in Douglas's poem is partly the imaginative parenthesis, with its detached or pinnacled alertness and its strange relation to hearing and saying. Indeed, much of this essay by Hill on Douglas[36] is bent upon the taxing achievement of a decent detachment, a freedom from unjust appropriation of suffering and horror and war. Hill quotes from Douglas such things as 'We stood here on the safe side of it', and 'I in another place'; and this might call up the relation between the word 'safe' and the ensuing parenthesis in the second of Hill's 'Two Formal Elegies', or a sentence like this from his criticism: 'The prime significance of Swift's "sin of wit" is that it challenges and reverses in terms of metaphor the world's routine of power and, within safe parentheses, considers all alternatives including anarchy'.[37] Hill admires Douglas precisely for his sense that sometimes 'We stood here on the safe side of it'; 'You reach a new world'; 'I in another place'; 'the same hours':

Each of these phrases, far from asserting a 'unifying generalization' [quoting Ted Hughes] about experience, conveys a sense of alienation, exclusion, of a world with its own tragi-comic laws. . . . And much of the acuteness of the perception is in the recognition that not

[35] *The Lords of Limit*, p. 102.
[36] *Stand*, 6:4 (1963), 9, 11.
[37] (1968); *The Lords of Limit*, p. 75.

everyone has to go through with this; that two absolutely different worlds co-exist at about a day's journey from each other.

Yet a simple bracket may establish a co-existing zone which is only a contained breath away and yet which breathes the pure serene of another planet. '(There is nothing, over the white fields, amiss)'.

It is the hush of brackets which answers to Hill's deepest sense of things, or rather it is the antagonism between two different kinds of hush: the hush of contained breath, and the hush of contained anger or violence. The subject is that of one of the jealous coplas in Hill's 'Songbook of Sebastian Arrurruz':

> It is to him I write, it is to her
> I speak in contained silence. Will they be touched
> By the unfamiliar passion between them?

That contained silence (which is both peace and war) may gravitate towards brackets: the contrariety is not unlike that which Eliot established with his four parentheses in 'The Love Song of J. Alfred Prufrock': the exasperated timorousness of

> (They will say: 'How his hair is growing thin!')

and of the quick succession:

> (They will say: 'But how his arms and legs are thin!')

heard against the awed erotic hush of imagining another's body:

> Arms that are braceleted and white and bare
> (But in the lamplight, downed with light brown hair!)

—and then, within twenty lines, the fourth and last parenthesis, cut down to a feebly factual baldness and to only a third of a line instead of the full parenthetical sigh:

> Though I have seen my head (grown slightly bald)
>   brought in upon a platter

Hill needs a comparable contrariety of impulses within the play of parentheses. The bitterly sardonic parenthesis can too easily become a métier for him.

> Some keep to the arrangement of love
> (Or similar trust)
>   ('The Distant Fury of Battle')

The pun there on 'trust' is certainly true to the metaphorical ensconcement within the brackets: the security of loving trust, and the very different security of (as the lines unfold) a financial trust. But the effect is of a sudden gust of feeling; there is more to the related pun on 'trust' in 'Requiem for the Plantagenet Kings': 'At home, under caved chantries, set in trust . . .' 'Set in trust': Hill had originally published this as 'locked in trust';[38] either way, it is germane to his decision elsewhere to set, or lock, 'trust' within brackets. The comparison, when it comes to these sardonic turns, might be with the moment in Swift's 'Verses on the Death of Dr. Swift' which Hill praised:

> My female Friends, whose tender Hearts
> Have better learn'd to act their Parts
> Receive the News in *doleful Dumps*,
> 'The Dean is dead (*and what is Trumps?*)'

'The rhyming wit', Hill remarks, 'itself works like a "trump" or triumph to snatch brilliant personal success from a position of elected disadvantage'.[39] But it is not only a rhyme, it is a rhyme within and without a bracket; the triumph is the fiercely witty sense that the brackets might better enclose what is really the parenthetical item, 'The Dean is dead'. As it stands, the aside—'(and what is Trumps?)'—is really the heart of the (heartless) matter, a point which flickers in Swift's having 'Trumps' as a bracketed rhyme-word and having the punning 'Hearts' ('whose tender Hearts') rhymingly out there in the open. What we see is the strange play of an utterly authentic voicing against a notation which defies exact vocalization.

Hill is aware that brackets, which can resist prurience (by detachment and a *cordon sanitaire*) can as easily encourage it (by snug smug private-booth gratifications of the secreted imagination). He has deplored 'the mild and modish pornography of Prior':

> At last, I wish, said She, my Dear—
> (And whisper'd something in his Ear.)
> ('Paulo Purganti')

'Whisper'd something' is truly symptomatic of the mode and perhaps helps to explain by contrast the nature of Swift's verse, which cuts

[38] *Paris Review*, No. 21 (Spring-Summer 1959); then *For the Unfallen* (1959).
[39] *The Lords of Limit*, p. 71.

through that barrier of shame and coquetry where it is only too easy
to excite a snigger with gestures of mock reticence.[40]

Yet there is a clear axis which connects Prior's bracketed igno-
bility of whispering-in-ears with Eliot's (and Hill's) bracketed
nobility of such things,

> a voice descanting (though not to the ear,
> The murmuring shell of time, and not in any language)

Hill often uses brackets to indict prurience, usually of a
crueller sort than Prior's. It is there in the juxtaposition of one
kind of imagination—sadistic relish—with an imagined bracketed silence:

> we are dying
> To satisfy fat Caritas, those
> Wiped jaws of stone. (Suppose all reconciled
> By silent music; imagine the future
> Flashed back at us, like steel against sun,
> Ultimate recompense.)
>   ('Funeral Music:2')

(The right place for 'silent music' is there, within brackets.)
The evocation of a prurience of violence is there too—again
with a kind of rhyming at once totally overt (the same word
repeated) and covert (one occurrence is within brackets)—when
Hill contrasts the gross realities and the delicate prurient art:

> Now at a distance from the steam of beasts,
> The loathly neckings and fat shook spawn
> (Each specimen-jar fed with delicate spawn)
> The searchers with the curers sit at meat
> And are satisfied.
>   ('Annunciations:I')

It is the brackets which enforce the sense of being—this time
corruptly—'at a distance', and which then themselves function
as that 'specimen-jar' which they enclose. This same vigilance
about prurience takes a very different tone when it imagines
the heat—this time not steaming—which is immediately shaded
by brackets, in one of Hill's prose-poems, 'A Letter from Ar-

menia', a poem likewise about heat, delicacy, pillage, disasters, and glazings:

> So, remotely, in your part of the world:
> the ripe glandular blooms, and cypresses
> shivering with heat (which we have borne
> also, in our proper ways) I turn my mind
> towards delicate pillage, the provenance
> of shards glazed and unglazed, the three
> kinds of surviving grain. I hesitate amid
> circumstantial disasters. I gaze at the
> authentic dead.

The tone of those lines could scarcely be more remote from, and yet the technical and emotional grounding has much in common with, Milton's great shading parenthesis in *Paradise Regained*, Satan's plea that Christ's reign

> Would stand between me and thy Fathers ire
> (Whose ire I dread more than the fire of Hell)
> A shelter and a kind of shading cool
> Interposition, as a summers cloud.
>   (iii 219-22)

The fire and the shade, and the forthright and the tentative, and the forthright and the treacherous, are alive in the interposition of the brackets.

Clearly there is an art, an allegiance, a strong choice of life, which will distrust any amalgam of the forthright and the tentative, or of the forthright and the treacherous. 'He disapproved of parentheses', says Boswell about Johnson, 'and I believe in all his voluminous writings, not half a dozen of them will be found' (iv 190). But there is need for the art of dubiety as well as the art of indubitability. Hill has observed how Hopkins, 'against this specious flowing away . . . poised a faith and a technique',[41] and he has written eloquently about the meeting of a faith and a technique in Wordsworth:

When Wordsworth says, of the female vagrant, that:

> She ceased, and weeping turned away,
> As if because her tale was at an end
> She wept;—because she had no more to say
> Of that perpetual weight which on her spirit lay

---

[41] Hill, interviewed by Hallam Tennyson.

he is indeed implying that words are 'in some degree mechanical' compared to the woman's action and suffering. But in order to bring out the difference Wordsworth puts in a collateral weight of technical concentration that releases the sense of separateness: the drag of the long phrasing across the formalities of the verse, as if the pain would drag itself free from the constraint. In 'as if' and 'because', pedantically isolating her, we glimpse the remoteness of words from suffering and yet are made to recognize that these words are totally committed to her existence. They are her existence. Language here is not 'the outward sign' of a moral action; it is the moral action.[42]

The sense of separateness, of isolation, of remoteness: these evoke a gulf between words and feelings as well as between the sufferer's feelings and the poet's. The scruple, the honesty, is in the compassionate separateness; and it is a compassionate (often fiercely so) separateness that Hill's simple subtle brackets can encompass. He is aware that just as there is a torrid art of prurience, so there is a frigid art of decorum, the wrong remoteness:

A PASTORAL

Mobile, immaculate and austere,
The Pities, their fingers in every wound,
Assess the injured on the obscured frontier;
Cleanse with a kind of artistry the ground
Shared by War. Consultants in new tongues
Prove synonymous our separated wrongs.

We celebrate, fluently and at ease.
Traditional Furies, having thrust, hovered,
Now decently enough sustain Peace.
The unedifying nude dead are soon covered.
Survivors, still given to wandering, find
Their old loves, painted and re-aligned—

Queer, familiar, fostered by superb graft
On treasured foundations, these ideal features!
Men can move with purpose again, or drift,
According to direction. Here are statues
Darkened by laurel; and evergreen names;
Evidently-veiled griefs; impervious tombs.

Hill seeks something which both is and is not 'evidently-veiled', something truly and not falsely 'impervious'. It may be medi-

[42] (1975); *The Lords of Limit*, pp. 116-7.

ated through a resurrected cliché, as in the superimposition there of officious inquisitive solicitude upon Doubting Thomas: 'The Pities, their fingers in every wound'. Or it may be an art of the parenthesis. The composer of the words 'The tongue's atrocities' is the poet who writes, in 'The Lowlands of Holland', of Europe as

> Shrunken, magnified—(nest, holocaust)—

The double punctuation, dashes and brackets, as in '—(studied reflex, contained breath)—', points up the particular metaphoricality of the brackets, and what they enclose is then itself not just two but double. For 'nest' is both a natural security and a collusive treachery (a nest of vipers, thieves, or robbers); and 'holocaust' is both a reverential act and an evil totality of massacre. How unsettlingly the two words settle side by side, ensconced within the nest of their brackets: '—(nest, holocaust)—'. Yet even here Hill's art respects and fears much from the past. The Jewish God, the Christian poet, and the pagan legend met long ago in an earlier collocation of nest and holocaust, in *Samson Agonistes*:

> Like that self-begott'n bird
> In the *Arabian* woods embost,
> That no second knows nor third,
> And lay e're while a Holocaust . . .

An art of the holocaust must also be an art of the phoenix. The first poem, 'Genesis' (1952), in Hill's first book of poems, *For the Unfallen* (1959), speaks of:

> A brooding immortality—
> Such as the charmed phoenix has
> In the unwithering tree.

Hill is a religious man without, it must seem, a religion; a profoundly honest doubter. 'The Pities, their fingers in every wound'; 'But I want the poem to have this dubious end; because I feel dubious; and the whole business is dubious'. So if we might suppose a patron for Hill, it might be Thomas.

CANTICLE FOR GOOD FRIDAY

> The cross staggered him. At the cliff-top
> Thomas, beneath its burden, stood

While the dulled wood
Spat on the stones each drop
Of deliberate blood.

A clamping, cold-figured day
Thomas (not transfigured) stamped, crouched,
Watched
Smelt vinegar and blood. He,
As yet unsearched, unscratched,

And suffered to remain
At such near distance
(A slight miracle might cleanse
His brain
Of all attachments, claw-roots of sense)

In unaccountable darkness moved away,
The strange flesh untouched, carrion-sustenance
Of staunchest love, choicest defiance,
Creation's issue congealing (and one woman's).

A reader senses how bitterly 'cold-figured' is transfigured into
the parenthetical '(not transfigured)'; and then how cleansingly
the 'slight miracle' of brackets proffers, 'at such near distance',
something which is at once 'attachments' and detachment; and
then, finally, how simply and unutterably, with what gravity
and awe the silent music sinks to the human mystery, the incarnation and the unparalleled muted glory of Mary:

Creation's issue congealing (and one woman's).

The words are at once belated and perfectly timed; they are
supremely weighed, with *issue* against the entrance into those
brackets, brackets which may remind us not only of Hill's
words 'In unaccountable darkness', but also of John Donne's
words about Mary:

Thou 'hast light in darke; and shutst in little roome,
Immensity cloystered in thy deare wombe.
                    ('La Corona:2. Annunciation')

All creation against—and yet not *against*—one woman. Those
last three words incarnate a profound paradox, a crux and an
aside, an admonition and a reassurance, such as allow Geoffrey
Hill to share the studied reflex and the contained breath of
George Herbert.

GEOFFREY HILL 2:
AT-ONE-MENT

The poems of *Tenebrae* (1978), like Geoffrey Hill's version of *Brand* (1978), put up a profound resistance to a central tenet of Hill's inaugural lecture, 'Poetry as "Menace" and "Atonement"' (also 1978).[1] The poems resist the tenet, partly because it is the way of poems to resist even the best of tenets, and partly because this particular tenet does not hold firm. 'Ideally', said Hill, 'my theme would be simple'; but then he allowed the reservations intimated by the conditional 'would' and the unconditioned 'Ideally' to sidle away:

> simply this: that the technical perfecting of a poem is an act of atonement, in the radical etymological sense—an act of at-one-ment, a setting at one, a bringing into concord, a reconciling, a uniting in harmony; and that this act of atonement is described with beautiful finality by two modern poets: by W. B. Yeats when he writes in a letter of September 1936, to Dorothy Wellesley, that 'a poem comes right with a click like a closing box' and by T. S. Eliot in his essay of 1953, 'The Three Voices of Poetry':
>
> > when the words are finally arranged in the right way—or in what he comes to accept as the best arrangement he can find—[the poet] may experience a moment of exhaustion, of appeasement, of absolution, and of something very near annihilation, which is in itself indescribable.
>
> Anyone who has experienced that moment in which a poem 'comes right' must, I believe, give instinctive assent to such statements.[2]

One does not blithely accuse Geoffrey Hill of being blithe, but there is a hopefulness here in the criticism, an unremarked irreconcilability, such as the poetry of Hill would have had to extend to and attend to. For a start, the words of Eliot are not at one with those of Yeats. It is impossible to imagine a testimony which would less fit something's coming right with a click like a closing box than the pained protracted refusal to click of

---

[1] Published *University of Leeds Review*, xxi (1978), but delivered 5 December 1977. Reprinted in *The Lords of Limit* (1984).

[2] p. 2.

Eliot's prose, its arriving finally at the word 'indescribable'. So that when Hill concludes that anyone who has experienced that moment must give instinctive assent to such statements, the difficulty is not, as he goes on to posit, the word 'instinctive' but the plural 'statements'. Those of us who are not poets and have not experienced such a moment might be able to imagine a poet's instinctive assent to one or other of the statements, but not to both. Hill's search for at-one-ment has led him to two descriptions of 'this act of atonement', each of which has indeed a 'beautiful finality' in its evocation of atonement as a finality, but the two of which are finally irreconcilable, tonally and totally. There cannot be a reconciling, a uniting in harmony, of Yeats's and Eliot's acts of witness here, any more than there can be of their intransigently inimical poetry. Hill, who has chosen to write criticism in passionate praise of Yeats, has chosen not to write any criticism at all of the poet even more important to his own poetry: Eliot.

One reason for not choosing Yeats's sense of the matter might be that his apophthegm relies upon something prejudicially contrastive which Hill prudently omits: 'The correction of prose, because it has no fixed laws, is endless, a poem comes right with a click like a closing box'. The poet's pains on which Hill broods would be sweetly mitigated if it were the case that poetry had anything as gratifying as 'fixed laws'. But the point is not that Eliot's sense of the creative achievement as something at once ended and endless is the one that must be assented to; rather that Hill does not attempt to set at one these two so different descriptions of the act of atonement.

For Hill's critical argument is unwilling to acknowledge the stubborn resistance put up to its hopes for such atonement and at-one-ment, resistance embodied in the very terms of its hopes. The prose-argument may talk of 'the shocking encounter with "empirical guilt"', not as a manageable hypothesis, but as irredeemable error in the very substance and texture of his [the poet's] craft and pride';[3] indeed, the prose-argument is at its most poignant, unsurprisingly but revelatorily, when it recalls one of the most deeply-felt poems in *Mercian Hymns* ('It is one thing to celebrate the "quick forge", another to cradle a face hare-lipped by the searing wire': XXV).

[3] p. 17.

It is one thing to talk of literature as a medium through which we convey our awareness, or indeed our conviction, of an inveterate human condition of guilt or anxiety; it is another to be possessed by a sense of language itself as a manifestation of empirical guilt.[4]

But the prose-argument does talk of these things, not incarnate an acknowledgement that there is not only irredeemable error but also irrecoverable loss. For the word 'atonement' obdurately will not return to its radical roots, to 'at-one-ment'. At-one-ment is simply, and finally, and unanswerably, not a word in the English language; and it will not do to be told that the technical perfecting of a poem is 'an act of atonement, in the radical etymological sense—an act of at-one-ment, a setting at one, a bringing into concord, a reconciling, a uniting in harmony': it will not do to be told this unless, in the very act of telling, it is conceded that there can be no reconciling, no bringing into harmony, of words like 'a reconciling, a uniting in harmony' and the non-word 'at-one-ment'; indeed, more radically despite the etymology, that there can be no atonement of atonement and at-one-ment. For one thing, even if the latter were alive and well and living in our language, it would now be pronounced differently from atonement. (There is the unreality of giddiness in the very sound of the phrase when Merle Brown intones of Hill: 'Such a moment of atonement'.)[5] There are therefore sound reasons for believing that atonement is doggedly and most ironically irreconcilable with at-one-ment. The loss of the ancient concord may be grievous; it must be irrecoverable. When Eliot wrote in *Little Gidding* that 'Sin is Behovely', the pain was at the admission that though sin is inevitable, an acknowledgement of sin has become as archaic as the arcane and capitalized word Behovely.

The pain from which Hill's prose-argument averts its mortal gaze is the one which the poetry of *Tenebrae* and of *Brand*, in its averted conscience, turns against itself.

> Crucified Lord, you swim upon your cross
> and never move. Sometimes in dreams of hell
> the body moves but moves to no avail
> and is at one with that eternal loss.

[4] pp. 6-7.
[5] *Double Lyric* (1980), p. 71.

> You are the castaway of drowned remorse,
> you are the world's atonement on the hill.
>> ('Lachrimae: 1.Lachrimae Verae')

There 'at one' refuses to plead that it is or could be at one with 'atonement'. There is an unbridgeable distance between 'at one' and 'atonement'. The quatrain space within the sonnet signals the distance, and so does the acknowledged difference of sound. 'Atonement' here, even while it laments 'that eternal loss', is not to be pronounced 'at-one-ment', not least because if it were it would lost any true uttering of atonement.

So near and yet so far:

> And suffered to remain
> At such near distance
>> ('Canticle for Good Friday')

A sense of loss when 'one' is not quite rhymed animates the elegiac apprehension of what it may be to be 'made one', in Hill's early poem 'Merlin' (1953):

> I will consider the outnumbering dead:
> For they are the husks of what was rich seed,
> Now, should they come together to be fed,
> They would outstrip the locusts' covering tide.
>
> Arthur, Elaine, Mordred; they are all gone
> Among the raftered galleries of bone.
> By the long barrows of Logres they are made one,
> And over their city stands the pinnacled corn.

For a particular unfulfilment attaches there to 'made one', since the two stanzas do not matchingly turn their off-rhyming monosyllables. The sequence *gone/bone/one/corn* is changed by the one that had gone before: *dead/seed/fed/tide* was a sequence which had proffered an indisputably full rhyme (*dead . . . fed*) at exactly the point in the stanza where 'gone' and 'made one' do not then offer such indisputable fulfilment.[6]

Hill's *Brand*, since it is a work of great powers, is very much more than a gloss on *Tenebrae*, but its amplitude does permit of its ministering as creative commentary, and *Brand* is fertile in

---

[6] On the record *The Poetry and Voice of Geoffrey Hill*, Hill does not read 'gone' and 'one' as full rhymes.

its insistence that between 'atone' and 'at one' there is a great
gulf fixed. Here is its first occurrence:

> You flirt and play the fool
> and leave the bitter toil
> to that poor Holy One
> sweating blood to atone,
> your dear Christ hurt with thorns,
> the savior of your dance.
>
> (Act I)[7]

For 'one', even when it is 'One', is no more at one with 'atone'
than 'fool' will agree to 'toil', or than 'thorns' harmonize with
'dance'. *Brand*'s off-rhyming is perfectly aligned for pledging
that the act of uttering 'atone' must decree that there can be no
reconciliation of it and the word 'one'.

Hill the critic, expatiating and conferring, does sometimes
yield to hopes of attaining without miracle the cruelly unattainable; but his art attains, among other things, an exact apprehension of what is for him unattainable. For him, or for *one*?
His sentence is unsettled:

If critics accuse me of evasiveness or the vice of nostalgia, or say that *I*
seem incapable of grasping true religious experience, I would answer
that the grasp of true religious experience is a privilege reserved for
very few, and that one is trying to make lyrical poetry out of a much
more common situation—the sense of *not* being able to grasp true
religious experience.[8]

One aspect of this is Hill's making lyrical poetry, not out of any
perfected at-one-ment of atonement and at-one-ment, but out
of the sense of honourably *not* being able to grasp such a perfect
concord, such a true religious experience. 'One main reason
for this', to apply the praise which William Empson gave to the
range of Eliot's 'Marina', 'is the balance maintained between
otherworldliness and humanism; the essence of the poem is the
vision of an order, a spiritual state, which he can conceive
and cannot enter'.[9] Hill turns this into something fearfully

---

[7] Quotations are from the Second Edition, Revised (1981); p. 14. For other rhymes
on 'atone', see *Brand*, pp. 50-1, 52, 66, 117, 131.

[8] *Viewpoints: Poets in Conversation* with John Haffenden (1981), p. 89.

[9] *Nation and Athenaeum*, 21 February 1931.

consolatory; it may be a mercy that we can only conceive and
not enter a vision that might prove a nightmare:

> Averroes, old heathen,
> If only you had been right, if Intellect
> Itself were absolute law, sufficient grace,
> Our lives could be a myth of captivity
> Which we might enter: an unpeopled region
> Of ever new-fallen snow, a palace blazing
> With perpetual silence as with torches.
>
> ('Funeral Music: 4')

> As with torches we go, at wild Christmas,
> When we revel in our atonement
>
> ('Funeral Music: 5')

For poems are themselves torches, and

> Heaven doth with us, as we, with Torches doe,
> Not light them for themselves: For if our vertues
> Did not goe forth of us, 'twere all alike
> As if we had them not.
>
> (*Measure for Measure*, I.i)

In hopes of perfect concord, Hill says:

The proof of a poet's craft is precisely the ability to effect an at-one-
ment between the 'local vividness' and the 'overall shape', and . . .
this is his truthtelling. When the poem 'comes right with a click like a
closing box', what is there effected is the atonement of aesthetics with
rectitude of judgement.[10]

Yet Hill's needing the two forms of the word is itself an admission (insufficiently an acknowledgement) that this whole business will *not* come right with a click like a closing box; and the
same goes for the use in quick succession of the different prepositions ('an at-one-ment between . . .' and 'an atonement of
aesthetics with'), instead of that perfectly simple conjunction
which would be the conjunction *and*.

To speak of atonement *between* x and y (instead of an atonement of x and y) is to concede that it is not truly an at-one-
ment, since it would have to be an at-one-ment (a setting at
one) of x and y, not between them. This same untrustworthi-
ness within the etymological plea is betrayed by *between* when

---

[10] *The Lords of Limit*, p. 10.

Hill says, of T. H. Green, that 'a Green lecture appears as an act of atonement, in the arena of communication, between the "unconscious social insolence" of the listener and what Coleridge termed the seeming "assumption of superiority" on the part of the speaker'.[11]

Hill, who yearns to trust the etymology of atonement, is not willing to be as imperious as Coleridge:[12]

> What is MUSIC? *Poetry* in its grand sense?
> Answer.
> Passion and order aton'd! Imperative Power in Obedience!

All of Hill's work is concerned, in a concurrence with Coleridge, with reconciliation. *Tenebrae* quotes Coleridge for one of its epigraphs (and as 'STC' moreover) and is close in occupation to 'Poetry as "Menace" and "Atonement" ' where Coleridge explicitly and importantly figures. *Tenebrae* is at the same time the most ambitious of all Hill's aspirations to atonement and at-one-ment. The ambition to imagine, at least, the union of sacred and profane love; the ambition to imagine, at least, the union of English poetry and European poetry, and of all the conflicting traditions and developments within English poetry; of England and its empire ('A Short History of British India'); of Protestant and Catholic: not even all these exhaust the ambitions of the book and of its masterly sequences. There is the longing to unite knowledge and wisdom, or to re-unite them, a longing which is responsible for a reader's thinking that, even more than with others of Hill's books, what would be better than any critical study would be a truly annotated edition. Moreover, in its sequences and within individual poems, *Tenebrae* seeks to incarnate the union of the One and the Many, and it is therefore metaphysical poetry. 'Verse properly called metaphysical is that to which the impulse is given by an overwhelming concern with metaphysical problems; with problems either deriving from, or closely resembling in the nature of their difficulty, the problem of the Many and the One' (James Smith).[13]

Yet it is not only the ear which refuses to trust that there

---

[11] (1975); *The Lords of Limit*, p. 114.

[12] *Notebooks*, entry 3231.

[13] *Scrutiny*, ii (1933), 228.

could be any perfect consonance of atonement and at-one-ment. For the eye sees the hyphens as forever both holding together and holding apart the elements which seek to constitute the non-word as a word. All punctuation is at once a uniting and a separating. Like mortar, it holds bricks together and holds them apart. When Eric Partridge begins his chapter on the hyphen by saying: 'The hyphen (-) has two main and entirely distinct functions: dividing and compounding',[14] he makes practical sense but only that. The hyphen has the capacity which Hill sees as 'an essential quality of Swift's creative intelligence: the capacity to be at once resistant and reciprocal'.[15] 'Their spades grafted through the variably-resistant soil' (*Mercian Hymns*, XII): there the variably-resistant hyphen at once joins and divides, at once grafts and grafts through.

The hyphen cannot but acknowledge, in the moment when it conceives of two things coming together, that they are nevertheless two not one, just as Hill's need not exactly to spell but to articulate the word 'atonement' differently when he means at-one-ment is tacitly an admission that the two, the same and not the same, will always be magnetically held apart and held together by being like-poles. 'Many of the poems in *Tenebrae* are concerned with the strange likeness and ultimate unlikeness of sacred and profane love' (Hill).[16] A hyphen may articulate strange likeness and unlikeness, conjoining for instance the word atonement and at-one-ment, the latter itself a declared conjunction of its elements.

Likeness and unlikeness meet: 'The Jesus-faced man walking crowned with flies' ('Lachrimae: 3.Martyrium'). Jeffrey Wainwright has said, truly but partially, that 'Jesus-faced' is 'uncomfortably and deliberately close to "Janus-faced"';[17] so it is, but such closeness itself then witnesses to immitigable difference, as it does in such a hyphenation as 'O near-human spouse and poet' ('Elegiac Stanzas'). The closer 'Jesus-faced' is to 'Janus-faced' the more indubitably—from one of the two Janus-viewpoints—it announces itself as other than 'Janus-faced'. The hyphened form is itself two-faced, a 'judas-kiss'.

[14] *You Have a Point There* (1953), p. 134.
[15] (1968); *The Lords of Limit*, p. 67.
[16] *The Poetry Book Society Bulletin*, No. 98, Autumn 1978.
[17] *Agenda*, 13:3 (1975), 33.

('Consigned by proxy to the judas-kiss': 'Lachrimae: 6.Lachrimae Antiquae Novae'.) Two-faced, or two-edged: 'What is carried over? The Frankish gift, two-edged, regaled with slaughter' (*Mercian Hymns*, XVI).

So the hyphen is likely to have much to do within a poetry concerned with the strange likeness and unlikeness of sacred and profane love, not least because the hyphen itself may be an acknowledgement of love, the conjunction of two as one, the bringing together of two 'under one' (hyphen: ὑφ' ἕν). The head and the body, for instance, as the children's book *Punctuation Personified* (1824) knew when it exactly located and named the hyphen as the neck. ('Churchwardens in wing-collars bearing scrolls': 'An Apology for the Revival of Christian Architecture in England: 12. The Eve of St Mark'.) Metaphysics, the One and the Many, and love, may marry in such articulation.

> Single Natures double name,
> Neither two nor one was called.
> ('The Phoenix and Turtle')

Neither and both. Or a troth-plight: 'What happens here', said Hill of Spenser's *Amoretti* LXVIII, 'is more solemn than a play of wit; it is a form of troth-plight between denotation and connotation'.[18]

The entry in Johnson's *Dictionary* under 'hyphen' is itself a poem in embryo, aspiring to the best relationships: '*Hyphen*. A note of conjunction: as, *vir-tue, ever-living*'. For the hyphen that divides 'virtue' only brings out that in its integrity, virtue is indivisible: and the hyphen that unites 'ever-living' carries a conviction about the relation of virtue to everlasting life. Virtue then chiefly lives. Coleridge was not truly attentive to either hyphens or virtue when he issued his rule: 'The rule for the admission of double epithets seems to be this: either that they should be already denizens of our Language, such as blood-stained, terror-stricken, self-applauding: or when a new epithet, or one found in books only, is hazarded, that it, at least, be one word, not two words made one by mere virtue of the printer's hyphen'.[19]

In a discussion of Emily Dickinson (a discussion which,

[18] (1983); *The Lords of Limit*, p. 144.
[19] *Biographia Literaria*, ch. i.

incidentally, has an epigraph from Geoffrey Hill), Geoffrey
Hartman makes much of her punctuation, naturally, but he
does take a liberty with it:

> Dickinson's ellipses bear study, though they put an interpreter in
> the uncomfortable position of arguing from silence. This silence
> becomes typographic in one formal device, baffling, but at least
> obtrusive. In many poems an idiosyncratic mark—dash, hyphen, or
> extended point—replaces the period sign and all other punctuation. It
> can appear at any juncture, to connect or disconnect, generally to do
> both at once. It is a caesura or *coupure* more cutting than that of
> Williams. It introduces from the beginning the sense of an ending
> and both extends and suspends it. The semantic value of this hyphen
> is zero, but it allows the asyndetic sentences to become an indefinite
> series of singular and epigrammatic statements. The zero endows
> them with the value of one, with loneliness or one-liness as in an
> amazing poem that begins "The Loneliness One dare not sound"
> (777).
> Why does this formal mark, this hyphen with zero meaning, have
> intraverbal force? Perhaps because it both joins and divides, like a
> hymen.[20] Perhaps because it is like the line between dates on tomb-
> stones. It may be an arbitrary sign or it may be nakedly mimetic. In
> any case, the decorous proposition that nature is style is radicalized:
> this elliptical, clipped mark evokes style as nature. That hyphen-
> hymen persephonates Emily.[21]

These pages say much that is true, especially as to that simultaneous connecting and disconnecting which is the mark of this
punctuation as, in different ways, of all; and they mention
much that happens to be pertinent to Hill (atonement and juncture). But Hartman's attentions to Emily Dickinson rest upon
a sleight, since the Dickinson mark is not a hyphen. Neither of
the poems which Hartman quotes in full contains a hyphen at
all; indeed, Emily Dickinson scarcely ever uses a hyphen.
Hartman is not the first to link hyphen and the hymen, but he
may be the first to croon over the pun (hyphenating it) when
there was no hyphen as warrant. James Joyce played with
'loveliest pansiful thoughts touching me dash in-you through
wee dots Hyphen, the so pretty arched godkin of bedding-

---

[20] Cp. Hill's remark that ' "Is about" is a pathetically frail locution to act as the
ontological membrane between two such "dinglich" clauses'; *The Lords of Limit*,
p. 133.
[21] *Criticism in the Wilderness* (1980), pp. 125-6.

nights',[22] but even in play Joyce knew the difference between a
dash and a hyphen, especially when relating the hyphen to both
hymen and Hymen. So despite the acuteness in Hartman's
speculations, the upshot is fickleness. As it was not when Emily
Dickinson herself used the word 'Hyphen', in a poem of obscure
depth:

> Those not live yet
> Who doubt to live again—
> "Again" is of a twice
> But this—is one—
> The Ship beneath the Draw
> Aground—is he?
> Death—so—the Hyphen of the sea—
> Deep is the Schedule
> Of the Disk to be—
> Costumeless Consciousness—
> That is he—

'Death—so—the Hyphen of the sea—': I take 'of' there to
mean mainly that the sea is a hyphen: the sea at once divides
and links the lands of the globe; if (as for Matthew Arnold) the
sea estranges, it also ties, and it constitutes the great transition,
the greatest passage of rites. Death too is such a hyphen, and
death's linkage is immediate, close-pressed, without as much
space even as is offered by the dashes that link the elements of
that line of Emily Dickinson's: 'Death—so—the Hyphen of the
sea—'.

> What if some litle paine the passage haue,
> That makes fraile flesh to feare the bitter waue?
>   (*The Faerie Queene*, I ix XL)

It is the conjunction of death, the hyphen, and the sea (a conjunction plumbed by Emily Dickinson) which saturates many
of the early hyphenations in Hill's poetry; the sea had soaked
his heart through.

> And found a rough sea-bitten island.
>   ('Saint Cuthbert on Farne Island')[23]

[22] *Finnegans Wake* (1939), p. 446.
[23] *Oxford Poetry 1952.*

O Ishmael, singing at the sea-starred helm,
                              ('An Ark on the Flood')[24]

And now the sea-scoured temptress, having failed
To scoop out of horizons what birds herald:
            ('Metamorphoses: III. The Re-birth of Venus')

Sea-preserved, heaped with sea-spoils,
                              ('Picture of a Nativity')

Through poisonous baked sea-things Perseus
Goes—
            ('Of Commerce and Society: III. The Death of Shelley')

T. S. Eliot's sea-girls and sea-wood are germane, but so, later, is 'The sea howl':

                    The sea howl
      And the sea yelp, are different voices
      Often together heard: the whine in the rigging,
      The menace and caress of wave that breaks on water,
      The distant rote in the granite teeth,
                              (*The Dry Salvages*)[25]

Hill gave this his own voice by the simple double stroke of dropping the definite article and of hyphening:

            Through sea-howl I heard Him call.
                    (*Brand*, Act IV)[26]

Hill gives salience to his hyphens, tactfully but pointedly, by having the unhyphenated word in the vicinity of its hyphened sibling.[27] In Eliot likewise, the unmelodramatic insistence that comes to settle gravely upon the first half of the compound 'half-look' is a consequence of our having first heard the word 'look', so that a discrimination may be made, a fear acknowledged, without mere alarm:

---

[24] *Oxford Poetry 1954*.

[25] Hill may have remembered 'menace and caress' when pondering poetry as 'menace and atonement', and 'The distant rote in the granite teeth' when pondering *The Mystery of the Charity of Charles Péguy*: 'or those who worship at its marble rote' (7).

[26] p. 98.

[27] E.g., in 'Holy Thursday', wolf and she-wolf; in 'Requiem for the Plantagenet Kings', blood and blood-marks; in 'Two Formal Elegies', witnesses and witness-proof; in *Mercian Hymns* II, pet-name and name: in XIII, self-possession and possession; in *Brand* (Act V), war-clouds and clouds.

> The backward look behind the assurance
> Of recorded history, the backward half-look
> Over the shoulder, towards the primitive terror.
> (*The Dry Salvages*)

Hill has learnt from such art.

> High voices in domestic chapels; praise;
> praise-worthy feuds;
> ('An Apology . . . :3. Who are these
> coming to the Sacrifice?')

Here is no feud between 'praise' and 'praise-worthy' (the 'high voices' are raised in praise not in anger), but there is some slight antagonism, some distance and distaste, as there is in the strictly unnecessary hyphen in 'praise-worthy'. Or one compound may lop-sidedly refuse to square itself exactly with another:

> like carapaces of the Mughal tombs
> lop-sided in the rice-fields, boarded-up
> near railway-sidings and small aerodromes.
> ('An Apology . . . :6. A Short History
> of British India, III')

There it is natural but futile to try to align '-sided' and '-sidings'.

The pressure in the vicinity, when the transition is from the compounded to the uncompounded form, may give a particular edge to what might otherwise have been so unremarked as scarcely to impinge; as when Hill banters Yeats.

> where wild-eyed poppies raddle tawny farms
> and wild swans root in lily-clouded lakes.
> ('An Apology . . . :7. Loss and Gain')

Pretty Coole, the wild swans, especially when followed by 'lily-clouded lakes', a phrasing which ribs 'the mackerel-crowded seas' of 'Sailing to Byzantium'. Hill's 'root in' suspects the swans, for all their beauty, of being piggish truffle-hunters; but then Hill himself is rooted in and has been rooting in those lily-clouded lakes of Yeats. Again, there are

> those muddy-hued and midge-tormented ghosts.
> ('An Apology . . . :1. Quaint Mazes')

—a line which has its small sting at Yeats and 'That dolphin-torn, that gong-tormented sea' ('Byzantium').

Tennyson too is among the ghosts, though likewise for an affectionate chaffing vassalage, feudal not feuding:

> High voices in domestic chapels; praise;
> praise-worthy feuds; new-burgeoned spires that sprung
> crisp-leaved as though from dropping-wells. The young
> ferns root among our vitrified tears.
>   ('An Apology . . . :3. Who are these coming to
>   the Sacrifice?')[28]

And if we ask, Who taught those new-burgeoned spires to rise? Alfred Tennyson, each lisping babe replies.

> Bring orchis, bring the foxglove spire,
>   The little speedwell's darling blue,
>   Deep tulips dashed with fiery dew,
> Laburnums, dropping-wells of fire.
>   (*In Memoriam*, LXXXIII)

It is the 'dropping-wells' which compound the 'spires'. Hill's lines are a new-burgeoning compound of Tennyson and himself; Tennyson's art is itself, newly-compounded, a dropping-well of fire. An allusion is a two-in-one, like a hyphenation. It can return to its roots, and Hill signals this, not only by using the word 'root' or 'roots', but by using it in the immediate vicinity of an allusion itself compounded like 'dropping-wells'. On several occasions Hill avails himself of the junction which a hyphen can effect in this very matter of roots:

> But when he tore his flesh-root and was gone,
>   ('Metamorphoses, V')

> (A slight miracle might cleanse
> His brain
> Of all attachments, claw-roots of sense)
>   ('Canticle for Good Friday')

The uncollected early poem 'Pentecost' (*Oxford Poetry 1952*) is a compendium of Hill's preoccupation with the root-secure or -insecure:

> The sudden putting-on of grace
> Though fresh, new-nerved, is all the more

---

[28] When the poem was first published, 'new-burgeoned' was 'far-dreamed-of'.

> Dependent on its neutral base
> That, root-secure through commonplace,
> Has stood the test of strength before.

But this early poem does not altogether trust the commonplace (the 'hedge-root' to which it later turns), and there is a stretching for something which, in the bizarrerie of its hyphenation, does not feel like a true fusion at all:

> The surety of growth is where
> Root stem and flower are brought to light—
> Integral as the hawthorn's rare
> True-fusion of deep earth and air—
> Held and expressed in terms of white.

It was not until *The Mystery of the Charity of Charles Péguy* (1983) that Hill got this rootedness secure:

> Woefully battered but not too bloody,
> smeared by fraternal root-crops and at one
> with the fritillary and the veined stone,
> having composed his great work, his small body,
>
> (10)

For there 'root-crops' must be at once deeply suggestive and perfectly down-to-earth ('root-secure through commonplace'); and in obdurately declining to rhyme with 'stone', 'at one' does not claim any finality of atonement, aware now that the word's root, the 'radical etymological sense', is not root-secure but is a forked radish, 'root-crops'.

The Mystery of the Charity of Charles Péguy does effect a true fusion because it does not strive for a 'true-fusion' (where the very hyphen resists fusion). The conjunction with 'true-' aspires to running exactly true, something which a hyphen will both minister to and baulk. This longing for perfect consonance must acknowledge that what seeks to be miraculous may be only fictive:

> Self-wounding martyrdom, what joys you have,
> true-torn among this fictive consonance,
>   ('Lachrimae:5. Pavana Dolorosa')

The consonance, like a hyphen, is fictive; the hyphen in 'true-torn' both clasps together and tears apart the elements.

The Mystery of the Charity of Charles Péguy has in some ways an intent of *entente*. It seeks to imagine (this English poet writing about that French poet) the ways in which England and France were at one in the Great War. This entails seeing the root sense atone/at-one as English and not French. Hill turns naturally to the link which acknowledges differences, two 'under one', a link which may bring not just two words but two languages under one: 'pâtisserie-tinklings of angels' (2). Or:

> you dream of warrior-poets and the Meuse
> flowing so sweetly; the androgynous Muse
> your priest-confessor, sister-châtelaine.
>
> (9)

The Muse is androgynous not only as male and female but as English and French; 'sister-châtelaine' (and this is brought home by its being both like and unlike the compound 'priest-confessor' immediately before) accommodates the two languages handsomely, even while recognizing that the word 'châtelaine', though socially welcome, remains some corner of an English field that is for ever foreign.

Hill had won for himself a new freedom in the writing of his *Brand*. *Brand*'s off-rhyming momentum had often required a hyphenated spelling to pass across the line-ending, sometimes availing itself of an existent hyphen, sometimes calling one into existence. There was the sliding gravity of a cleft and a drift:

> a great cleft
> in the rock, where the drift-
> ing snow, and ice have built
> the roof of a huge vault.
>
> (Act I)

There was the sudden twist of a knife:

> He turned the knife on him-
> self, and screamed Satan's name.
>
> (Act II)

There was the pathos that is ceaselessly agitated but never moves away from grief:

> and hear the ceaseless sparrow-
> flutterings of sorrow
> in the eaves of the heart's house.
>
> (Act IV)

There was damnation's mortal vertigo:

> Press forward; or fall, back-
> sliding into the grave.
>   (Act V)

And there was the bitter comedy of the worldly:

> Then they took stock
> of the new building-work.
> Dazzled by what they saw,
> with a good deal of awe-
> struck relish, one might say,
>   (Act V)

> Just give them something big
> and they're happy: church, pig-
> sty, it doesn't matter.
>   (Act V)[29]

These dramatic transitions Hill chastened to the elegiac timbre of *The Mystery of the Charity of Charles Péguy*. Even an explosion is handled with care:

> What is this relic fumbled with such care
> by mittened fingers in dugout or bomb-
> tattered, jangling estaminet's upper room?
>   (7)[30]

Or there is the exquisite intersection of time and the timeless in the stanzaic transition across a hyphen; the lulled and peaceful sense that there is all the time in the world is enough to pierce the heart:

> and in the fable this is your proper home;
> three sides of a courtyard where the bees thrum
> in the crimped hedges and the pigeons flirt
> and paddle, and sunlight pierces the heart-
>
> shaped shutter-patterns in the afternoon,
> shadows of fleurs-de-lys on the stone floors.
>   (3)

---

[29] pp. 22, 30, 98, 163, 138, 141.

[30] 'The word italicized in the next example may well puzzle a good many readers without its hyphen; it has quite lately come into use in this country ("Chiefly U.S.", says the *Oxford Dictionary*, which prints the hyphen, whereas Webster does not), and is in danger of being taken at first sight for a foreign word and pronounced in strange ways. "The soldiers . . . have been building *dugouts* throughout April.—*Times*"'

Art, which is gladdened and saddened by such hopes, resists
evolutionary optimism. The handbook-account of one kind of
hyphenation announces a simple evolution: 'In the life of compound words there are three stages: (1) two separate words (*cat
bird*); (2) a hyphenated compound (*cat-bird*); (3) a single word
(*catbird*)'.[31] The three stages are elsewhere spoken of as 'degrees
of relationship' or of 'intimacy':

> There are three degrees of intimacy between words, of which the first
> and loosest is expressed by their mere juxtaposition as separate words,
> the second by their being hyphened, and the third or closest by their
> being written continuously as one word.[32]

This makes workaday sense, but it is partial. For there may be
just as much relationship or intimacy between words side by
side as between those hyphened or run together; the nub is not
degrees of relationship or intimacy but kinds. To hold the
adjacent word at arm's length could manifest a high degree of
relationship and even of intimacy. To join two words by a
hyphen effects a union, a closeness, to which the two may happily agree or from which the two may strain to break free. This
is announced by 'close-' compounds: 'Being close-pressed still
kept storms out and storms in' ('Asmodeus'), or 'and kept close-
hidden at my heart!' (*Brand*, Act IV).[33]

> churchwardens in wing-collars bearing scrolls
> of copyhold well-tinctured and well-tied.
> ('An Apology . . . :12. The Eve of St Mark')

How well 'well-' accommodates itself to the balanced properties
and proprieties; how well-tied each compound is, and how well-
tied the two of them, with 'well-tied' a succinct and equable
contraction of 'well-tinctured'. *Modern English Usage* is a lesser
thing than poetry when it insists: 'This possible confusion
between adjective and adverb probably accounts for the unnecessary hyphen that often appears with *well* and *ill*'.[34] A special

(H. W. and F. G. Fowler, *The King's English*, 2nd edn. 1925, p. 280). *The Mystery* . . .
has 'in dugout': 'The Distant Fury of Battle' has a different turn: 'Some, dug out of
hot-beds, are brought bare'.
[31] *Usage and Abusage* (New Edn, 1957), p. 148.
[32] *The King's English*, p. 275.　　[33] p. 130.
[34] H. W. Fowler, *Modern English Usage* (2nd Edn, rev. Sir Ernest Gowers, 1965),
p. 256.

intimacy may be effected by other compounds:

> without vantage of vanity, though mortal-proud
> (*The Mystery* . . . , 2)

—there the link is partly that of an oxymoron, with '-proud'
surprised at the audacity of 'mortal-'. Or this:

> But rest assured, bristly-brave gentlemen
> (8)

—where '-brave' bristles to find itself being given a military
French buss by 'bristly-'.

The oxymoron is not the only form of hyphenation to challenge the 'three stages' equanimity, but it is the most
unignorable, and Hill can do wonders with it: 'the rooms of
cedar and soft-thudding baize' ('An Apology . . . , 9. The
Laurel Axe'). Sickening, how imperceptive we usually are
about thudding.

One pressing paradox is the apprehension that a great
author from the past is both dead and alive. There is an entry
(3270) in Coleridge's Notebooks where (the editor remarks)
'the spacing suggests that there may have been a thought of
verse':

> Shakespere, Milton, Boyle, all the
> great living-dead men of our Isle.

'Living-dead' is the compacted wisdom of the matter, and I
think that perhaps Coleridge was remembering a passage in
one of the dead poets whom he revered: Samuel Daniel. Yet
Daniel's hyphenation had a reversed emphasis, as was appropriate to its being devoted not, in the first place, to great
authors but to that which is the condition of their greatness: the
very alphabet, the letters that became humane letters:

> O blessed Letters, that combine in one,
>   All Ages past, and make one live with all:
>   By you, we do conferre with who are gone,
>   And the dead-living unto Councell call;
>   By you, th' unborne shall have communion
>   Of what we feele, and what doth us befall.
> (*Works*, 1602)

The rhyme sequence *one / gone / communion*, is itself an act

of combining in one, but the incarnation of such combining
in one, such setting at one, is the hyphened oxymoron 'dead-
living'. *Tenebrae* seeks to set at one 'all the great living-dead
men of our Isle'; and it does 'the dead-living unto Councell
call'.

Largest of all the reconciliatory aspirations in *Tenebrae*, there
is the seeking of that union which Eliot limned as beyond even
Valéry (Eliot is everywhere alive in *Tenebrae*, and Hill's art
calls up Valéry's):

Intelligence to the highest degree, and a type of intelligence which
excludes the possibility of faith, implies profound melancholy. Valéry
has been called a philosopher. But a philosopher, in the ordinary
sense, is a man who constructs or supports a philosophic system; and
in this sense, we can say that Valéry was too intelligent to be a philosopher. The constructive philosopher must have a religious faith, or
some substitute for a religious faith; and generally he is only able to
construct, because of his ability to blind himself to other points of
view, or to remain unconscious of the emotive causes which attach
him to his particular system. Valéry was much too conscious to be
able to philosophise in this way; and so his "philosophy" lays itself
open to the accusation of being only an elaborate game. Precisely, but
to be able to play this game, to be able to take aesthetic delight in it, is
one of the manifestations of civilised man. There is only one higher
stage possible for civilised man: and that is to unite the profoundest
scepticism with the deepest faith. But Valéry was not Pascal, and we
have no right to ask that of him.[35]

Hill asks a great deal of himself. 'A Pre-Raphaelite Notebook' was first published with the words 'Adapted from Pascal';
the acknowledgement in *Tenebrae* is that it 'adapts a sentence
from Pascal's *Pensées*' (Pensée 96). Originally published sixteen
years before *Tenebrae*, this is a poem of atonement, and it repeatedly needs the symbol or mark (something less grand than
a symbol, and more mysterious than a mark) by which things
are set as or set at one. A hyphen can be what Hill calls 'the
precise detail of articulation';[36] and 'the writing of every poem
presents its unique problems, of finding the right articulation
for the particular moment'.[37] So a single short poem such as
'A Pre-Raphaelite Notebook' may need a variety of hyphened

[35] 'Leçon de Valéry', *Paul Valéry Vivant* (1946), pp. 74-6.
[36] *The Lords of Limit*, p. 111.
[37] *The Illustrated London News*, 20 August 1966.

forms. There is the hyphen which most reminds us that a union may be reiteratedly driving or driven in sequence, at once followed by the contrasting unhyphened form:

> Gold seraph to gold worm in the pierced slime:
> greetings. Advent of power-in-grace. The power
> of flies distracts the working of our souls.

The repeated hyphenation yearns for 'unity and simultaneousness' (Coleridge on compounds),[38] but there are cross-purposes such as Hill greeted in exactly the same terms in praise of Shakespeare: 'Shakespeare is perhaps ready to accept a vision of actual power at cross-purposes with the vision of power-in-grace'.[39] Then there is in 'A Pre-Raphaelite Notebook' the hyphen which comprehends the divine acts of issuance and utterance as being simply not imaginable as severance or disjunction, since the hyphen preserves relationship even in the act of describing a breach: 'The God-ejected Word'. And there is the hyphen which most admits the incomplete, the prefix 'half-': 'a half-eaten ram'. All of Hill's volumes bring out how a hyphen doubles and halves; *Tenebrae* elsewhere has (very different in their operations): 'half-way', 'half-faithful', 'half-built', 'half-gloom', and 'half-effaced'. The hyphens of *Tenebrae* embody the desire and seeking which are everywhere the poems' explicit energy; a hyphened 'half-' may embody the desire and pursuit of the whole.[40]

Tenebrae is unique and yet perfectly continuous with Hill's earlier work. He has always been a strong (and sometimes idiosyncratic) hyphenator. 'Genesis', the first poem in his first volume of poems,[41] sees the six days of the Creation as one creation, and sees all creation as one ('a repetition in the finite mind of the eternal act of creation in the infinite I AM', in the words of *Biographia Literaria*). 'Genesis' commands its sequence of compounds, from 'The tough pig-headed salmon', through

---

[38] *The Friend*, No. 18, 21 December 1809.

[39] (1969); *The Lords of Limit*, p. 66.

[40] In 'The Turtle Dove', half-sleep; in 'The White Ship', half-appear; in 'Of Commerce and Society, IV', Half-erased and half-dead; in VI, half-under; in 'Funeral Music', half-unnerved; in 'The Stone Man', Half-recognized; in 'The Songbook of Sebastian Arrurruz', Half-mocking and half-truth; in *Mercian Hymns* VII, half-bricks.

[41] Preceded by the pamphlet, *The Fantasy Poets, Number Eleven* (1952).

'The soft-voiced owl' and 'the glove-winged albatross', to 'The phantom-bird'. These work very differently. 'The tough pig-headed salmon' depends not only on the tribute to up-river stubbornness and on the odd accuracy of the physical likening (as if the joining of pig and salmon were vindicated as something much more simply true than either the tragic chimera or the comic child's-book animal-strips), but also on the fact that though you can say 'pig-headed', there are things you can't say. 'We do not usually talk of anyone having *an absent mind, a pig head, a chicken heart, a wrong head* or *raw bones*'.[42]

In its context, 'The soft-voiced owl' (in a way that looks 'deliberate' to those who have 'eyes') recalls 'the quiet-voiced elders' of the elderly Eliot, wise old owls. Hill:

> 'Beware
> The soft-voiced owl, the ferret's smile,
> The hawk's deliberate stoop in air,
> Cold eyes . . . '

Eliot:

> And the wisdom of age? Had they deceived us,
> Or deceived themselves, the quiet-voiced elders,
> Bequeathing us merely a receipt for deceit?
> The serenity only a deliberate hebetude,
> The wisdom only the knowledge of dead secrets
> Useless in the darkness into which they peered
> Or from which they turned their eyes.
>
> (*East Coker*)

'The glove-winged albatross' in 'Genesis' suggests the unfitting collusion between the victim and its persecutor (there is a different slant on this in Hill's next poem but one, where 'Child and nurse walk hand in glove'). And 'The phantom-bird' is explicitly paralleled by and perhaps identified with 'the phoenix', so that the very hyphen becomes a way in which

> Reason in it selfe confounded,
> Saw Division grow together,
> ('The Phoenix and Turtle')

'The phantom-bird' offers a quite different conjunction from those before it in 'Genesis', with its hyphen insisting (since 'phantom bird' would have made perfect sense) upon a linkage

[42] Valerie Adams, *An Introduction to Modern English Word-formation* (1973), p. 100.

which might have seemed needless or forced but which has a compacted reality: 'The phantom-bird goes wild and lost'. Hill's Brand was to ask the deranged and sharp-eyed Gerd about her silver bullet ('They say it works / wonders against demons'):

> And hawks?
> Real phantom-hawks?
> (Act V)[43]

Those words in *Brand* look not only to the first poem of *For the Unfallen* and its 'phantom-bird', but also to the words of 'Funeral Music: 7': 'A hawk and a hawk-shadow', and to the words of 'The Pentecost Castle: 8' in *Tenebrae*:

> fulfilment to my sorrow
> indulgence of your prey
> the sparrowhawk the sparrow
> the nothing that you say

'The Pentecost Castle', the sequence of fifteen lyrics which begins *Tenebrae*, famously has no punctuation, not even at the end of a poem or of the sequence. It has been argued by W. S. Milne[44] that this sequence's 'unpunctuated tones of innocence (true innocence which has incorporated the facts of experience and transcended them) compromise the "worldly" punctuation of the succeeding sequences' ('Lachrimae', 'An Apology for the Revival of Christian Architecture in England', and 'Tenebrae'), and that Hill 'sets up an idealistic artifice of poetic voice at the beginning of the volume which the succeeding, punctuated sequences are "placed" or compromised by, through comparison'. There can be no doubt of the contrast of the totally unpunctuated and the heavily punctuated sequences: but there is some sentimentality in Milne's feeling no qualms about 'innocence', both in the world and in Hill's poetry.[45] That is, to speak innocently, as Milne does, of 'the lack of punctuation indicating an unchecked flow of the living spirit' (as against 'the succeeding poems in the volume' which are checked 'by

---

[43] p. 179.

[44] *Agenda*, 17:1 (1979), 27-9.

[45] Hill confronts innocence in, for example, 'Holy Thursday', 'Ovid in the Third Reich', and 'Locust Songs'. As to unpunctuation in *Tenebrae*: when first published, 'Te Lucis Ante Terminum' ('Two Chorale-Preludes: 2') had no punctuation—except a hyphen.

what Hill . . . called ''the inertial drag of speech'' ') is to avert
one's eyes from the fact that the unchecked flow of the living
spirit may manifest itself as, for instance, murderousness.

Anyway, every device of the poet, every technical or formal
disposition, is an axis and not a direction; its flow of spirit runs
between two points, along such and such a line, but not necessarily in this as against that direction. The very quality which
makes for such-and-such can in other circumstances make for
the exact opposite. 'The thing that causes instability in another
state—of itself causes stability—as for instance wet soap slips
off the ledge, detain it till it dries a little & it *sticks*' (Coleridge,
Notebooks, entry 1017). Hill shares in 'Hopkins's ambiguous,
ungraspable ''world-wielding'' force ('' . . . something that
makes, builds up and breeds . . . something that unmakes or
pulls to pieces . . . '')'.[46] It may be ungraspable, but the hyphen
tries to seize upon it, as Hill does when he turns the 'ambiguous
ungraspable ''world-wielding''' to this: 'The word-monger,
word-wielder, is brought to judgement'.[47]

'The Pentecost Castle' does not just have no punctuation; it
has un-punctuation or non-punctuation. Yet two of Eliot's
deepest remarks about punctuation and technique (and 'we
cannot say at what point ''technique'' begins or where it ends')
press upon Hill's sequence. First, that 'verse, whatever else it
may or may not be, is itself a system of *punctuation*; the usual
marks of punctuation themselves are differently employed'.[48]
Second, that in a poem punctuation 'includes the *absence* of
punctuation marks, when they are omitted where the reader
would expect them'.[49]

> If the night is dark
> and the way short
> why do you hold back
> dearest heart
>
> though I may never
> see you again
> touch me I will shiver
> at the unseen

[46] *The Lords of Limit*, p. 147.
[47] *The Lords of Limit*, p. 158.
[48] *Times Literary Supplement*, 27 September 1928.
[49] Eliot's words on the sleeve of his record of *Four Quartets*.

the night is so dark
the way so short
why do you not break
o my heart   (11)

This poem is and is not punctuated, or rather is both non-punctuated and punctuated. It is punctuated because verse, with its lineations sketching its lineaments and with its stanzas taking a stand, is itself a system of punctuation. It is non-punctuated because it not only has none of the conventional marks of punctuation but it has an absence of such marks where the reader would have expected them.

> marked
> visible absences, colours of the mind,
> ('Terribilis est Locus Iste')

One mark in particular is visibly absent: the question-mark. The question-mark presses upon the poem, wishing to steady the lonely sufferer:

> why do you hold back
> dearest heart
>
> why do you not break
> o my heart

For the double cry (positive and negative) both is and is not a question; it is interrogative in its hunger for an answer, it is exclamatory in its protest, and it is declarative in its stoicism. It beseeches a question-mark, an exclamation-mark, and a full stop; all or none of these. Hill would not have effected his very different poignancy had it not been for the Eliot of 'Marina' and its fog-lifting:

> What seas what shores what grey rocks and what islands
> What water lapping the bow
> And scent of pine and the woodthrush singing through the fog
> What images return
> O my daughter.

Non-punctuation is like non-being, and it has its depths:

> depths of non-being
> perhaps too clear
> my desire dying
> as I desire

Yet, as this concluding unstopped quatrain of 'The Pentecost
Castle' shows, there is one simple and deep respect in which it
is simply not true to say that 'The Pentecost Castle' has no
punctuation. W. S. Milne says of the lack of punctuation in
'The Pentecost Castle' that Hill represents 'a condition beyond
knowing', 'by abandoning those aspects of language which are
designed to break down reality into component parts'.[50] But
one mark of punctuation which signally breaks down reality
into component parts is not abandoned. For the hyphen ('depths
of non-being') both is and is not a mark of punctuation. It
is, after all, a mark by which the particular pointing of the
language is manifested and controlled, and handbooks of punctuation have for centuries included a discussion of the hyphen.
But it is anomalous, since our first thought, and even our
central thought, may be that punctuation is a mark of the articulation of word to word, and not within a word. The equivocation
of the hyphen is perfectly at one with the way in which 'The
Pentecost Castle' both is and is not punctuated (there is what
Eliot called 'the disposition of lines on the page', the strongly-
felt presence of lineation and stanza, and there is the strongly-
felt absence of particular marks of punctuation at crucial points).
The presence of hyphens within the poem is, to say the least,
a complication of any simple innocence.

> St James and St John
> bless the road she has gone
> St John and St James
> a rosary of names
>
> child-beads of fingered bread
> never-depleted heart's food
> the nominal the real
> subsistence past recall
>
> bread we shall never break
> love-runes we cannot speak
> scrolled effigy of a cry
> our passion its display
>
> (10)

It is the hyphen which threads the rosary of child-beads, never-
depleted, and love-runes; it is the hyphen which brings home

[50] *Agenda*, 17:1 (1979), p. 29.

what it is to conceive of 'love-runes we cannot speak', since the human voice cannot speak a hyphen.[51]

If there are brought together the hyphens and the impinging absence of other punctuation-marks, then the question may arise of the absence of hyphens when they are omitted where the reader would expect them, here in 'The Pentecost Castle' or elsewhere. Tennyson was reproved by Coleridge, and attributed the reproof to a poetical mannerism in 'Œnone':

> I had an idiotic hatred of hyphens in those days, but though I printed such words as 'glénrĭver', 'téndriltwĭne' I always gave them in reading their full two accents. Coleridge thought because of these hyphened words that I could not scan.[52]

The first dozen lines of 'Œnone' included in 1832 'glenriver', 'steepdown', 'tendriltwine', 'cedarshadowy', 'Godbuilt', 'snowycolumn'd', and 'darkblue'; this opening did permit itself 'Far-seen', as if Tennyson either baulked at the odd form 'Farseen' or had run out of resistance to the hyphen.[53] Hill, who writes as if only an idiot would have a hatred of hyphens, is aware of how a Tennysonian colouring can be given, sometimes banteringly, by declining—as in Tennyson's 'cedarshadowy'—to furnish a hyphen. As in this Tennysonian landscape:

> and the marsh-orchids and the heron's nest,
> goldgrimy shafts and pillars of the sun.
> ('An Apology . . . :11. Idylls of the King')

This is one extremity of the absent hyphen, the Tennysonian passion of the past becoming a passion of the pastiche. The opposite extremity is not to run the words together but to let them float free, even compounding their not being a compound

---

[51] Gone from the French translation of 'The Pentecost Castle': 'runes d'amour pour nous imprononçables'. Likewise 'chapelet d'enfant' and 'inépuisable' (tr. René Gallet, *Obsidiane*, No. 18, March 1982).

[52] Tennyson, in the Eversley edition; cp. Hallam Tennyson, *Alfred Lord Tennyson: A Memoir* (1897), i 50. The 22 lines of an early poem by Tennyson have 11 such unhyphenated compound words and the poem's title is 'Dualisms'.

[53] "It is stated that the train service on the Hsin-min-tun-Kau-pan-tse-Yingkau section of the Imperial Chinese Railway will be restored within a few days—*Times*". 'Hsinmintun, Kaupantse, and Yingkau. These places can surely do without their internal hyphens in an English newspaper; and one almost suspects, from the absence of a hyphen between *Ying* and *kau*, that the *Times*' stock must have run short' (*The King's English*, pp. 276-7).

by how they are lineated:

> At dawn the Mass
> burgeons from stone
> a Jesse tree
> of resurrection
>
> budding with candle
> flames the gold
> and the white wafers
> of the feast
>
> and ghosts for love
> void a few tears
> of wax upon
> forlorn altars
>
> ('The Pentecost Castle:4')

Not 'candle-flames', not even 'candle flames', but

> budding with candle
> flames the gold

—and this within a sequence of lines none of which had hitherto run over. The candles and their flames both are and are not one; they drift poignantly apart even in their celebration. It is the opposite of the unascetic prolongation which Eliot stirred here:

> stirred by the air
> That freshened from the window, these ascended
> In fattening the prolonged candle-flames,
> Flung their smoke into the laquearia,
> Stirring the pattern on the coffered ceiling.
>
> (*The Waste Land*)

Eliot's lines make your eyes prick and tingle, but not with sad tears. Hill's lines are close to tears, again with a sense of so near and yet so far:

> budding with candle
> flames the gold

Moreover, the words 'for love' yearn to be at one with the 'forlorn',[54] to assuage with love such sadness. The 'few tears' were

---

[54] When the poem was first published, 'forlorn' was 'their quenched'.

in *Brand* the settled bereavement of Agnes which Brand with cruel integrity unsettles:

> And a whole year has gone;
> and the candle shines clear
> over the place where he lies.
> And he can see us
> if he chooses to come
> and gaze in, quietly,
> at the still candle-flame.
> But now the window blurs
> with breath-mist, like tears.
>
> (Act IV)[55]

For there the candle-flame is still, as are not the

candle

flames

It may be said that to make this much of hyphens is far-fetched and murderously dissecting ('. . . murderously / To heal me with far-fetched blood': 'Three Baroque Meditations: 3. The Dead Bride'). But the general case for attention to minutiae in Hill's poetry is corroborated by his own sense that nothing is beneath notice. 'I would claim the utmost significance for matters of technique'.[56] As for this particular point of technique, hyphenation: Hill's revisions of 'The Pentecost Castle' in particular, and of *Tenebrae* more widely, and of all his poetry most widely,[57] show that he attends meticulously to this very matter. For 'under the briar rose' (twice in 'The Pentecost Castle, 2') was first published as 'under the briar-rose'; 'my love meet me half-way' (9), conversely, was first published as 'my love meet me half way'; and 'Splendidly-shining darkness' (13) as 'Splendidly shining darkness'.

Such an adverbial hyphenation in 'ly-' is an insistent one in Hill. Perhaps he is refusing to be intimidated by Churchill, who wrote to Edward Marsh: '*Richly embroidered* seems to me two words, and it is terrible to think of linking every adverb to

[55] p. 119.
[56] *The Lords of Limit*, p. 2.
[57] 'The plum-tree' and 'horse-flies' of 'Te Lucis . . .' were first published without their hyphens. Of earlier poems, 'Two Formal Elegies: I' revised 'sand-graves' to 'sand graves'; 'Canticle for Good Friday' revised 'carrion sustenance' to 'carrion-sustenance'.

a verb by a hyphen'.[58] Eric Partridge says roundly that 'an adverb in *-ly* never takes a hyphen, whether before or after a participle, present or past'.[59] But Hill's art is, in its own terms, 'greatly-aloof' from, and 'variably-resistant' to, such a dogma; as an art which is 'splendidly-shining', 'evidently-veiled', 'newly-stung', 'rawly-difficult', 'roughly-silvered', 'truly-chastened', 'blazingly-supreme' and 'nicely-phrased', the one thing it isn't is 'blindly-ignorant' of the handbooks' urgings. Hill praised the poetry of Robert Lowell: 'The writing is deeply-felt and strongly-mannered: the feeling is embodied in the mannerism'.[60] In Hill's own poetry, the deep feeling is embodied in that strong mannerism of adverbial hyphenation. So 'Splendidly shining darkness' became 'Splendidly-shining darkness'.

That is, Hill knows the difference between 'Hearthstones' in *Mercian Hymns* (XXVIII)[61] and 'hearth-stone' in his *Brand* (Act II). He is not oblivious of the strange likeness and unlikeness ('At such near distance') when the 'same' word takes minutely different forms:

> Dawnlight freezes against the east-wire.
>> ('I had hope when violence was ceas't')
> In dawn-light the troughed water floated a damson-bloom of dust.
>> (*Mercian Hymns*, XXV)
> Then turn your backs on the dawn-light.
>> (*Brand*, Act II)[62]
> Down in the river-garden a grey-gold
> dawnlight begins to silhouette the ash.
>> (*The Mystery of the Charity of Charles Péguy*, 10)

'Not only is the use of the hyphen a matter of indifference in an immense number of cases . . . ' (*OED*, 'General Explanations: Combinations'). Not in poetry, it isn't. 'Car-dealers' are so nearly those other untrustworthy people who deal cards, especially if they are to be found in the company of 'shuffle'

---

[58] *Modern English Usage*, rev. Gowers, p. 256.
[59] *You Have a Point There*, p. 145.
[60] *Essays in Criticism*, xiii (1963), 190.
[61] On 'Hearth-stones', see Martin Dodsworth, *Stand*, 13:1 (1971-2), 62.
[62] p. 36.

and 'carls'; Hill uses the momentary flicker of mis-spelling and mis-hyphenation rather as Robert Lowell did.

> Merovingian car-dealers, Welsh mercenaries;
> a shuffle of house-carls.
>
> (*Mercian Hymns*, XXVII)

Hill is a poet preoccupied (some would say obsessed) with such minutiae. Coleridge's observation is true for the critic because it is first true for the poet: 'And I must not forget in speaking of the certain Hubbub, I am to undergo for hyper-criticism, to point out how little instructive any criticism can be which does not enter into minutiae'.[63]

> When the sky cleared above Malvern he lingered in
> his orchard; by the quiet hammer-pond. Trout-fry
> simmered there, translucent, as though forming the
> water's underskin. He had a care for natural min-
> utiae.   (*Mercian Hymns*, XIV)

The lines are evidence of a care for artistic minutiae too, as in the way the hyphen in 'hammer-pond' permits the eerie juxta-position of 'quiet' and 'hammer' to be so tellingly unmelo-dramatic ('by the quiet hammer-pond'); for the hyphen paces and points the sequence of words so that 'quiet' is unobtrusively held at a very slightly greater distance from 'hammer-pond' than it would be from 'hammer pond' and yet not so distant as it would be from 'hammerpond'.

When Hill refers to 'Ash-Wednesday feasts', he remembers the hyphen which Eliot had and which even Eliot's best critics sometimes fail to remember. In *Tenebrae*, Hill offers 'Two Chorale-Preludes', not, as John Peck[64] has it, 'Two Chorale Preludes' (the two poems are both two and one; their autonomy is preserved, and the hyphen does the more than trick). Hill might ask, chasteningly, what Andrew Waterman means by distinguishing the adverb 'selfchasteningly' from the noun which he uses three pages later: 'the poetic self-chastening'.[65] *Self-* is perhaps Hill's most frequently needed hyphenation; it is certainly the form which dominates *Tenebrae, Brand* and 'Poetry as "Menace" and "Atonement"'.

[63] *Notebooks*, entry 3970.
[64] *Agenda*, 17:1 (1979), 22.
[65] *British Poetry Since 1970*, ed. Peter Jones and Michael Schmidt (1980), pp. 91, 94.

Compounds with 'self-' at once incarnate the utmost singleness of a hyphenation and strike at its roots, since they turn
the doubleness upon itself and make the matter perversely one.
Hill's distrust of self-expression,[66] and of every such 'self-inspiring
self-deceiver',[67] even when sitting 'in gaunt self-judgment on
their self-defeat',[68] is responsibly desperate for a contrasting
honourable word of self. He finds it in selfhood. 'Selfhood is
more vital, recalcitrant, abiding, than self-expression'.[69] It is
in the poet's acknowledgement of 'irredeemable error in the
very substance and texture of his craft and pride . . . that his
selfhood may be made at-one with itself'.[70]

For selfhood, unlike 'at-one', is indeed one, and it has no
room for even the best-intentioned hyphen. *Tenebrae* brings
this home when 'selfhoods' are threatened by splits and by
hyphened faceting:

> Moods of the verb 'to stare',
> split selfhoods, conjugate
> ice-facets from the air,
> the light glazing the light.
> ('Two Chorale-Preludes:1. Ave Regina Coelorum')

The ice-facets are not conjured from the air, but are learnedly
conjugated; the selfhoods do offer at least a vision of integrity,
unsplit, refusing the violent scholarly yoking.

> Already, like a disciplined scholar,
> I piece fragments together, past conjecture
> Establishing true sequences of pain.
> ('The Songbook of Sebastian Arrurruz, 1')

No less painful, and no less true though never above suspicion,
are the sequences which are pieced not from fragments but
from wholes. Hill is much more sceptical of multiple hyphen-
ings than are his critics. Yet the critics' mannerism is caught
from the poet, even if he is not only more sceptical than they
are but more sceptical than his much-loved Hopkins. Hill per-

---

[66] See *The Poetry Book Society Bulletin*, No. 98, Autumn 1978; 'What Devil Has Got
Into John Ransom?'; and the sermon preached by Hill at Great St Mary's, Cambridge, 8 May 1983.
[67] *Brand*, Act V, p. 175.
[68] *The Mystery* . . ., 6.
[69] Sermon preached by Hill, 8 May 1983.
[70] *The Lords of Limit*, p. 17.

mits himself neither the callisthenics of 'Amansstrength' at one extreme, nor the self-advertisement of 'drop-of-blood-and-foam-dapple', of 'wimpled-water-dimpled, not-by-morning-matchèd', or of 'Miracle-in-Mary-of-flame'. Yet Hill greatly admires Hopkins's indeflectibility.

> Our hearts' charity's hearth's fire, our thoughts' chivalry's throng's
>   Lord.
>   ('The Wreck of the Deutschland')
> I cannot entirely agree with [Elisabeth Schneider's] suggestion that
> 'the effect is arbitrary and labored'. The method, I would accept,
> is arbitrary and laboured but the effect is one of hard-won affirm-
> ation.[71]

But it was not simply the fact that Charles Péguy's title had been *Le Mystère de la Charité de Jeanne d'Arc* that made Hill call his poem *The Mystery of the Charity of Charles Péguy* rather than *Charles Péguy's Charity's Mystery*. Hill admires Hopkins and does otherwise. English ought to be kept up. And so should the English distrust of compounding compounds.

>   I wake
>   To caress propriety with odd words
>   And enjoy abstinence in a vocation
>   Of now-almost-meaningless despair.
>   ('The Songbook of Sebastian Arrurruz, 11')

'The phrase ''now-almost-meaningless''', said Jeffrey Wainwright, 'is hyphenated to point up its accession into cliché, though here a cliché restored to hint at the real despair of the poet—the possibility of no longer, through the contraction of valid speech, being able to say anything meaningful'.[72] Such hyper-hyphenated phrases are not to be trusted, though this awkwardly has to include the fact that you can't trust them to be false either. You must simply exercise 'A busy vigilance of goose and hound' ('Asmodeus, II'). Especially when near such a lithe paradigm of doubled-hyphenation as this:

>   I am shadowed by the wise bird
>   Of necessity, the lithe
>   Paradigm Sleep-and-Kill.
>   ('Three Baroque Meditations, 1')

[71] *The Lords of Limit*, p. 113.   [72] *Stand*, 10:1 (1968), 49.

Necessity, the tyrant's paradigm, is winged by hyphens.

Even, or particularly, the grandest of these turns may be twists:

> Whose passion was to find out God in this
> His natural filth, voyeur of sacrifice, a slow
> Bloody unearthing of the God-in-us.
> But with what blood, and to what end, Shiloh?
>
> ('Locust Songs: Shiloh Church, 1862')

Brand has its comic preposterousness:

> that Fear-and-Trembling School
> has taught you very well!
> . . .
> high-stepping Meek-and-Mild!
>
> (Act I)[73]

Tenebrae more darkly declines to adjudicate between the authentic and the inauthentic, pressing the reader to take the responsibility of response to such finely judged withholdings as: 'Stupefying images of grief-in-dream' and 'this is true marriage of the self-in-self' ('Tenebrae'). Those last three words, that last one word, might not ring like a true marriage.

In his essay on *Cymbeline* (a text with 'a strong taste for hyphens'),[74] Hill refers to 'James VI and I, the unifier and pacifier'.[75] Divinely rightly unhyphenated, James VI and I was something of a metaphysical as well as political feat, and when in his Jonson essay Hill quotes Coleridge, the form used is again evidence that the handbooks on punctuation have (as Eric Partridge insisted) a point:

> The *anachronic* mixture of the Roman Republican, to whom Tiberius must have appeared as much a Tyrant as Sejanus, with the *James-and-Charles-the-1st* zeal for legitimacy of Descent.[76]

James-and-Charles-the-1st? That looks to be at once a succession and a simultaneity, unifying and pacifying. There is likewise something happy, a touch of the trouvaille, in its being

[73] p. 14.
[74] The (Cambridge) New Shakespeare, ed. John Dover Wilson and J. C. Maxwell (1960), p. 126.
[75] *The Lords of Limit*, p. 56.
[76] *Coleridge on the Seventeenth Century*, ed. R. F. Brinkley (1955), p. 643; Hill (1960), *The Lords of Limit*, p. 50.

the United Committee of Framework-Knitters which moves Hill to invoke such knittings as 'time-signature', or to this sequence:

To do justice to the quality of his seeing [Hopkins's, of Wordsworth] one must refer again to Richard Oastler and to the Nottingham framework-knitters. Writers on linguistics employ a term 'stress-pitch-juncture'. ' "Juncture" is that particular configuration of pause and pitch characteristics by which the voice connects linguistic units to each other or to silence' (Seymour Chatman). In this case one requires a modified term, 'stress-pitch-disjuncture'.[77]

When Eric Partridge pondered the way in which, thanks to hyphens, 'a number of distinct entities—apprehended, it is true, as a collectivity or a collective idea—becomes an intellectual, aesthetic, stylistic unit', he found himself gravitating to a unit not intellectual, aesthetic, or stylistic, but religious and metaphysical. The gravity of the instance pricked Partridge to a certain uneasy levity about high-style hyphenation:

Thus, whereas most of us would write:
The ideal of the mystic is oneness with God, the stylist would perhaps write:
The ideal of the mystic is oneness-with-God.
If the collectivity be put first, i.e. made the subject of the sentence, most of us would write:
Oneness with God is the ideal of the mystic,
but the stylist would probably prefer:
Oneness-with-God is (or, constitutes) the ideal of the mystic.
The relationship of the theory to the practice can be more clearly seen in a sentence no stylist would permit himself:
The idea oneness-with-God forms the very basis of mystical philosophy, that of God everywhere-and-in-everything-whether-animate-or-inanimate, the basis of pantheism; and that of God-in-the-form-of-man or, at the least, God-with-the-(better)-feelings-and-the-(superior)-attributes-of-man, the basis of anthropomorphism.[78]

The hope (beyond hope) of setting at one the two soundings of atonement is the impulse of religious consciousness. It was the philosopher F. H. Bradley who furnished one of the great high and dry moments of philosophical comedy when his Table

of Contents summarized the arguments of Book I (Appearance)
Section III of *Appearance and Reality*:

III. RELATION AND QUALITY
    I.   Qualities without relations are unintelligible. They cannot
        be found, 26-27. They cannot be got bare legitimately,
        27-28, or at all, 28-30.
    II. Qualities with relations are unintelligible. They cannot be
        resolved into relations, 30, and the relations bring internal
        discrepancies, 31.
   III. Relations with, or without, qualities are unintelligible,
        32-34.

It was Bradley's disciple, T. S. Eliot, who perpetrated the comic
totality of a related footnote:[79] 'Ultimately, it must be remembered, there are not even relations'. Even so, that very footnote
bore some relation to Eliot's text.

Bradley hoped to reconcile the Atonement and atonement:

> You can not understand the recognition of and desire for the divine
> will; nor the consciousness of sin and rebellion, with the need for
> grace on the one hand and its supply on the other; you turn every fact
> of religion into unmeaning nonsense, and you pluck up by the root
> and utterly destroy all possibility of the Atonement, when you deny
> that the religious consciousness implies that God and man are ident-
> ical in a subject.
>
> For it is the atonement, the reconciliation (call it what you please,
> and bring it before your mind in the way most easy to you), to which
> we must come, if we mean to follow the facts of the religious con-
> sciousness. Here, as everywhere, the felt contradiction implies, and is
> only possible through, a unity above the discord: take that away, and
> the discord goes.
>
>   (*Ethical Studies*, 'Concluding Remarks')[80]

It was a great turn, so to retort Ulysses' words as to make the
discord go in peace:

>   Take but Degree away, un-tune that string,
>   And hearke what Discord followes.
>   (*Troilus and Cressida*, I iii)

If, in these highest reaches of philosophy and religion, Bradley
is right to insist that 'the felt contradiction implies, and is only

---

[79] *Knowledge and Experience in the Philosophy of F. H. Bradley* (1964), p. 131.
[80] *Ethical Studies* (2nd edn, 1927), pp. 323-4.

possible through, a unity above the discord', it is equally true that at those rare opposite moments of the felt atonement there is implied a discord below the unity. It is this double truth that in Bradley so makes against any complacency of utterance.

Yet 'a unity above the discord'—not obliterating or oblivious of the discord—may, on occasion and by grace, be incarnated by virtue of a poet's hyphen:

> and abstinence crowns all our care
> with martyr-laurels for this day.
>   ('Veni Coronaberis')

Like the spiritual Platonic old England which Coleridge revered, Hill, when he rests, rests in not on his martyr-laurels:

> Platonic England, house of solitudes,
> rests in its laurels and its injured stone,
>   ('An Apology . . . ,9. The Laurel Axe')

But mostly there is little rest; rather there is what Hill in 1954, precariously hyphening, called the need 'to walk the tight-rope over the jaw-hole.'[81] His poems are some versions of what *The Mystery of the Charity of Charles Péguy* compactly calls 'militant-pastoral'. They are 'variably-resistant' to criticism.

'Any-mad-versions of an Author's meaning now a days pass for animadversions'. Hill might agree with Coleridge.[82] But as a child his first recorded word was 'jam-jar'.[83]

---

[81] *The Isis*, 17 February 1954.
[82] *Notebooks*, entry 4124.
[83] *The Isis*, 18 November 1953.

CLICHÉS

The only way to speak of a cliché is with a cliché. So even the best writers against clichés are awkwardly placed. When Eric Partridge amassed his *Dictionary of Clichés* in 1940 (1978 saw its fifth edition), his introduction had no choice but to use the usual clichés for clichés. Yet what, as a metaphor, could be more hackneyed than *hackneyed*, more outworn than *outworn*, more tattered than *tattered*? Is there any point left to—or in or on—saying of a cliché that its 'original point has been blunted'? Hasn't this too become blunted? A cliché is 'a phrase "on tap"' as it were'—but, as it is, is Partridge's 'as it were' anything more than a cool pretence that when, for his purposes, he uses the cliché *on tap* it's oh so different from the usual bad habit of having those two words on tap? His indictment of 'fly-blown phrases' has no buzz of insect wings, no weight of carrion.

Even George Orwell (whom William Empson, with an audacious compacting of clichés, called the eagle eye with the flat feet)—even Orwell had to use the cliché-clichés (*hackneyed, outworn*), and could say, 'There is a long list of fly-blown metaphors which could similarly be got rid of if enough people would interest themselves in the job,' without apparently being interested himself in whether *fly-blown* wasn't itself one of those very metaphors which could be got rid of. That was in 1946, in his famous piece 'Politics and the English Language.'[1] More than thirty years later, a sociological treatise *On Clichés: The Supersedure of Meaning by Function in Modernity* (1979), by Anton C. Zijderveld, finds itself trapped as usual, but—also as usual—without wincing enough and without pondering enough the implications of this trap. Clichés 'roll ever so easily over our tongues' (like those words themselves); they are 'like the many coins of our inflated economic system' (itself a metaphor which has long since gone off any linguistic gold standard); they are 'reach-me-downs,' 'off the peg'; or they are 'rubbed smooth by use.' This last is a cliché which the best literary critic of dead metaphors, Donald Davie, could not do without in his fine book *Purity of Diction in English Verse*. But if the phrase 'rubbed

[1] *Horizon*, April 1946; *Collected Essays* (1968), 1970 edn, iv 156-70.

smooth by too much handling' hasn't itself been rubbed so
smooth as not to come in handy when discussing this very matter, don't we have to think again about whether it makes sense
to urge that clichés should be—in Orwell's words—scrapped,
got rid of?

Partridge's blurb still says in 1978 exactly what it said in
1940, that his book 'is full of the things better left *unsaid*'—but
there was no way his introduction could, or can, say the things
it needs to say except by saying many of these phrases better
left unsaid, clichés about clichés. Instead of banishing or shun-
ning clichés as malign, haven't we got to meet them imaginatively, to create benign possibilities for and with them?

But then Orwell's darkest urgings, in the words which end
his essay, have a weirdly bright undertow.

From time to time one can even, if one jeers loudly enough, send
some worn-out and useless phrase—some *jackboot, Achilles' heel, hotbed,
melting pot, acid test, veritable inferno* or other lump of verbal refuse—into
the dustbin where it belongs.

For what is most alive in that sentence is not the sequence
where Orwell consciously put his polemical energy—his argumentative train of serviceable clichés from 'worn-out' and 'useless' through 'lump of verbal refuse' to 'the dustbin where it
belongs'—but rather the sombre glints lurking in the sequence
of the scorned clichés themselves: the way in which, even while
he was saying that they were useless phrases, Orwell used them
so as to create a bizarre vitality of poetry. The *jackpot* has, hard
on its heels, *Achilles' heel*; then the *hotbed* at once melts in the
heat, into *melting pot*, and then again (a different melting) into
acid test—with perhaps some memory of Achilles, held by the
heel while he was dipped into the Styx; and then finally the
veritable inferno, which not only consumes *hotbed* and *melting pot*
but also, because of *veritable*, confronts the truth-testing *acid test*.
Orwell may have set his face against those clichés, but his
mind, including his co-operative subconscious, was another
matter.

The feeling lately has been that we live in an unprecedented
inescapability from clichés. All around us is a rising tide of
them; we shall drown and no one will save us. A great poet,
Pope, expected to 'win my way by yielding to the tyde.'[2] It is

2 Epistles of Horace, Book I, Epistle I 34.

hard to know whether the gloomy sense that we are more than
ever threatened by clichés is historically grounded. For it is
easy to forget that there were a great many clichés in the past
which are now entirely forgotten. We are conscious of our time's
clichés as we can never be of past times', and one of the
pleasures of reading Swift's derangedly meticulous *Polite Conversation*, a tissue of eighteenth-century clichés, is discovering
how many of the moribund vacancies it records have since died
away entirely from the language. Again, there is certainly a
morbid propensity just now to claim that clichés are springing
up to endanger us. The sociologist Zijderveld musters the predictable sense of outrage:

> Since modernization has progressed the farthest in the USA,
> American English and much of its *slang* has become the *lingua franca* of
> modernity. Thus, wherever a nation modernizes on the scale of
> North-America (which is called significantly, though falsely, 'Ameri-
> canization'), hackneyed American words like 'jeans', 'sneakers',
> 'hamburgers', 'disc-jockeys', and the all-American 'hi' as a means of
> greeting, are liable to penetrate into the native language, just as
> American-based multi-nationals are liable to well-nigh invisibly
> sneak into the native economic system.[3]

But even if some words (*viable*, for instance) can manage single-
handed to become clichés, *jeans*—since it is an object—isn't
exactly one of them. Trousers of that material which is named
after Genoa aren't a product of any new Americanization; the
first reference to them cited in the *Oxford English Dictionary* is
from that sturdily English figure Robert Surtees (in 1843), and
it describes Septimus 'with his white jeans.' An entry for 1846
gives us 'my friend in the jeans', and as recently—so to speak—
as 1923 it was John Galsworthy who remarked that 'he wore,
not white ducks, but blue jeans.' If an American writer has to
be enlisted, it shouldn't be someone from our era of multi-
nationals, but Mark Twain just over a century ago: 'They were
dressed in homespun "jeans", blue or yellow.' A tiny instance,
but these cries of alarm are often ridiculously late in the day, as
when people speak as if such demotic terms as *no way* or *slush
money* hadn't been around for a very long time indeed.

Yet the feeling that those valuable dangerous things, widespread literacy and the mass media, have helped to create a

[3] *On Clichés* (1979), p. 26.

new torrent of clichés is unlikely to be simply mistaken. Language has its ecology and its spoliations; for every landscape being raped, there may be a language too. Conspicuous consumption and planned obsolescence are features of the linguistic as well as of the social scene. Words and idioms are created and worked to death with a ruthless speed that would have shocked earlier ages—the process resembles one of those eerie films which speed up a flower's life from budding to withering. No sooner had President Nixon's press secretary Ronald Ziegler uttered his lying word for lying, *inoperative*, than it had itself become inoperative. No sooner floated than sunk.

Yet as is suggested by the nemesis which so soon rendered Ziegler and his master inoperative, this obsolescence doesn't have to be a cause for gloomy indignation, for the wringing of hands or of necks. Just as there is no opportunity which cannot be abused, so there is no abuse which cannot be an opportunity. The writers against clichés tacitly recognize this, even if they don't openly acknowledge it, when they find that they themselves can illuminate clichés by—can do so only by—calling up clichés to aid them. By using clichés. But using is the nub. Not being used by them.

Marshall McLuhan is one of the few who have explicitly delighted in the opportunities presented by clichés. *From Cliché to Archetype* (1970) insists that a cliché can be a probe, or even that it cannot but be a probe. McLuhan deplores those who simply cry out at clichés, 'Avaunt and quit my sight!' For a cliché is

an active, structuring, probing feature of our awareness. It performs multiple functions from release of emotion to retrieval of other clichés from both the conscious and unconscious life . . . The banishing of the cliché from serious attention was the natural gesture of literary specialists. The Theater of the Absurd has shown us some of the creative contemporary uses of cliché.[4]

Not just the theatre of the absurd either; McLuhan seizes on Hamlet's response to the clichés of the players: 'It is the very cliché, or stereotype qualifying of the actor's performance, that awakens him. Such can be the function of cliché at any time for anybody.'[5]

[4] *From Cliché to Archetype* (1970), 1971 edn, p. 55.   [5] *From Cliché to Archetype*, p. 58.

McLuhan had an air of professional high hopes. Still, we should welcome his voice against the doom-dealing despairers. I am less sure that we should welcome Anton Zijderveld. For although he too knows that we mustn't simply suppose that we can avoid clichés, his fear of them is inordinate. Countless times he warns of their *tyranny*; he shudders at the way they are *moulds* of our consciousnesses; and he laments the simple stimulus/ response way they artfully work upon us—as if stimulus / response psychology were authoritatively unimpeachable. 'It is a kind of brainwashing, and in order to be successful, a rather crass kind of behaviourism has to be applied: the cliché as stimulus has to be repeated over and over again in order to achieve the thoughtless, mechanical response it set out to elicit.'[6] I doubt whether clichés do in fact work by 'a rather crass kind of behaviourism,' but I am sure that this argument about them does.

True, Zijderveld comes in the end to acknowledge that all is not lost. But even then he is lugubrious. The most we can hope for is 'stratagems to relativize the power of clichés,' and these —especially his pages about 'comic sublimation'—turn out to be a dourly defensive business. 'Aesthetic sublimation' too is a bitter battle. There is no feeling that a cliché may become the artist's—or the witty humane conversationalist's—delighting ally. Instead, we are in a grim world where if you don't sourly subjugate clichés they will subjugate you. A feat of imagination is no more than the inflicting of defeat. What we must do is make sure that the brutal boot is on the right foot. Thus Brecht used clichés 'cynically' (a good thing, apparently), used them 'cynically in order to shatter them'. Such art gains 'a temporary victory over the power of clichés.'[7] For Zijderveld, the right metaphor is of military might. The artistic gracing of clichés, or their imaginative redemption, coarsens here into a replacing of tyranny-by-clichés with tyranny-over-clichés. Clichés are to be *attacked*. An oppressive campaign and not likely to issue in any heartfelt play of mind, whether in ordinary life or in extraordinary literature.

But it is heartfelt play of mind which the best writers elicit from a vigilant—not beady-eyed—engagement with clichés.

---

6 *On Clichés*, p. 13.   7 *On Clichés*, p. 99.

There is a continual creation of delight from the opportunities presented by the countless clichés of the times, clichés which are not to be scorned or expelled (your writing will only become haughty and *outré*), and not to be truckled to, but which are to be imaginatively, wittily, touchingly co-operated with. Clichés invite you not to think—but you may always decline the invitation, and what could better invite a thinking man to think?

Zijderveld is right to say that it is of the nature of a cliché that it has 'a capacity to bypass reflection,' but he is melodramatic when he gloomily inspissates this into 'gradually making everyone immune to reflection.' 'One suddenly realizes how easily clichés are exchanged, how rarely we hesitate to use them in daily life, and above all how seldom we apologize for their use.'[8] Speak for yourself. (But then clichés discourage that.) For a great deal of daily conversation finds wit and humour and penetration in a conscious play with clichés. Irony, not sarcasm; irony has respect for what was once a living truth within what has become a truism, and the difference between an irony and a sarcasm is—as William Empson has shown[9]—that a worthwhile irony is to some degree true in both senses.

One serious and various way you may resist a cliché's propensity to bypass reflection is by using the cliché self-reflexively, with a sense of how the very words of a particular cliché have some relation to what makes a cliché. McLuhan's anecdote doesn't say so, but it enacts this:

A teacher asked her class to use a familiar word in a new way. One boy read: 'The boy returned home with a cliché on his face'. Asked to explain his phrase, he said: 'The dictionary defines *cliché* as a "worn-out expression" '.[10]

An accident? A felicity? A trouvaille, perhaps—we live in an age which especially delights in *objets trouvés* and in found poems and which appreciates the fine fluke which is a trouvaille.

In the art of Geoffrey Hill, there is a supple and diverse sense of how a witty or rueful or sardonic reflexiveness may animate a cliché. 'It seems to be a modern fallacy that "living speech" can be heard only in intimate situations; in fact the clichés and

---

[8] *On Clichés*, p. 55.
[9] *Some Versions of Pastoral* (1935), p. 56.
[10] *From Cliché to Archetype*, p. 54.

equivocations of propaganda or of "public relations" are also part of the living speech of a society'.[11] Hill achieves dignity by rising above clichés; he achieves truthfulness by not eschewing cliché. What fascinates him is the appalling gulf between the way we usually mutter such-and-such a phrase and how we might use it if the doors of perception were cleansed. Take the end of his sombre poem 'The Guardians,' which tells how the old gather the bodies of the drowned young:

> There are silences. These, too, they endure:
> Soft comings-on; soft after-shocks of calm.
> Quietly they wade the disturbed shore;
> Gather the dead as the first dead scrape home.

'Scrape home' is a triumph, though it winces at a defeat. It is unforcedly literal, 'scrape' being the dead body as like a keel that runs ashore, and 'home' being nothing but the truth. But in the gap between such a way of scraping home and our usual application (in American, *scrape by?*—just winning, just safe, gulping with relief)—in that gap is the appalling heart-break of the poem, the gap between what we always hope of life and what we often get. Yet a full recognition of why the cliché here is so alive, even while it gazes upon the bodies of the dead, would have to incorporate some feeling of the cliché *scrape home* as itself here scraping home. Only just. Our relief is partly (only partly, because Hill doesn't give in to the fashionable wish that poems should have *no* subject other than their own workings) a matter of how the cliché itself is brought home to us. To use a cliché is to take a risk. But then nothing is more dangerous than playing safe.

In Hill's poems, as in those of Marvell and Jonson which he has praised, 'the perspective requires the utterance of deliberate cliché, but cliché rinsed and restored to function as responsible speech.'

Jonson's language is frequently literary in the best sense of the term. That is, its method requires that certain words and phrases, by constant repetition in popular literary modes, shall have been reduced to easy, unquestioned connotations. These connotations are then disturbingly scrutinized. Pope's:

> Oblig'd by hunger and Request of friends

[11] (1960); *The Lords of Limit* (1984), p. 39.

requires for its effect the common formula of gentlemanly apologia, on the part of coy amateurs bringing out verse. It is 'hunger' that blasts the cliché into a new perspective.[12]

'A new perspective'—that is, something to break through our unseeing blandness. As with Robert Lowell, the accusation of tastelessness is not risked but courted; 'The Humanist' suddenly erupts within brackets: '(Tasteless! tasteless!)'. So often have we seen St Sebastian pierced with arrows, that we cannot but be glazed to it, see it through glass. But not here, in 'The Martyrdom of Saint Sebastian' ('Of Commerce and Society: VI'):

> Naked, as if for swimming, the martyr
> Catches his death in a little flutter
> Of plain arrows. A grotesque situation,
> But priceless, and harmless to the nation.

'Catches his death' is certainly shockingly tasteless in its evocation of the common cold, but who could deny that it is altogether accurate as a description of Sebastian's way of death? And if it first of all tells the truth, what is the objection to its being shocking? Anyway, with again a sardonic reflexiveness, the cliché doesn't just tell of the death, it does what a poem, like a painting, has to do: it 'catches his death'. The likeness, like the moment, is caught all right. Added to which, 'catches' doesn't sneer at the martyr, since it catches his decisiveness, his skill, and his power to will what God wills.

The word that has a very telling look is 'grotesque'. Its range of conflicting emotions is at work again on 'a little flutter'. Once more this is both literally accurate, as the arrows wing home, and desolatingly inadequate in its reduction of martyrdom to the petty thrill of laying a small bet. '*Flutter*: *OED* 4. *slang*. An attempt or "shy" at anything; an exciting venture at betting or cards'; to which the 1972 Supplement adds: 'Now usually used of speculation or betting on a small scale'. Pascal's wager, with its concomitant martyrdom, has dwindled to a moment at the races, the comfiest of calculated roguish risks, 'a little flutter'. Yet the risk that the poet has taken is not comfy; 'a little flutter' (self-reflexively, though not only that) bets the whole

---

[12] *The Lords of Limit*, pp. 45-6.

poem, and stakes its author's reputation, on being able to snatch the victory of art from the defeat that is ordinarily cliché. But then the martyr had done likewise. The rhyme *martyr/flutter* flaps with grim limpness, but St Sebastian had not gone limp.

The climax of these contrarieties is 'priceless'—is there any other epithet which we can apply quite casually both to an invaluable work of art and to a preposterously comic situation? The woundingly comic effect here is achieved by a method resembling that which Hill pinpointed in Isaac Rosenberg's poetry, 'the skilful juxtaposing of elevated and banal diction'.[13] Except that Hill compacts this, since we are given not juxtaposition but interpenetration: 'catches his death', like 'scrape home', is both elevated *and* banal. Hence the remarkable economy of Hill at his best. The ironic mode, as Yvor Winters showed,[14] is often a very wasteful one, since it may spend words on doing something and then more words on undoing it. The simultaneous duplicity (in the best sense) of Hill's poems is a very different matter.

The deliberate and responsible use of cliché can foster critical self-consciousness; not a paralyzed self-consciousness of the narcissistic kind that disappears into itself, but the kind that properly grounds its imaginative flights in the cliché's unservile acknowledgement that it is a cliché. In 'Ovid in the Third Reich,' Hill has written a poem which says what can be said for those Germans who remained silent. The remarkable thing is that at the same time he says what must be said against them.

> I love my work and my children. God
> Is distant, difficult. Things happen.
> Too near the ancient troughs of blood
> Innocence is no earthly weapon.

Eloquence is saved from becoming oratory because that last line teeters on the edge of a collapse into self-pitying despair. But the (unspoken) cliché—'Innocence is no earthly good,' no earthly use—does offer a faint hope that innocence may be a heavenly weapon, a heavenly good or of heavenly use. For where else did the cliché *earthly* come from, where but in a con-

---

[13] *The Concise Encyclopedia of English and American Poets and Poetry*, ed. Stephen Spender and Donald Hall (1963), p. 278.

[14] 'The Double Mood', *In Defense of Reason* (1960), pp. 65-74.

trast of the earthly and the heavenly? Once more, though, the tragic wit is salted with a sense that in the ordinary way—if imagination were not to take its opportunity—the cliché, these very words, would be no earthly good, no earthly use.

Yet if the innocence of a German would not protect him, how much more must this have been true of a Jew?

> I have learned one thing: not to look down
> So much upon the damned.

'Look down', with the profound uncertainty of 'despise' or 'see from Heaven'—and with a further uncertainty unfolding: is the reference to the traditional pastime-reward of contemplating the tortures of the damned? Or are we hearing of a prudence that is by no means entirely ignoble, and that warns us against staring for ever at suffering? For that way, either madness or hardheartedness lies.

Or there is the end of Hill's 'Orpheus and Eurydice':

> Love goes, carrying compassion
> To the rawly-difficult;
> His countenance, his hands' motion,
> Serene even to a fault.

The shrivelled phrase blossoms wonderfully. 'Even to a fault': it admits our doubts about the ideal of self-sacrificial love, yet at the same time it offers an unforgettable feeling for what true forgiveness is, 'serene even to a fault.' Others' faults are twined so simply with its own. But then what might ordinarily be a fault is here redeemed: the use of a cliché like *to a fault*.

Geoffrey Hill's poems are not aloof, but they are high. Yet he has his own proper accommodation with our casually down-to-earth clichés. So does an artist of a very different kind. Bob Dylan's art does not traffic in clichés, but it travels far and near by the vehicle of cliché. For what could a popular song be which scorned or snubbed cliché? Those who wish to disparage the art of Dylan ought to make sure, at least, that they go no further than did William James in his affectionate disparagement of William Shakespeare:

He seems to me to have been a professional *amuser*, in the first instance, with a productivity like that of a Dumas, or a Scribe; but possessing what no other amuser has possessed, a lyric splendor added to his

rhetorical fluency, which has made people take him for a more essentially serious human being than he was. Neurotically and erotically,
he was hyperaesthetic, with a playful graciousness of character never
surpassed. He could be profoundly melancholy; but even then was
controlled by his audience's needs . . . Was there ever an author of
such emotional importance whose reaction against false conventions
of life was such an absolute zero as his?[15]

For Shakespeare, read Dylan? But would it anyway be the best
thing for an artist to do with false conventions of life, or of
language: to *react against* them?

Dylan has a newly instinctive grasp of the age-old instincts
which created a cliché in the first place, and this is manifest on
all the occasions when he throws new light on an old cliché, or
rotates a cliché so that a facet of it catches a new light. At the
same time, like the very unlike Geoffrey Hill, he often grounds
his wit, humour, and pathos on an intuition as to how a cliché
may incite reflection, and not preclude it, by being self-reflexive.

> Well, ask me why I'm drunk alla time,
> It levels my head and eases my mind.
> I just walk along and stroll and sing,
> I see better days and I do better things.
>   ('I Shall Be Free')

The phrase *seen better days* has itself seen better days—that would
do as the definition of a cliché. But Dylan brings it from its past
into his and our present, by turning it into the present tense, 'I
see better days'; and by marrying it to 'and I do better things,'
he does a far better thing with it than usual. He eases it from
a dim past into a bright present. He helps us see it in a better
light, so that instead of its ordinary sad backward glance, there
is a step forward, the strolling of an unaggressive intoxication
which refreshes the flat old phrase. Just an accident? There are
too many such happy accidents in Dylan's songs for them not
to be felicities. Anyway, Dylan knows perfectly well that the
tired phrase *seen better days* is usually imprisoned within its ex-
hausted meaning—you can hear him sing the glum words in
someone else's song on a tape from 1961. His own 'I Shall Be
Free' is free from the clichéness of its clichés, without getting

[15] To T. S. Perry, 22 May 1910; *The Letters of William James* (1920), ii 336.

proudly trapped in the illusion that you can free yourself from clichés by having no truck with them.

'I see better days' has its appealingly wide-eyed hopefulness. But Dylan can narrow his eyes, suspicious of too easy a sympathy with those who are dangerously wrong. So take the cliché *see through your eyes*. Ordinarily, casually, it means putting yourself in the other man's place, seeing things through his eyes. Far harder to do than the easy saying of it would suggest. Possibly a very misguided thing to do, too. So Dylan wrests the cliché into the more stringent sense which goes with sharp-eyed suspicion: 'seeing through things' as knowing their cunning and hypocrisy.

> A world war can be won
> You want me to believe
> But I see through your eyes
> And I see through your brain
> Like I see through the water
> That runs down my drain.
>
> ('Masters of War')

For the first verse had sung 'I just want you to know / I can see through your masks'—the vigilant sense of 'see through'— so that when we hear 'But I see through your eyes,' we see that it doesn't mean the usual blandly magnanimous thing ('from your point of view'), but the stubborn opposite: I see what your eyes are trying to hide. The cliché has been alerted, and we are alerted to its clichéness, seeing the words from a new perspective, a different point of view, and seeing penetratingly through them.

A cliché begins as heartfelt, and then its heart sinks. But no song about lovers and their hearts can afford to turn away from those truths which may never get old but whose turns of phrase have got old and grey and full of sleep. The trouble with a cliché like *take it to heart* is that by now it's almost impossible to take it to heart. Yet genius with words is often a matter, as T. S. Eliot said,[16] of being original with the minimum of alteration, and such is one of the evidences of Dylan's genius.

> So if you find someone that gives you all of her love,
> Take it to your heart, don't let it stray . . .
>
> ('I Threw It All Away')

[16] Introductory Essay to *London* and *The Vanity of Human Wishes* (1930).

THE FORCE OF POETRYTHE FORCE OF POETRY

'Take it to heart' becomes 'take it to your heart,' just enough
to take it into the heartfelt; *it* stands for 'all of her love,' and
there is the tiny touching swerve from 'someone' in the previous
line—you'd think it was going to be 'So if you find someone
that gives you all of her love / Take *her* to your heart,' and
take her in your arms.

'Make it new,' commanded Ezra Pound from the captain's
tower. It goes for clichés too. Not one is irredeemable, thanks
especially to the grace of that self-reflexiveness which, so long
as it doesn't escalate its claim as if it were the only thing which
art were ever preoccupied with, can rightly be valued as a great
deal of late twentieth-century criticism has valued it: as a power
for wit, humour, true acknowledgement, thought, and feeling
in the renovation of the state of the language.

LIES

The epigraph for the 1975 conference of the Northeast Modern Language Association, on 'Language, Literature, and Change,' was this:

In every culture, language and literature have served both to cause and to reflect economic, political, philosophical, social changes. The conference will explore the relationship of language and literature to cultural change.

Such considerations are, among other things, anthropological in the interplay of the human condition and a cultural condition or conditioning. Taking heart from the fact that Raymond Firth said that 'One of the functions of anthropology is to ask questions about the obvious,'[1] I should like to ask some questions about a particular instance of the obvious: that *lie* in English means both to say something false while knowing it to be so, and to rest or (expressive of bodily posture) to be in a prostrate or recumbent position. A pun, after all, is likely to be a compacting or a constellating of language and literature, of social and cultural circumstance.

There is potency in the pun or the suggestive homophone. 'Miscegenation' must be a bad thing. Does it not confess that it is a mis-something? (All it really confesses is that it is a *miscere-*something, but the word still carries its infection.) Similarly, 'What's good for General Motors is good for America' presses us to concede the claim made by *general* (not invidiously particular or sectional, and with a touch of 'captains of industry' authority); a quite other route would have to be taken if the language were to press us to concede that 'What's good for A. B. Dick is good for America.' Again, the political energy of a *strike* (and perhaps the credulity as to its effectiveness) profits from the crisp energy of the word, a word—*strike*—which accords to an enterprise which is one of withdrawal, passivity, and attrition the associations of something which is on the offensive, active, and speedy.

---

[1] *Times Literary Supplement*, 21 February 1975. My essay is much indebted to Mary Douglas.

George Steiner has described the poles of such associative contingencies:

The associative content which contingencies import into letters, numbers, syllables, and words can be private or social or both. The associative contour lies along a spectrum which extends the whole way from the solipsism of the maniac to human generality . . . At one pole we find a 'pathology of Babel,' autistic strategies which attach hermetic meanings to certain sounds or which deliberately invert the lexical, habitual usage of words. At the other extreme, we encounter the currency of banal idiom, the colloquial shorthand of daily chatter from which constant exchange has all but eroded any particular substance. Every conceivable modulation exists between these two extremes.[2]

But notice the equivocation in 'all but eroded': in 'daily chatter,' 'constant exchange has all but eroded any particular substance.' Is the inescapable habit of certain associative contingencies (the verbal identity of *lie* and *lie*, for instance) inevitably a process which all but erodes any particular substance of associative content? The opposite assertion could no less persuasively be made: that it is the daily chatter, the constant exchange, the altogether-unnoticed coincidings and associations which work most strongly upon their users. For these are insinuatingly and insidiously unremarked: no conscious vigilance will secure a speaker against those subliminal associations which proffer themselves—or, rather, do nothing so obtrusive as proffer themselves—as natural, innocent and neutral rather than, as they more probably are, potencies. The 'collective consciousness' posited by some anthropologists—for example, in the matter of ritual classifications for left hand and right hand—is the more telling when we envisage it as a collective unconsciousness or subconsciousness which is nevertheless historically, culturally, and linguistically created and creative. Take the fact that alone of the pronouns I is capitalized in English. Insofar as we are conscious of the fact, most of us find it a fact scarcely visible through the strong colouring of E. E. Cummings, or, rather, e. e. cummings. We do not go about perpetually conscious of the privileged capitalization of *I*. Does this mean ('constant exchange has all but eroded any particular substance') that this striking linguistic fact scarcely impinges upon

[2] *After Babel* (1975), p. 171.

us? Or does it mean—and this is no less likely—that it impinges
with the great and enduringly active power of a constant pressure, like that of the weight of the air upon our heads, which
does not seem to *strike* us at all? And the French, who say
lower-case *je* with a commitment to *égalité* and *fraternité* that does
not set it apart from you and he and we and they, are they not
fed by the daily bread of *their* language? The effect of the nutri-
ment is another matter; it could be said that the English, thanks
to their language (which itself exists thanks to them), are comfortable egotists, happy to erect *I* (although not *me*) above the
rest of you. Or it could be said that the English acknowledge
that *I* is, unavoidably, a pronoun different from all the rest,
since its user must be in this sense privileged, and that what
the English language asks recognition of, or embodies recognition of, is this unegotistically realistic consideration. Do not
pretend—the language might remind us—that you *can* speak of
yourself as you speak of others. Whereas the French, who go
about egalitarianly *je*, humbly lower-case, have not paid more
than lip service to this *égalité* and *fraternité* any more than to the
larger ones, and really mean JE. What matters is that *I/je* does
suggest an axis, an axis for egotism, its forms and pressures;
which way the considerations then run along the axis is a
different and difficult question. One does not have to be
Marshall McLuhan to believe that these daily pressures both
create and are created by frames of mind, lines of thought,
conduits of feeling. When Professor Steiner says 'constant exchange has all but eroded any particular substance', it sounds
as if he is making light of the ubiquitous unnoticed features of a
language; but then his metaphor—'currency' and 'exchange'—
may remind us that as long as coins continue to be in circulation it doesn't make any difference how worn or eroded they
are.

Lie/lie: Barbara Herrnstein Smith has said that this is 'probably the most poetically fruitful homonym in English.'[3] I should
go further and say that *lie/lie* is—or rather, has been for centuries, as it is now under threat from historical and cultural
changes—simply the most important pun in the language. It is
even more important than its grand contestant, the constellation
of *sense*—a word upon which those two great students of words

---

[3] *Poetic Closure* (1968), p. 166.

and their cultural contexts and implications, William Empson
and C. S. Lewis, bent their eliciting powers.[4] As with *sense*, so
with *lie* the importance of a pun must be in the first place a
matter of the enduring and central matters which it encom-
passes. Lies are important irrespective of any pun that may
visit them. For one thing, the telling of the truth is necessary to
those social and cultural agreements without which there cannot be a society or a culture. Even the devils know this, for as
Sir Thomas Browne said, 'so also in Moral verities, although
they deceive us, they lie not unto each other; as well understanding that all community is continued by Truth, and that of
Hell cannot consist without it.'[5] For another thing, telling the
truth is a necessary condition for the existence of a language at
all. Which is why in the language—indeed, in most or all
languages, one may guess—there is no truth verb that is the
counterpart to the verb to lie. (And there are, from similar
causes or with similar effects, no puns on *true* and *truth* that
amount to anything.) You cannot truth, a fact which both makes
the telling of the truth a less glib matter than lying ('the truth,
the whole truth, and nothing but the truth'), and also brings
out that speaking has to be posited on a presumption of the
speaking of the truth.[6] Even if it were not accepted that words

[4] William Empson, *The Structure of Complex Words* (1951); C. S. Lewis, *Studies in Words* (1960).

[5] Sir Thomas Browne, *Pseudodoxia Epidemica*. Dr. Johnson adopted and adapted these lines in his *Adventurer*, No. 50 (28 April 1753).

[6] Yet the deflection of the verb *sooth/soothe* (from Old English Soðian) is instructive: from 'to prove to be true' (*OED* instances from 950 to 1588); through 'to declare to be true; to uphold as the truth' (1553-1616); into 'to put forward a lie or untruth as being true' (1591-1616); and so into the current 'to smoothe, gloss over, flatter, or render calm' (1697 on). So that *soothe*, far from meaning 'tell you the truth,' has come to mean 'make you feel better, probably by off-white lies'—a dismaying index of social and cultural change. And was it a sense both of the urgency of ascertaining the truth and of the deep uneasy longing that it might be confidently ascertained and assev-erated, might miraculously be—in Hamlet's words—'as easy as lying,' which created in the riven years from 1638 to 1689 a sudden and unique birth of stillborn truth verbs?

OED: Truth, *v.*

+ 3. *trans.* To name or call truly; to describe with truth as.

Obs. nonce-use.

1638 FORD *Fancies* II.ii, The ancients Who chatted of the golden age, feign'd trifles. Had they dreamt this, they would have truth'd it heav'n.

+ 4. *intr.* with *it*: To speak or deal truly (nonce-rendering of Gr. ἀληθεύειν in Eph.iv. 15). *Obs.*

1648 T. HILL *Serm. Truth & Love* 21 Truthing it in love, which were an admirable motto for saints. 1656 S. WINTER *Serm.* Ep. Ded., I have without gall. . . . manag-

about words all have a special force, though not necessarily a greater force than other words (for this claim might be merely a literary critic's professional predilection), it is nevertheless the case that *lie* has the special potency of immediately paradoxical possibilities, since it strikes at the roots of language and may strike, self-incriminatingly, at itself. The importance of lying therefore ranges from all those daily falsehoods in the ordinary world to such abstract but intense considerations of language, society, and philosophy. In 1970 there was published a book wholly devoted to the paradox of the liar.[7]

Yet the importance of the phenomenon of lying is a necessary but not a sufficient condition of any claimed importance for the pun on *lie* and *lying*. Then there are the linguistic pressures on the word *lie* which themselves make the word a creator of pressure. There is, first, a depopulation around *lie* which gives it the potency of salience. For instance, *lie* calls up no manifest etymology for us; as a short and simple Old English word, it seems—as does the word *truth*—to be a root concept behind or below which we cannot penetrate. (The contrast would be with the words *veracity* and *mendacity* which send our thoughts abroad, in both senses.) Next, there is the fact that there are no profound or memorable proverbs about lies or truth, so that the words themselves have to muster all the energy of the phenomena. A comparable depopulation, lending prominence and salience to *lie* and *truth*, is that by which a great many lie and truth terms have fallen out of the language, as if by some evolutionary concentration upon the survival of the fittest words. Middle English *gab*, to lie, survives only in its weakened child, *gabble*; *leasing* has gone, as has the plural *lyings*; the adjective *lie* (from Old English *lyȝe*, lying); various transitive and quasi-transitive uses of to lie (*OED* 3 and 4); and 'to give the lie to'

ed this controversie, truthing it in love.
    Truthify, *v. nonce-wd.* [f. TRUTH + (1) FY.] *intr.* To act according to truth; to deal truly. (Cf. TRUTH *v.* 4).
    1647 TRAPP *Comm. Eph.* iv. 15 Speaking the truth, or Doing the truth, as the Vulgar hath it. Truthifying, or following the truth, as one rendereth it. 1689 M. SYLVESTER *Serm. Heb.* x 24-5 (1690) 334 b. This is indeed . . . to truthifie in Love, if I may make an English Word to express the valor of the Greek Word, ἀληθεύοντες ἐν ἀγάπῃ.

[7] Robert L. Martin, ed., *The Paradox of the Liar* (1970).

(accuse of lying). You can no longer 'make a lie,' you can only
tell it; you can now lie only *about*, not—as you once could—of,
on, or upon (*OED* 1b).[8]

Again, there is the salience given by the marked absence of
synonyms for *lie*; all we have is either ephemeral or infantine slang (bounce, crammer, whopper, fib—to cite Roget's
Thesaurus) or euphemisms: *falsehood* and *untruth*, neither of which
strictly speaking means *lie* and both of which therefore can on
occasions have the special offence of a euphemism. Dr. Johnson
knew perfectly well what *lie* means, and yet 'Johnson had
accustomed himself to use the word *lie*, to express a mistake or
an errour in relation; in short, when the *thing was not so as told*,
though the relator did not *mean* to deceive. When he thought
there was intentional falsehood in the relator, his expression
was, "He *lies*, and he *knows* he lies." '[9] Boswell remarks that
this usage was 'to the great offence of those who did not know
him.' Yet *falsehood* then has to be called in exculpatingly as even
more offensive, once Johnson has given offence with his idiosyncratic use of the word *lie*; Mrs. Piozzi records that Burney
had asked her whether she had indeed subscribed £100 to
building a bridge:

'It is very comical, is it not, Sir?' said I, turning to Dr. Johnson, 'that
people should tell such unfounded stories.' 'It is,' answered he, 'neither
comical nor serious, my dear; it is only a wandering lie.' This was
spoken in his natural voice, without a thought of offence, I am con-

---

[8] We need to remember that there is this distinction between *lie with* and *lie on* (tell
lies about) as well as the opposite thing, their sexual overlapping, if we are to feel fully
the cruel imagination of Iago's words to Othello, which persist in intimating mendacity
while insisting on carnality:

Othello. Hath he said anything?
Iago.   He hath (my Lord) but be you well assur'd,
     No more than he'le un-sweare.
Othello. What hath he said?
Iago.   Why, that he did: I know not what he did.
Othello. What? What?
Iago.   Lye.
Othello. With her?
Iago.   With her? On her: what you will.
Othello. Lye with her? lye on her? We say lye on her, when they be-lye-her. Lye with her: that's
     fullsome . . .   (IV i)
[9] James Boswell, *Life of Johnson*, ed. G. Birkbeck Hill, rev. L. F. Powell (1934-64),
iv 49.

fident; but up bounced Burney in a towering passion, and to my much amaze, put on the hero, surprising Dr. Johnson into a sudden request for pardon, and protestation of not having ever intended to accuse his friend of a falsehood.

Falsehood there suffers the nemesis of euphemism; what Johnson meant, after all, was rather that he *had* intended to attribute to his friend a falsehood but had *not* intended to accuse him of a lie. If we ask why Johnson, who of all men was the most scrupulously concerned with the truth (including lexicographical truth),[10] should have wished to fly in the face of the language, and use *lie* neutrally (otherwise saying 'he *lies*, and he *knows* he lies,' as if *lie* didn't *mean* knowing it to be so)—if we ask why Johnson embraced this idiosyncrasy, an answer might be that, while knowing full well that a man does not have to be in haste when he says all men are liars, he nevertheless had a deep wish to think better of mankind than that. He had a deep wish both to acknowledge the prevalence of lying[11] and yet to salvage something for human dignity through the wishful pretence that perhaps somehow all men are liars and yet don't 'know' they are lying when they do so.

The final linguistic consideration is one of the many asymmetries between *lie* and *truth*, one which lends to *lie* (and to its pun) a range of suggestions which are denied to or disdained by *truth*. This is the fact that rhymes for *truth* are few, and only one of them has much potentiality for discovering or urging insights. *Booth* and *tooth* and *uncouth* have little to offer in a relationship with *truth*;[12] *ruth* (pity) did have, but has now left the English language to dwell in the realms of Poesy; as has *sooth*, which had the truth of a tautology in rhyming with truth.[13] Which leaves, as perhaps the only word into metaphorical

[10] Johnson 'would not allow his servant to say he was not at home when he really was,' and argued this out (Boswell, i 436).

[11] 'He was indeed so much impressed with the prevalence of falsehood, voluntary or unintentional, that I never knew any person who, upon hearing an extraordinary circumstance told, discovered more of the *incredulus odi*' (Boswell, iii 229); see, too, *Adventurer*, No. 50 (28 April 1753).

[12] Thomas Hardy added to his copy of Walker's *Rhyming Dictionary*, under 'youth,' the word 'blooth' (bloom), but the word has not flourished (Robert Gittings, *Young Thomas Hardy*, 1975, p. 84).

[13] *OED* sooth. *sb.* 'In common use down to the first half of the 17th cent.; after this apparently obsolete (exc. perhaps in ['by my sooth'] until revived as a literary archaism, chiefly by Scott and contemporary writers.'

relation with which a rhyme can creatively bring *truth*, the word *youth*—a rhyme which has indeed done things for poets from Shakespeare (Sonnet 138) to Philip Larkin (the bitter end of 'Send No Money')—and to Bob Dylan, who in 'Something There Is about You' deftly supplements his rhyme of *youth* and *truth* with the names of *Ruth* and *Duluth*.

This marked paucity of suggestive rhyming for *truth*, which lends it a lonely dignity and integrity, contrasts sharply with the manifest and manifold rhymes which crowd upon or from *lie*: *fly* (with its altruism or cowardice), *die* (with its moment of truth and its horizontality), *I* and *my* (with their sincerity or insincerity), *eye* (with its honesty or shiftiness), and so on. Shakespeare's sonnets are haunted by such rhymes:

> If *I* could write the beauty of your *eyes*,
> And in fresh numbers number all your graces,
> The age to come would say this Poet *lies*,
> Such heavenly touches nere toucht earthly faces.
>   (Sonnet 17)

> For *I* have sworne thee faire: more perjurde *eye*,
> To swere against the truth so foule a *lie*.
>   (Sonnet 152)[14]

Shakespeare rhymes *eye* with the nonmendacious *lie* in Sonnets 1, 2, 31, and 153; and on three occasions does the same thing but differently—that is, with an anti-pun, not simply meaning *lie* and not meaning mendacious *lie*, but meaning the whole unit '*lie*: not mendacious *lie*,' so that the mendacious sense is called to mind but is fended off. The rhyme on each of these occasion is *eyes*:

> To finde where your true Image pictur'd lies.
>   (Sonnet 24)

> And says in him their faire appearance lyes.
>   (Sonnet 46)[15]

> They know what beautie is, see where it lyes,
> Yet what the best is, take the worst to be.
>   (Sonnet 137)

---

[14] Where the usual emendation from *eye* to *I* blurs the pun.
[15] Editors emend *their* to *thy*.

It is Shakespeare's work which provides the transition from those linguistic considerations which give salience to the *lie/lie* pun, to the more largely human considerations which give importance to it. For there is a *prima facie* likelihood that a pun which is so ubiquitously necessary to the greatest writer in the language is a very important pun.[16] Shakespeare, who needs and wants the words *lie*, *lies*, and *lying* hundreds of times in his work, has only three times the punless form *lied*. We should ask ourselves whether the fretfulness or impatience which we sometimes feel with those puns is to Shakespeare's discredit or to ours—have we lost, or become blinded to, the important considerations that presumably seemed to Shakespeare to raise above triviality such an insistence as this?

> That Lye, shall lie so heavy on my Sword,
> That it shall render Vengeance, and Revenge,
> Till thou the Lye-giver, and that Lye, do lye
> In earth as quiet, as thy Fathers Scull.
> *(Richard II, IV i)*

Or there is the opposite of insistence, there is the anti-pun of *Much Ado about Nothing*:

> Done to death by slanderous tongues,
> Was the Hero that here lies:
> Death in guerdon of her wrongs,
> Gives her fame which never dies:
> (V iii)

Such intimations are everywhere alert in Shakespeare:

> Who tels me true, though in his Tale lye death,
> I heare him as he flatter'd.
> *(Antony and Cleopatra, IV ii)*

> That I may tell pale-hearted Feare, it lies;
> And sleepe in spight of Thunder.
> *(Macbeth, IV i)*

> There is no shuffling, there the Action lyes
> In his true Nature.
> *(Hamlet, III iii)*

Hamlet, indeed, is one of the two plays which most challenge us to retrieve, or else to despair of, the depth of Shakespeare's pre-

[16] P. B. Taylor has a note on lie and die in *Romeo and Juliet* (*Archiv*, ccxi, 1974, 65).

occupation with this pun. Can we gratefully accommodate, within the seriousness of Claudius' lying and of Hamlet's bitter truths ('That's a faire thought to ly between Maid's legs,' or ''Tis as easie as lying', III ii), such exchanges as those between Hamlet and the Gravedigger, or must they be grudgingly tolerated as tiring and tiresome?

Hamlet. I thinke it be thine [thy grave] indeed: for thou liest in it.
Gravedigger. You lye out on't Sir, and therefore it is not yours: for my part, I doe not lye in't; and yet it is mine.
Hamlet. Thou dost lye in't, to be in't and say 'tis thine: 'tis for the dead, not for the quicke, therefore thou lyest.
Gravedigger. 'Tis a quicke lye Sir, 'twill away againe from me to you.

(V i)

The other play which issues the same challenge to our powers of recovery is *Othello*, a play about lethal lying which asks us to take seriously both its tragic puns—

Othello. What hath he said?
Iago. Why, that he did: I know not what he did.
Othello. What? What?
Iago. Lye.
Othello. With her?
Iago. With her? On her: what you will.

(IV i)

—and its tiresome comedy about the same *he*, directed at that same *her*:

Desdemona. Do you know Sirrah, where Lieutenant Cassio lyes?
Clown. I dare not say he lies any where.
Desdemona. Why man?
Clown. He's a Soldier, and for me to say a Souldier lyes, 'tis stabbing.
Desdemona. Go too: where lodges he?
Clown. To tell you where he lodges, is to tel you where I lye.
Desdemona. Can any thing be made of this?
Clown. I know not where he lodges, and for mee to devise a lodging, and say he lies heere, or he lies there, were to lye in mine owne throat.

(III iv)

We are impelled to ask the question which Desdemona asks about all this *lie/lie* business: 'Can any thing be made of this?' An answer can begin with what Shakespeare made of it in Sonnet 138.

When my love sweares that she is made of truth,
I do beleeve her though I know she lyes,
That she might thinke me some untuterd youth,
Unlearned in the worlds false subtilties.
Thus vainely thinking that she thinkes me young,
Although she knowes my dayes are past the best,
Simply I credit her false speaking tongue,
On both sides thus is simple truth supprest:
But wherefore sayes she not she is unjust?
And wherefore say not I that I am old?
O loves best habit is in seeming trust,
And age in love, loves not t'have yeares told.
   Therefore I lye with her, and she with me,
   And in our faults by lyes we flattered be.

It is an extraordinary evocation, positively Proustian, of 'simple truth' and of complex lying; indeed, I should have said that this sonnet is unquestionably a profound treatment of the *lie/lie* pun were it not that someone has questioned the very presence of that pun. We should be grateful to Douglas Hamer[17] for alerting us to the further pun on the swordsmanship sense of *lie*; but we should be ungrateful to him for trying to extirpate the other pun.

The sonnet tells how Shakespeare and the woman made a love-game of telling white lies about themselves in the hope of making themselves more acceptable: Beatrice and Benedick 'lie with' each other in much the same way. Though now always taken in its crude sexual sense, the phrase has only two primary meanings: (*a*) 'therefore I tell her lies, and she me,' and (*b*) 'Therefore I fence with her (in lies), and she with me (likewise).' The sexual sense is accidental, not primary, and is best seen as an associated sexual quibble of the kind so loved by Shakespeare. In sense (*b*) he uses an image derived from fencing, one ignored by *O.E.D.* and Onions, but not by Schmidt: (i) 'Thou knowest my old ward [guard in fencing]. Here I lay, and thus I bore my point' (I *Henry IV*, II.iv.216), where 'Here I lay' means that he assumed the posture of self-defence, which implies counterattacking, which posture he illustrates; (ii) 'One knows not at what ward you lie' (*Troilus*, I. ii. 283), and 'at all these wards I lie' (288), but here, because the topic is Cressida's behaviour, the punning is indeed sleazily sexual, though the primary reference is to the posture of

---

[17] Douglas Hamer, review of P. Martin, *Shakespeare's Sonnets: Self, Love and Art*, in *Review of English Studies*, n.s. xxv (1974), 78.

self-defence in fencing. The two lines in the sonnet thus mean, 'Therefore I fence with her in lies, and she with me, and by lying about our own shortcomings we present ourselves as better than we are.' Beds, in short, are out.

A man who finds the tone of this tragically embittered poem,

> When my love sweares that she is made of truth,
> I do beleeve her though I know she lyes,

to be that of 'a love-game of telling white lies' (white lies? the man lying about his age and the woman about her infidelity?) —a man who feels that the feelings of this sonnet are like the love-game banter of Beatrice and Benedick in *Much Ado*—wants his feelings seen to. But more important, Mr. Hamer has to acknowledge that his own *Troilus* instances are 'sleazily sexual,' and for all the shortness of his conclusion—'Beds, in short, are out'—he doesn't himself seem to have been very good at excluding them, since he has earlier said: 'The sexual sense is accidental, not primary, and is best seen as an associated sexual quibble of the kind so loved by Shakespeare.' Accidental, primary, and associated all seem to me to be quibblings; but what is sure is that, if the sexual sense of *lie* is best seen as a sexual quibble of the kind so loved by Shakespeare, beds, in short, are in.

The importance of the *lie/lie* pun is that it concentrates an extraordinarily ranging and profound network of truth-testing situations and postures. It brings mendacity up against those situations and postures which constitute the great moments or endurances of truth: the child-bed, the love-bed, the bed of sleep and dreams, the sick-bed, the death-bed, the grave. . . . And even perhaps the modern secular counterpart to the confessional's kneeling: the psychiatrist's couch. It concentrates this network, or rather concentrated it, since historical and cultural circumstances are now disintegrating it.

Notice that *lie/lie* disconcerts, while it nevertheless does not simply overturn or deny, the widespread association of the upright with the strong and good, and of the prostrate or supine with the weak and bad. (Correct upstanding rectitude, as against the prone who take it lying down.)

> Let us honour if we can
> The vertical man,

Though we value none
But the horizontal one.
(W. H. Auden)

What happens is not that *lie/lie* denies or overturns this align-
ment or allegiance but that the pun questions it or resists its
complacent application. Mendacity in the pun is neither identified with the supine, nor is it opposed by the supine: it is confronted with a posture which is frequently an important test of
truth, a moment importantly of truth, or of lies. Not a reversal,
but a proper recalcitrance. So that the pun is not of the kind
which asks recognition for the parallel or cognate (when, say,
whole and *holy* are brought back into that congruity which pre-
vailed in their etymological root), nor is it of the right-angled or
antithetical kind (as when *cleave*, cut apart, plays against *cleave*,
cling together),[18] but is a pun of, in both senses, the most testing kind.

Most puns are intimations of a metaphorical relationship, in
which each of the two words may be seen under the aspect of
the other; thus the *heart/hart* and the *dear/deer* puns invite us to
see something about love by viewing it as hunting, and something about hunting by viewing it as love. Such puns are no less
socially circumstanced than any others. What for Shakespeare
clearly embodied some important insights into love has now—
thanks largely to the decay of hunting—dwindled into a pun
which can figure seriously in a poem only when its decay is itself
part of the subject, as in Bernard Bergonzi's 'Descartes and the
Animals,' which ends:

> Man, born to think, and out of thinking born,
> was that one beast that felt its natural part.
> And from the woods a shrill triumphant horn
> sounded for the swift and broken hart.

Now the *lie/lie* pun does not embody an aspect or image or
metaphor: it embodies a test or vigilance or admonition. Such a
vigilance must not, then, be confused with a reversal, though it
may amount to one, in that a man lying may be a man being

---

[18] See Freud, 'The Antithetical Sense of Primal Words,' *Jahrbuch*, bk. 2 (1910),
reprinted in *Collected Papers* (1925), vol iv. It is striking that 'upright' used also to mean
'flat on one's back,' as in Donne's punning line: 'There lyes are wrongs, here safe
uprightly lye' ('Loves Warre').

very truthful—or may not. Rodney Needham, observing that 'the theme of reversal is itself one of the most pervasive and fundamental problems in social anthropology,' has said:

> All these examples involve relations between categories, i.e. they are problems in classification. They are of outstanding importance, for if our first task as social anthropologists is to discern order and make it intelligible, our no less urgent duty is to make sense of those practically universal usages and beliefs by which people create disorder, i.e. turn their classifications upside down or disintegrate them entirely.[19]

But the value of *lie/lie*, the reason why it has for centuries been such a centre of profound values, is that it neither endorses nor turns upside down; it tests. Edmund Leach has discussed the relation of puns to taboos and has said of *queen/quean* (royal consort, and prostitute or homosexual):

> Although these two words pretend to be different, indeed opposites, they really denote the same idea. A queen is a female of abnormal status in a positive virtuous sense, a quean is a person of depraved character or uncertain sex, a female of abnormal status in a negative sinful sense.

Yet *lie/lie* transcends such handy-dandy two-ends-of-a-seesaw; Leach is cogent when he urges, of the *god/dog* twist,

> No doubt there is a sense in which such facts as these can be deemed linguistic accidents, but they are accidents which have a functional utility in the way we use our language.[20]

Nevertheless 'functional utility' would not be eloquent enough for the *lie/lie* coinciding, which is a network of profound adjurations and admonitions.

Coinciding, at a particular moment in history: the two distinct verbs for lie (Old English licgan, lie down, and Old English leoȝan, tell a lie) settled their differences and settled down as *lie* in about 1300. Profound, partly because this relates love (and sex) to language. George Steiner, who is all eloquence, has dilated upon what he calls 'eros and language': 'The

---

[19] Rodney Needham's introduction to his translation of *Primitive Classification* by Emile Durkheim and Marcel Mauss (1963), pp. xxxix-xl.

[20] Edmund Leach, 'Anthropological Aspects of Language: Animal Categories and Verbal Abuse,' in *New Directions in the Study of Language*, ed. Eric H. Lenneberg (1964), pp. 25, 27.

seminal and the semantic functions (is there, ultimately, an etymological link?) [asked Steiner, and did not stay for an answer] determine the genetic and social structure of human experience. Together they construe the grammar of being.'21 Such doings can easily be overdone, and yet a pun which marries love and truth, or love and untruth, must be potentially potent.

Clearly there are many values other than truth, and it would be worth thinking about the puns and perhaps the postures which constitute the testing grounds for, say, courage or order. But equally clearly there is—or has been—in our culture a central place for a pun which brings dishonesty up against . . . not honesty or dishonesty—but an honesty-testing situation. Bacon warned against 'the false appearances that are imposed upon us by words,' but the interest of his own words is that they have to be taken very differently if the word against whose pressures he warns happens to be a word whose suggestive pressure itself constitutes a warning, as *lie/lie* does:

certain it is that words, as a Tartar's bow, do shoot back upon the understanding of the wisest, and mightily entangle and pervert the judgment . . . It must be confessed that it is not possible to divorce ourselves from these fallacies and false appearances, because they are inseparable from our nature and condition of life; so yet nevertheless the caution of them (for all elenches, as was said, are but cautions) doth extremely import the true conduct of human judgment. (*Of the Advancement of Learning*, Book ii)

But *lie/lie* is not what it was—sadly, because a crucial focus for vigilance lives in, and is kept alive by, the pun's concentration. Partly, it is the situations and postures themselves—rather than any linguistic change—which are losing their centrality (losing it to another centrality, or to centrelessness?). So the birth-bed, which was once a focus both for the intensities of the daily family and for those of legendary mystery, is now in the realm of institutions and professions. Women do not give birth at home; bastardy is no longer a profound issue; legendary births, and mighty changelings or foundlings, have shrunk to the mere rumour that hospitals are always doling out the wrong babies to their proud nonparents. An anthropologist would know that this trivializing of the birth-bed is not a feature of all

21 *After Babel*, pp. 38-9.

societies; and a historian would know that it has not always
been a feature of ours. Yet the birth-bed remains a powerful,
though slighted, truth-testing situation—a time for a mother
and father seriously to contemplate the truth about one's life
and one's love, and a time for their child later to test discovered
truths against.

The sick-bed, too, has been increasingly handed over to the
same institutions, and the medical profession is finding its
burden of truth-telling or lie-telling increasingly hard to bear;
nurses and doctors are crying out for relief from the pressures
of truth and lies which their all-but-total takeover of caring for
the sick has subjected them to.[22] The same is even more true of
the death-bed. Most of us no longer either witness or achieve
truth—or lies—in what were the profound experiential front-
ings of the sick-bed and the death-bed. We become strangers to
those who were close to us, the sick ensconced within the
'Ambulances' of Philip Larkin's poem, which needs the anti-
pun on *lies* (and *true*) for the passersby who

> sense the solving emptiness
> That lies just under all we do,
> And for a second get it whole,
> So permanent and blank and true.
>   Far
> Fiom the exchange of love to lie
> Unreachable inside a room
> The traffic parts to let go by.

But it is not a trivial matter that for almost everyone (and
'everyone' includes philosophers) an immediate and important
focus for intense concern as to whether one should ever lie is
inevitably the sick or dying recipient of the truth or lie. Dr.
Johnson's passion, even if his judgment is not concurred with,
represents an enduring reminder of how important a truth-test
this is:

But I deny the lawfulness of telling a lie to a sick man for fear of
alarming him. You have no business with consequences; you are to
tell the truth. Besides, you are not sure what effect your telling him
that he is in danger may have. It may bring his distemper to a crisis,

---

[22] See Robert Kastenbaum and Ruth Aisenberg, *The Psychology of Death* (1972),
pp. 214-25.

and that may cure him. Of all lying, I have the greatest abhorrence of this, because I believe it has been frequently practised on myself.

(Boswell, iv 305-6)

And the posture of death? Surely that sombre pun is indestructible?

> And was not death a lusty struggler
> In overthrowing James the Juggler?
> His life so little truth did use
> That here he lies—it is no news.[23]
>
> (John Hoskins, 1566-1638)

> Now from the chamber all are gone
> Who gazed and wept o'er Wellington,
> Derby and Dis do all they can
> To emulate so great a man.
> If neither can be quite so great,
> Resolved is each to LIE *in state*.
>
> (Walter Savage Landor, 1852)

> An old dissembler who lived out his lie
> Lies here as if he did not fear to die.
>
> (J. V. Cunningham, *c*.1940)

But the epitaph itself is rapidly becoming a thing of the past, so to speak. For fewer and fewer people are buried, and fewer and fewer graves are visited; and not many public figures now lie in state, and even fewer private persons lie at home in death. Our culture is not concerned to validate *these* experiences as moments of truth (though it is not clear what else is to be validated). We will soon be as far from any living continuity with the buried dead as we are from the funeral sculpture which Philip Larkin ponders in 'An Arundel Tomb,'[24] a poem which occupies itself with seeking the truth of such commemoration:

> Side by side, their faces blurred,
> The earl and countess lie in stone . . .

> They would not think to lie so long.
> Such faithfulness in effigy
> Was just a detail friends would see . . .

---

[23] J. William Hebel and Hoyt H. Hudson, *Poetry of the English Renaissance* (1929), p. 527. The poem is the subject of two excellent pages in Barbara Herrnstein Smith's *Poetic Closure,* pp. 166-7.

[24] The whole poem may be found on pp. 274-5.

> Time has transfigured them into
> Untruth. The stone fidelity
> They hardly meant has come to be
> Their final blazon, and to prove
> Our almost-instinct almost true:
> What will survive of us is love.

If time is transfiguring the child-bed, the sick-bed, the death-bed, and the grave into untruth, or at least making them no longer the focuses for truth that they once were, what is left of *lie/lie*? There is still the bed of sleep and dreams. And there is the love-bed, which has increasingly become for more and more people the only profound truth-testing situation. The love-bed offers—or may claim to—a resistance to all systems, whether social, political, religious, or ethical; it asks us to believe that the most important truth that can be uttered is also the most important, easiest, and most contemptible lie: 'I love you.' In this as in so much else, 'Dover Beach' catches for all time a great historical movement of mind and heart, and Arnold too needs an anti-pun on *lie*, braced between *true* and *dreams*:

> Ah, love, let us be true
> To one another! for the world, which seems
> To lie before us like a land of dreams,
> So various, so beautiful, so new,
> Hath really neither joy, nor love, nor light,
> Nor certitude . . .

That 'certitude' was to become the 'certainty, fidelity' which 'pass' from W. H. Auden's 'Lay your sleeping head, my love'—a poem which has its deep unease about lying:

> But in my arms till break of day
> Let the living creature lie,
> Mortal, guilty, but to me
> The entirely beautiful.

A similarly deep unease underlies William Empson's 'Aubade,' with its tragic refrain:

> The language problem but you have to try.
> Some solid ground for lying could she show?
> The heart of standing is you cannot fly . . .
>
> I slept, and blank as that I would yet lie.
> Till you have seen what a threat holds below,
> The heart of standing is you cannot fly.

Yet the pun is under threat even here, even in the love-bed. For although lovers will no doubt continue to avail themselves of the posture, the word has already lost its amatory suggestions. Eric Partridge speaks of 'lie with', as 'perhaps the oldest euphemism for ''to copulate'' in the English language'; yet it was already 'somewhat archaic' for the *OED*, and in the world we live in, lovers do not lie with one another. In remote and unliberated areas, they can still sometimes perhaps be found sleeping together—which is why the New English Bible, whose language is a monument of dithering and of bet-hedging, has 'sleep with' at *Genesis*, iii 15 while retaining 'lie with' at *Genesis*, xix 34. All euphemisms have lately taken a hammering, but the case of *lie* is more perilous. For even its postural meaning is threatened—by *lay*. Bob Dylan, like many Americans, sometimes finds the mendacious suggestions of *lie* unwelcome; he could hardly begin a song 'Lie lady lie' unless he were happy that our minds might race ahead to that second line of his from another song, 'Don't waste your words, they're just lies.' 'Lay lady lay' has that lovely languorous assonantal stretching;—on the other hand, it too has its disadvantages, at least to an Englishman, in that it could proceed to 'the table' or 'an egg.' Still, linguistic solecisms don't just happen, and *lay* wants to oust *lie* because it finds the mendacity possibilities of *lie* either an embarrassment or an unsolicited admonition. But it is an admonition which our poets are trying to preserve, as in this poem by Philip Larkin.

TALKING IN BED

Talking in bed ought to be easiest,
Lying together there goes back so far,
An emblem of two people being honest.

Yet more and more time passes silently.
Outside, the wind's incomplete unrest
Builds and disperses clouds about the sky,

And dark towns heap up on the horizon.
None of this cares for us. Nothing shows why
At this unique distance from isolation

It becomes still more difficult to find
Words at once true and kind,
Or not untrue and not unkind.

Yet words tell different truths and different lies in different languages. The French no doubt have elsewhere their own linguistic nodes or constellations which have the range and penetration of *lie*, but their word for *lie* intimates something very different from the English. The inevitable pressure from and toward *mensonge* is *songe*, so that a lie is seen as a kind of dream or a dream as a kind of lie. Proverbially, 'songe, mensonge'; poetically, every French poet has had recourse to this resource: La Fontaine, Corneille, Boileau, Voltaire, Théophile, Lamartine, Baudelaire.

> Laissez, laissez mon coeur s'enivrer d'un mensonge,
> Plonger dans vos beaux yeux comme dans un beau songe.
>
> ('Spleen et idéal,' *Fleurs du mal*)

It is not for an Englishman to claim to be able to plumb those depths which the *mensonge/songe* pun may plunge down into; but he may safely notice some things about it. First, that it relates the lie, *mensonge*, not to truth but to reality, the dream that is *songe*. Second, that this overlaps with part, but only part, of what *lie/lie* intimates: the bed of sleep and dreams. Third, that both *mensonge* and *songe* are on the unreality side of the line, and neither necessarily constitutes a vigilance about the other (though the pun can be vigilantly used). And fourth, that as *mensonge* has its relation to *songe*, so *vrai* has its relation to that other dream, *rêve*, a coincidence which is thus part of a double coincidence, and one which the French poet may learn from and teach from—as when, in their Pléiade translation of *Romeo and Juliet*, P.-J. Jouve and Georges Pitoëff deny themselves the obvious *mensonge/songe* in order to avail themselves of *rêves/vrais*:

> *Mercutio.* That dreamers often lye.
> *Romeo.* In bed a sleepe while they do dreame things true.
> (I iv)

> *Mercutio.* C'était que ceux qui rêvent
> Sont souvent mis dedans.
> *Romeo.*   Dedans le lit
> Où ils dorment en rêvant des rêves vrais.

Some sense of the differences between *mensonge/songe* and *lie/lie* may be gained if we think of the greatest writer on lying, Proust. Thus the English translation has no living tissue when a sentence which begins 'Why do we not reflect at the time. . . . ,' and reiterates 'Why do we not reflect,' is grafted to the next sentence which speaks of 'the lie itself'; whereas the sequence in the French is 'Que ne songe-t-on alors, . . . que ne songe-t-on . . . le mensonge même' (*La prisonnière*). The same passage shows *lie/lie* naturally surfacing in the English:

But at the very moment when she speaks of something else beneath which lies hidden the thing that one does not mention, the lie is immediately perceived.   (*Remembrance of Things Past: The Captive*)[25]

where the French has simply:

Mais au moment même où elle parle, où elle parle d'une autre chose sous laquelle il y a cela, qu'elle ne dit pas, le mensonge est perçu instantanément.

The same thing happens in *A l'ombre des jeunes filles en fleurs*, where the liar Bloch says in the French, 'Crois-moi . . . si hier en pensant à toi . . . je n'ai pas sangloté toute la nuit,' whereas in the English this becomes 'Believe me . . . if yesterday, when I thought of you . . . I did not lie awake weeping all night long'—and this in a paragraph where we are told of Bloch: 'Whenever he began to grow sentimental and wished his hearer to grow sentimental over a falsehood, he would say: "I swear it," more for the hysterical satisfaction of lying than to make people think that he was speaking the truth.'[26]

But perhaps the right instance is not Proust but the writer whose only book of criticism is on Proust: Samuel Beckett. For Beckett writes both in English and in French, and in his self-translation we have a unique opportunity to contemplate *lie/lie*. Two pages of *The Unnamable*[27] speak endlessly of lies:

it's not the moment to tell a lie, but how can you not tell a lie,
that's all hypotheses, lies,
more lies . . . all lies,
all lies

—and in the middle of this we find:

and what lies between us, how the land lies,

[25] Trans. C. K. Scott Moncrieff (1924), iv 237-8.
[26] *Within a Budding Grove*, trans. C. K. Scott Moncrieff (1924), iv 61.
[27] (1958), pp. 174-5.

—for which Beckett's French offers no such thing:

et comment c'est entre nous, quel genre de terrain,
(*L'Innommable,* p. 186)

Or take the last of Beckett's *Texts for Nothing*: his English here wonderfully compacts the birth-bed, the sick-bed, the death-bed, and the grave, and concludes with *lie*:

Last everlasting questions, infant languors in the end sheets, last images, end of dream, of being past, passing and to be, end of lie.

Beckett's French gives salience not to that bitterly curtailed *lie* (not *lying*, it will be noted), but to two differently related words in his death sentence, *songes* and *mensonges*:

Dernières questions de toujours, poses de petite fille dans les draps de la fin, dernières images, fin des songes, de l'être qui vient, de l'être qui passe, de l'être qui fut, fin des mensonges.

But the life is going out of *lie/lie*, and when it has gone, our language, our literature, and our culture will lack what has constituted a powerful concentration of vigilance. It will be a pity when not a single reader of the *New York Review of Books* gets pleasure from the fact that the Association of Existential Psychology and Psychiatry could advertise among the attractions of its two-day meeting 'On Lying and Liars' (March 8-9, 1975) a talk on 'Lying in Groups.' (Group sex? Natural childbirth?) It will be a pity when no one wishes to supply Arthur Carr's title question: 'English Department Administrators: Where Do Our Talents Lie?'[28] with some such answer as 'In and through your teeth.' It will be a pity when no one takes the anti-pun on *lie* with which Philip Larkin ends 'Church Going':

A serious house on serious earth it is,
In whose blent air all our compulsions meet,
Are recognised, and robed as destinies.
And that much never can be obsolete,
Since someone will forever be surprising
A hunger in himself to be more serious,
And gravitating with it to this ground,
Which, he once heard, was proper to grow wise in,
If only that so many dead lie round.

[28] Association of Departments of English, meeting at the Université de Montréal, 5 April 1975.

For *lie* has been a word 'in whose blent air all our compulsions meet'—compulsive lying and compulsive truth-telling—and this in a compacting of our mental mendacity and our physical self in the great truth-testing postures; and unfortunately it simply isn't true that 'that much never can be obsolete.' When it ceases to be true 'that so many dead lie round,' the dead will not be around to speak tacitly such truths.

Which leads finally to a poem by J. V. Cunningham which may stand as both the epigraph and the epitaph for all this:

> Here lies New Critic who would fox us
> With his poetic paradoxes.
> Though he lies here rigid and quiet,
> If he could speak he would deny it.

WALTER PATER, MATTHEW ARNOLD
AND MISQUOTATION

'To see the object as in itself it really is': so Arnold entered upon 'The Function of Criticism at the Present Time'. Pater retorted that 'in aesthetic criticism the first step towards seeing one's object as it really is, is to know one's own impression as it really is'.[1] Oscar Wilde then took the next step: 'The highest criticism, then, is more creative than creation, and the primary aim of the critic is to see the object as in itself it really is not'.[2] As when the critic misquotes it?

There is an innovative essay called 'Misquotation as Re-creation' by Matthew Hodgart. Hodgart's earliest example of a critic's quasi-creative misquoting of the lines by Burns which he was instancing was Thomas Carlyle in 1828, and Carlyle at once followed his misquotation by of course insisting:

This clearness of sight we have called the foundation of all talent; for in fact, unless we see our object, how shall we know how to place or prize it, in our understanding, our imagination, our affection?[3]

Misquotation goes directly to the nub of the confrontation between Pater and Arnold: the distinction between criticism and creation. 'Everybody', said Arnold, 'would be willing to admit, as a general proposition, that the critical faculty is lower than the inventive.'[4] But a critic in the school of Harold Bloom would admit no such thing. Bloom glories in the claim that Pater's 'writings obscure the supposed distinction between criticism and creation', and at once asks, un-interrogatively, ' "Supposed", because who can convince us of that distinction?' But one plain place to locate the distinction is in a writer's very words, and in some sane restrictions upon a critic's right to rewrite them. As someone who believes that Arnold's little finger is worth Pater's whole hand of little fingers, I regret its

---

[1] *The Renaissance* (1873), 1910 edn, p. viii.

[2] Quoted in part by Harold Bloom, Introduction to *Selected Writings of Walter Pater* (1974), p. viii. It is from 'The Critic as Artist'.

[3] *Essays in Criticism*, iii (1953), 28-38.

[4] 'The Function of Criticism', *Lectures and Essays in Criticism*, ed. R. H. Super (1962), p. 259.

not simply being the case that Arnold's modest shrewdness about the function of criticism leads him to quote impeccably, while Pater's quasi-creative arrogation misleads him to misquote peccably.

In Shakespeare's words,

> Spirits are not finely touch'd,
> But to fine issues.
> (*Measure for Measure*, I i)

Pater wanted something finer than fineness. 'In *Measure for Measure*', he begins his essay, 'as in some other of his plays, Shakespeare has remodelled an earlier and somewhat rough composition to "finer issues" '[5]—and already Pater's own remodelling has begun. The *raison d'être* of his syntax is that it should usher in the word 'finer', inaugurating an essay which will consummate the word as its concluding paragraph, moving there from 'finer knowledge' to 'finer justice', and so to the last sentence of Pater's essay and 'just those finer appreciations'—*Appreciations* being the title of this book, a book which indeed speaks of an author's obligation to 'justify the title of his book'.[6]

Pater had a greed for fineness; but something other than greed is involved, as is clear from his not grinding on up to the word 'finest'. He uses 'finest', as he uses every word cognate with 'fine', but this one infrequently, perfunctorily. For, unlike the comparative, the superlative implies a climax, a completion, an outcome rather than an endless process and 'a tension of nerve'. ('A passion of which the outlets are sealed, begets a tension of nerve'.[7]) If what you desire is 'ear and finger refining themselves infinitely, in the appetite for sweet sound',[8] then you need, not 'fine' or 'finest' (each of which has its resting satisfaction), but 'finer' and 'refine'. Hence Pater's characteristic ring, whether it be a self-regarding quotation—'those "men of a finer thread" who have formed and maintain the literary ideal'[9]—or Pater being his own man and talisman: 'the finer accommodation of speech to that vision within', 'the finer

[5] *Appreciations* (1889), 1910 edn, p. 170.
[6] *Appreciations*, p. 234.
[7] 'Aesthetic Poetry', *Appreciations* (first edn); *Selected Writings*, p. 193.
[8] *The Renaissance*, p. 151.
[9] *Appreciations*, p. 18.

edge of words', 'this finer, more delicately marvellous super-
naturalism', 'that gift of handling the finer passages of human
feeling, at once with power and delicacy, which was another
result of his [Coleridge's] finer psychology'[10]—it is worth risking a satiety of what Pater undistressedly calls 'reiterated refine-
ments',[11] because such a list is a reminder that here Pater was
insatiable. Just as he was obliged to remodel 'fine issues' into
'finer issues', so he was obliged—though here he was not directly
quoting—to remodel 'finely touched' into 'more finely touched':

The modern mind, so minutely self-scrutinizing . . . needs to be more
finely touched than was possible in the older, romantic presentment.[12]

Pater's temperament is one thing; his critical enterprise is
not another. What drew him to *Measure for Measure* was that
Shakespeare was here remodelling something rougher. Shakespeare 'has refashioned . . . materials already at hand, so that
the relics of other men's poetry are incorporated'[13]—and so has
Pater. The rough had become the fine; the fine is now to become the finer. Literature, as Pater often (and sometimes itali-
cizedly) says, is the '*fine* art'; criticism has then to be the finer
art. Hence such a spiral as this:

It is a finer ideal, extracted from what in relation to any actual world
is already an ideal. Like some strange second flowering after date, it
renews on a more delicate type the poetry of a past age, but must not
be confounded with it.[14]

Pater is speaking of an artistic movement, 'Aesthetic Poetry',
but he is contemplating too his own criticism—or, to him,
criticism. Criticism too is a strange second flowering, a renewing on a more delicate type of the poetry of a past age. A great
picture may be a play of light, 'but refined upon, and dealt
with more subtly and exquisitely than by nature itself';[15] to the
critic, it then itself has to be refined upon, and dealt with more
subtly and exquisitely than by art itself.

[10] *Appreciations*, pp. 10, 16, 98, 100; also pp. 179, 200; *Selected Writings*, pp. 190, 1,
230, 235; *The Renaissance*, p. 207.
[11] *The Renaissance*, p. 170.
[12] *Appreciations*, p. 98.
[13] *Appreciations*, pp. 181-2.
[14] 'Aesthetic Poetry', *Selected Writings*, p. 190.
[15] *The Renaissance*, p. 133.

In this late age we are becoming so familiarised with the greater works of art as to be little sensitive of the act of creation in them: they do not impress us as a new presence in the world.[16]

A half-truth wholeheartedly aggrandizes itself, and the 'new presence in the world' becomes the altitudinous critic. His act of creation is even more miraculous than the original one. Like God—in the first substantial quotation from Sir Thomas Browne which Pater gives in his essay—'He was driven to a second and harder creation—of a substance like Himself'.[17] Indeed, it is only such art as parallels a second creation, and so parallels the critic's creativity, which comes home to Pater:

With him [Michelangelo] the beginning of life has all the characteristics of resurrection: it is like the recovery of suspended health or animation, with its gratitude, its effusion, and eloquence.[18]

But what does eloquence say when it finds itself chafing at reproducing other men's eloquence? Misquotation is one way for it to practise its high chemistry:

What the enthusiastic young student expected from Browne, so high and noble a piece of chemistry, was the 're-individualling of an incinerated plant'—a violet, turning to freshness, and smelling sweet again, out of its ashes, under some genially fitted conditions of the chemic art.

Palingenesis, resurrection, effected by orderly prescription—the 're-individualling' of an 'incinerated organism'—is a subject which affords us a natural transition to the little book of the *Hydriotaphia*, or *Treatise of Urn-Burial*.[19]

It is clear that Pater is more moved at the thought of a resurrected violet than he would ever be to see a common or garden violet. What Pater says of the artist, he means of the critic: that he is one of those 'who, starting with acknowledged types of beauty, have refined as far upon these as these refine upon the world of common forms'.[20] Just as 'The Child in the House' raises memory above itself, above the ordinary retrospect of life—

the finer sort of memory, bringing its object to mind with a great

[16] *Appreciations*, p. 80.
[17] *Appreciations*, p. 126.
[18] *The Renaissance*, p. 75.
[19] *Appreciations*, p. 152.
[20] *The Renaissance*, p. 105.

clearness, yet, as sometimes happens in dreams, raised a little above itself, and above ordinary retrospect[21]

—so the critic raises art above itself. Criticism, finer than fine, is to be at least the peer of art, in that it too is an awareness of 'all those finer conditions wherein material things rise to that subtlety of operation which constitutes them spiritual, where only the finer nerve and the keener touch can follow'.[22] Art raises material things to subtle spirituality, but art itself then is seen as a material thing which criticism raises to the subtler and the more spiritual. But the revolution devours its children, and criticism was to find itself further subtilized and spiritualized into the heights of meta-criticism. At which point it has become time for an insistence that spirits are not finely touched but to less fine issues.

But then Pater, like many who are more sure of the need for spirituality than of the existence of the spirit, does not know quite what to make of the word *spirit*. So he can say that Isabella in *Measure for Measure* is 'respected even by the worldly Lucio as "something ensky'd and sainted, and almost an immortal spirit"',[23] where Lucio's respect for Isabella, abated though it drastically is in Pater's version, is markedly greater than Pater's respect for Shakespeare. 'I hold you as a thing en-skied, and sainted' (*Measure for Measure*, I v): let us pass over Pater's substitution of 'something' for 'a thing', it is of little interest except as showing—as do others of his misquotations—that Pater, who would talk lavishly about cadence and about such rhythm as 'gives its musical value to every syllable', and even about 'the rhythm of a whole book',[24] was less than refined in his sense of that smaller thing, the rhythm of a whole line. What matters (and this too is a rhythmical débâcle) is Pater's re-modelling of 'By your renouncement, an imortal spirit' into 'and almost an immortal spirit.' Nothing could make clearer the factitiousness of Pater's commitment to renunciation than his erasing of it here. On the face of it, Shakespeare's line was made for him. 'Hence a contention, a sense of self-restraint and renunciation, having for the susceptible reader the effect of

<hr/>

[21] *Selected Writings*, p. 1.
[22] *The Renaissance*, p. 116.
[23] *Appreciations*, p. 177.
[24] *Appreciations*, pp. 12, 30.

a challenge for minute consideration':[25] such is the spiritual reward of the finer style. But as soon as this 'challenge for minute consideration' has to confront a real—a religious and not a religiose—renunciation, it fails lamentably; or rather, succeeds lamentably in rewriting Shakespeare to flatter its own susceptibilities. In its place, Pater makes one of the oddest, and most betraying, substitutions he ever made: 'and almost an immortal spirit'. For Pater mollifies religion into religiosity, itself 'almost an immortal spirit'. But then it is a ubiquitous feature of Pater's style that it uses 'almost' in conjunction with strong, extreme, or absolute terms, in order to create an emotional tremor, a simulation of a forthcoming delicate discrimination which proves not to come forth. We should heed Pater's own injunction, and attend to

those weaknesses of conscious or unconscious repetition of word, phrase, motive, or member of the whole matter, indicating, as Flaubert was aware, an original structure in thought not organically complete.[26]

His *almosts* are those of a man who winces into verbalism: almost painful, almost insane, almost diseased; almost animal, almost coarse; almost natural, almost supernatural, almost clairvoyant; almost endless, almost nameless, almost expressionless; almost impassive, almost disembodied, almost dead . . . Again, one wants to list enough of what Pater calls 'almost wearisome reiteration'[27] to suggest that he never wearied of it. Moreover, 'almost' has direct filaments to his other reiterated rhetorical turn, 'a kind of x y', a verbal device for combining a maximum air of uncomplacent discrimination with a minimum effort to achieve it. The corrugated brow is on a mask. Thus, the frisson words which Pater factitiously qualifies with 'almost' often take a place in the 'a kind of x y' formula too.

> Almost visual: a sort of visual power.
> Almost grotesque: a kind of spectral grotesque.
> Almost physical: a sort of physical beauty.[28]

[25] *Appreciations*, pp. 13-14.

[26] *Appreciations*, p. 23.

[27] *Appreciations*, pp. 58, 108 (and 251); *Selected Writings*, p. 6; *Appreciations*, pp. 177, 188, 137, 197; *The Renaissance*, p. 87; *Appreciations*, p. 32; *The Renaissance*, pp. 20, 87, 53; *Selected Writings*, p. 232; *The Renaissance*, pp. 7, 169.

[28] *Appreciations*, p. 23: *Selected Writings*, p. 234. *Appreciations*, p. 207 (and 209): p. 114. *The Renaissance*, p. 178 (and 191): *Appreciations*, pp. 152-3.

The important cluster, the one which is cognate with 'almost an immortal spirit', is of those flirtations with religion which are eager not actually to propose lest God dispose, or, 'a sort of religious sentimentalism'.[29] As with:

> Almost mystical: a sort of half-playful mysticism; a sort of mystical sensuality; a kind of mystical appetite.[30]

This turn of speech is apt not only to Pater's temperament ('a sort of divided imperfect life'; 'a sort of delicate intellectual epicureanism'; 'a kind of unimpassioned passion'; 'a kind of passionate coldness'[31]), and not only to this particular re-rendering of Shakespeare's immortal—or almost immortal—words, but to all those liberties of more-than-interpretation which Pater feels free to take. For 'those associative conceptions of the imagination . . . would have a kind of prevenient necessity to rise at some time to the surface of the human mind'.[32] One such, in this shape itself, rises when, in the final paragraph of the Conclusion to *The Renaissance*, Pater translates Victor Hugo, 'Les hommes sont tous condamnés à mort avec des sursis indéfinis', as 'we are all under sentence of death but with a sort of indefinite reprieve'.[33] Another instance of 'a kind of prevenient necessity' rises when Pater possesses Ian Fletcher to say that 'Much of the highly methodized aesthetics of Yeats exist in a kind of evasive or tangential state in Pater'.[34]

Among the many things which Pater evaded was any suggestion that he might be evasive. Is he not explicitly committed to the utmost attentiveness, alertness, exactitude? Yet praise of his author's exactness diverts attention from his own inexactness. Thus a sentence which speaks of 'a singular watchfulness for the minute fact' and 'a closeness to the exact physiognomy' will misquote Coleridge's poetry; a sentence which praises

---

[29] *The Renaissance*, p. 108. Also: A sort of cloistral refuge; a kind of religious influence; a sort of inborn religious placidity; a sort of biblical depth; a kind of languid visionariness; a sort of religious duty; a kind of sacramental efficacy; a kind of mortified grace; a kind of sacred grace; a sort of material shrine; a kind of sacred transaction; a sort of religious melancholy. (*Appreciations*, pp. 18, 26, 44, 53, 83, 95, 121, 153; *The Renaissance*, p. 69; *Selected Writings*, pp. 4, 13; *The Renaissance*, p. 51.)

[30] *Appreciations*, p. 71: pp. 58, 121, and *Selected Writings*, p. 13.

[31] *Appreciations*, pp. 71, 112; *Selected Writings*, p. 231; *The Renaissance*, p. 229.

[32] *Appreciations*, p. 79.

[33] *The Renaissance*, p. 238.

[34] *Walter Pater* (1959), 1971 edn, p. 36.

Wordsworth's poetry for 'its precise and vivid incidents' will furnish four quotations with each of which there is something slightly wrong, in three cases the error apparently being Pater's own; and a sentence which says 'in his own words'[35] will misquote Wordsworth as if Wordsworth's *own* words were somehow slightly different from his words. Is such protestation a twinge of that 'scholarly conscience'[36] of which Pater speaks? Pater cares so much that poetry should be particular ('For Rossetti, as for Dante, without question on his part, the first condition of the poetic way of seeing and presenting things is particularization'[37]) that he is not particular about how he presents things, and he will say that Wordsworth 'has celebrated in many of his poems the "efficacious spirit", which, as he says, resides in these "particular spots" of time'.[38] Wordsworth did not say '"particular spots" of time', but— magnificently unadjectival—'There are in our existence spots of time'.[39] The 'efficacious spirit' of Wordsworth is powerless in the face of Pater's even more efficacious spirit, 'the relative spirit'. 'To the modern spirit nothing is, or can be rightly known, except relatively and under conditions.'[40] Including, presumably, the words of a poem. 'What the moralist asks is, shall we gain or lose by surrendering human life to the relative spirit?'[41] What we might ask is, what do we gain and what do we lose by surrendering art to the relative spirit? The answer is that we gain some Pater, and lose some Shakespeare, Wordsworth, Coleridge.

It was à propos of Coleridge that Pater said that 'the modern mind . . . needs to be more finely touched', and the phrase 'finer influence' occurs in Coleridge in another passage which Pater remodels. ' "I had found", Coleridge tells us [Pater tells us]',[42]

> That outward forms, the loftiest, still receive
> Their finer influence from the world within;
> Fair ciphers of vague import, where the eye
> Traces no spot, in which the heart may read
> History and prophecy.

[35] *Appreciations*, pp. 90, 45, 63. [36] *Appreciations*, p. 12.
[37] *Appreciations*, p. 208. [38] *Appreciations*, p. 46.
[39] Wordsworth has 'particular spot' in 'The Brothers' 81 and *The Excursion*, vi 500.
[40] *Appreciations*, p. 66. [41] *Appreciations*, p. 103.
[42] *Appreciations*, pp. 90-1, quoting 'Lines Written in the Album at Elbingerode'.

'Finer' there was already provided; Pater's present remodelling is the change of 'Life' to 'world', for Coleridge had written
that

> the loftiest, still receive
> Their finer influence from the Life within.

Pater's heart reads, and his eye traces, what he wishes to have
been said; he receives Coleridge's words as 'Fair ciphers of
vague import', and imports into them his self, his importance.
For to Pater, 'the Life within' would not do, because it did
not—as 'the world within' does—sufficiently disjoin the higher
inner world of impressions and sensations from the lower outer
world of facts and data and commonness. The critic who puts
into Coleridge's mouth the words 'the world within' is the critic
whose mouth utters these same words as his own on a matter
where his heart was confident that it importantly read history
and prophecy:

> It makes him [Browning] pre-eminently a modern poet—a poet of the
> self-pondering, perfectly educated, modern world, which having
> come to the end of all direct and purely external experiences, must
> necessarily turn for its entertainment to the world within.[43]

The paradox or irony of the situation is then that Pater can
create this 'world within'—'the inward world of thought and
feeling'[44]—only by a violation of a world without, another
man's 'world within' as it had become embodied—'the visible
vesture and expression of that other world it sees so steadily
within'[45]—in the world which is the words of a poem.

But Pater will have had another objection to 'the Life within':
his objection to life, to which he mostly preferred the alternative ('the refinement of the dead', 'corpse-like in her refinement'[46]). Elsewhere in Coleridge, he did not need to find a
substitute for 'life', since the neighbouring words 'anxious',
'cruel', and 'taskmaster' sufficiently refined it into submission:

> Dim similitudes
> Weaving in mortal strains, I've stolen one hour
> From anxious self, life's cruel taskmaster![47]

---

[43] *Essays from The Guardian* (1896), p. 43.   [44] *The Renaissance*, p. 234.
[45] *Appreciations*, p. 31.   [46] *The Renaissance*, pp. 112, 205.
[47] 'On Observing a Blossom on the First of February, 1796'; *Appreciations*, p. 84.

Here it is not 'life' then, which is the occasion for Pater's 'weaving' of his 'anxious self' ('that strange, perpetual weaving and unweaving of ourselves',[48] as he calls it in the Conclusion to *The Renaissance*); the word of Coleridge which Pater here unweaves is 'moral', for Coleridge wrote, not 'mortal strains', but 'Dim similitudes / Weaving in moral strains.' 'Dim similitudes', rather than exact renderings, are what Pater is indeed weaving, rather as he felt free—or freed—because of the words 'Fair ciphers of vague import'. Pater does not wish Coleridge to have said 'moral'. The aesthete frets at the merely moral; and yet the aesthete is always irked into insisting that what he proffers is a morality larger than Morality with its large M ('His morality is all sympathy',[49] says Pater of Botticelli). T. S. Eliot said of Pater that, 'being primarily a moralist, he was incapable of seeing any work of art simply as it is'.[50] Pater was seldom more the remodelling moralist than when replacing the word 'moral' with his even more moral word 'mortal'. 'For with this desire of physical beauty mingled itself early the fear of death—the fear of death intensified by the desire of beauty.'[51] Such a mingling is clear in Pater's thrilling to Browne, to whom—Pater says—'the visible function of death is but to refine, to detach from aught that is vulgar.'[52]

The 'anxious self' has become Pater's, not Coleridge's; and Pater's anxiety is intimated by the word 'self'. For it raises those questions about a proper respect for others' selves and for their creations which Pater wished always to elide. Coleridge is praised for 'his finer psychology . . . his exquisitely refined habit of self-reflection';[53] but does Coleridge reflect upon himself or merely reflect himself, the mirror and the Narcissus?

Yet Pater's is an anxious self, never able to brazen out his supreme arrogatings, and always paying his respects (as in the notorious ending of 'Style') to respectable concessions. He would have liked to earn his own praise of Winckelmann:

Occupied ever with himself, perfecting himself and developing his genius, he was not content, as so often happens with such natures, that the atmosphere between him and other minds should be thick,

---

[48] *The Renaissance*, p. 236.
[50] *Selected Essays* (1932), 1951 edn, p. 440.
[52] *Appreciations*, p. 153.

[49] *The Renaissance*, p. 56.
[51] *Selected Writings*, p. 11.
[53] *Appreciations*, pp. 100-1.

and clouded; he was ever jealously refining his meaning into a form, express, clear, objective.[54]

But what happens to the objective, to a transparent access to other minds, if it be not your meaning but theirs which you are ever jealously refining?

Arnold could say that a critic's duty was to let his author 'speak for himself', and to gain 'readers for his author himself, not for any lucubrations on his author';[55] but Pater would repeatedly pre-empt the matter by building his lucubrations in as misquotations. Arnold could say that 'the great art of criticism is to get oneself out of the way'.[56] Pater may inaugurate his praise of Charles Lamb in such terms—

It was as loyal, self-forgetful work for others, for Shakespeare's self first, for instance, and then for Shakespeare's readers, that that too was done: he has the true scholar's way of forgetting himself in his subject[57]

—but Pater is not forgetting himself in thus speaking twice of the matter, and by the next page he is his old audacious, evasive self with the words 'really the creator':

To feel strongly the charm of an old poet or moralist . . . and then to interpret that charm, to convey it to others—he seeming to himself but to hand on to others, in mere humble ministration, that of which for them he is really the creator—this is the way of his criticism.

The creator, not even *a*? The wistful note—'he seeming to himself but to hand on to others, in mere humble ministration'—is a consequence of Pater's proud, self-conscious longing for Lamb's humble unselfconsciousness, and it is signalled by Pater's obsessive turn: 'he seeming to himself but to . . .' For the two most important quotations—as against misquotations— in Pater are the following, and the one is a benign counterpart of the other while they are built upon the same syntactical turn:

that long quiet life . . . in which 'all existence', as he [Browne] says, 'had been but food for contemplation'.[58]

[54] *The Renaissance*, p. 220.
[55] 'Byron', *English Literature and Irish Politics*, ed. R. H. Super (1973), p. 235.
[56] 'Pagan and Mediaeval Religious Sentiment', *Lectures and Essays in Criticism*, p. 227.
[57] *Appreciations*, p. 111.
[58] *Appreciations*, pp. 128-9.

'I did but taste a little honey with the end of the rod that was in mine hand, and lo! I must die.'[59]

Pater, mild and obdurate as only a lover of the relative spirit can be, needs this turn because it is uncoercive in tone while being fiercely exclusive in substance. Most of his innumerable statements which include the *is but* or *does but* formula are cunning constrictions of the truth, and in particular those which famously include the words 'in truth': 'For in truth all art does but consist in the removal of surplusage.'[60] Does but?

Pater yearns for a world in which he can be guiltlessly sure that

License again, the making free with rule, if it be indeed, as people fancy, a habit of genius, flinging aside or transforming all that opposes the liberty of beautiful production, will be but faith to one's own meaning.[61]

But what if the thing which opposes the liberty of beautiful production is the rights of someone else's beautiful production, towards which even genius, 'flinging aside or transforming all that opposes the liberty of beautiful production', may feel some inescapable responsibility? What if 'faith to one's own meaning' can be achieved only by faithlessness to another's meaning? *Will be but* is the ritual to exorcise all such perplexities. 'In him [Plato], the passion for truth did but bend, or take the bent of, certain ineradicable predispositions of his nature.'[62]

The ineradicable predispositions of Pater's nature lead him to say that 'Coleridge could never have abandoned himself to the dream, the vision, as Wordsworth did, because the first condition of such abandonment must be an unvexed quietness of heart';[63] and one sentence later he quotes 'Resolution and Independence': 'My whole life I have lived in quiet thought!' Or rather misquotes, since Wordsworth wrote: 'My whole life I have lived in pleasant thought'. Pater will have had reasons for wanting 'pleasant' out, since his epicureanism was of the sort which finds less pleasure in contemplating the pleasant than the

[59] *I Samuel*, xiv 43; *The Renaissance*, p. 222.

[60] *Appreciations*, p. 19. *Is but* and *are but* provide this reassurance in the three successive sentences which end the first paragraph of the Conclusion to *The Renaissance*.

[61] *Appreciations*, p. 35.

[62] *Selected Writings*, p. 225.

[63] *Appreciations*, p. 86.

painful. A whole life lived in pleasant thought would have
seemed to him worse than unlikely: vulgar. But he had, too, his
reasons for wanting 'quiet' in. For Pater would have given
anything for a 'quiet life', so that he could assimilate it to those
quiet lives of his: Luca della Robbia, with 'a life of labour and
frugality, with no adventure and no excitement except what
belongs to the trial of new artistic processes'; Flaubert, and his
'really quiet existence'; Wordsworth, with his 'life of much
quiet delicacy'; 'Lamb's quiet subsequent life'; and Sir
Thomas Browne with his 'long quiet life'.[64]
Pater wished to assimilate all these to each other so that he
might assimilate them all to himself. 'The Child in the House'
murmurs that 'there are those who pass their days, as a matter
of course, in a sort of "going quietly"';[65] and the Child in the
House was the don in the college.
Pater speaks often of the exact; indeed, since it is the comparative form of any epithet which is more necessary to him, it
is not surprising that the first sentence of *Appreciations* should
say 'to speak more exactly'. 'A more exact estimate', 'exact
trial', 'exact apprehension', 'exact proportion', 'exact manner',
'exact physiognomy', 'exact expression', 'exact equivalence',
'an exact sense', 'exact relation', 'great exactness'[66]—these
crystallize in Pater's insistence upon an exact and exacting process: 'the exaction from every sentence of a precise relief', that
the writer should 'scrupulously exact of it, from syllable to
syllable, its precise value'.[67] Again, the writer is 'a lover
of words for their own sake, to whom nothing about them is
unimportant, a minute and constant observer of their physiognomy'.[68] Pater asks us to be alive to 'unfading minutest circumstance', to 'a host of minute recognitions', to be 'minutely
systematic in our painstaking'; he asks us to see that art is
'perfect in minute detail'.[69]

The one word for the one thing, the one thought, amid the multitude
of words, terms, that might just do: the problem of style was there!—

[64] *The Renaissance*, p. 70; *Appreciations*, pp. 32, 40, 107, 128.
[65] *Selected Writings*, p. 7.
[66] *Appreciations*, pp. 67, 18, 34 (twice), 90, 126, 204, 243; *The Renaissance*, pp. viii, x.
[67] *Appreciations*, pp. 17, 21.
[68] *Appreciations*, p. 20.
[69] *Selected Writings*, pp. 7, 248, 241; *The Renaissance*, p. 170.

the unique word, phrase, sentence, paragraph, essay, or song, absolutely proper to the single mental presentation or vision within.[70]

But the problem for Pater was not there where it was for Flaubert; it was to combine an explicit announcement that the great writer found the one word that was absolutely proper, with an implicit assurance that the life of a critic was worth anything only if it was worth at least no less than that of an artist, and that therefore it was absolutely proper for the critic to substitute his own uniqueness for the earlier and other creation.

The essay on 'Style' is therefore characterized by one of Pater's grandest unions of audacity and evasion, in the higher prudential assurance: it quotes not one single instance of that consummated style which it invokes; its only quotations are about, and not of, style; and the thing which its quoted authors —Montaigne, Schiller, Flaubert, and Maupassant—have in common is that in no case is Pater giving us, since they did not write in English, their 'one word for the one thing', their 'unique word, phrase, sentence'.

It is the word 'transcribe' which yokes Pater's re-creative mistranscriptions and his whole sense of what creation is. For the simplest way to become something else than a transcriber is to mistranscribe.

Livy, Tacitus, Michelet . . . each, after his own sense, modifies—who can tell where and to what degree?—and becomes something else than a transcriber; each, as he thus modifies, passing into the domain of art proper. For just in proportion as the writer's aim, consciously or unconsciously, comes to be the transcribing not of the world, not of mere fact, but of his sense of it, he becomes an artist, his work *fine* art.[71]

For 'transcribe' is on good terms with Pater's rhetorical terms ('do but', 'refining', 'almost') when he sets the fine against the finer art:

Giotto, . . . Masaccio, Ghirlandajo even, do but transcribe, with more or less refining, the outward image; they are dramatic, not visionary painters; they are almost impassive spectators of the action

---

[70] *Appreciations*, p. 29.

[71] *Appreciations*, pp. 9-10. It is pleasant that Arnold mistranscribed 'Transcribblers' as 'transcribers' in quoting Gray's remark that Aristotle 'has suffer'd vastly by the Transcribblers'. 'Thomas Gray', *English Literature and Irish Politics*, p. 193.

before them. But the genius of which Botticelli is the type usurps the data before it as the exponent of ideas, moods, visions of its own; in this interest it plays fast and loose with those data, rejecting some and isolating others, and always combining them anew.[72]

The question is whether it is the same thing to 'usurp the data' if the data are not the world, nature, and life but the specific works of particular artists. Harold Bloom, an unreconstructed re-constructing Paterian, is in no way perturbed by the ongoing equivalence: 'To adapt Shelley's idea of the relation between poetry and the universe, let us say that criticism creates the poem anew, after the poem has been annihilated in our minds by the recurrence of impressions blunted by reiteration.'[73] To the creative writer, the world's his oyster, which he with pen will open. Arnold may have deplored Tennyson's 'dawdling with its [the Universe's] painted shell';[74] yet it is one thing to claim that the painted shell of the universe is your oyster, it is another to claim that Botticelli's painted shells are your oyster. When Pater says of the grotesques in Dante's *Inferno* that they 'make one regret that he [Botticelli] has not rather chosen for illumination the more subdued imagery of the *Purgatorio*',[75] Harold Bloom notes: 'A mistake on Pater's part, as Botticelli did illustrate the whole of Dante's poem'. But Bloom at once recovers himself, and our author, by putting 'mistake' into quotation marks: 'But the "mistake" is revelatory and brings Botticelli closer to Pater.' All Pater's subjects have to be close to him, and are haled there if necessary. 'Revelatory'? But what is revealed is nothing about Botticelli, and about Pater merely his inappropriate appropriatingness.

'What is this song or picture', asks Pater,

this engaging personality presented in life or in a book, to *me*? What effect does it really produce on me? Does it give me pleasure? and if so, what sort or degree of pleasure? How is my nature modified by its presence, and under its influence? The answers to these questions are the original facts with which the aesthetic critic has to do; and, as in the study of light, of morals, of number, one must realise such primary data for one's self, or not at all.[76]

72 *The Renaissance*, pp. 53-4.
73 *Selected Writings*, pp. vii-viii.
74 Letter to Clough, *c*. 6 December 1847.
75 *The Renaissance*, p. 52.
76 *The Renaissance*, p. viii.

Everything turns on whether one agrees with Pater that 'the original facts', the 'primary data', are one's answers to these questions about one's impressions; or whether one agrees with Arnold, that the original facts, the primary data, are the objects, not the impressions; or whether—a third realm—one agrees with, say, F. R. Leavis, that the original facts, the primary data, are neither objectivities of an object nor subjectivities of an experiencer, but the intersubjectivities which create art as they create language, the human world, the third realm. Such creative co-operation—

all the mighty world
Of eye, and ear,—both what they half create,
And what perceive
('Tintern Abbey')

will not grant primacy, let alone tyranny, to either.

It would be for a philosopher to argue out the crux of the matter: rights. Pater's rights leave little room for anyone else's or anything else's. He admires artists because they have their way with life: 'the individual genius which contrived after all, by force of will, to have its own masterful way with that environment'; 'No one ever ruled over the mere *subject* in hand more entirely than Leonardo, or bent it more dexterously to purely artistic ends'.[77] But if your subject is Leonardo's art, if your environment is what an artist made of his environment, the case is altered. 'Art', says Pater (and those of us who do not believe it of art will believe it still less of criticism) is 'always striving . . . to get rid of its responsibilities to its subject or material.'[78] But since art is itself Pater's subject and material, his is an art which is always wilful in its self-serving self-thwarting impulse to create an art which will get rid of its responsibilities to art. 'The basis of all artistic genius lies in the power of conceiving humanity in a new and striking way, of putting a happy world of its own creation in place of the meaner world of our common days.'[79] But the critic's artistic genius (as it wishes itself) finds itself confronted not by the meaner world of our common days—'the commonness of the world',[80] as Pater calls it elsewhere—but by a happy world of another's creation;

---

[77] *Selected Writings*, p. 224; *The Renaissance*, p. 119.   [78] *The Renaissance*, p. 138.
[79] *The Renaissance*, p. 213.   [80] *The Renaissance*, p. 216.

the only hope is then to treat that happy world of art as if were really no better than the meaner world (slighting not just the world but art, as it is the nemesis of all aestheticism to do). Pater is confident that he belongs among 'the creative minds of all generations—the artists and those who have treated life in the spirit of art.'[81] He belongs with neither, but in a third category: those who treat art in the spirit of art. This, which will be revered, as a lofty compounding of art, by those present-day exponential exponents of highly self-regarded criticism who are Pater's heirs, will seem to Arnold's heirs to be a decadent downward spiral of inbreeding.

'Rights' are defined by Pater as 'achieved powers'—'but by way of an estimate of its rights, that is, of its achieved powers'[82] —and in that case they may be owed to the achievedness which is art as they are not owed, or are differently owed, to the non-achieved multifariousness which is the world. 'The idea of justice', says Pater, 'involves the idea of rights. But at bottom rights are equivalent to that which really is, to facts.'[83] Yet Pater, when the rights of his authors are out of question, plays loose with that which really is, with facts, as they are embodied in the very words.

Pater's misquotations are the rewriting of his authors so that they say special Paterian things. Arnold's misquotations—and let me acknowledge here my debt to R. H. Super's magnificent edition—are the rewriting of his authors so that they say unspecial things. Where Pater demeans his authors by outdoing them, escalating their phrases into his fugitive noosphere, Arnold demeans his authors by bringing them down to earth, de-escalating them, as if they have not outdone him—or rather us.

So it is characteristic of Arnold, as it would not be of Pater, to lapse into a traditional misquotation, of the sort which reduces something individual to something commonplace.

After all that has been said, it remains immutably true that 'a little knowledge is a dangerous thing', unless he who possesses it knows that it *is* a little.[84]

---

[81] *Appreciations*, p. 241.
[82] *Appreciations*, p. 6.
[83] *Appreciations*, p. 183.
[84] *The Popular Education of France*; *Democratic Education*, ed. R. H. Super (1962), p. 160.

But it remains immutably true, too, that Pope said no such thing; Pope's line, because of the insinuating alliteration of 'learning' with 'little', and because of the assonance of 'learning' with 'thing', elevates to salience the one word 'dangerous'; the conventional misquotation is conventional in foisting in 'knowledge' (a very different possession from 'learning') to pair phonetically with 'dangerous'. Pope's glint of surprise is replaced by a proverb. What is Arnoldian about the substitution is simply that Arnold has no commitment to any especial Arnoldianness.

What Arnold effects, then, is not a re-creation, but a mild de-creation. Whereas Pater's praise of exactitude, 'perfect in minute detail',[85] sits oddly with his inexactitude, Arnold's sense of life's natural speed and its insouciance can make use of a phrase like 'perfectly well' so that we appreciate its good-natured approximation as something very different from Pater's theoretical perfectionism. It is in this spirit that, unlike Pater's re-creation of Shakespeare in his own image, Arnold de-creates Shakespeare into our own image.

The translator must not, indeed, allow himself all the liberty that Shakspeare allows himself; for Shakspeare sometimes uses expressions which pass perfectly well as he uses them, because Shakspeare thinks so fast and so powerfully, that in reading him we are borne over single words as by a mighty current; but, if our mind were less excited, — and who may rely on exciting our mind like Shakspeare? — they would check us. 'To grunt and sweat under a weary load;' — that does perfectly well where it comes in Shakspeare; but . . .[86]

But Arnold, as we are, is 'borne over single words'; the single word here being 'load', since Shakespeare did not write what we almost hear Hamlet say (it being what we would ourselves have said), 'To grunt and sweat under a weary load', but 'To grunt and sweat under a weary life'. To Hamlet, it is not that there is a load in life, but that life itself is the load. 'Life' is itself a substitution, but by Shakespeare himself; what Arnold does is remove Shakespeare's creative substitution, a small act of de-creation by Arnold such as reduces an individual genius, not to nullity, but to the tradition and the unindividual talent of the

[85] *The Renaissance*, p. 170.
[86] *On Translating Homer*; *On the Classical Tradition*, ed. R. H. Super (1960), p. 155.

general mind. Whereas Pater, likewise banishing the word
'Life', substitutes 'the world within' for 'the Life within'
because he needs to create something Paterian, Arnold does
not substitute anything of his own, anything Arnoldian, when
he puts 'a weary load' for 'a weary life'—what he does is remove
Shakespeare's dramatic substituting. Pater wants Wordsworth
or Shakespeare to be Paterian; Arnold wants them not to be
quiet so signally Wordsworthian or Shakespearean.

So the characteristic misquotation by Arnold of Wordsworth
is not—like Pater's re-writing of Wordsworth's 'pleasant
thought' as 'quiet thought'—the insistent creation of something
personal to the critic, but the erasing of something personal to
the poet. 'Poets', says Arnold,

> receive their distinctive character, not from their subject, but from
> their application to that subject of the ideas (to quote the *Excursion*)
>
> On God, on Nature, and on human life,
>
> which they have acquired for themselves.[87]

But it was the distinctive character of Wordsworth that he wrote,
not 'On God, on Nature, and on human life', but 'On Man,
on Nature, and on Human Life'. The near-tautology (as in
'With rocks, and stones, and trees') is the surprise and the individuality of the line. Arnold—and it is the price which he pays
for his justified fear of the merely personal and the singular,
and for his advocacy of the non-idiosyncratic and the central—
Arnold de-creates, he removes the surprise and the individuality
of Wordsworth's line, but not in order to substitute a surprise
and an individuality of his own—rather, to replace it by the
sober sense of the commonplace. 'On God, on Nature, and on
human life' is, in its inventorial uninventiveness, the line
which you or I, no less than Arnold (but less indeed than Wordsworth), might have come down with.

It is natural to Pater to introduce near-tautology when misquoting, near-tautology being evidence that each man overkills
the thing he overloves.

> Why have they dared to march
> So many miles upon her peaceful bosom,

---

[87] *On Translating Homer*; *On the Classical Tradition*, p. 210. But Arnold has the quotation (from 'The Recluse') right in his essay on Wordsworth.

> Frighting her pale-fac'd visages with war?
> (*Richard II,* II iii)[88]

'Pale-fac'd visages' is a surprise in its near-tautology, 'pale-fac'd villages' being Shakespeare's cooler understatement. It is natural to Arnold to remove near-tautology, replacing the individually biblical 'high and lofty' with the trite 'high and holy',[89] or removing words which are quirky in their uninspected surplusage. If Keats speaks of 'my own domestic criticism', Arnold silently drops 'domestic'; if John Smith says that the spirit 'could forcibly enter and penetrate into the souls of men', Arnold silently drops 'and penetrate'[90]—a thing which Pater, who can hardly survive for more than a few pages without some form of 'penetration', would never have done. If Ruskin, like his pupil Pater an escalator, speaks of 'principles of the most perfect beauty', Arnold will silently tone down the exorbitance and remove the solecism: 'principles of such perfect beauty'.[91]

Pater incises what is his own; Arnold excises what is other men's. Wordsworth says that 'Nature never did betray the heart that loved her' ('Tintern Abbey'), and 'betray' has a sudden edge (malevolence, promise-breaking, infidelity, treachery); Arnold says that 'Wordsworth says: "Nature never did forsake the heart that loved her"',[92] and we have glided into a softer, more conventional world than Wordsworth's. Wordsworth, according to Arnold,

calls the earth 'the mighty mother of mankind', and the geographers call her 'an oblate spheroid'; Wordsworth's expression is more proper and adequate to convey what men feel about the earth, but it is not therefore the more scientifically exact.[93]

Yet Wordsworth's expression was something more than proper and adequate; he did not offer the conventionality (and the conventionally mumming alliteration) of 'mighty mother of mankind', but the surprise of 'doleful Mother of Mankind' ('Invocation to the Earth'), with its large-sympathied whole-

---

[88] *Appreciations*, p. 193.

[89] *God and the Bible*, ed. R. H. Super (1970), p. 156.

[90] 'John Keats', *English Literature and Irish Politics*, p. 209; 'A Psychological Parallel', *Essays Religious and Mixed*, ed. R. H. Super (1972), p. 127.

[91] *God and the Bible*, p. 385.

[92] *God and the Bible*, p. 233.

[93] *Literature and Dogma; Dissent and Dogma*, ed. R. H. Super (1968), p. 189 n.-90.

earth evocation of Ceres at one with the Mater Dolorosa.

Or if we think, not of the fecund mother and the virgin mother, but of the young virgin:

I feel disposed to say that a single line is enough to show the charm of Chaucer's verse; that merely one line like this—

> 'O martyr souded in virginitee!'

has a virtue of manner and movement such as we shall not find in all the verse of romance-poetry.[94]

But in 'The Prioress's Tale' Chaucer did not see, conventionally, the virgin-martyr as soldered in virginity, as if virginity were something which soldered her up or within which she was soldered up, but as soldered *to* virginity: 'O martyr souded to virginitee', indissolubly at one with her calling, as the Bride of Christ is wedded and welded to Christ.

Pater substitutes the word 'quiet' so that it will create a Paterian world: 'My whole life I have lived in quiet thought!'. Arnold substitutes the word 'quiet' because Keats has left it out, Keats having intimated quietness while saying something more sharply paradoxical:

> What little town, by river or seashore,
> Or mountain-built with quiet citadel,
> Is emptied of its [*read* this] folk, this pious morn?
> ('Ode on a Grecian Urn')

Arnold may say of this vignette that 'it is composed with the eye on the object',[95] but his own eye is not on his object, since Keats wrote 'peaceful citadel', a quiet oxymoron. 'Quiet' is the conventional word which is expressly not expressed; 'peaceful' is surprisingly, yet decorously, at war with 'citadel', whereas 'quiet' is a mere atmospheric conventionality of the explicit. But Arnold is not exactly foisting the word in; it is rather that, insufficiently alert to the commonplace, he will not permit Keats to have foisted it out.

Likewise with Tennyson.

> For all experience is an arch, wherethrough
> Gleams that untravelled world, whose distance fades
> For ever and for ever, as we gaze.   ('Ulysses')

---

[94] 'The Study of Poetry', *English Literature and Irish Politics*, p. 175.
[95] *On the Study of Celtic Literature*; *Lectures and Essays in Criticism*, pp. 377-8.

It is no blame to the thought of those lines, which belongs to another order of ideas than Homer's, but it is true, that Homer would certainly have said of them, 'It is to consider too curiously to consider so'. It is no blame to their rhythm, which belongs to another order of movement than Homer's, but it is true that these three lines by themselves take up nearly as much time as a whole book of the *Iliad*.[96]

But is it to consider too curiously to consider that Tennyson's lines are more individual, less conventional, than Arnold's rendering of them down? Tennyson did not write 'For all experience', with its graceless chiming with 'For ever and for ever', and with its suggestion of a reassuring dependence of concatenation; he wrote 'Yet all experience', with its unreassuring rotation. Tennyson did not write 'whose distance fades' (which is unimaginedly vague), but 'whose margin fades', where the equivocation which is built into 'margin' (is it the line or the space?) is the very embodiment of Tennyson's sense of this taunting tragic recess-process. And Tennyson did not write 'For ever and for ever, as we gaze', but 'For ever and for ever when I move'. No solidarity of *we*, and no galleried acquiescent contemplation of *gaze*. 'Move' is a word which comes hauntingly within Ulysses's immobile cadences, a word which should have been alive—as it could not be, since he had conventionally re-written the lines—in Arnold's profound evocation of the auditory imagination: 'It is no blame to their rhythm, which belongs to another order of movement than Homer's, but it is true that these three lines by themselves take up nearly as much time as a whole book of the *Iliad*.'

Little things? But remember what Arnold said about the orthographical antics of *The Times*:

Some people will say these are little things; they are not; they are of bad example. They tend to spread the baneful notion that there is no such thing as a high, correct standard in intellectual matters; that every one may as well take his own way; they are at variance with the severe discipline necessary for all real culture; they confirm us in habits of wilfulness and eccentricity, which hurt our minds, and damage our credit with serious people.[97]

Yet severe discipline is compatible with our feeling an affectionate amusement when Arnold cites 'a saying . . . of the great

[96] *On Translating Homer; On the Classical Tradition*, p. 147.
[97] 'The Literary Influence of Academies', *Lectures and Essays in Criticism*, pp. 242-3.

John Hunter: "*Don't think*; try and be patient'''',[98] and has managed to mangle and amputate the surgeon's saying: 'Don't think; try; be patient; *be accurate.*'

In starting, I mentioned Matthew Hodgart's essay, 'Misquotation as Re-creation', and I should like to end with one of his instances, a famous one: T.S. Eliot's preference for the incorrect 'bewildering' over the correct 'bewitching' in his essay on Tourneur: 'For the poor benefit of a bewildering minute.' Eliot, with the masterly discretion which always attended his use of parentheses, says:

(*Bewildering* is the reading of the 'Mermaid' text; both Churton Collins and Mr Nicoll give *bewitching* without mentioning any alternative reading: it is a pity if they be right, for *bewildering* is much the richer word here.)[99]

It is characteristic of Eliot that he should not engage in a second creation himself, but should adopt and make his own another's second creation; characteristic, too, that he should in effect both acknowledge that 'bewildering' is not the word to hold to, and yet make clear that he has no intention of letting the word escape his grip. (When Eliot quoted these lines in 'Tradition and the Individual Talent', 'bewildering' acknowledged no opposition.) What matters more, though, is the way in which this 'misquotation as re-creation' is intimate with Eliot's profoundest sense of what creation is: the creation of one's self, and the creation of others' selves, in society and in procreation and through or within art's imaginings.

At this point I shall venture to generalise, and suggest that with the disappearance of the idea of Original Sin, with the disappearance of the idea of intense moral struggle, the human beings presented to us both in poetry and in prose fiction to-day, and more patently among the serious writers than in the underworld of letters, tend to become less and less real. It is in fact in moments of moral and spiritual struggle depending upon spiritual sanctions, rather than in those 'bewildering minutes' in which we are all very much alike, that men and women come nearest to being real.[100]

That, from *After Strange Gods* (1934), needs to be complemented

[98] 'A Liverpool Address', *Philistinism in England and America*, ed. R. H. Super (1974), p. 82.

[99] *Selected Essays* (1932), 1951 edn, p. 192.

[100] *After Strange Gods* (1934), p. 42.

by a letter in 1935 from Eliot to Stephen Spender in which Eliot put no quotation (or misquotation) marks around that misquotation which had become so much a part of himself:

Even just the bewildering minute counts; you have to give yourself up, and then recover yourself, and the third moment is having something to say, before you have wholly forgotten both surrender and recovery. Of course the self recovered is never the same as the self before it was given.[101]

Eliot is there speaking of criticism, but there is no usurpation in its manifest applicability to creation and to love.

Paradoxically, the misquotation, which is an instance of Eliot's inability to surrender himself to Tourneur's created world (perhaps Eliot too fervidly believed that the sexual act was bewildering not bewitching), is central to Eliot's evocation of the act of creation:

and when the words are finally arranged in the right way—or in what he comes to accept as the best arrangement he can find—he may experience a moment of exhaustion, of appeasement, of absolution, and of something very near annihilation, which is in itself indescribable. ('The Three Voices of Poetry')[102]

Eliot is indebted to both Arnold and Pater; Eliot insists that for all their flexing and loggerheads, it was six of Arnold and half a dozen of Pater; and Eliot's re-creative misquotation relates directly to his stricture on Arnold in *The Use of Poetry and the Use of Criticism*:

One feels that the writing of poetry brought him little of that excitement, that joyful loss of self in the workmanship of art, that intense and transitory relief which comes at the moment of completion and is the chief reward of creative work.[103]

Eliot's re-creative crux is pertinent likewise to Pater's unconditional un-surrender, Pater's conviction that criticism, like creation for him, is not a loss of self, joyful or otherwise, but is a matter of never finding yourself at an end rather than of acknowledging that there is a point at which you end and at

[101] *T. S. Eliot : The Man and His Work*, ed. Allen Tate (1966), 1971 edn, p. 59.
[102] *On Poetry and Poets* (1957), p. 98.
[103] *The Use of Poetry and the Use of Criticism* (1933), p. 108.

which someone, something, else begins. 'The literary artist',
for Pater,

sustained by yet restraining the productive ardour . . . somewhere
before the end comes, is burdened, inspired, with his conclusion, and
betimes delivered of it, leaving off, not in weariness and because he
finds *himself* at an end, but in all the freshness of volition.[104]

Such volition stales, in Pater and in his heirs.

[104] *Appreciations*, p. 24.

AMERICAN ENGLISH AND
THE INHERENTLY TRANSITORY

American English is often disparaged, not least by Anglophile Americans. But disapproval of how people use language—as of everything that people do—ought at least to ask whether there is anything which a particular suspected act may be able to effect which a more proper one might miss. Not that it need then be six of one and half a dozen of the other; simply that it may be salutary to grant that, with these choices of language as with other choices, it will not very often turn out to be none of one and a dozen of the other. The greatest novelist who was both American and English (and both nineteenth and twentieth century), Henry James—'Novelist. Citizen of two countries. Interpreter of his generation on both sides of the sea', in the perfect words of his gravestone, in Cambridge, Massachusetts:— even James did not always ask himself whether there was anything that demotic American speech could honourably effect which was not possible to the proprieties. Addressing the graduating class at Bryn Mawr College in 1905 on 'The Question of Our Speech', James was right to insist that even the most minute decisions about pronunciation, for instance, are up to something; but he was narrow in supposing that the something up to which they were must be no good.

Hence the undefined noises that I refer to when consonantal sound drops out; drops as it drops, for example, among those vast populations to whose lips, to whose ear, it is so rarely given to form the terminal letter of our 'Yes', or to hear it formed. The abject 'Yeh-eh' (the ugliness of the drawl is not easy to represent) which usurps the place of that interesting vocable makes its nearest approach to deviating into the decency of a final consonant when it becomes a still more questionable 'Yeh-ep'.[1]

Questionable, but *not* then questioned by James; who (preoccupied by the relation between a consonant and social consonance) does not stay for an answer to such a question as: 'Is there any truth to which "yeh-ep" can do justice to which "Yes"

---

[1] *The Question of Our Speech; The Lesson of Balzac* (1905), pp. 26-7.

cannot?' The answer is 'Yeh-ep', or 'yeh-eh', or 'yes'; but they
would not be the exactly the same answer. There is the well-
known story of the English philosopher, said to be J. L.
Austin, who drew his American audience's attention to the fact that,
though two negatives make a positive, there are no circumstances in which two positives make a negative. From the floor:
'Yeah, yeah'. To such an American incisiveness of exposure,
our response might be those very different words of enthusiastic
concurrence, 'Yes, yes'. James is right to praise 'yes' as 'that
interesting vocable', but wrong to imply that 'yeh-eh' is unin-
teresting—or indeed disinterested.

The marriage between the English language and the American
people is thought likely not actually to be till death them do
part, but until divorce does. R. W. Burchfield, the chief editor
of the Oxford dictionaries, and therefore the man who may
know more about the language than anyone in the world, and
who certainly is responsible for more knowledge of it than anyone, has said:

> I am convinced that the structure of the English language is not
> seriously at risk. I am equally sure that the two main forms of English,
> American English and British English, separated geographically from
> the beginning and severed politically since 1776, are continuing to
> move apart, and that existing elements of linguistic dissimilarity be-
> tween them will intensify as time goes on, notwithstanding the power
> of the cinema, TV, *Time* Magazine, and other two-way gluing and
> fuelling devices.[2]

Dr Burchfield may be right; but the run always has a way of
being so long that few are likely to notice whether he was or
not. It is two centuries since Noah Webster was insisting:

> As an independent nation, our honor requires us to have a system of
> our own, in language as government. Great Britain, whose children
> we are, and whose language we speak, should no longer be *our* stan-
> dard; for the taste of her writers is already corrupted and her language
> on the decline. But if it were not so, she is at too great a distance to be
> our model, and to instruct us in the principles of our own tongue . . .
> [For] within a century and a half, North America will be peopled with
> a hundred millions of men, *all speaking the same language*. [Isolation,
> new ideas, intercourse with native peoples] will produce, in a course

of time, a language in North-America, as different from the future language of England, as the modern Dutch, Danish and Swedish are from the German, or from one another.[3]

One further thing would have surprised Webster, as it would have surprised James a century later: the competition to English now mounted by those other languages of *America*, particularly Spanish. The expansion which James saw as North America's linguistic destiny has turned out to be an expansion not only of English but of opportunities other than English:

Keep in sight the so interesting historical truth that no language, so far back as our acquaintance with history goes, has known any such ordeal, any such stress and strain, as was to await the English in this huge new community it was so unsuspectingly to help, at first, to father and mother. It came *over*, as the phrase is, came over originally without fear and without guile—but to find itself transplanted to spaces it had never dreamed, in its comparative humility, of covering, to conditions it had never dreamed, in its comparative innocence, of meeting; to find itself grafted, in short, on a social and political order that was both without previous precedent and example and incalculably expansive.[4]

The English language in America is necessarily affected by the new sensitivities about the very word *America*, and so by the present state of languages other than English. Even a woman as formidable as she who once penned the following letter to a newspaper (and such formidable American women still exist) would no longer be able to write so unmisgivingly about these matters:

To the Editor of the [St Louis] Post Dispatch.
Naturalization is all too easily obtained by the foreigner who comes to America and becomes in a short time a citizen of a free republic. Do we properly prepare him for this inestimable privilege? The moment almost in which he sets foot on our shores we should begin to 'Americanize' him by requiring him to learn the English language, to speak it and read it. As long as he thinks, speaks or perchance reads in another tongue, he cannot sympathize with the spirit nor share the ideals of our republic, whose future depends on the unification of many peoples from many lands.[5]

[3] *Dissertations on the English Language* (1789); quoted by Susie I. Tucker, *English Examined* (1961), pp. 136-7.
[4] *The Question of Our Speech*, pp. 38-9.
[5] Box I, envelope 10, of Charlotte Eliot's scrap-book of her poems and other publications. Preserved in the Houghton Library, Harvard.

This letter was by the mother of Thomas Stearns Eliot. Such confident accents as hers have gone, at least for our age; not only as to the larger ethnic assimilative questions, but as to the equanimity with which an alert person could once say—as if it presented no wrinkle or ruckle—'we should begin to "Americanize" him by requiring him to learn the English language'.

It is her son, T. S. Eliot, who is still the most penetrating creative commentator upon the English language in America. He is Henry James's counterpart, the greatest poet who was both American and English; he is also the last—let us hope, the latest—great poet and great critic in English.

In 1922—the year of *The Waste Land*—Eliot needed to compare English and American poetry. This involved him in comparing the English language as it was in the two countries; and this in turn meant invoking a third term, French, in order to get purchase on the other two. (On the same principle, Eliot was later to urge that, if we were to get any purchase on the poetry/prose distinction, we should need to invoke the third term *verse*.[6] Purgatory may have been invented for the same reason.) In his 'London Letter' to *The Dial* in New York, Eliot wrote:

The English language is of course badly written in both countries. In England it is not ungrammatical, but common; it is not in bad taste, but rather tasteless. English imposes less upon the writer than French, but demands more from him. It demands greater and more constant variation; every word must be charged afresh with energy every time it is used; the language demands an *animosity* which is singularly lacking in those authors who are most publicly glorified for their style.[7]

That the distinctions do, for Eliot, go very deep is clear from the way in which what he says here of words—'English imposes less upon the writer than French, but demands more from him'—he was later to echo when thinking of the word of God: Christianity 'demands more and expects less' than other creeds.

If we take the implications of Eliot's metaphor, 'every word must be charged afresh with energy every time it is used', then we might contrast different kinds of battery. English is a smaller battery than French; it goes flat more quickly, but it has the

[6] Introduction to Paul Valéry, *The Art of Poetry* (1958), p. xvi.
[7] *Dial*, lxxii (1922), 510-13.

advantage that it is much more portable, and does not take an inordinate time to re-charge. The French language would then be a much larger battery; it doesn't have to be charged afresh with energy every time it is used, but when it does go flat (when it has ceased to be current), it needs to go into the garage for a century, and it is a very large object to have to lug to the garage, even for forty immortals of the French Academy. By extension, the American language is to English, what English is to French; the American language, or rather those characteristically American elements within English in America, cannot be charged afresh; you simply had better throw the words away once they go flat. 'Laid back', once you hear your mother use it, had better be flatly laid to rest.

Four years later, in 1926, Eliot wrote a review of Joseph Warren Beach on *The Outlook for American Prose* and of Fred Newton Scott on *American Slang*:

We are impressed, reading Mr. Beach's criticism and the quotations from the authors whom he criticizes, that none of these eminent men of letters seems to employ, or to be engaged in the formation of, that curious chimera 'the American language'. 'The American language'— if by that is meant a possible literary vehicle of thought and feeling, and not merely the transient slang of the time—must exist chiefly in the patriotic mind of Mr. Mencken, a journalist, by the way, whom Mr. Beach shows to be capable of writing extremely good, straightforward English prose.

That 'American language', indeed, is a ghost which walks only when the lights are very low. Mr. Beach turns the light on to several apparitions of the ghost, and reveals much bad language and a little good language, but nothing positively 'American'. But we are told that there is a peculiar American vocabulary of racy popular speech.

Eliot's touch here—the touch of an anonymous reviewer in the *Times Literary Supplement* (2 September 1926)—was light, but again the sensibility was grave, graver than he yet admitted. For the word 'chimera' ('that curious chimera "the American language"') was to figure in *Burnt Norton* as the conclusive climax of the passage on the relation of words to the Word: 'The loud lament of the disconsolate chimera'. As for Eliot's other reflection—'That "American language", indeed, is a ghost which walks only when the lights are very low'—this haunting thought was never to be exorcised until what is in effect Eliot's last poem, *Little Gidding*, when he was to imagine a ghost, walking when the lights are very low (in the war-time London black-out indeed), and engaging in a profound poetic disquisition about language, and tacitly about the strengths of English, American and French, since Eliot's line, 'To purify the dialect of the tribe', is an Englishing of the French line— 'Donner un sens plus pur aux mots de la tribu'—in which Mallarmé had honoured the tomb of Edgar Allan Poe.

In 1926, Eliot ended his anonymous review roundly (perhaps the more roundly, and not altogether squarely, for the review's never having let on that it was by an American—an American who next year was to become an Englishman):

For the rest—as Mr. Beach's book and a rapid examination of American slang combine to show—America is not likely to develop a new language until its civilization becomes much more complicated and more refined than that of Britain; and there are no indications that this will ever happen. Meanwhile, America will continue to provide a small number of new words which can usefully be digested by the parent language.

But again Eliot's words betrayed an honourable inability to be quite as coolly dismissive as he wished; for 'a rapid examination of American slang'—because of a tacit link between 'rapid' and 'slang'—takes you back to the nub of the matter: ' "The American language" '—if by that is meant a possible literary vehicle for thought and feeling, and not merely the transient slang of the time— . . .'. For this is the crux: first, that American English more deeply acknowledges slang constitutionally than does British English; second, that American English is not so concerned to separate 'a posssible literary vehicle for thought and feeling' from 'the transient slang of the time', and indeed believes that there are certain thoughts and feelings for which the only true literary vehicle is slang; and third, that American English is more deeply considerate of the relation between transience and slang than Eliot's words, 'the transient slang of the time', would suggest. For a good deal of slang is much less transient than one would suppose, or rather than it likes to pretend; and there are many other features of language than slang which are intimate with transience. Yet, as G. K. Chester-

ton said, 'The one stream of poetry which is continually flowing is slang'.[8]

Transience is the issue. The point is not so much whether
American society, or American English, really is more transient,
more susceptible of change, than English society or British
English, but whether Americans and Englishmen agree to believe that this is so. Transience—within a spectrum of seriousness from the frivolities of fashion to the vistas of apocalypse—
presses differently upon the language. It was this which prompted
Eliot's first example of 'racy popular speech' and 'current
American slang' that had entered England: 'the verb to *double-
cross*'. For what Eliot was at once able to seize upon was the fact
that 'double-cross' had no sooner established itself than it
began to pass away, not into a void but into the null. 'This useful and expressive word is already in decay; its original meaning of a betrayal of *both* sides is reduced to plain betrayal, which
renders it superfluous'. Eliot does not say more than that, but
one application of his acumen here would be to say that the
word 'double-cross'—exactly as inaugurative slang in a world
of built-in obsolescence—carried the seeds of its own betrayal;
almost at once it was betrayed—doublecrossed, even; betrayed
on both sides, American and English.

It was the transitory to which Eliot gave salience:

Certain words, like the verb *to boost*, and its substantive *booster*, reflect
aspects of contemporary American life so accurately as to obtain a
documentary value. But the majority of the words and phrases
(especially the phrases) are inherently transitory. One class is that of
synonyms, which can retain their value only so long as they retain
some novelty, and which are certain to be superseded by later inven-
tions: the synonyms for 'money' (*bones, bucks, iron men*, for 'dollars')
and the synonyms for strong liquors and for intoxication (*hooch* means
rather illicit liquor, and succeeds the antiquated *moonshine*) are certain
to pass away. So are the innumerable terms of opprobrium, which
have their Elizabethan and Jacobean analogues (*e.g., bonehead, boob,
simp, skate, dub, zob*). The more elaborate metaphors cannot endure
(*soup and fish* for 'evening dress').

The young Eliot took a stern view, and urged resistance. Of
such a verbal phrase as 'put over', he wrote:

[8] *The Defendant* (1901). I owe this to *The Oxford Book of Aphorisms*, ed. John Gross
(1983).

It does not represent the evolution of a new language so much as the degradation of an old one. Every language contains its own potentiality of deterioration, and the tendency illustrated by these verbal phrases [get by with, put across, put over] exists, independently, in this country: notice the success, among certain classes in England, of *phone through* instead of *telephone* or the acceptable *ring up*. We can strive against this tendency more competently if we recognize that it is indigenous.

But, as always, there is the question of what you do once resistance has become hopeless. If you can't beat them because they have already beaten you, should you not join them? American writers have often been far more imaginative than their English counterparts in turning to creative advantage these very conditions of language. There is an analogy with the challenge to American English of American non-English. Some of the best writers of American English have turned to advantage these pressures to unsettle or unseat English as *the* language. Dr. F. R. Leavis was scathing about any such creative friction, and pointed at Theodore Dreiser:

He represents the consequences of the later influxes from Europe and the sudden polyglot agglomeration of big raw cities, and may with some point be said to belong to the culturally dispossessed. It is possible, of course, to call the state of those who have lost their distinctive heritage, and acquired nothing comparable in its place, distinctively American; but the tendency to treat this state as a positive American tradition out of which a great national literature may be expected to come is depressing. Out of the conditions represented by Dreiser (who writes as if he hasn't a native language) no great literature *could* come; and nothing that can properly be called the beginnings of literature came in his case.[9]

But to other Englishmen it has seemed at least possible that there are beneficiaries as well as victims of such conditions. There are certain things that a writer may be able to do who writes as if not securely in possession of a native language.

Something analogous goes for obsolescence. For some of the best American writers, there has been a reward—for them and for their readers—in seeing the decay of language, or its transitoriness (not necessarily the same thing), or its prompt obsole-

---

[9] Introduction to Marius Bewley, *The Complex Fate* (1952), p. x.

scence, as not simply a condition of life but a condition for art. The distinctive poignancy of American English within American literature has much to do with its making its own linguistic transience—the unlikelihood that the battery could be charged afresh with energy—an acknowledgment and not just an admission. The sense that some of the most vivid words in today's language are—to take up Eliot's terms of disparagement—'inherently transitory', 'certain to be superseded', 'certain to pass away', and 'cannot endure': this sense can then itself be constitutive of some of the great effects of distinctively American literature, so that the degradation and deterioration of the language become, though always losses, the source of new gains.

Every user of language, whatever his or her politics, is engaged not only in conversation but in conservation. In any language, 'the conservative interest' predominates. The terms are those of Henry James:

> The question is whether it be not either no language at all, or only a very poor one, if it have not in it to respond, from its core, to the constant appeal of time, perpetually demanding new tricks, new experiments, new amusements of it: so to respond without losing its characteristic balance. The answer to that is, a hundred times, 'Yes' [not 'Yeh-eh' or 'Yeh-ep'], assuredly, so long as the conservative interest, which should always predominate, remains, equally, the constant quantity; remains an embodied, constituted, inexpugnable thing. The conservative interest is really as indispensable for the institution of speech as for the institution of matrimony.[10]

But the *extent* to which the conservative interest within language predominates varies greatly from one society to another. It predominates more in Britain and in British English than in American and American English. One simple index is the *Barnhart Dictionary of New English* (the second volume of which appeared in 1980); it includes much more American English than British English, and not just because of the book's provenance. More importantly, the conservative interest is *believed* to predominate less in America. Never was Henry James more American than when, urging the young women of Bryn Mawr to fight for propriety in speech, he found that he could not make his point impinge without recourse to slang, slang which,

10 *The Question of Our Speech*, pp. 46-7.

as soon as he utters it, is touchingly revealed as en route for the
obsolete or the dated:

You will have, indeed, in any at all aspiring cultivation of tone, a vast
mass of assured impunity, of immunity on the wrong side of the line,
to reckon with. There are in every quarter, in our social order,
impunities of aggression and corruption in plenty; but there are
none, I think, showing so unperturbed a face—wearing, I should
slangily say, if slang were permitted me here, so impudent a 'mug'—
as the forces assembled to make you believe that no form of speech is
provably better than another, and that just this matter of "care" is an
affront to the majesty of sovereign ignorance.[11]

But it is not only a question of the proportion of words that
stay put to words that don't; it is also a question of the relation
of that which changes to that which does not;—a relation which
is always a central preoccupation of culture in general and of
literature—because of its medium—in particular. The American writer, or citizen, will sometimes not even try to arrest a
process of toxic decay. The English writer, or citizen, will
sometimes not even try to apprehend that a process of decay
need not be toxic. The *present* state of the English language in
America and in England differs partly because of a different
relation of language to the present.

The American poet Ed Dorn has said:

Our articulation is quite different from other people's; we arrive at
understanding and meaning through massive assaults on the language, so no particular word is apt to be final. It's rapidly rerun all the
time. And I think that can be healthy usage. On the other hand,
there's so much of it that it gets the reputation for being loose. A lot of
it in fact is.[12]

Put like that, it might sound blithe. The best American poets
convey the poignancy of there being nothing final. Bob Dylan,
for instance. 'It's rapidly rerun all the time'. With personal
experience and with American technology in his mind's eye,
Dylan sings, in 'If You See Her, Say Hello':

> Sundown, yellow moon
> I replay the past
> I know ev'ry scene by heart
> They all went by so fast.

[11] *The Question of Our Speech*, pp. 17-18.
[12] Quoted by Donald Davie, *Trying to Explain* (1980), p. 15.

There is no such thing as a video of the heart; replaying the past does depend on knowing every scene by heart; but what makes this heartfelt is the unspoken 'And yet' between the lines:

> I know ev'ry scene by heart
> They all went by so fast.

'And yet they all went by so fast'; not 'because they all went by so fast'. You'd have been right to expect that it would have been by their having gone by so slowly that they were known by heart. It isn't that by some audacity 'fast' means 'slow' (black English sometimes likes 'bad' to mean 'good'); simply that you have to be quick on the uptake as Dylan kisses the joy as it flies, in both senses of *it flies*. Again, in 'Is Your Love in Vain?', he sings: 'Are you so fast that you cannot see that I must have solitude?'—where 'fast' means slow on the emotional uptake because of being so determinedly ahead of the game. To say of someone, especially of a woman, that she was 'fast' was itself once a fast (indecorous and suggestive) thing to say; but this sense faded. The language, sensitive to these glowings and fadings, is in sympathy with the love-experience which likewise has its glowing and fading.

'No time to think'? That is the title, and the refrain, of a Dylan song. But in terms of the transitory language, it is not that there is no time to think, but rather that one of the things that must be promptly thought about is that there's no time. The refrain in this Dylan song is always 'And there's no time to think'—until the last verse. Then the refrain-line both expands and contracts: it expands, in that it takes over the whole of the last verse; it contracts, in that in the final end when it is time for the last refrain, time so presses ('no time to lose') that instead of 'And there's no time to think', the refrain is curtailed to 'And no time to think'.

> No time to choose when the truth must die
> No time to lose or say goodbye
> No time to prepare for the victim that's there
> No time to suffer or blink
> And no time to think.

The point is not that British English is insensitive to time (no language ever can be); rather that, because it gives a less important role than does American English to the ephemeral or

transitory or obsolescent, there are certain effects occluded
from it—effects which cannot as clearly be seen and shown from
the vantage-point of this one form of English as against the
other. Effects, for example, of rueful admission; of American
English itself conceding that much of it not only is not built to
last, but is built not to last. Some love-affairs are like that, and
a poet or singer is likely to create something worth his and our
while when his love-affair with his medium, language, is intimate with this sense of what a *while* is (in language and in life)
that something should be worth it. Dylan sings, as no English
singer quite could,

> You will search, babe,
> At any cost.
> But how long, babe,
> Can you search for what's not lost?
> Ev'rybody will help you,
> Some people are very kind.
> But if I can save you any time,
> Come on, give it to me,
> I'll keep it with mine.
>   ('I'll Keep It with Mine')

An English counterpart could have effected the spectral presence
there of 'keep . . . time'; but could not have trusted British
English so perfectly to compact, as American English here
does, the smallest social offer and the largest offer of salvation:

> But if I can save you any time . . .
> But if I can save you   anytime . . .

It is not only the compacting of the two senses within the one
line which shows the sheer egalitarian width of American
English, but the compacting within the second sense—'But if
I can save you   anytime'—of the most serious magnanimity
with the casual largesse of conversational acknowledgement—
'any time' in that sense is pure American in the way in which,
socially at ease, it fosters such ease. It can even be printed as
one word in American English; when *sung* by Dylan it is not
unmistakably two words as it is when he prints his words.
Within art (and the daily language too can be used with art),
'any time' gets some of its force, breezily fresh, from the sense
that it is not itself a phrase which could have figured in Ameri-

can society and American English '*any* time'.

'No particular word is apt to be final', said Ed Dorn. But *finally* to be apt, that is a different matter; and the word 'final' or 'finally' stands differently to experience in American English for this very reason: that a consciousness of how little is final in words or out of them pervades the saying. There is a gambling song by Dylan, 'Rambling, Gambling Willie', which has the line: 'When the game finally ended up, the whole damn boat was his'. The game didn't just end, it ended up (those verbal phrases which Eliot deprecated); and it didn't just end up, it finally ended up. ('No particular word is apt to be final'.) There is a mild surprise at its being possible to say 'finally ended up' without sheer tautology; and yet it makes perfect sense, since a gambling game is always ending and beginning again, until the last hand, when it finally ends up; in this, the gambling game is like the song itself, which is always coming to an end with each verse (ending with the refrain 'Wherever you are a-gamblin' now, nobody really knows'), but does finally end up. Or again, Dylan sings to Ramona: 'You've been fooled into thinking / That the finishin' end is at hand'. Not one of those temporary or tentative ends, but the finishing end. In 'All I Really Want to Do', Dylan sings:

> I ain't lookin' to block you up,
> Shock or knock or lock you up,
> Analyze you, categorize you,
> Finalize you, or advertise you.
> All I really want to do
> Is, baby, be friends with you.

—where 'Finalize' gets its pouncing power not just from being a word that was American before English (though Australian before American), but also—given the American sense of how finality fleets away, like an advertisement ('Finalize you or advertise you')—from being such a shrug of a word. And one might (in passing . . .) notice Dylan's dexterity with the phrase which is apocryphally taken as getting the Englishman into trouble, when he asks for an early call in the morning:

> I ain't lookin' to block you up,
> Shock or knock or lock you up.

The sly propriety tactfully, pregnantly, separates 'knock' from 'you up' for a couple of words; after all, the preceding 'shock' would more suggest 'shock you' than 'shock you *up*' (though one of the things that Dylan is doing is giving a shake to the phrase 'shake you up'). Nobody need feel embarrassed; it all goes by so fast.

You can hear the acknowledgement of the transient, the obsolescent, in the imaginative use in American English of such a sturdily old-time phrase as 'come to pass'. In British English, this could be well-used with simple archaic dignity, with the sense of something more grave than any simple happening: under 'come to pass', *Collins Dictionary* (1979) is flatly reduced to '*Archaic*. To happen'. But the creative use of the phrase within American English is likely to pick up the poignancy of 'come *to pass*', a poignancy which the English poet may believe has to be spelt out rather than intimated; spelt out, for instance, as Christina Rossetti does when she makes her two-stanza poem 'May' turn upon a change of these words:

> I cannot tell you how it was;
> But this I know: it came to pass—
> Upon a bright and breezy day
> When May was young, ah pleasant May!
> As yet the poppies were not born
> Between the blades of tender corn;
> The last eggs had not hatched as yet,
> Nor any bird forgone its mate.
>
> I cannot tell you what it was;
> But this I know: it did but pass.
> It passed away with sunny May,
> With all sweet things it passed away,
> And left me old, and cold, and grey.

This is altogether more explicit, more explicated even, than the American way with the phrase. There is a poem by John Crowe Ransom, 'Spectral Lovers', which has the stanza:

> And gesturing largely to the moon of Easter,
> Mincing his steps and swishing the jubilant grass,
> Beheading some field-flowers that had come to pass,
> He had reduced his tributaries faster
> Had not considerations pinched his heart
> Unfitly for his art.

'Jubilant' swings on into 'Beheading some field-flowers', but does sadden at 'that had come to pass'. Ransom uses the phrase with an Anglophile elegance that is yet tinged with what is now an unEnglish shivering of the phrase. Dylan, in a song ('I Pity the Poor Immigrant') which has its connections with the 'polyglot' immigrations that perturbed Dr Leavis, ends his vision of this suffering with:

> I pity the poor immigrant . . .
> Whose visions in the final end
> Must shatter like the glass.
> I pity the poor immigrant
> When his gladness comes to pass.

'In the final end' finds some resilience in the fact that this is itself nearing the *last* ending of a verse; furthermore its near-tautology is effectively American. Moreover, those last lines of the song, 'I pity the poor immigrant / When his gladness comes to pass', sharply challenge the British English sense of the phrase. You can of course imagine kinds of gladness for the happening, the arrival of which somebody is to be pitied (sadistic kinds, for instance); but the pressure of the phrase is essentially to make you acknowledge that gladness comes *to pass*. 'We Poets in our youth begin in gladness; / But thereof come in the end despondency and madness'.

'The conservative interest' is present in the old-world phrase 'come to pass', but in the Dylan song it does not predominate. Something has happened since the old days of the phrase; has come to pass. Sometimes, though, Dylan does need to help the conservative interest predominate. Then he will move from a quintessentially American phrase like 'big dreams' to a British English way of speaking.

> God don't make promises that he don't keep.
> You've got some big dreams, baby, but in order
>   to dream you've gotta still be asleep.
> When you gonna wake up, when you gonna wake
>   up, when you gonna wake up,
> Strengthen the things that remain.
>   ('When You Gonna Wake Up')

For there the language to which he means to awaken his audience is not American English, with its 'big dreams', but the conservative and conserving force of the *Revelation* of the King

James Bible: 'Be watchful, and strengthen the things which
remain, that are ready to die'.[13] The line is itself one of the
things which remain; and it impinges newly within a sense of
the language itself as elsewhere so 'ready to die'.

For American English is especially alive with words and
phrases that are ready to die; this can be a great resource, provided that the words and phrases admit it—not so much admit
that they *have* seen better days as admit that before very long
they will have seen better days. In every language there are
clichés (phrases which have seen better days), and slang;
clichés and slang can be very different, but they are both likely
to have a short life-expectancy, if life is vividness and vitality.
Then they can become zombies or ghosts; dead but they won't
lie down, like that phrase itself. In every language an artist, or
an imaginative conversationalist, can unexpectedly show that
they are not really dead but sleeping; or not quite dead, and so
can be given the kiss of life; or quite dead, but can be resurrected. Yet it is in American English—with its constitutional
need to be novel, since how else could it free itself from British
English?—that there can most often be created this particular
poignancy, of a language acknowledging that much of it is not
long for this world, and building an art which lasts out of a
medium which admits that many of its characteristic com-
ponents will not last. 'The order is / Rapidly fadin'', sings
Dylan (in 'The Times The Are A-Changin''), with some play
of *rapidly* against *fading*.

Writing about slang in *Time* Magazine recently (8 November
1982), Lance Morrow did summary justice:

As the University of Cincinnati's William Lasher remarks, 'Slang
doesn't get written down, so it doesn't endure. If you do write it
down, it gets into the language, and stops being slang'. In a maniacally
open electronic society, the news and entertainment industries sift
hungrily through the culture searching for color, anecdote, personality, uniqueness and, of course, slang. All these items instantly
become part of the show. Slang is wonderful entertainment. But its
half-life is shorter now. Good slang gets commercial in a hurry, like
certain country-music singers.

But the glory and peril of American English may be that the

---

[13] Dr Eric Griffiths pointed out the Biblical allusion to me.

matter won't separate out so simply and so totally. For slang does not stop being slang the moment it hits the page, any more than it stops being fresh the moment it is uttered.

Eliot, so that he might escape having his inculpation of American English be an exculpation of British English, acknowledged that 'Every language contains its own potentiality of deterioration'. So American English does differ, does have something of 'its own': first, in that so many of its characteristic features and strengths are of the sort that are likely to be quick to deteriorate (no preservatives); and second, in that this very fact is one from which the reflective and imaginative user of the language may wrest distinction.

American English, distinctively effective, will often not just contain its potentiality of deterioration but will advert to it (not the same as advertising it or finalizing it); and will realize, in this more-than-*potentiality* of deterioration, a potentiality for imaginative redemption. We might just take Eliot's word 'contain' as seriously as he later took it in *Burnt Norton*, and say that American English will 'contain its own potentiality of deterioration' not only as harbouring it but as keeping it within bounds, yet not so utterly as not to reveal that this is what is happening.

> Go, said the bird, for the leaves were full of children,
> Hidden excitedly, containing laughter.

Containing laughter means not entirely containing it; means its showing through the restraint. It is in this large sense that American English, more than British English because of the greater centrality to American English of words and phrases that are in transit, may be said to contain its own potentiality of deterioration.

Ed Dorn related his conviction that American English is 'rapidly rerun all the time' to its getting 'the reputation for being loose. A lot of it in fact is'. Again one question is what imaginatively may be made available by such looseness. Take 'kind of'. The *H-N* Supplement (1976) to the *Oxford English Dictionary* was able to give earlier examples than had the Dictionary itself, of 'kind of' as 'in a way, as it were, to some extent'; the earliest citation had been Dickens, but this is now antedated by the New Hampshire poet T. G. Fessenden (1804): 'I kind of love you, Sal—I vow'; and by the *Massachusetts Spy* in

1830: 'I was kind of provoked at the way you came up'. Though decently accommodated within British English, 'kind of' has never been perfectly at home there. Clearly it is a phrase which can minister to every kind of (not kinda) unclarity, laziness, vagueness, and evasion, and so it does in writers as different as Walter Pater and Iris Murdoch in the corrugated pseudo-precise form 'a kind of x y'. But by the same token it can be, not abused, but used imaginatively to capture precisely the social functions of such laziness, vagueness, and evasion. No writer of British English would be able to be so resourceful with the unstrict phrase because it is not, strictly, an English resource. I think of Dylan in 'Honey, Just Allow Me One More Chance', pleading exactly for kindness while hinting that he is granting a good deal of latitude, singing the word 'kind' so that it 'kinda' expands: 'Just one kind(a) favour I ask you'. Or Dylan using it at the end of a song'. 'Don't Think Twice, It's All Right', to capture a final precisely-calculated refusal vaguely to forgive, moving from 'unkind' to 'kinda':

> I ain't sayin' you treated me unkind
> You could have done better but I don't mind
> You just kinda wasted my precious time
> But don't think twice it's all right.

'You just wasted my precious time', he can be heard singing in an early unofficial recording of the song, tight-lipped and self-righteous, whereas 'You just kinda wasted my precious time' is precious for its unruffled steely approximation—comic more-over because on other lips 'kinda', after all, is usually itself a waste of precious time.

Or there is John Berryman, who wrote 'I am a monoglot of English / (American Version)' (*The Dream Songs*: 48). Berryman relates 'kindly' not to the unspoken 'kind of' but to its brother 'sort of', in ending *The Dream Songs*: 27 by touchingly evoking a double hopelessness: the hopelessness or wrongheadedness of resisting transience, and the hopelessness of striving for an unachievable exactitude hereabouts:

> My friends,—he has been known to mourn,—I'll die;
> live you, in the most wild, kindly, green
> partly forgiving wood,
> sort of forever and all those human sings

> close not your better ears to, while good Spring
> returns with a dance and a sigh.

'Sort of forever': the wistful wishful quality of that is at one with American English (the language itself saying: 'My friends,—he has been known to mourn,—I'll die'), as it could never be with British English, to which 'sort of' remains forever sort of foreign. Like the unEnglish cadence of a great Berryman line: 'The patient is brought back to life, or so' (*The Dream Songs*: 67).

Or there is Norman Mailer. *The Executioner's Song* (a work of genius and a national feat) repeatedly finds its strength in the loose generosity of those everywhere-repeated phrases 'kind of' and 'sort of'. The first page of the book recalls of the young Gary Gilmore: 'Gary was kind of quiet', where 'kind of' bides its time. Mailer can use—report—the phrase a thousand ways, sensitive to the thousand social occasions at which it can assist. It can be egalitarian: Gary and Nicole as 'a kind of democratic Romeo and Juliet', with the democratic truly in touch with the demotic. It can tell an exact truth about inexactitude: 'She had only kind of told Gary the truth'; or about the vague wish not to hurt ('She didn't mean to be rude to Johnny, but she did kind of forget he was there'); or about the relatively easy way of admitting to uneasiness ('They kind of got along'), or to room for manoeuvre ('kind of promised each other'), or to sheer bafflement ('kind of a cross . . . between Boris Karloff and Andy Warhol'). Finally there is the poignancy of this turn as Gilmore, about to embrace at last the execution upon which he has insisted, has his last meeting with Stanger: 'and they looked in each other's eyes, kind of a final embrace'. Perhaps not final; Gilmore had religious faith. But certainly kind of final; sort of forever.

There is the same potentiality in another American turn of phrase which—like 'kind of' and 'sort of'—is itself about potentiality, untapped, uncertain, gestured-towards, unrealized: 'and all'. It is in the *OED*: *And all*: 'And everything *else*, and everything connected therewith, *et cetera*; hence, Too, also, as well (especially in dial. speech; Sc. ''Woo'd an' married an' a'''')'. But the instances then given from British English are not strong, or rather they are more like the strong impatience of 'and so on and so forth' or like the strongly specific ('Old

Uncle Tom Cobbleigh and all'—all of them available to be
named). This is quite other than the sidling sliding sidelong
movement of the current American 'and all'. In 'Visions of
Johanna', Bob Dylan can turn the acquiescent helplessness
and uselessness of 'and all' into the far-from-hopeless or -use-
less energies of aggression and baffled anger:

> Now, little boy lost, he takes himself so seriously
> He brags of his misery, he likes to live dangerously
> And when bringing her name up
> He speaks of a farewell kiss to me
> He's sure got a lotta gall to be so useless and all
> Muttering small talk at the wall while I'm in the hall . . .

—where 'and all' is itself a kind of muttering but is not small
talk; threateningly, it is talking big.

John Berryman can make 'and all' the epitome of self-pity's
vague yawning and yearning for something unspecified, self-
pity as insatiably unspecific; as in his poem about a poetry-
reading.

THE DREAM SONGS: 118

> He wondered: Do I love? all this applause,
> young beauties sitting at my feet & all,
> and all.
> It tires me out, he pondered: I'm tempted to break laws
> and love myself, or the stupid questions asked me
> move me to homicide—
>
> so many beauties, one on either side,
> the wall's behind me, into which I crawl
> out of my repeating voice—
> the mike folds down, the foolish askers fall
> over theirselves in an audience of ashes
> and Henry returns to rejoice
>
> in dark & still, and one sole beauty only
> who never walked near Henry while the mob
> was at him like a club:
> she saw through things, she saw that he was lonely
> and waited while he hid behind the wall
> and all.

The first time it comes, it is '& all' (ampersand); the next time
and the final time, when it twice has a whole line to its little
self, Berryman spells it out: 'and all'.

Such an imprecision as 'and all' can be infuriatingly ingratiating, so conscious of how relaxed it is; but it can also within its native tongue, American English, focus very precisely upon such imprecision. Conversely, British English can do wonders with the other phrase which was for the *OED* a synonym of 'and all' though it is, when in action, no such thing: *et cetera*. For *et cetera*—with its tribute to the dear departed language of precision, Latin—ordinarily lays claim not to the helpless loveable shrug of 'and all', but to a helpful admirable firmness of gesture, pointing to a docile marshalled list. No American poet (and I am not forgetting E. E. Cummings's 'my sweet old etcetera') could do with *et cetera* what Byron did, at his most laconic, beginning Canto III of *Don Juan* with the sharp despatch of: 'Hail Muse! et cetera. We left Juan sleeping . . . ' Or rather, an American poet can do this best if mocking an Englishman, as in the opening of Anthony Hecht's 'The Dover Bitch':

> So there stood Matthew Arnold and this girl
> With the cliffs of England crumbling away behind them,
> And he said to her, 'Try to be true to me,
> And I'll do the same for you, for things are bad
> All over, etc., etc.'
> Well now, I knew this girl . . .
> *(The Hard Hours,* 1967)

The English language, like its favourite form the iambic pentameter, is crumbling away (into American—'For things are bad all over', and into crumbled crumpled Latin: 'etc., etc.'.)

For a final, or 'kind of final', focus I take a word, *real*, which with its derivatives brings together thoughts of the vague and the precise, the transitory and the unchanging. For if American English, especially at present, has a special opportunity in those very intimations of vagueness and transience to which it accords an important place, it is still necessary always to ask how its good effects are made real, are—in both senses—realized. When Robert Frost honoured the Presidential Inauguration of 1961 by reciting a poem, he chose one, 'The Gift Outright', which had at its heart a characteristic American oxymoron (an advance from its earlier line 'But we were England's, still colonials')—a paradox caught in the words 'vaguely realizing'. For those words are *not* applied to a person ('vaguely realizing', as one might say 'dimly apprehending'), but to the land itself:

> Such as we were we gave ourselves outright
> (The deed of gift was many deeds of war)
> To the land vaguely realizing westward,
> But still unstoried, artless, unenhanced,
> Such as she was, such as she would become.

The *O—Scz* Supplement (1982) to the *Oxford English Dictionary* is a revelation as to the changes that have taken place for this word. One of the most important is the belated acknowledgment of usages which were perfectly available to the original compilers of the *OED* but were strikingly unrecognized. Thus the *OED* itself did not acknowledge one hard-headed economic sense of *real*: 'Reckoned by purchasing power rather than monetary or nominal value', although this sense is (we now learn) as old as Dr. Johnson and Adam Smith. 'In real terms . . .': oh yes, those terms are now understood to be all too real. And to this old but unacknowledged economic sense, the Supplement to the *OED* is able to add our characteristic extensions: *real money*, in American English (at first) as 'a large sum of money'; and *real money*, in British English, as 'the coinage or currency in which one habitually reckons, frequently as opposed to foreign currency'.

Another of the important usages which the *OED* declined to notice is *real life*, though this is as old as Thomas Jefferson and Maria Edgeworth. We should not be surprised that the Supplement's earliest citation is Jefferson's American English (if that term is altogether right for the year 1771): 'Considering history as a moral exercise, her lessons would be too infrequent if confined to real life'. 'Real life', like its brother 'the real world', has been suspected of being both soft-headed and hard-nosed. Those who believe that the bourgeoisie, or whoever, will oppressively claim that particular social arrangements are ineluctable reality are quick to put sneering quotation-marks around the word *real* ('real'). Those who, often from the opposite flank, object to the implication that factories are real whereas universities aren't, are quick to find unreal this use of 'real', especially when a university man is guilty of this *trahison des clercs*: 'The Vice-Chancellor of Lancaster University strongly believes "that the university must keep contact with the real world outside." May I take this opportunity to ask . . . : (*a*) what is real about the real world? (*b*) why is it always outside?' (a letter from Oxford to *The Listener*, 19 May 1966).

But then there are all those applications of *real* which were subsequent to the *OED* and which are pointers to the way we live now, the relation of our times to time. 'Real time': 'the actual time during which a process or event occurs, especially one analyzed by a computer, in contrast to time subsequent to it when computer processing may be done, a recording replayed, or the like'. ('It's rapidly rerun all the time'; 'I replay the past'.) More grimly, there is the newly-felt need for the sense of *real* which is at work in 'real coffee' ('coffee made, directly from ground coffee beans, as opposed to "instant" coffee'—*opposed* is good). This dates from 1964; and from 1972 there is the Campaign for Real Ale ('a name sometimes applied to draught beer that has been brewed and stored in the traditional way'). This usage too can escalate, as in the equivocal graffito: 'Ban the Bomb. Campaign for Real War'.

Our world has become increasingly suspicious of both the real and the unreal. Hence the gingerly way in which the word *real* gets handled, as if the very thought of it were unreal. 'The real thing' ('True love, as distinct from infatuation, flirtation, etc. [a great *et cetera*]') goes back as far as 1857, we now learn from the Supplement (the *OED* did not acknowledge it); but as the years went by, 'the real thing' became suspected of the very unreality it was challenging. People felt that it was being capitalized upon, and the only way to protect us against this was to capitalize it back: the Real Thing. Mary McCarthy (1941): 'All that conjugal tenderness had been a brightly packaged substitute for the Real Thing'—where the capitals on the Real Thing make it look as if it too is a bit of bright packaging.

Real as meaning ' "genuine" ', free from nonsense, affectation, or pretence' is likewise much older than one would have thought (it is in Tennyson); but it has lately been having its work cut out, stemming the tide of inauthenticity and insincerity, of illusions of feeling. Hence the escalation into the comparative form, 'realler' (not something you can usually do with the word 'real', after all).

He [Seymour Krim] . . . finds that criticism gets in the way of his 'truer, realer, imaginative bounce.' (1961)

This was a realler America than I had known in the past, hitching on this or that bandwagon or presidential campaign. (1966)

Time Magazine gives a more wistful tone to its escalation: 'Billy is very sweet and very gentle and very real' (1977).

Then there has been the proliferation of reality-hyphenations (or -hypes, for short). Reality-content, reality-control, reality-based, reality-centred, reality-principle, reality-testing, reality-value, and (now in the second *Barnhart Dictionary of New English*) reality-therapy; the stock-piling of these being enough to make reality seem, yet again, unreal. The very devices which seek to emphasise the real then have the effect of scepticizing it. Leslie Fiedler, in his fiery emphasis, goes for the double 'really', with the second one underlined: 'what the self-appointed censors have always objected to . . . is not really, *really* the fact that they are violent . . .' Czeslaw Milosz defines poetry as 'a passionate pursuit of the Real', whereupon Henry Gifford was drily though sincerely solicitous: 'The capital letter may increase rather than disarm the scepticism of many readers'.[14] The 3rd edition of the *Oxford Dictionary of Quotations* (1979) no longer has room for Longfellow's 'Life is real! Life is earnest!'. I suspect that it was censored.

Which leads—finally—to a notable American invention to cope with some aspects of this, an invention which is itself then tinged with evanescence: 'for real'. *Real* no longer feeling real, American English calls into existence a demarcated variant. As meaning 'genuine, (in) earnest, true, sincere', the earliest citation in the *O-Scz* Supplement to the *OED* is Billie Holiday in 1956 ('The only joints fancy enough to have a victrola and for real enough to pick up on the best records'). If in 1984 John Glenn had one thing to offer—other than the obvious one—which none of the other Democratic Presidential hopefuls could claim, it was his having furnished the earliest *OED* Supplement citation for a sub-section of a word: under 'for real': 'adv. Really, truly, actually; in reality: 1962 J. Glenn, *Into Orbit*: Everyone seemed to sense that we were going for real this time'. Senator Glenn, as he then wasn't, may claim to have put the adverbial usage into orbit. But it was John Berryman who made the most of 'for real', making real—realizing—the fact that it too is hastening towards unreality. *The Dream Songs*: 7 longs for the old (young) freshness which time has undone:

---

14 *Times Literary Supplement*, 9 September 1983.

'THE PRISONER OF SHARK ISLAND'
WITH PAUL MUNI

Henry is old, old; for Henry remembers
Mr Deeds' tuba, & the Cameo,
& the race in *Ben Hur,* — *The Lost World*, with sound,
& *The Man from Blankley's*, which he did not dig,
nor did he understand one caption of,
bewildered Henry, while the Big Ones laughed.

Now Henry is unmistakably a Big One,
Fúnnee, he don't féel so.
He just stuck around.
The German & the Russian films into
Italian & Japanese films turned, while many
were prevented from making it.

He wishing he could squirm again where Hoot
is just ahead of rustlers, where William S
forgoes some deep advantage, & moves on,
where Hashknife Hartley having the matter taped
the rats are flying. For the rats
have moved in, mostly, and this is for real.

What Berryman does is combine the conviction that the reality
is now known to be very ugly and is no play-acting, dummy-run
or film fantasy ('For the rats / have moved in, mostly, and this
is for real'), with the conviction—given the instant obsolescence
of a phrase like 'for real'—that these days no apprehension of
the real can last for long. Even happy apprehensions of nemesis,
as when Dylan sings, in 'When The Ship Comes In':

Oh the foes will rise
With the sleep still in their eyes
And they'll jerk from their beds and think they're dreamin'.
But they'll pinch themselves and squeal
And know that it's for real,
The hour when the ship comes in.

INDEX

Italics within entries denote some sustained consideration of a particular poet or topic.